Ruy Barr__

Jesus

without

Paul of Tarsus

Faithful to Jesus Christianity

Ruy Barraco Mármol

The author is a victim of identity theft. There is somebody using his name, who even got a valid Photo ID (Driver's License or ID Card), with a picture that belongs to the identity thief, and the information of the victim. In addition, the identity thief got a new social security number, under the name of the author, and uses that social security number to work and to sign contracts. He might have gotten a birth certificate of the author. This identity thief most likely lives in one of the states of Rhode Island, Maryland or Massachusetts, and has FBI records.

Jesus without Paul of Tarsus

Ruy Barraco Mármol

Contents

Chapter II. The Book of Revelation, the Signs of the Coming of the Son of Man, the Coming of the Son of Man and the Great Tribulation, the Final Judgment and the New Jerusalem........391

Ruy Barraco Mármol

Acknowledgments

First, I want to thank God. I want to thank the Father, the Son and the Holy Spirit, for guiding me to write this book, and for all that this book means and says. Second, I want to acknowledge the help that the following persons gave me while I was writing this book: my wife, Gabriela Bursa Davies, for all the support and help she gave me during these years, for all the virtue, love and happiness that she showed, and for her hard work; my sons, Eliseo and Constantino, who understood that I had to write the book, and accepted my full time occupation; my sister María Virginia Barraco Mármol, her husband and their sons, who opened up their home for us, in order that this book could be better done; my mother, Virginia Lee Edwards, who helped me with my English and with the Edition of the book; and my father, Mario Domingo Barraco Mármol, who died in 2006 and personally gave me a Christian education and a great desire for the truth.

About the Author

There are certain books in which because of their subject the reader might justifiably have more interest in knowing personal information about the author. This is one of them. For that reason, without turning this prologue into an autobiography, I will provide some information about my life.

I was born in 1972, in Washington, D.C., United

States of America. I was raised Catholic. I was baptized in Saint Matthew's Church of Washington D.C.. When I was six years old, after my parents' divorce, my sisters María, Consuelo, and I moved with my father, Mario Domingo Barraco Mármol, to the Argentine Republic.

I had my first communion in the Society of Jesus Catholic Church, and I received confirmation in the Father Claret Catholic Church. I studied at the "Colegio Nacional de Monserrat", a traditional three-hundred year old humanist high school, where Latin and Greek are taught among other languages. Afterwards, I studied law at the National University of Córdoba, School of Law and Social Science. I have been married since 2001 and I have two sons. I practiced law since I graduated in 1999, until June 2008; all in the Province of Córdoba, Argentine Republic. At the end of June 2008, I moved to the State of Texas, United States of America.

My father was born in the Province of Córdoba, Argentine Republic, in 1932, and he died in 2006. Before getting married with my mother, Virginia L. Edwards, he studied to be a priest at the Major Seminary of Our Lady of Loreto of Córdoba, Argentine Republic, and at the Pontifical Gregorian University of Rome, Italy, where he graduated in philosophy. In the United States of America he worked as a chief editor of the Spanish edition of the magazine published by the Organization of American States (O.A.S.), called "Americas". From him I inherited a Christian education and a good religious, political and philosophical library.

My mother, Virginia Lee Edwards, was born in 1942, in Saint Louis, Missouri, United States of America. She graduated from Vassar College with a bachelor of arts, a major in English, and a minor in Zoology. She also worked as an assistant and associate editor of the magazine published by the Organization of American States (O.A.S.), but in the English edition. There is where my parents met.

My paternal grandfather, Rodolfo Barraco Mármol, was born in 1900, in Rosario City, Province of Santa Fe, Argentine Republic. He was a federal judge in Córdoba, Río Cuarto and Bell Ville; all of them cities of the Argentine Republic. His wife, my paternal grandmother, was Cándida Rosa Aguirre Cámara, born in 1901, in Córdoba city, Province of Córdoba, Argentine Republic.

My maternal grandfather, Joseph C. Edwards, was born in 1909, in Springfield, Missouri, United States of America. He was a cardiologist, who graduated from Harvard University in 1934. During World War II, he served in Italy, France, North Africa, and participated in D-day. His wife, my maternal grandmother, was Virginia Anne Moser, born in 1914, in Saint Louis, Missouri, United States of America.

I feel deeply thankful to all the ministers and people that help the world with faith. I have a high concept and esteem for the Catholic Church, its authorities, and its members; the same way I have a high concept and esteem for the other Christian Churches, their authorities and their members, who live and spread the essential truths of Christianity[1].

---

[1] The Gospel according to Saint Luke, New King James Version (N.K.J.V.) says: "10:26 He said to him, "What is written in the law? What is your reading of it?" 10:27 So he answered and said, "'You shall love the LORD your GOD with all your heart, with all your soul, with all your strength, and with all your mind,' and 'your neighbor as yourself.'" 10:28 And He said to him, "You have answered rightly; do this and you will live." 10:29 But he, wanting to justify himself, said to Jesus, "And

Ruy Barraco Mármol

This is the second book that I have written. The first is called "Protección de la Vida e Igualdad Prenatal del Hombre en la República Argentina" (Before birth protection of human life and equality in the Argentine Republic), U.S.A., Xlibris, 2010.

I first published this book under the title "Gotcha Saint Paul", but then I decided to retitle the book and to make a few changes because, even though this book is about the recognition of Paul as a false prophet, it is principally about recognizing Jesus as our only leader and about encouraging a faithful to Jesus Christianity, and I thought the new title "Faithful to Jesus Christianity", would communicate better the subject of the book, although after writing the book in Spanish I

---

who is my neighbor?" 10:30 Then Jesus answered and said: "A certain man went down from Jerusalem to Jericho, and fell among thieves, who stripped him of his clothing wounded him, and departed, leaving him half dead. 10:31 "Now by chance a certain priest came down that road. And when he saw him, he passed by on the other side. 10:32 "Likewise a Levite, when he arrived at the place, came and looked, and passed by on the other side. 10:33 "But a certain Samaritan, as he journeyed, came where he was. And when he saw him, he had compassion. 10:34 "So he went to him and bandaged his wounds, pouring on oil and wine; and he set him on his own animal, brought him to an inn, and took care of him. 10:35 "On the next day, when he departed, he took out two denarii, gave them to the innkeeper, and said to him, 'Take care of him; and whatever more you spend, when I come again, I will repay you.' 10:36 "So which of these three do you think was neighbor to him who fell among the thieves?" 10:37 And he said, "He who showed mercy on him." Then Jesus said to him, "Go and do likewise."" Scripture quotations marked with (N.K.J.V.) in this work are taken from the New King James Version, Copyright c 1979, 1980, 1982 by Thomas Nelson, Inc. Used by permission. All rights reserved. The Gospel according to Saint Luke (N.K.J.V.) says: "9:49 Now John answered and said, "Master, we saw someone casting out demons in Your name, and we forbade him because he does not follow with us." 9:50 But Jesus said to him, "Do not forbid him; for he who is not against us is on our side." The Gospel according to Saint Matthew (N.K.J.V.) says: "12:50 For whoever does the will of My Father in heaven is My brother, and sister, and mother."" This is the spirit which every Christian must have.

decided to title the book "Jesus without Paul of Tarsus."

Preface

Despite having read the four Gospels many times, as the great majority of Christians, I had never read in a complete, dedicated, and free manner the book of Acts of the Apostles and the Epistles of Paul.

Several times, readings of passages of the Epistles of Paul had left me with serious doubts about them, but the sound trust that I have been taught to have in the Bible, and that I still maintain, allowed me to live with those doubts until I studied the epistles. This book is the result of that study.

Certainly, whoever reads this work without having read the Epistles of Paul in a complete, dedicated and free manner, might decide to do so. To those persons who attempt to, I forewarn you that you will find the epistles, at times, writings very difficult to read. However, I encourage you to do it regardless of the difficulty, because there are fundamental reasons that demand it. It is preferable, in the reading of the epistles, to follow what is believed to be their chronological order[2], rather than the order they are presented in the

---

2 The Spanish Bible called "La Nueva Biblia de Jerusalén" says the chronological order most likely is the following: 1) First Epistle to the Thessalonians. 2) Second Epistle to the Thessalonians. 3) First Epistle to the Corinthians. 4) Second Epistle to the Corinthians. 5) Epistle to the Galatians. 6) Epistle to the Romans. 7) Epistle to the Philippians. 8) Epistle to the Colossians. 9) Epistle to the Ephesians. 10) Epistle to Philemon. 11) First Epistle to Timothy. 12) Second Epistle to Timothy. 13) Epistle to Titus. 14) Epistle to Hebrews. Nueva Biblia de Jerusalén, Nueva Edición revisada y

Bible.

Methodology

I have tried to write this book in the simplest way possible and I have tried to reason mostly based on premises taken from the Bible, so that it should not be necessary to consult other documents to verify the correctness of the reasoning and the truth of the premises and conclusions. The most important books of human history, the Gospels, are presented in a very simple manner.

I worked using the King James Version; the Revised Standard Version, Second Catholic Edition; the New King James Version; the New American Bible; the New American Standard Bible; the New International Version; the English Standard Version; and also the Nestle-Aland Greek-English New Testament, the Merk Greek-Latin New Testament, and the Latin Vulgate, among other Bibles, some of them Spanish translations.

I took the precaution of comparing different versions of the Bible. That job is indispensable to whomever wants to study the Bible, because there are differences between versions and translations, and it is necessary to be aware of them. In those cases in which I found significant differences between the mentioned English versions of the Bible I quoted them all, and when I judged necessary I went to the Greek text.

This is a book that it is specially written for, and will delight, simple Christians, no matter what Christian

ampliada. Edición Española. (Spain; Desclee de Brouwer, 1999) p.1554.

Church they belong to, who are those who love the pure truth, simple as it is; those who love freedom of thought, and have faith in the reason that God gave us. It is a book that is especially written for, and will delight, straight-thinking people. It is a book that is going to express the feelings and thoughts of many Christians, especially of those who truly love Christ.

Even more, I hope that It will be a work that will help the development of the revolution that Christianity and the world need, strengthening the Christianity of those who are already Christians; attracting to true Christianity people who have turned away because of vices of the Christian Churches; and calling the attention of people that have never been interested in Christianity.

It is a work that is going to give many answers. It is going to explain many of the most important mistakes that the Christian Churches have made, and hopefully will help the Christian Church grow and get stronger.

- Part I -

Ruy Barraco Mármol

Prologue

Jesus says and asks in the Gospel according to Saint Luke (Revised Standard Version, Second Catholic Edition): "18:8 ...Nevertheless, when the Son of man comes, will he find faith on earth?"

How hard it is to imagine a world without faith in Jesus...! It is very hard to imagine a world without faith...Notwithstanding, I want to ask you now, for a moment, that you close your eyes and try to imagine a world without faith in Jesus; and that then you imagine a world in which the Christian Church, instead of teaching the words that Jesus taught to the twelve apostles, and of building its doctrine upon them, is teaching a doctrine partially built upon the words of Jesus, and partially built upon the words of another man, who came after Jesus; a man who came after Jesus falsely claiming that Jesus appeared to him, and that Jesus talked to him. Imagine that Jesus and his passion were being used to teach the doctrine of another man. Imagine that you are living in that world and that you have the opportunity to do something to help Christianity return to the pure words of Jesus: to help Christianity return to the words of Jesus just as Jesus taught them to the twelve apostles that he chose, prepared and credited publicly and that are preserved in the Gospels. And ask yourselves: What would you do in that world? Would you recognize the difference between the words of this man and the words of Jesus? Would you recognize the error? Would you pay attention to it? Would you be among those who remain faithful to the word of Jesus and promote a faithful to Jesus Christianity? Or, would you leave things just as they are?

Now open your eyes..., read this book..., and allow yourselves to see that this is the case of the world we are living in today. After Jesus ascended into heaven to be with the Father until the Second Coming, Paul of Tarsus joined the Christian Church, saying that he saw Jesus, after his Ascension, and that Jesus talked to him. And then Paul of Tarsus said that Jesus named him the apostle to the gentiles and that Jesus talked through him. And at some point of the development of the Church, the Christian Church started to teach the words of Paul, preserved in the Epistles of Paul, as if they were the word of God, with equal authority as the words that Jesus talked personally and publicly to the twelve apostles.

In this book I will explain how this happened and why it is an error. I will explain that we, as Christians, should nurture ourselves and remain faithful to the words that Jesus spoke to the twelve apostles, just as they are preserved in the Gospels; and how our personal salvation and the salvation of the world depend on this.

To do it, I will start with an introduction that it is meant to identify and highlight some facts concerning the life of Jesus and Paul of Tarsus, and also to explain with more details the content and the object of this book. I wish that the peace of the Lord is with you during the reading of this book, and that the Holy Spirit gives you strength and understanding.

Chapter I. Introduction

It is often said that reality greatly surpasses dreams and even imaginations. That sentence has never been truer than in regard to Jesus.

Way beyond any dream, or imagination, and in spite of being announced and prophesied, God became a man, to come to the world with signs and proofs, to proclaim to us very good news, to announce the kingdom of God,[3] life beyond death,[4] to bring hope,[5] to give us knowledge of salvation through forgiveness of our sins,[6] and to preach and have the word of God preached in his name to all the nations of the world, so that men repent, convert and enter to the kingdom of God.[7]

---

[3] The Gospel according to Saint Luke (N.K.J.V.) says: "*4:43 but he said to them, "I must preach the kingdom of God to the other cities also, because for this purpose I have been sent.*"

[4] The Gospel according to Saint Matthew (N.K.J.V.) says: "*22:31 But concerning the resurrection of the dead, have you not read what was spoken to you by God, saying, 22:32 'I am the God of Abraham, the God of Isaac, and the God of Jacob'? God is not the God of the dead, but of the living.*""

[5] The Gospel according to Saint Matthew (N.K.J.V.) says: "*12:21 And in his name Gentiles will trust.*"

[6] The Gospel according to Saint Luke (N.K.J.V.) says: "*1:76 "And you, child, will be called the prophet of the Highest; For you will go before the face of the Lord to prepare His ways, 1:77 To give knowledge of salvation to His people By the remission of their sins,*"

[7] The Gospel according to Saint Luke (N.K.J.V.) says: "*24:46 Then He said to*

Ruy Barraco Mármol

The man who God became was Jesus. His mother was a virgin, the Virgin Mary,[8] a descendent of David.[9]

them, "Thus it is written, and thus it was necessary for the Christ to suffer and to rise from the dead the third day, 24:47 "and that repentance and remission of sins should be preached in His name to all nations, beginning at Jerusalem."

[8] The Gospel according to Saint Luke (N.K.J.V.) says: "1:26 Now on the six month the angel Gabriel was sent by God to a city of Galilee named Nazareth, 1:27 to a virgin betrothed to a man whose name was Joseph, of the house of David." The virgin's name was Mary. The Gospel according to Saint Luke (N.K.J.V.) says: "1:34 Then Mary said to the angel, "How can this be, since I do not know a man?"'. In my opinion, this answer of Mary implies that she was a virgin. The Bible, book of the prophet Isaiah, (N.K.J.V.) says: "7:14 Therefore the Lord Himself will give you a sign: Behold, the virgin shall conceive and bear a son, and shall call His name Immanuel." The Greek word translated as virgin in the Bible (Septuagint), book of the prophet Isaiah, and in the New Testament, is παρθενος (parthenos), which means maiden, virgin, young woman. This same word is used with the meaning of virgin in the Bible (Septuagint), book Genesis 24:16. In my opinion, the word is correctly translated as virgin. It seems that this sign announced by Isaiah had to be something extraordinary, supernatural. A sign by definition must be something extraordinary, supernatural. A virgin conceiving and bearing a son was something supernatural. A young woman doing the same was not. Besides, it is easier to believe that a man is the son of God if his mother is a virgin. For that reason, it makes sense that God decided that a virgin was going to conceive and bear his son. Sir Lancelot C.L. Brenton "The Septuagint with Apocrypha" Greek and English, Hendrickson Publishers, Originally published by Samuel Bagster & Sons, Ltd., London 1851. United States of America, 2009. Robert Young LL.D, "Analytical Concordance to the Bible", Funk & Wagnalls Company, New York, 1912

[9] The Bible, book of the prophet Isaiah (N.K.J.V.), says: "11:1 There shall come forth a Rod from the stem of Jesse, And a Branch shall grow out of his roots. 11:2 The Spirit of the Lord shall rest upon Him, the Spirit of wisdom and understanding, the Spirit of counsel and might, the Spirit of knowledge and of the fear of the LORD. 11:3 His delight is in the fear of the LORD. And He shall not judge by the sight of His eyes, Nor decide by the hearing of His ears; 11:4 But with righteousness He shall judge the poor, And decide with equity for the meek of the earth; He shall strike the earth with the rod of His mouth, And with the breath of His lips He shall slay the wicked. 11:5 Righteousness shall be the belt of His loins, and faithfulness the belt of His waist. 11:6 "The wolf also shall dwell with the Lamb, The leopard shall lie down with the young goat, The calf and the young lion and the fatling together; And a little child shall lead them. 11:7 The cow and the bear shall graze; Their young ones shall lie down together; And the lion shall eat straw like the ox. 11:8 The nursing child

He was conceived while she was betrothed to Joseph. His place of birth was Bethlehem of Judea,[10] and he lived in a private way until he was around 30 years old.[11] From around his 30 years to his 33 he carried out his public life of signs, wonders and preaching, teaching us that he is God[12] become Man,[13] the Messiah and the Christ foretold by many prophets a long time before.[14]

---

shall play by the cobra's hole, And the weaned child shall put his hand in the viper's den. 11:9 They shall not hurt nor destroy in all My holy mountain, For the earth shall be full of the knowledge of the LORD As the waters cover the sea."

[10] The Bible, book of the prophet Micah, (N.K.J.V.) says: "5:1 Now gather yourself in troops, O daughter of troops; He has laid siege against us; They will strike the judge of Israel with a rod on the cheek. 5:2 "But you, Bethlehem Ephrathah, Though you are little among the thousands of Judah, Yet out of you shall come forth to Me The One to be Ruler in Israel, Whose goings forth are from of old, From everlasting." 5:3 Therefore He shall give them up, Until the time that she who is in labor has given birth; Then the remnant of His brethren Shall return to the children of Israel. 5:4 And He shall stand and feed His flock in the strength of the LORD, In the majesty of the name of the LORD His God; And they shall abide, For now He shall be great To the ends of the earth;"

[11] The Gospel according to Saint Luke, Verse 3:23.

[12] The Gospel according to Saint John (N.K.J.V.) says: "8:57 Then the Jews then said to Him, "You are not yet fifty years old, and have You seen Abraham?" 8:58 Jesus said to them, "Most assuredly, I say to you, before Abraham was, I AM." I believe this is one of the many ways with which Jesus taught us he is God. The Bible, book of Exodus, (N.K.J.V.) says: "3:13 Then Moses said to God, "Indeed, when I come to the children of Israel and say to them, 'The God of your fathers has sent me to you,' and they say to me, 'What is His name?' what shall I say to them?' 3:14 And God said to Moses, "I AM WHO I AM." And He said, "Thus you shall say to the children of Israel, 'I AM has sent me to you.'" The Gospel according to Saint John (R.S.V.), Second Catholic Edition, says: "10:30 I and My Father are one."

[13] The Gospel according to Saint Luke (N.K.J.V.) says: "24:39 Behold My hands and My feet, that it is I Myself. Handle Me and see, for a spirit does not have flesh and bones as you see I have."

[14] The Gospel according to Saint John (N.K.J.V.) says: "4:25 The woman said to Him, "I know that Messiah is coming" (who is called Christ). "When He comes, He

Ruy Barraco Mármol

In this last period of around 3 years, the public period of his life, he personally and publicly prepared, credited and sent disciples, especially twelve chosen from among them, the twelve apostles,[15] to testify to all the nations of the world his announcements, his preaching, and his other proofs. Those twelve were the first ministers of the Christian Church founded by Christ.

And although Christ, during his earthly life, must have lived many beautiful and wonderful moments, he did not come on a pleasure trip. His message would not be welcomed by the people of the world from the Jews, especially by the Jews' hierarchy.[16]

To accomplish his goals he had to carry out an immeasurably hard labor. On behalf of men's salvation Christ had to experience during his life the premature death of Joseph, his foster father, the beheading of John the Baptist,[17] his cousin, and many other brothers'

---

will tell us all things." 4:26 Jesus said to her, "I who speak to you am He.""

[15] The list of names of the apostles is: Peter, originally named Simon; Andrew; James; John; Philip; Bartholomew also called Nathanael; Thomas; Matthew also called Levi; James the son of Alphaeus; Judas also called Thaddeus; Simon the Cananean; and Judas Iscariot.

[16] The same way many Jews rejected Christ at the beginning of Christianity, the rejection has continued in all the nations of the world. Still, the message of Christ is not welcomed by the people of the world. Among those people there are persons of all the beliefs, sons of Christians, ex Christians, and even persons who call themselves Christians but choose to live ignoring Christ.

[17] The Gospel according to Saint Matthew (N.K.J.V.) says: *"14:9 And the king was sorry; nevertheless, because of the oaths and because of those who sat with him, he commanded it to be given to her. 14:10 So he sent and had John beheaded in prison. 14:11 And his head was brought on a platter and given to the girl, and she brought it to her mother. 14:12 Then his disciples came and took away the body and*

sufferings. He had to bear hate, dispraise, rejection, humiliations, insults,[18] mockeries, torture, and even had to give his life for men's salvation. And he had to give it facing flagellation. He had to let one of his chosen betray him, Judas Iscariot,[19] and allow other people, who had Christ as an enemy without a reason, to nail him to a cross, until death, and in the presence of his own mother. Sorrow even unto death, is the way the

---

buried it, and went and told Jesus. 14:13 When Jesus heard it, He departed from there by boat to a deserted place by Himself. But when the multitudes heard it, they followed Him on foot from the cities. 14:14 And when Jesus went out He saw a great multitude; and He was moved with compassion for them, and healed their sick. 14:15 When it was evening, His disciples came to Him, saying, "This is a deserted place, and the hour is already late. Send the multitudes away, that they may go into the villages and buy themselves food." 14:16 But Jesus said them, "They do not need to go away. You give them something to eat." 14:17 And they said to Him, "We have here only five loaves and two fish." 14:18 He said, "Bring them here to me." 14:19 Then He commanded the multitudes to sit down on the grass. And He took the five loaves and the two fish, and looking up to heaven, He blessed and broke and gave the loaves to the disciples; and the disciples gave to the multitudes. 14:20 So they all ate and were filled, and they took up twelve baskets full of the fragments that remained. 14:21 Now those who had eaten were about five thousand men, besides women and children". I believe that Christ experienced a great sorrow in that moment, and he felt a big compassion for the disciples of John the Baptist, which motivated him to perform the significant sign of the miracle of the feeding of the five thousand, which surely brought them comfort.

[18] The Gospel according to Saint Mark (N.K.J.V.) says: "15:29 And those who passed by blasphemed Him, wagging their heads and saying, "Aha! You who destroy the temple and build it in three days, 15:30 "save Yourself, and come down from the cross!" 15:31 Likewise the chief priests also, mocking among themselves with the scribes, said, "He saved others; Himself He cannot save. 15:32 "Let the Christ, the King of Israel, descend now from the cross, that we may see and believe." Even those who were crucified with Him reviled Him."

[19] The Gospel according to Saint Matthew (N.K.J.V.) says: "26:24 The Son of man indeed goes just as it is written of Him, but woe to that man by whom the Son of Man is betrayed! It would have been good for that man if he had not been born." 26:25 Then Judas, who was betraying Him, answered and said, "Rabbi, is it I?" He said to him, "You have said it."

sorrow felt by Christ just before the Passion is described; all this with him being God, which really is not a minor detail.[20] This truly is love.

And his goals, his mission, were completed. Christ accomplished his mission. Everything was accomplished as Christ confirms to us on the cross before expiring.[21] And everything was accomplished in the way it was prophesied. Men do not need a new name, or to wait for another man, to reach salvation.[22] His preaching neither needs complement, nor admits supplement or substitution[23].

After being killed, three days passed, he resurrected, he appeared to his disciples, he gave them power to forgive and retain sins,[24] and he strengthened their

---

[20] The Gospel according to Saint Matthew (N.K.J.V.) says: "26:38 Then He said to them, "My soul is exceedingly sorrowful, even to death. Stay here and watch with Me." 26:39 He went a little farther and fell on His face, and prayed, saying "O My Father, if it is possible, let this cup pass from Me; nevertheless, not as I will, but as You will."

[21] The Gospel according to Saint John (N.K.J.V.) says that Christ on the cross before expiring said: "19:28 After this, Jesus, knowing that all things were now accomplished, that the Scripture might be fulfilled, said, "I thirst!" 19:29 Now a vessel full of sour wine was sitting there; and they filled a sponge with sour wine, put it on hyssop, and put it to His mouth. 19:30 So when Jesus had received the sour wine, He said, "It is finished!"And bowing His head, He gave up His spirit."

[22] The book of Acts of the Apostles (N.K.J.V.) says: "4:12 Nor is there salvation in any other, for there is no other name under heaven given among men by which we must be saved."

[23] The Gospel according to Saint John (N.K.J.V.) says: "15:15 No longer do I call you servants, for a servant does not know what his master is doing; but I have called you friends, for all things that I have heard from My Father I have made known to you." It says all things that I have heard.

[24] The Gospel according to Saint John (N.K.J.V.) says: "20:23 "If you forgive the sins of any, they are forgiven them; if you retain the sins of any, they are retained.""

knowledge of the scriptures.[25] He also promised them the power to perform miracles, and he told them to wait for the promise of the Father: the Holy Spirit.[26]

Then Jesus ascended to Heaven to be with the Father until the Second Coming.[27] And when the day of Pentecost came, being all together in one place, they received the Holy Spirit.[28]

After that the apostles dedicated themselves to the preaching of the word of Jesus, the word of God, naming a new apostle, the apostle Matthias,[29] to

---

[25] The Gospel according to Saint Luke (N.K.J.V.) says: "24:45 And He opened their understanding, that they might comprehend the Scriptures."

[26] The book of Acts of the Apostles (N.K.J.V.) says: "1:8 But you shall receive power when the Holy Spirit has come upon you; and you shall be witnesses to Me in Jerusalem, and in all Judea and Samaria, and to the end of the earth."

[27] The book of Acts of the Apostles (N.K.J.V.) says: "3:21 whom heaven must receive until the times of restoration of all things, which God has spoken to the mouth of all His holy prophets since the world began." The book of Acts, Verse 1:11. The Gospel according to Saint John (N.K.J.V) says: "16:7 Nevertheless I tell you the truth. It is to your advantage that I go away; for if I do not go away, the Helper will not come to you: but if I depart, I will send Him to you."

[28] The book of Acts of the Apostles, Chapter 2.

[29] The book of Acts of the Apostles (N.K.J.V.) says: "1:20 "For it is written in the Book of Psalms, 'Let his dwelling place be desolate, And let no one live in it'; and, 'Let another take his office.' 1:21 "Therefore, of these men who have accompanied us all the time that the Lord Jesus went in and out among us, 1:22 "beginning from the baptism of John to that day when He was taken up from us, one of these must become a witness with us of His resurrection." 1:23 And they proposed two: Joseph called Barsabas, who was surnamed Justus, and Matthias. 1:24 And they prayed and said, "You, O Lord, who know the hearts of all, show which of these two You have chosen 1:25 "to take part in this ministry and apostleship from which Judas by transgression fell, that he might go to his own place." 1:26 And they cast their lots, and the lot fell on Matthias. And he was numbered with the eleven apostles."

complete the number of 12 apostles that God had chosen and institutionalized for the apostolic ministry,[30] which had been left incomplete by the treason and death of Judas, so that the new apostle could bear testimony with them of the resurrection of Jesus.

The one chosen to be one of the twelve could not have been anyone. It had to be one of the men who had accompanied the apostles during all the time that the Lord Jesus went in and out among them, beginning from the baptism of John until the day when Christ was taken up from them. The book of Acts of the Apostles, Revised Standard Version (R.S.V.), Second Catholic Edition,[31] says: "*1:21 So one of the men who have accompanied us during all the time that the Lord Jesus went in and out among us, 1:22 beginning from the baptism of John until the day when he was taken up from us-one of these men must become with us a witness to his resurrection.*" The Gospel according to Saint John (R.S.V.), Second Catholic Edition, says: "*15:26 But when the Counselor comes, whom I shall send to you from the Father, even the Spirit of truth, who proceeds from the Father, he will bear witness to me; 15:27 and you also are*

---

[30] The book of Acts of the Apostles (N.K.J.V.) says: "*1:24 And they prayed and said, "You, O Lord, who know the hearts of all, show which of these two You have chosen 1:25 "to take part in this ministry and apostleship from which Judas by transgression fell, that he might go to his own place.*" The book of Acts of the Apostles (N.K.J.V.) says: "*1:17 for he was numbered with us and obtained a part in this ministry.*"

[31] Scripture quotation taken from "*The Holy Bible*", Revised Standard Version, Second Catholic Edition, Printed in China, published by Thomas Nelson Publishing for Ignatius Press, 2006. Scripture quotations marked with (RSV) are from the Revised Standard Version, Second Catholic Edition.

witness, because you have been with me from the beginning."

The number of twelve apostles corresponds with the number of tribes of Israel,[32] and it is very meaningful and symbolical. It is used symbolically many times in the Old Testament, and also in the New Testament.

The Gospel according to Saint Matthew (R.S.V.), Second Catholic Edition, says: *"19:28 Jesus said to them, "Truly, I say to you, in the new world, when the Son of man shall sit on his glorious throne, you who have followed me will also sit on twelve thrones, judging the twelve tribes of Israel."* The same Gospel (R.S.V.), Second Catholic Edition, says: *"26:52 Then Jesus said to him, "Put your sword back into its place; for all who take the sword will perish by the sword. 26:53 Do you think that I cannot appeal to my Father, and he will at once send me more than twelve legions of angels?"* The Gospel according to Saint John (R.S.V.), Second Catholic Edition, says: *"11:9 Jesus answered, "Are there not twelve hours in the day? If any one walks in the day, he does not stumble, because he sees the light of this world."* And the book Revelation (R.S.V.), Second Catholic Edition, teaching about the New Jerusalem, says: *"21:12 It had a great, high wall, with twelve gates, and at the gates twelve angels, and on the*

---

[32] The Bible, book of Genesis, (N.K.J.V.) says: *"49:28 All these are the twelve tribes of Israel, and this is what their father spoke to them. And he blessed them; he blessed each one according to his own blessing."* The Bible, book of Exodus, (N.K.J.V.) says: *"24:4 And Moses wrote all the words of the LORD. And he rose early in the morning, and built an altar at the foot of the mountain, and twelve pillars according to the twelve tribes of Israel."* The Bible, book of Exodus, (N.K.J.V.) says: *"28:21 And the stones shall have the names of the sons of Israel, twelve according to their names, like the engravings of a signet, each one with its own name; they shall be according to the twelve tribes."*

gates the names of the twelve tribes of the sons of Israel were inscribed; 21:13 on the east three gates, on the north three gates, on the south three gates, and on the west three gates. 21:14 And the wall of the city had twelve foundations, and on them the twelve names of the twelve apostles of the Lamb."

At that point, when the twelve apostles began preaching, everything indicated that the Christian Church would be built on doctrine starting from the word of Jesus taught personally to them. Moreover, at that point, everything indicated that in the hierarchical institutional matters the Church would be built on the basis of these twelve apostles, who had been publicly taught, educated, prepared and credited by God in person for that mission, for that ministry.[33]

When I read in the gospels episodes like the washing of feet,[34] I see Christ leaving us important teachings, and also preparing the twelve apostles for the mission he

---

[33] Except, of course, the case of Judas replaced by Matthias.

[34] The Gospel according to Saint John (N.K.J.V.) says: "13:1 Now before the Feast of the Passover, when Jesus knew that His hour had come that He should depart from this world to the Father, having loved His own who were in the world, He loved them to the end. 13:2 And supper being ended, the devil having already put it into the heart of Judas Iscariot, Simon's son, to betray Him. 13:3 Jesus, knowing that the Father had given all things into His hands, and that He had come from God and was going to God, 13:4 rose from supper and laid aside His garments, took a towel and girded Himself. 13:5 After that, He poured water into a basin, and began to wash the disciples' feet, and to wipe them with the towel with which He was girded. 13:6 Then He came to Simon Peter. And Peter said to him, "Lord, are you washing my feet?" 13:7 Jesus answered and said to him, "What I am doing you do not understand now, but you will know after this." 13:8 Peter said to him, " You shall never wash my feet!" Jesus answered him, "If I do not wash you, you have no part with Me." 13:9 Simon Peter said to him, "Lord, not my feet only, but also my hands and my head!"

would commission them. This makes me believe that those who were going to be part of the ministry of the twelve apostles needed to be prepared by Christ. So important was it for Christ for the Christians to be humble that Christ himself, God, even took the job to wash personally the feet of the apostles, among other reasons, so that they would learn to be humble and teach others to be humble.

However, unexpectedly, unpredictably, astonishingly, the course of events would take another direction. A man, who did not accompany Christ during his earthly life, and who had not been personally and publicly taught, prepared, educated and credited by him, would show up saying that he had been privately called by Jesus to bear his name, with great sufferings, to all the nations, kings and to the sons of Israel.

And this man would later allege to have been privately chosen and supernaturally instructed by Christ to be the apostle of the gentiles, witness of what he had seen and of other apparitions of Jesus that he would witness, and to preach new words of God. And he would take a place equal or greater than the place of most of the apostles, if not all of them, at least in the scriptures. This, when he started to be considered a new apostle, with equal hierarchy than the twelve, and when his epistles became known and considered the word of God, spoken by Christ through him, and their content considered dogma of faith.

Moreover, the words pronounced by this man who showed up, written in the epistles that are attributed to him, would share in an important measure, altogether with the words of God taught to the twelve apostles by

Christ in his earthly life, a fundamental position in the construction of the Christian doctrine. This privileged position would be placed principally in moral, but also in theological and institutional subjects.

The Christian doctrine on which man would reach salvation, and how he would, no longer would be built exclusively on the basis of what Christ taught to the twelve apostles, nor on the basis of the words Christ chose during his public life. Another man would come with other words of God. Something likewise can be said about the marriage and divorce doctrine, about the best form of government, about the way Christians should maintain their relationships, about the relationships between church, Christians and civil society, about freedom of religion, women's rights, celibacy, about richness, that no longer would be built exclusively on the basis of the words of God which Christ taught to the apostles. The word of Christ expressed to the twelve apostles would share that place with the supposed word of Christ expressed to a new man, which on some occasions would relegate the words of Christ expressed to the twelve apostles to a second or even an ignored place.[35]

The man we are talking about was called Saul or Paul and he is almost universally known as Saint Paul. Who is Saul or Saint Paul or simply Paul? According to the information found in the book of Acts of the Apostles and from the epistles attributed to him, he was born in

---

[35] Today such a position regarding the words of this man has lost ground, but his words still have a great influence on the substance and basis of certain positions of the Christian Church, fundamentally the Catholic Church, which, in my opinion, are very erroneous and prejudicial.

Tarsus in Cilicia,[36] in Asia Minor.

It is taught that Paul's birth took place between the years 1 to 10 A.D.[37] He was educated in Jerusalem.[38] He would have been between 23 and 33 years old, more or less, in the year of the crucifixion of Christ, who, according to what may be concluded from the gospels and the astronomic information, was crucified in the year 33 A.D.[39]

He was a Jew with Roman citizenship since birth,[40]

---

[36] The book of Acts of the Apostles (N.K.J.V.) says: "22:3 "*I am indeed a Jew, born in Tarsus of Cilicia, but brought up in this city at the feet of Gamaliel, taught according to the strictness of our fathers's law, and was zealous toward God as you all are today.*"

[37] Josef Holzner "San Pablo Heraldo de Cristo", (Barcelona; Editorial Herder, 1959), p. 479 says that Paul was born probably between the years 1 to 5 A.D. He says that because Paul is called young at the time of the death of Saint Stephen, which he says happened in the year 33 or 34 A.D., and yet he was already an important figure, which means he must have been more or less 30 years old at that time.

[38] The book of Acts of the Apostles (N.K.J.V.) says: "22:3 "*I am indeed a Jew, born in Tarsus of Cilicia, but brought up in this city at the feet of Gamaliel, taught according to the strictness of our fathers's law, and was zealous toward God as you all are today.*" When Paul says "in this city" he refers to Jerusalem.

[39] Mario Domingo Barraco Marmol "When Was Jesus Born?" said that in the year 33 A.D. there was a full moon in Jerusalem at noon on Friday, the third of April, according to the Julian calendar which was in use at that time, which would have been the first of April in the Gregorian calendar which we use today. This is why the Jews celebrated Passover on the following day, our Holy Saturday, the day on which our Lord Jesus rested in the tomb, since there was a full moon from Friday through Saturday after the spring equinox (in the northern hemisphere.) BARRACO MARMOL, Mario Domingo, "When Was Jesus Born?". The citation states: This conclusion was published in 1933 by Father John Schaunmberger, C.S.S.R. in "Tabella Neomeniarum Vitae Publicae Domini"..., as cited by Father Juan Leal, S.J. in "Sinopsis de los Cuatros Evangelios" [Synopsis of the Four Evangelists] page 105, published by the B.A.C. (Biblioteca de Autores Cristianos) [Library of Christian Authors]

and he would be unexpectedly a Pharisee. Who were the Pharisees? They were a group of Jews, a sort of religious party of Jews.[41] I believe it is appropriate to say a religious and political party (some teach that their ultimate political goal was to restore a National State of Israel with a theocratic regime),[42] or maybe a Jewish Church, who in the time of Christ were considered the defenders of the Jewish law, the sacred scriptures, and the tradition. The Pharisees had great fame and prestige among the Jews, and even though they were not priests, the vast majority of them, in regard to the knowledge of the law and the observance of the traditions of the fathers, took precedence over the priests[43]. And in fact, they were the leaders in the teaching of the sacred scriptures[44].

How is that they were not priests and they taught the law? The book "Introducción a la Biblia", by Manuel

---

[40] The book of Acts of the Apostles (N.K.J.V.) says: "22:28 The commander answered, "With a large sum I obtained this citizenship." And Paul said, "But I was born a citizen.""

[41] The book of Acts of the Apostles (N.K.J.V.) says: "23:9 Then there arose a loud outcry. And the scribes of the Pharisees' party arose and protested, saying, "We find no evil in this man; but if a spirit or an angel has spoken to him, let us not fight against God." 23:10 Now when there arose a great dissension, the commander, fearing lest Paul might be pulled to pieces by them, commanded the soldiers to go down and take him by force from among them, and bring him into the barracks."

[42] De Tuya Manuel and José Salguero "Introducción a la Biblia" [Introduction to the Bible], vol II, p. 547.

[43] De Tuya Manuel and José Salguero, "Introducción a la Biblia", vol. II, p. 547.

[44] The Gospel according to Saint Matthew (N.K.J.V.) says: "23:2 The scribes and the Pharisees sit in Moses' seat."

de Tuya and José Salguero, says that after the exile, the teaching of the Torah (first five books of the bible, Jewish law, sacred scripture) stopped being a monopoly of the priests. In that way the teaching of the priests started to be carried out separately from the ritual, and in the synagogues. Even more, when the scribes and doctors of the law appeared, they soon became the teachers of the nation.[45] These scribes and doctors of the law were almost all Pharisees[46]. The Pharisees had great support in the Jewish nation and an important representation in the Sanhedrin. The Sanhedrin was a senate of the Jews that assisted the chief of the community.[47]

Who and what kind of men were the Pharisees

---

[45] De Tuya Manuel and José Salguero, "Introducción a la Biblia", vol. II, p. 471.

[46] De Tuya Manuel and José Salguero, "Introducción a la Biblia", vol. II, p. 547.

[47] According to Manuel De Tuya and Jose Salguero, in "Introducción a la Biblia", vol II., p. 560, the high priest was the president by right. The members of the Sanhedrin (the supreme council and tribunal of the Jews in the times of the New Testament having religious, civil and criminal jurisdiction) belonged to three groups: the priestly aristocracy, the lay aristocracy, represented by the elders, and the scribes and doctors of law. This latter group was dominated almost exclusively by the Pharisees. The jurisdiction of the Sanhedrin differed according to the times. Above all it was the highest religious court, and as such, handled all matters which concerned the religious life of the Jewish nation. It also had power in civil matters. It could declare a sentence of death, but this sentence could not be executed without previous ratification by the Roman attorney general. The Sanhedrin had its own police and could arrest and jail criminals, administer corporal punishment, levy fines, and exclude criminals from the Israeli community. In the provinces and the Diaspora there were also local courts which were called Sanhedrins which heard local matters according to the laws of the Sanhedrin of Jerusalem, whose decisions were communicated to the Jews all over the world. The decisions and sentences of the Great Sanhedrin of Jerusalem were not subject to appeal.

according to the gospels?: The ones who had sat on the chair of Moses;[48] men whose righteousness was not enough to enter the kingdom of heaven;[49] men who did not know what mercy is;[50] men who loved the place of honor at feasts, salutations in the market places, and being called rabbi;[51] men who shut the kingdom of heaven against men, and did not enter themselves;[52]

---

[48] The Gospel according to Saint Matthew (N.K.J.V.) says: "23:2 *The scribes and the Pharisees sit in Moses' seat. 23:3 "Therefore whatever they tell you to observe, that observe and do, but do not do according to their works; for they say, and do not do."*

[49] The Gospel according to Saint Matthew (N.K.J.V.) says: "5:20 *For I say to you, that unless your righteousness exceeds the righteousness of the scribes and Pharisees, you will by no means enter the kingdom of heaven."*

[50] The Gospel according to Saint Matthew (N.K.J.V.) says: "9:11 *And when the Pharisees saw it, they said to His disciples "Why does your Teacher eat with tax collectors and sinners?" 9:12 When Jesus heard that, He said to them, "Those who are well have no need of a physician, but those who are sick. 9:13 "But go and learn what this means: 'I desire mercy and not sacrifice.' For I did not come to call the righteous, but sinners, to repentance."*

[51] The Gospel according to Saint Matthew (N.K.J.V.) says: "23:2 *The scribes and the Pharisees sit in Moses' seat. 23:3 "Therefore whatever they tell you to observe, that observe and do, but do not do according to their works; for they say, and do not do. 23:4 "For they bind heavy burdens, hard to bear, and lay them on men's shoulders; but they themselves will not move them with one of their fingers. 23:5 "But all their works they do to be seen by men. They make their phylacteries broad and enlarge the borders of their garments. 23:6 "They love the best places at feasts, the best seats in the synagogues, 23:7 "greetings in the marketplaces, and to be called by men, "Rabbi, Rabbi.' 23:8 "But you, do not be called 'Rabbi'; for One is your Teacher, the Christ, and you are all brethren. 23:9 "Do you not call anyone on earth your father; for One is your Father, He who is in heaven. 23:10 "And do not be called teachers; for One is your Teacher, the Christ. 23:11 "But he who is greatest among you shall be your servant. "And whoever exalts himself will be humbled, and he who humbles himself will be exalted."*

[52] The Gospel according to Saint Matthew (N.K.J.V.) says: "23:13 *"But woe to you, scribes and Pharisees, hypocrites! For you shut up the kingdom of heaven against men; for you neither go in yourselves, nor do you allow those who are*

lovers of money;[53] hypocrites; the brood of vipers;[54] the ones who called Jesus the prince of demons;[55] men like whitewashed tombs, which outwardly appear beautiful, but within are full of dead men's bones and all uncleanness;[56] the ones who took counsel against Jesus to destroy him;[57] the ones who, along with the chief of priests,[58] found him guilty,[59] and the ones who went

---

entering to go in."

[53] The Gospel according to Saint Luke (N.K.J.V.) says: "*16:13 "No servant can serve two masters; for either he will hate the one and love the other, or else he will be loyal to the one and despise the other. You cannot serve God and mammon. 16:14 Now the Pharisees, who were lovers of money, also heard all these things, and they derided Him."*

[54] The Gospel according to Saint Matthew (N.K.J.V.) says: "*3:7 "But when he saw many of the Pharisees and Sadducees coming to his baptism, he said to them, "Brood of vipers! Who warned you to flee from the wrath to come?"*

[55] The Gospel according to Saint Matthew (N.K.J.V.) says "*9:34: But the Pharisees said, "He casts out demons by the ruler of the demons.""*

[56] The Gospel according to Saint Matthew (N.K.J.V.) says: "*23:27 "Woe to you, scribes and Pharisees, hypocrites! For you are like whitewashed tombs which indeed appear beautiful outwardly, but inside are full of dead men's bones and all uncleanness."*

[57] The Gospel according to Saint Matthew (N.K.J.V.) says: "*12:14. Then the Pharisees went out and plotted against Him, how they might destroy Him."*

[58] The Gospel according to Saint John (N.K.J.V.) says: "*18:1 When Jesus had spoken these words, He went out with His disciples over the Brook Kidron, where there was a garden, which He and His disciples entered. 18:2 And Judas, who betrayed Him, also knew the place; for Jesus often met there with His disciples. 18:3 Then Judas, having received a detachment of troops and officers from the chief priests and Pharisees, came there with lanterns, torches, and weapons."*

[59] The Gospel according to Saint Luke (N.K.J.V.) says: "*22:66 As soon as it was day, the elders of the people, both chief priests and scribes, came together and led Him into their council, saying, "If You are the Christ, tell us." But He said to them,*

before Pilate to ask for Christ's tomb to be secure.[60] That kind of men were the Pharisees and Paul was one of them.

Certainly, there were many exceptions among the Pharisees, but this does not seem to be the case of Paul. The information that comes from the book of Acts of the Apostles implies that during the passion of Christ he already might have been a Pharisee very well related to the hierarchy of the Jews, and that he was not exactly a humble, merciful, gentle and harmless Pharisee.

I say that during the passion of Christ he most likely already was a Pharisee very well related to the hierarchy of the Jews, because he was present the day of the murder, the execution, of the first Christian martyr, Saint Stephen, committed by the members of the Sanhedrin and some other Jews who supported them. That murder was committed more or less 2 years after the passion of Christ[61] as a result of a sort of

---

22:67 "If I tell you, you will by no means believe. 22:68"And if I also ask you, you will by no means answer Me or let Me go. 22:69 "Hereafter the Son of Man will sit on the right hand of the power of God." 22:70 Then they all said, "Are You then the Son of God?"So He said to them, "You rightly say that I am." 22:71 And they said, "What further testimony do we need? For we have heard it ourselves from His own mouth."

[60] The Gospel according to Saint Matthew (N.K.J.V.) says: "27:62 On the next day, which followed the Day of Preparation, the chief priests and Pharisees gathered together to Pilate 27:63 saying, "Sir, we remember, while He was still alive, how that deceiver said, 'After three days I will rise.' 27:64 "Therefore command that the tomb be made secure until the third day, lest His disciples come by night and steal Him away, and say to the people, 'He has risen from the dead.' So the last deception will be worse than the first.""

[61] It is calculated that this occurred more or less two years after the death of Jesus, because according the book of Acts at the time of his death the Church already had reached a certain level of development, and it could not have

judicial procedure like the one that finished with the condemnation of Jesus. The reason for the execution of Saint Stephen was the preaching of the word of Christ, the performance of healings and other miracles.

Saint Stephen was a very important man for the Christians. He was not one of the twelve apostles, but was one of the seven chosen by the twelve to help in the daily distribution of assistance. He was full of the Holy Spirit, and not only helped with the daily distribution, but also did great wonders and signs, and preached with great wisdom.[62] After Christ's death and resurrection, and in the time of the apostles, not many received the power of doing wonders and signs and miracles; at least not many are mentioned in the book of Acts of the Apostles as having those gifts. Two of the seven chosen by the twelve appear in the book with them: Saint Stephen and Saint Philip.

And Paul, the book of the Acts of the Apostles says, approved that savage stoning to death, and participated in it being present and keeping the garments of those who killed him, and made ravages in the Christian Church during the persecution unleashed that day against the Christians, against the preachers of the word of God, entering house after house, and dragging men and women to commit them to prison.[63] To do that he

---

happened much later because if it had, certain events related in the Epistles of Paul would not have been relevant, such as the periods of three years, and fourteen years mentioned in the Epistle of Paul to the Galatians.

[62] The book of Acts of the Apostles, Verses 6:1-9.

[63] The book of Acts of the Apostles (N.K.J.V.) says: "*8:1 Now Saul was consenting to his death. At that time a great persecution arose against the Church*

Ruy Barraco Mármol

must have had an important rank in the Jewish hierarchy. In fact, at the time of the execution of Saint Stephen, he probably was a member of the Sanhedrin.[64]

The rank of Paul at the time of the execution of Saint Stephen, that was committed more or less two years after Christ was crucified, strongly suggests that Paul had already been very well related to the hierarchy of the Jews, two years before, at the time of Christ's crucifixion.

I say that he was not a humble, merciful, gentle, and harmless Pharisee, in addition to what I have just said, because the book of Acts of the Apostles says that Paul acknowledged to have been not only a persecutor,[65] but a calumniator,[66] a flagellator,[67] torturer,[68] and multiple

---

which was at Jerusalem; and they were all scattered throughout the regions of Judea and Samaria, except the apostles. 8:2 And devout men carried Stephen to his burial, and made great lamentation over him. 8:3 As for Saul, he made havoc of the Church, entering every house, and dragging off men and women, committing them to prison."

[64] The book of Acts of the Apostles (N.K.J.V.) says: "26:9 "Indeed, I myself thought I must do many things contrary to the name of Jesus of Nazareth. 26:10 "This I also did in Jerusalem, and many of the saints I shut up in prison, having received authority from the chief priests; and when they were put to death, I cast my vote against them." Some people interpret that the vote he is talking about is the vote that the members of the Sanhedrin gave, and that this implies that he was a member by that time.

[65] The book of Acts of the Apostles 26:9-10. Idem note 65.

[66] The book of Acts of the Apostles (N.K.J.V.) says: "6:8 And Stephen, full of faith and power, did great wonders and signs among the people. 6:9 Then there arose some from what is called the Synagogue of the Freedmen (Cyrenians, Alexandrians, and those of Cilicia and Asia), disputing with Stephen. 6:10 And they were not able to resist the wisdom and the Spirit by which he spoke. 6:11 Then they secretly induced men to say, "We have heard him speak blasphemous words against Moses and God." And they stirred up the people, the elders, and the scribes; and

murderer of Christians:[69] In actual terms a torturer, a state terrorist, a perpetrator of genocide and crimes against humanity. In medieval terms he would have been a Jewish counterpart of what was late called an inquisitor. Christ called Judas a son of the devil.[70] In gospel language, it does not seem inappropriate to call Paul son of the devil before his calling. Jesus called some Jews, who did not believe in him and wanted to kill him, son of the Devil.[71]

---

they came upon him, seized him, and brought him to the council. 6:13 They also set up false witnesses who said, "This man does not cease to speak blasphemous words against this holy place and the law; 6:14 "for we have heard him say that this Jesus of Nazareth will destroy this place and change the customs which Moses delivered to us." 6:15 And all who sat in the council, looking steadfastly at him, saw his face as the face of an angel."

67 The book of Acts of the Apostles (N.K.J.V.) says that Paul stated: "22:19 "So I said, 'Lord, they know that in every synagogue I imprisoned and beat those who believe on You. 22:20 "And when the blood of Your martyr Stephen was shed, I also was standing by consenting to his death, and guarding the clothes of those who were killing him." The Greek work translated as beat, is ΄δερων (deron), which means to skin, flay; to cudgel (Karl Feyerabend "Langenscheidt Pocket Greek Dictionary- Greek-English" (Germany, Langenscheidt) under δερω (dero).

68 The book of Acts of the Apostle (N.K.J.V.), Second Catholic Edition, says that Paul acknowledged: "26:11 And I punished them often in every synagogue and compelled them to blaspheme; and being exceedingly enraged against them, I persecuted them even to foreign cities."

69 The book of Acts of the Apostles (N.K.J.V.) says: "26:9 Indeed, I myself thought I must do many things contrary to the name of Jesus Nazareth. 26:10 "This I also did in Jerusalem, and many of the saints I shut up in prison, having received authority from the chief priests; and when they were put to death, I cast my vote against them."

70 The Gospel according to Saint John (N.K.J.V.) says: "6:70 Jesus answered them, "Did I not choose you the twelve, and one of you is a devil?" 6:71 He spoke of Judas Iscariot, the son of Simon, for it was he who betray Him, being one of the twelve."

No, Paul was not an exception among the Pharisees. As I said, he must have been between 23 and 33 years old at the time of the Passion; and because it was customary for the Jews to go to Jerusalem during the feast of Passover, it is most likely that he had been in Jerusalem at the same time Jesus had been; at least during one of the feasts of Passover of Jesus' public life, which were three, according to the Gospel of Saint John (2,13; 6,4; 13,1); and it is very likely, very likely, that Paul might not only have rejected Christ's doctrine, which is a fact, but he might also have done so having seen Christ personally. Christ, his signs and wonders, did not pass unnoticed among the Pharisees. They knew perfectly his teachings and using that knowledge did not cease to tempt Christ with questions - - and not only in Jerusalem. Because of Paul's temperament, it is not hard to imagine him taking the initiative, tempting Christ with questions and participating in the process Christ had to endure before his crucifixion.[72]

---

[71] The Gospel according to Saint John (N.K.J.V.) says: "*8:43 Why do you not understand My speech? Because you are not able to listen to My word. 8:44 "You are of your father the devil, and the desires of your father you want to do. He was a murderer from the beginning, and does not stand in the truth, because there is no truth in him. When he speaks a lie, he speaks from his own resources, for he is a liar and the father of it. 8:45 "But because I tell the truth, you do not believe Me. 8:46 "Which of you convicts Me of sin? And If I tell the truth, why do you not believe Me? 8:47 "He who is of God hears God's words; therefore you do not hear, because you are not of God.*"

[72] The book of Acts of the Apostles (N.K.J.V.) says: "*26:16 'But rise and stand on your feet; for I have appeared to you for this purpose, to make you a minister and a witness both of the things which you have seen and of the things which I will yet reveal to you. 26:17 "I will deliver you from the Jewish people, as well as from the Gentiles, to whom I now send you*". If these words were true, then Paul would had seen things of Christ or at least known about Christ during his earthly life, which suggest that Paul knew Christ personally during Christ's earthly life. □

It is worth bringing out, that Paul probably carried on the genocide of the first Christians authorized and empowered by high authorities of Rome, maybe even by the Emperor himself. The Gospel according to Saint John says that Jesus was taken to Pilate because the Jews did not have the authorization to put any man to death.[73] That suggests that when Paul, shortly after the passion of Christ, more or less two years, persecuted, imprisoned and condemned Christians to death, he was acting under authorization and power given by Rome. In fact, the book of Acts of the Apostles (R.S.V.), Second Catholic Edition, narrating the liberation of Saint Peter and Saint John from the hands of the Sanhedrin, says: "*4:27 for truly in this city there were gathered together against your holy servant Jesus, whom you anointed, both Herod and Pontius Pilate, with the Gentiles and the peoples of Israel*". Herod and Pilate were high authorities of Rome.

In any case, the inquisition that Paul carried on seems to have stopped when he abandoned it, which is also very suggestive, for more than one reason.

Certainly, for some readers this matter of the precedents of Paul will be the hardest to understand concerning his election as an apostle and minister of new words of God, words not taught to the twelve apostles. And indeed they have good reasons for it.

There is no record that any other prophet in all the

---

[73] The Gospel according to Saint John (N.K.J.V.) says: "*18:31 Then Pilate said to them, "You take Him and judge Him according to your law." Therefore the Jews said to him, "It is not lawful for us to put anyone to death.""*

history of the Jewish religion had ever had evil antecedents even remotely close. There is no record that other Christians considered to be 'saints' had ever had that kind of background. Not even Judas did. Judas' betrayal was not part of his background because it was committed after his election as an apostle. Besides, although he betrayed Christ, which is not irrelevant, he was chosen so that the scriptures would be accomplished[74] and seems to have an infamous destiny forever and ever - - not a destiny of glory like Paul seemed to have, at least among men.

Saint Matthew did not have antecedents even remotely close. Being a tax collector, if it was a sin for a Jew, was nothing compared to being a persecutor and a perpetrator of genocide against Christians. Not even being a soldier of the Roman Empire was as bad for a Jew. In the Gospel according to Saint Luke (R.S.V.), Second Catholic Edition, John the Baptist, says: "*3:12 Tax collectors also came to be baptized, and said to him, "Teacher, what shall we do?" 3:13 And he said to them, "Collect no more than is appointed you." 3:14 Soldiers also asked him, "And we, what shall we do?" And he said to them, "Rob no one by violence or by false accusation, and be content with your wages."* If being a tax collector or a soldier were as bad as being a persecutor, torturer and killer, John the Baptist would have not said to them what he said. These tax collectors were most likely Jews. In my opinion, even the soldiers were most likely Jews. This

[74] The Gospel according to Saint John (N.K.J.V.) says: "*17:12 "While I was with them in the world, I kept them in Your name. Those whom you gave Me I have kept; and none of them is lost except the son of perdition, that the Scripture might be fulfilled."*

happened before the public life of Jesus. It seems that it was too early to have gentile tax collectors and soldiers being baptized by John the Baptist. The Gospel according to Saint Luke, (R.S.V.) Second Catholic Edition, says: "*19:1 He entered Jericho and was passing through. 19:2 And there was a man named Zachae'us; he was a chief tax collector, and rich. 19:3 And he sought to see who Jesus was, but could not, on account of the crowd, because he was small of stature. 19:4 So he ran on ahead and climbed up into a sycamore tree to see him, for he was to pass that way. 19:5 And when Jesus came to the place, he looked up and said to him, "Zacchae'us, make haste and come down; for I must stay at your house today." 19:6 So he made haste and came down, and received him joyfully. 19:7 And when they saw it they all murmured, "He has gone in to be the guest of a man who is a sinner." 19:8 And Zacchae'us stood and said to the Lord, "Behold, Lord, the half of my goods I give to the poor; and if I have defrauded any one of anything, I restore it fourfold." 19:9 And Jesus said to him, "Today salvation has come to this house, since he is also a son of Abraham. 19:10 For the Son of man came to seek and save the lost."* The chief tax collector also seems to have been a Jew. Even if he were not a Jew, the words of Jesus imply that being a tax collector was not a sin for those who were not Jews. The tax collector was not abandoning his job, and still he was being saved. If it were not a sin for those who were not Jews to be tax collectors we know for sure that for a Jew being a tax collector was not even remotely close to being as bad as being a persecutor, torturer and killer of innocent Christians. In the Gospel according to Saint Matthew (R.S.V.), Second Catholic Edition, Jesus says about a Roman Soldier: "*8:10 When Jesus heard him, he marveled, and said to those who followed him, "Truly, I say to you, not even in Israel I have found such faith".*

Not only the other prophets, apostles and saints chosen by God did not commit those kinds of crimes and sins against innocents before their election, but also they were not chosen while they were carrying on persecutions, tortures and murders against innocent men.

The prophets and saints certainly have not been perfect: Only God is perfect. And surely some of them committed serious crimes and sins, but none of them were before their election by God torturers and perpetrators of a religious genocide that had as victims men of faith in God, and much less Christians; none of them were chosen while they were committing a genocide of men of faith.

To punish men and women of faith for the only reason of being Christians, to torture them to get them to blaspheme against Christ, to beat to death those who would rather die before denying Christ, requires a heart defiled with evil, especially if the author of such crimes had a privileged education in sacred scriptures.[75]

Let us remember that Christ taught that the most important matters of the Jewish Law were "justice, mercy and faithfulness", so nobody can use as an excuse zeal for the law as a reason for committing those acts.

If Paul was really chosen by God, then God would

---

[75] The Gospel according to Saint Matthew (N.K.J.V.) says: "*15:18 "But those things which proceed out of the mouth come from the heart, and they defile a man. 15:19 "For out of the heart proceed evil thoughts, murders, adulteries, fornications, thefts, false witness, blasphemies. 15:20 "These are the things which defile a man, but to eat with unwashed hands does not defile a man."*

have made an exception which it seems he would have never repeated in electing others who have been blessed with the chance to do signs, wonders, and healings, in the history of the Christian Church. After Paul, it seems at least, all those who have been chosen by God, have not been persecutors, torturers, murderers, and perpetrators of genocide against Christians.

In the Old Testament, Noah found favor with the Lord before being chosen[76]. In the New Testament, Gospel according to Saint Luke, Verse 1:30, (R.S.V.), Second Catholic Edition, the angel told Virgin Mary in the moment of the annunciation: "Do *not be afraid, Mary, for you have found favor with God*"[77]. Zechariah and his wife were both righteous before God, walking in all the commandments and ordinances of the Lord blamelessly, before the conception of John the Baptist was foretold to Zechariah. Everything seems to indicate that Abraham, Moses, Elijah and Elisha were chosen because of their moral virtues, and certainly were not perpetrators of genocide of men of faith in God at the time they were chosen.

That is why it is very hard to understand the election of Paul, who, even after supposedly being chosen by God as an apostle, did not recognize that when he

---

[76] The Bible, book of Genesis, (N.K.J.V.) says: "*6:8 But Noah found grace in the eyes of the LORD.*"

[77] The Gospel according to Saint Luke (N.K.J.V.) says: "*1:30 Then the angel said to her. "Do not be afraid, Mary, for you have found favor with God. 1:31 "And behold, you will conceive in your womb and bring forth a Son, and you shall call His name JESUS.*"

Ruy Barraco Mármol

persecuted the Christian Church, he did not walk blamelessly in the justice of the Lord, as he stated,[78] on the contrary.

The most important matters of the Jewish law, as I have said, according to what Jesus taught, are: justice, mercy and faithfulness; Thus Paul did not walk blamelessly in the justice of the law, when he was perpetrating the torture and genocide of the first Christians.

For me it is very hard to understand this matter of the precedents of Paul and the kind of man he was at the time of his supposed calling, but it is even harder to understand the issue of doctrine. One thing is to be chosen to preach words already taught and preached by God in person, and another very different thing is to be chosen to teach and preach in the name of God new words of God, after God did it personally.

The Bible (R.S.V.), Second Catholic Edition, book of Acts of the Apostles, says: "*3:22 Moses said, 'The Lord God will raise up for you a prophet from your brethren as he raised me up. You shall listen to him in whatever he tells you. 3:23 And it shall be that every soul that does not listen to that prophet shall be destroyed from the people.'*" It mentions only one prophet who will have the words of God put in his mouth; not two.

To appreciate the influence, the position, of the teachings of Paul in the development of the Christian doctrine, it is enough to note how many times his teachings have been used to sustain the positions of the

---

[78] The Epistle of Paul to the Philippians (N.K.J.V.) says: "*3:6 concerning zeal, persecuting the church; concerning the righteousness which is in the law, blameless.*"

Catholic Church, in its Declarations, Constitutions and Councils, throughout history. In this book, I will give some examples of that influence. Indeed, the fact that his epistles are considered the word of God says it all.

For me it was very strange, for the reasons and circumstances before mentioned, that God chose Paul to preach new words of God at the time he was a brutal perpetrator of genocide against Christians; especially because for me there was no need for more preaching after the preaching of Christ, and Christ's doctrine does not need complement nor admits supplement, and because Jesus was supposed to remain with the Father until the Second Coming.

Nevertheless, it is taught that Paul would have been chosen by Christ, and baptized not later than three years after Christ's crucifixion. It is taught that after the ascension of Jesus, he appeared to Paul, instructed him, and that since then Paul would have carried on a ministry in which he would teach new words of God.

During his preaching he would have written some epistles. These epistles are considered part of the Bible. The Christian Bible can be divided in two main parts: the Old Testament and the New Testament. The Epistles of Paul are part of the New Testament.

There are 14 epistles preserved that are attributed to Paul. All of those epistles are considered to be divinely revealed, and committed to writing under the inspiration of the Holy Spirit. They are considered to have God as their author. They are considered to contain in writing everything and only those things, which God wanted. They are considered to be without error.

Ruy Barraco Mármol

The Catholic Church, in the Second Ecumenical Council of the Vatican, as well as on other opportunities, has declared that.[79] It is a doctrine of faith of the Catholic Church that the mentioned declaration has been made by the Catholic Church in an infallible way. The majority, if not all, of the other Christian Churches hold the Epistles of Paul as sacred scriptures, as the word of God.

In the first part of this work, I will argue that the Epistles of Paul contain errors and teachings opposed to the teachings of Christ; that they give a wrong spiritual message, and that their consequences have been extremely vicious.

I will argue that the errors contained in the Epistles of Paul imply that they are not inspired, they are not the word of God, they are not sacred scripture, and that the Catholic Church is not infallible. This proof of the fallibility of the Catholic Church is very special because it can be verified easily by the reading of few passages of the Bible.

I will argue that Christians do not need the doctrine of infallibility, and that the fact that in general the Christian Church is not infallible, neither means that it will be defeated, nor that the word of God will be defeated.

I will argue that the error about the Epistles of Paul neither compromise the fundaments of the Catholic Church, nor the fundaments of the other Christian Churches: On the contrary.

---

[79] Second Ecumenical Council of the Vatican, Dogmatic Constitution of Divine Revelation, Dei Verbum, Chapter III.

I will argue that given the seriousness of the errors all the doctrine built on the Epistles of Paul must be reviewed; especially the Christian doctrine about divorce, celibacy and women ministers.

I will argue that Paul was a false prophet and that he acted as if he were inspired by the Devil, if he were not somehow the Devil itself.

I will argue that many of the errors and defects of the Catholic Church, and of many other Christian Churches, involving authorities and secular members, have been caused to a greater or lesser extent by the Epistles of Paul, which, of course, does not excuse the responsibility of those who committed these errors.

I will argue that the Epistles of Paul caused the errors of the Christian Church in the matters of discrimination against women, origin of the power of civil authority, intromission of the Church in civil matters, the Inquisition, legitimacy of governments that are not constitutional democracies,[80] submission of people to ecclesiastic authority, freedom of thought and freedom of religion, capacity of men and women, among others. I will argue that the Epistles of Paul promoted vices in the Christians like the custom of judging, noting and driving apart brothers they judged wicked, and other vices like lack of humility, and disrespect for nonchristians.

I will argue that our world peace is still in danger because of vices like the ones Paul introduced into the Christian Church.

---

[80] When I use the expression constitutional democracy, I mean the form of State and Government that the U.S.A. has.

Ruy Barraco Mármol

I will argue that the Christian Church in general is in condition to give a spectacular impulsion to Christianity by remaining faithful to Jesus and recognizing Paul as a false prophet.

Furthermore, in the second part of this work, I will start by showing that Paul is the Second Beast of the book of Revelation or at least its first horn. After that, I will expose an interpretation of the last chapters of the book of Revelation, which talk about the bride getting clothed with fine linen and the Coming of the Word of God, which leaves me, with unfathomable perplexity, surprise and motivation. I will then expose an interpretation that will unveil the general message of the book of Revelation, and show how this interpretation is supported by the New Testament, and the Old Testament.

Finally, I will end up sharing some practical advice that may be useful for any Christian, but especially for those who have the courage to be faithful to Jesus and spread the true word of Christ.

Chapter II.
The Errors of the Epistles of Paul

I argued that the Epistles of Paul contain errors, teachings opposed to the teachings of Christ, that they give a wrong spiritual message, and they have had very noxious consequences. In this chapter I will treat some of the most important errors of the Epistles of Paul. I will use the word error with the meaning of contradiction of truth[81], whether or not it is caused unintentionally.

I ask the reader, at this point, to focus on determining whether or not it is true that the statements that I denounce are errors, if they are opposed to the teachings of Christ, if they give a wrong spiritual message, and if they have had very noxious consequences.

II.1. Discrimination against Women

The First Epistle of Paul to Timothy (R.S.V.), Second Catholic Edition, says: "*2:11 Let a woman learn in silence*

---

[81] The Webster's Seventh New Collegiate Dictionary gives as a 2b meaning of the word error: "*Christian Science: Illusion about the nature of reality that is the cause of human suffering: the contradiction of truth.*" "Webster's Seventh New Collegiate Dictionary", (Springfield, Massachusetts, U.S.A., G.&C. Merriam Company Publishers, 1965)

with all submissiveness. 2:12 I permit no woman to teach or to have authority over men; she is to keep silent. 2:13 For Adam was formed first, then Eve; 2:14 and Adam was not deceived, but the woman was deceived and became a transgressor. 2:15 Yet woman will be saved through bearing children, if she continues in faith and love and holiness, with modesty."

The First Epistle of Paul to the Corinthians (R.S.V.), Second Catholic Edition, says: "*11:1 Be imitators of me, as I am of Christ. 11:2 I commend you because you remember me in everything and maintain the traditions even as I have delivered them to you. 11:3 But I want you to understand that the head of every man is Christ, the head of a woman is her husband, and the head of Christ is God. 11:4 Any man who prays or prophesies with his head covered dishonors his head, 11:5 but any woman who prays or prophesies with her head unveiled dishonors her head — it is the same as if her head were shaven. 11:6 For if a woman will not veil herself, then she should cut off her hair; but if it is disgraceful for a woman to be shorn or shaven, let her wear a veil. 11:7 For a man ought not to cover his head, since he is the image and glory of God; but woman is the glory of man. 11:8 (For man was not made from woman, but woman from man. 11:9 Neither was man created for woman, but woman for man.) 11:10 That is why a woman ought to have a veil on her head, because of the angels. 11:11 (Nevertheless, in the Lord woman is not independent of man nor man of woman; 11:12 for as woman was made from man, so man is now born of woman. And all things are from God.) 11:13 Judge for yourselves; is it proper for a woman to pray to God with her head uncovered? 11:14*

Does not nature itself teach you that for a man to wear long hair is degrading to him, 11:15 but if a woman has long hair, it is her pride? For her hair is given to her for a covering. 11:16 If any one is disposed to be contentious, we recognize no other practice, nor do the churches of God."

The First Epistle of Paul to the Corinthians (R.S.V.), Second Catholic Edition, says: "*14:34 the women should keep silence in the churches. For they are not permitted to speak, but should be subordinate, as even the law says. 14:35 If there is anything they desire to know, let them ask their husbands at home. For it is shameful for a woman to speak in church. 14:36 What! Did the word of God originate with you, or are you the only ones it has reached? 14:37 If any one thinks that he is a prophet, or spiritual, he should acknowledge that what I am writing to you is a command of the Lord."*

The Epistle of Paul to the Ephesians (R.S.V.), Second Catholic Edition, says: "*5:21 Be subject to one another out of reverence for Christ. 5:22 Wives, be subject to your husbands, as to the Lord. 5:23 For the husband is the head of the wife as Christ is the head of the Church, his body, and is himself its Savior. 5:24 As the Church is subject to Christ, so let wives also be subject in everything to their husbands."*

The Epistle of Paul to the Colossians (R.S.V.), Second Catholic Edition, says: "*3:18 Wives, be subject to your husbands, as is fitting in the Lord."*

Ruy Barraco Mármol

Errors

It is an error to forbid women to teach men and to have authority over men. It is not true that women should not teach men, and have authority over men. Women will not be saved through bearing children if they continue in faith and love and holiness with modesty. Women will be saved through the same reasons and ways that men will be saved.[82]

The head of a woman is not her husband. Any woman who prays or prophesies with her head unveiled does not dishonor her head, does not dishonor man. It is not the same as if her head were shaven. Women do not need to have a veil on their heads, because of the angels. Women are permitted to speak in churches. If they desire to know anything, they can ask in Church to a priest or to a man other than their husband and they do not have to wait until they are home to ask their husbands. The husband is not the head of the wife, as Christ is the head of the Church. Man is not the head of woman and the comparison is very unfortunate. It is not shameful for a woman to speak in Church. Women do not have to be subject in everything to their husbands, as the Church is subject to the Jesus.

[82] Saint Justin Martyr, in his book "Dialogue with Trypho", written around the year 150 A.D., said: "Moreover, the fact that females cannot receive circumcision of the flesh shows that circumcision was given as a sign, not as an act of justification. For God also bestowed on women the capability of performing every good and virtuous act. We see that physical formation of male and female is different, but it is equally evident that the bodily form is not what makes either of them good or evil. Their righteousness is determined by piety and justice." St. Justin Martyr "Dialogue with Trypho", Translated by Thomas B. Falls, Edited by Michael Slusser, The Catholic University of America Press, Washington D.C., 2003, Chapter 23:5, p. 38.

Commentaries

At this point of Christianity understanding I do not need to stop too long to argue that these statements of Paul are wrong. I do not need to prove that it is wrong to forbid women to teach or to have authority over men. I do not need to prove that it is wrong to teach that women need to wear a veil over their heads because of the angels. I do not need to prove that it is wrong to teach that women cannot speak at church. I do not need to prove that it is wrong to teach that if a woman wants to know something she should ask her husband at home. I do not need to prove that it is wrong to teach that a group of people must be subject in everything to another, in the way the Church has to be subject to Jesus. I do not need to prove that it is wrong to put a group of people over other group of people, as if we were not all brethren. I do not need to prove that it is wrong to teach that a certain group of people is the head of another group of people.

These statements against women are opposed to the obligation to love God, and our neighbor as ourselves.[83] God loves women, wants good for them, and without doubt the good of women and the good of society depend on the recognition of these natural rights of

---

[83] The Gospel according to Saint Matthew (N.K.J.V.) says: "22:34 *But when the Pharisees heard that He had silenced the Sadducees, they gathered together. 22:35 Then one of them, a lawyer, asked Him a question, testing Him, and saying. 22:36 "Teacher, which is the great commandment in the law?" 22:37 Jesus said to him, "'You shall love the LORD your GOD with all your heart, with all your soul, and with all your mind. 22:38 "This is the first and great commandment. 22:39 "And the second is like it: 'You shall love your neighbor as yourself.' 22:40 "On these two commandments hang all the Law and the Prophets.""*

women disregarded in the epistles of Paul.

These statements have nothing to do with Christ's doctrine. Human equality is a basic principle of Christ's doctrine. Rich and poor, Jews and Gentiles, educated men and uneducated, freemen and slaves, men and women, are all called in the same terms. Christ's doctrine promotes equality between men and women; the statements in analysis from the Epistles of Paul promote discrimination against women. Christ's doctrine promotes rationality. The statements in analysis from the Epistles of Paul promote irrationality. Christ's doctrine promotes equality and freedom for human beings. The statements in analysis from the Epistles of Paul promote submissiveness and dependence. Christ's doctrine promotes a just religion, marital and social order that did not exist at the time of his earthly life. The statements in analysis from the Epistles of Paul made it harder to attain a more just order than the one that existed at the time of his life.

The Gospel according to Saint Matthew (R.S.V.), Second Catholic Edition, says: "*23:8 But you are not to be called rabbi, for you have one teacher, and you are all brethren. 23:9 And call no man your father in earth, for you have one Father, who is in heaven. 23:10 Neither be called masters, for you have one master, the Christ.*" These teachings of Jesus were directed to men and women. Christ taught that men and women are all brethren and must have Christ only as master, which means that husbands are not the head of the wives.

This is how things are today, and have always been, at least after the coming of Christ. The discriminatory statements of Paul against women are not the word of

God.

It is important to notice that the fundaments that Paul gives to sustain these statements are not directed to support a temporary discrimination against woman, but a permanent discrimination. He argues that the nature of man and woman, that creation, command this discrimination against women.

The First Epistle of Paul to Timothy, R.S.V. (Second Catholic Edition), says: "*2:11 Let a woman learn in silence with all submissiveness. 2:12 I permit no woman to teach or to have authority over men; she is to keep silent. 2:13 For Adam was formed first, then Eve; 2:14 and Adam was not deceived but the woman was deceived and became a transgressor. 2:15 Yet woman will be saved through bearing children, if she continues in faith and love and holiness with modesty.*" These arguments are still applicable today. If they are wrong today, they were wrong when they were first given by Paul. These are not temporary or circumstantial arguments.

The First Epistle of Paul to the Corinthians (R.S.V.), Second Catholic Edition, says: "*11:7 For a man ought not to cover his head, since he is the image and glory of God; but woman is the glory of man. 11:8 (For man was not made from woman, but woman from man. 11:9 Neither was man created for woman, but woman for man.) 11:10 That is why a woman ought to have a veil on her head, because of the angels.*" The same thing can be said about these arguments. These are not temporary or circumstantial arguments: or has creation changed? If these arguments are wrong today because of human rights, because of natural rights of women, which are, neither temporary nor circumstantial, then, they were

Ruy Barraco Mármol

wrong when they were first given by Paul.

Besides, even in the case these teachings of Paul were meant to be temporary, which they clearly were not, they would have been wrong anyway, because they were opposed to Christ's teachings which were given to have immediate application. The word of Jesus cannot even be temporarily contradicted. Jesus taught that men and women are not supposed to be masters or heads of any other men or women, and this teaching, as well as all his other teachings, were meant to have immediate application. Jesus taught that we are all brethren, and this teaching, as well, was meant to have immediate application.

It is also interesting to notice that, in fact, although in the First Epistle to Timothy, Paul forbids women to teach men, there are testimonies in the New Testament of women who taught.

The book of Acts of the Apostles (R.S.V.), Second Catholic Edition, says: "*18:26 He began to speak boldly in the synagogue; but when Priscilla and Aqui'la heard him, they took him and expounded to him the way of God more accurately.*" Priscilla was a woman teaching a man. And it was not presented as if it were unnatural or infamous.

There are even testimonies of women who prophesied. The Gospel according to Saint Luke (R.S.V.), Second Catholic Edition, says: "*2:36 And there was a prophetess, Anna, the daughter of Phan'uel, of the tribe of Asher; she was of a great age, having lived with her husband seven years from her virginity, 2:37 and as a widow till she was eighty-four. She did not depart from the temple, worshiping with fasting and prayer night and day. 2:38 And coming up at that very hour she gave thanks to God, and* spoke of him to all who were looking for the redemption of Jerusalem." This woman taught and prophesied to all who were looking for the redemption of Jerusalem, which included men as well as women.

The book of Acts of the Apostles (R.S.V.), Second Catholic Edition, also mentions prophetesses, saying: "21:8 The next day we departed and came to Caesare'a; and we entered the house of Philip the evangelist, who was one of the seven, and stayed with him. 21:9 And he had four unmarried daughters, who prophesied."

Whoever prophesies, also teaches, and the natural place for a prophetess to prophesy and teach is in the Church, and to the Church. In the First Epistle of Paul to Corinthians (R.V.S.), Second Catholic Edition, it is said about those who prophesy: "14:3 On the other hand, he who prophesies speaks to men for their upbuilding and encouragement and consolation. 14:4 He who speaks in a tongue edifies himself, but he who prophesies edifies the Church. 14:5 Now I want you all to speak in tongues, but even more to prophesy. He who prophesies is greater than he who speaks in tongues, unless someone interprets, so that the Church may be edified."

In addition, in the Old Testament, there are also testimonies of women prophesying. The book of Exodus (R.S.V.), Second Catholic Edition, says: "15:20 Then Miriam, the prophetess, the sister of Aaron, took a timbrel in her hand; and all the women went out after her with timbrels and dancing. 15:21 And Miriam sang to them: "Sing to the Lord, for he has triumphed gloriously; the horse and his rider he has thrown into the sea."

And also there is a testimony of a woman who not only prophesied and taught men, but was even a judge.

The book of Judges (R.S.V.), Second Catholic Edition, says: *"4:4 Now Deborah, a prophetess, the wife of Lap'pidoth, was judging Israel at that time. 4:5 She used to sit under the palm of Deborah between Ra'mah and Bethel in the hill country of E'phraim; and the sons of Israel came up to her for judgment."* For the purpose of looking for judgment it is said the Israelites came up to her.

From these and other testimonies of the Bible, it seems that the Epistles of Paul not only made the progress of the social position of women more difficult, but promoted a reversal of it.

In one way or another, the truth is that neither the husband must dominate the wife, nor the wife must dominate the husband. The original sin, according to the Bible, happened when Adam listened to Eve when she asked him to disobey God.[84]

Consequences

These statements of Paul helped discrimination against women to survive long after him, not only in the

---

[84] The Bible, book of Genesis, (N.K.J.V.) says: *"3:12 Then the man said, "The woman whom You gave to be with me, she gave me fruit of the tree, and I ate." 3:13 And the LORD God said to the woman, "What is this you have done?" The woman said, "The serpent deceived me, and I ate." 3:14 So the LORD God said to the serpent: "Because you have done this, You are cursed more than all cattle, And more than every beast of the field; On your belly you shall go, And you shall eat dust All the days of your life. 3:15 And I will put enmity Between you and the woman, And between your seed and her Seed; He shall bruise your head, And you shall bruise His heel." 3:16 To the woman He said: "I will greatly multiply your sorrow and your conception; In pain you shall bring forth children; Your desire shall be for your husband, And he shall rule over you." 3:17 Then to Adam He said, "Because you have heeded the voice of your wife, and have eaten from the tree of which I commanded you, saying, 'You shall not eat of it': Cursed is the ground for your sake; In toil you shall eat of it All the days of your life."*

Christian world but in the rest of the world as well.

Discrimination against women has caused great damage to society in general, and to innumerable women in particular. It has been responsible in human history for the death of many women, and the fact that many women have been beaten, denied instruction, frustrated and denied of others of their fundamental rights, with all the consequences that come from these injustices not only to them, but to their sons and daughters, their families and society in general. The men who were taught to have their wives submit to them have also been greatly damaged.

Moreover, these errors have tempted and still tempt women, and also men, to reject Christianity, and are used as basis of arguments against it. At least half of humanity has been tempted by these statements to reject Christianity. They give a wrong spiritual message and are not simple mistakes.

Besides, today when it is so important to condemn the immoral treatment of the women in the Muslim countries, and in other countries of the World, where extreme discrimination against women still affects - hundreds of thousands of women and their families, the Catholic Church, and the rest of the Christian Churches, that sustain that these statements of the Epistles of Paul are the word of God, lose strength and moral authority to do it.

I hope that at the end of this book the reader will see that it is unacceptable that some women are still publicly stoned to death because of discrimination against women, while every Sunday Christians are told to repeat that the Epistles of Paul, which contain these wrong statements, are the word of God. I hope that the reader will see that Christianity must stop teaching that these statements are the word of God, the product of Holy Spirit's inspiration, and start firmly to condemn them, publicly, and straightforwardly. It is a big offense to God to attribute to him words that do not belong to him, and that dishonor his name. This is truly taking the name of God in vain.

What I have said does not mean that without Christianity women's situation and human beings' situation in general would have been much better than it was and is. I believe that women's situation in nonchristian countries in general, for instance, Islamic countries, is a good proof of that. The unity of origin and destiny of woman regarding man, monogamy, and the general principle of marriage indissolubility that are part of Christian doctrine, without doubt have helped to make harder the existence of a social framework with greater indignity for women, and have saved them from many of the disastrous consequences that go with societies where polygamy is allowed, and where men are permitted to replace wives whenever they wish. This is very meaningful when it concerns a society in which all family power is concentrated in men, as it was until not long ago, in most of the world.

Difficulties

Do the passages of the Bible, book of Genesis, Verses 3:8-19, justify the statements of the Epistles of Paul that I have just denounced?

Some pretend to justify these statements of the

Epistles of Paul and discrimination against women in general through the book of Genesis (R.S.V.), Second Catholic Edition, that says: *"3:8 And they heard the sound of the Lord God walking in the garden in the cool of the day, and the man and his wife hid themselves from the presence of the Lord God among the trees of the garden. 3:9 But the Lord God called to the man, and said to him, "Where are you?" 3:10 And he said, "I heard the sound of you in the garden, and I was afraid, because I was naked; and I hid myself." 3:11 He said, "Who told you that you were naked? Have you eaten of the tree of which I commanded you not to eat?" 3:12 The man said, "The woman whom you gave to be with me, she gave me fruit of the tree, and I ate." 3:13 Then the* LORD *God said to the woman, "What is this that you have done?" The woman said, "The serpent beguiled me, and I ate." 3:14 The Lord God said to the serpent, "Because you have done this, cursed are you above all cattle, and above all wild animals; upon your belly you shall go, and dust you shall eat all the days of your life. 3:15 I will put enmity between you and the woman, and between your seed and her seed; he shall bruise your head, and you shall bruise his heel." 3:16 To the woman he said, "I will greatly multiply your pain in childbearing; in pain you shall bring forth children, yet your desire shall be for your husband, and he shall rule over you." 3:17 And to Adam he said, "Because you have listened to the voice of your wife, and have eaten of the tree of which I commanded you, 'You shall not eat of it,' cursed is the ground because of you; in toil you shall eat of it all the days of your life; 3:18 thorns and thistles it shall bring forth to you; and you shall eat the plants of the field. 3:19 In the sweat of your face you shall eat bread till you return to the ground, for out of it you were taken; you are*

Ruy Barraco Mármol

dust, and to dust you shall return."

But, it cannot be interpreted that these verses justify the statements of the Epistles of Paul in analysis, in the first place, because they evidently go against the obligation to love God and our neighbor; and the Bible cannot be interpreted to justify violations of these two most important commandments of God. All of the other commandments depend on them. And Jesus taught to the contrary that men and women must have Christ only as their masters, as their leaders.

In the second place, because the fact that in the book of Genesis God says that the husband will dominate over his wife does not mean that God has commanded man to dominate woman.

The book of Genesis also says that the consequence for men will be the following: in toil they will eat the ground's yield all the days of their lives; that the ground will produce to them thorns and thistles, and that they will eat plants of the field; that by the sweat of their face men will get bread to eat.

And even though the book of Genesis says so: does this mean men must not try, through honest means, to get food with the least effort possible? Should not women help men in that purpose? Of course they should, the same way men should try to build a society where men do not dominate over women.

Illustrative Quotes

The very important and recent Encyclical Castii Connubii of Pope Pius XI on Christian Marriage, from December 31, 1930, says on its point 26: *"Domestic society being confirmed, therefore, by this bond of love, there should flourish in it that "order of love", as St. Augustine calls it. This order includes both the primacy of the husband with regard to the wife and children, the ready subjection of the wife and her willing obedience, which the Apostle commends in these words: "Let women be subject to their husband as to the Lord, because the husband is the head of the wife, and Christ is the head of the Church."* The footnote says *(Eph., V,22-23)*.[85]

The Apostle mentioned is Paul. Very frequently, authors of the Catholic Church refer to him in that way. "The Apostle", is used to describe Paul, despite the fact that he was not even one of the twelve. The epistle referred to in the footnote is the Epistle of Paul to the Ephesians, Chapter 5, Verses 22 and 23.

The encyclical shows for certain a case in which a wrong Catholic doctrine in this matter was constructed on the Epistles of Paul.

II.2. About Men Wearing Long Hair

The First Epistle of Paul to the Corinthians (R.S.V.), Second Catholic Edition, says: *"11:13 "Judge for yourselves; is it proper for a woman to pray to God with her head uncovered? 11:14 Does not nature itself teach you that for a man to wear long hair is degrading to him, 11:15 but if a woman has long hair, it is her pride? For her hair is given*

[85] Pius XI, Casti Connubii (31/12/1930) Vatican official web site: http://www.vatican.va/holy_father/pius_xi/encyclicals/documents/hf_p-xi_enc_31121930_casti-connubii_en.html. Denzinger Henry "*The Sources of Catholic Dogma*", (U.S.A.; Loreto Publications, 2002), translated by Roy J. Deferrari, from the thirtieth edition of Enchiridion Symbolorum by Henry Denzinger, revised by Karl Rahner, S.J., published in 1954, by Herder & Co., Freiburg, p. 586.

to her for a covering."

Error

It is not degrading for a man to wear long hair.

Commentaries

This error requires no further refutation.[86] It is not the word of God that it is degrading for a man to wear long hair.

Consequences

Every time Christianity is made to appear as a religion opposed to reason, intelligent people are tempted to reject it. Every time Christianity sustains nonsensical positions, people are tempted to reject it; especially freethinkers; especially young freethinkers. This error tempted and tempts freethinkers to reject Christianity. Any error hides the "Light of the Gospel of Christ".

Besides, this kind of statement leads the way to other nonsensical positions in Christianity, bringing irrationality into Christian doctrine.

---

[86] I understand that it is part of Christian tradition that Christ used long hair, as many of his contemporaries did. Was this taken into account by the author of the Epistle to the Corinthians? If Christ did not use long hair, then why is Christ in so many times portrayed with it?

Illustrative Quote

The First Epistle of Paul to the Corinthians (R.S.V.), Second Catholic Edition, says: *"14:23 If, therefore, the whole Church assembles and all speak in tongues, and outsiders or unbelievers enter, will they not say that you are mad?"*

II.3. About Effeminacy and the Kingdom of God

The First Epistle of Paul to the Corinthians (R.S.V.), Second Catholic Edition, says: *"6:9 Do you know that the unrighteous will not inherit the kingdom of God? Do not be deceived; neither the immoral, nor idolaters, nor adulterers, nor homosexuals, 6:10 nor thieves, nor the greedy, nor drunkards, nor revilers, nor robbers will inherit the kingdom of God."*

The footnote of this verse says: *"homosexuals: Greek has "effeminate nor sodomites". The apostle condemns, not the inherent tendencies of such, but the indulgence of them."*

Error

Being effeminate does not exclude anyone from the Kingdom of God.

Commentaries

The footnote of the Revised Standard Version, Second Catholic Edition, says that the Greek text (the language in which the epistle was written) says "neither

Ruy Barraco Mármol

effeminate nor sodomites...will inherit the kingdom of God." And that is the way it has been read and interpreted for centuries.[87]

The King James Version of the Bible, First Epistle of Paul to the Corinthians, says: "*6:9 Know ye not that the unrighteous shall not inherit the kingdom of God? Be not deceived: neither fornicators, nor idolaters, nor adulterers, nor effeminate, nor abusers of themselves with mankind, 6:10 Nor thieves, nor covetous, nor drunkards, nor revilers, nor extortioners, shall inherit the kingdom of God.*" The New American Bible translates: *"nor boy prostitutes, nor sodomites."* The New American Standard Bible translates: *"nor effeminate, nor homosexuals."* The New International Version translates: *"nor male prostitutes, nor homosexual offenders."* The English Standard Version translates: *"nor men who practice homosexuality."*

The translations of this verse by the King James Version and the New American Standard Bible are accurate, as well as the footnote of the Revised Standard Version, Second Catholic Edition. The Greek text says: "...ούτε μαλακοί ούτε αρσενοκοίται...[88]"

---

[87] The Latin Vulgate, a transcendent version of the Bible, from the fifth century, says: "*6:9 An nescitis quia iniqui regnum Dei non possidebunt? Nolite errare: neque fornicarii, neque idolis servientes, neque adulteri, 6:10 neque molles, neque masculorum concubitores, neque fures, neque avari, neque ebriosi, neque maledici, neque rapaces regnum Dei possidebunt.*" According to the Harper Collins Latin Concise Dictionary mollis means: soft, tender, gentle; (character) sensitive, weak, unmanly.

[88] NESTLE – ALAND, "Greek-English New Testament', Greek text Novum Testamentum Graece, in the tradition of Eberhard Nestle and Erwin Nestle, edited by Barbara and Kurt Aland, Johannes Karavidopoulos, Carlo M. Martini, Bruce M. Metzger – English Text 2nd Edition of the Revised Standard Version – The critical apparatuses prepared and edited together with the Institute for New Testament Textual Research, Münster/Westphalia by Barbara and Kurt

Μαλακοι (malakoi) means effeminate.[89] Effeminate is used to describe the man who acts in a feminine way. Αρσενοκοιται (arsenokoitai) means male homosexual.[90] A man can be effeminate without being homosexual.

Considering the Greek text and the footnote of the (R.S.V.), Second Catholic Edition, the two words in this verse should have been translated in it, in the following

---

Aland. (Stuttgart, Deutsche Bibelgesellschaft. 1981) Other Greek Bible: P. Merk, Augustinus "Novum Testamentum Graece et Latine" septiman editionem. Other Greek Bible: Goodrich Richard J. and Albert L. Lukaszewski "A Reader's Greek New Testament", second edition, (China; Zondervan, 2007)

[89] Zerwick, Max "Analysis Philologica Novi Testamenti Graeci", (Romae; Sumptibus Pontificii Instituti Biblici, 1953), says under AD Corinthios I, 6:9, that μαλακοσ (malakos) means mollis, effeminatus, venereis deditus. According to the Harper Collins Latin Concise Dictionary mollis means: soft, tender, gentle; (character) sensitive, weak, unmanly...; and effeminatus means effeminate." Harper Collins Publishers "Harper Collins Latin Concise Dictionary" (Great Britain; Harper Collins Publishers Limited, 2003). Goodrich, Richard J. and Albert L. Lukaszewski "A Reader's Greek New Testament", ΠΡΟΣ ΚΟΡΙΝΘΙΟΥΖ Α translates the word μαλακοσ (malakos) as fine, delicate, effeminate, homosexual. Feyerabend, Karl "Langenscheidt Pocket Greek Dictionary" translates the word μαλακοσ (malakos) as: soft, tender, sickly; mild, gentle; tender, delicate; effeminate, cowardly; careless, remiss; luxurious, wanton.

[90] Zerwick, Max "Analysis Philologica Novi Testamenti Graeci", under Ad Corinthios I, 6:9, says that the word αρσενοκοιτνησ (arsenokoites) is formed by the word αρσεν (arsen) that means, in Latin, masculus, which according to the Harper Collins Latin Concise Dictionary means in English male, masculine, manly; and by the word κοιτη (koite) that means, in Latin, lectus, concubitus. The Harper Collins Latin Concise Dictionary translates the word lectus-i as couch, bed, bier; and translates the word concubitus-us as reclining together (at table); sexual union. Richard J. Goodrich and Albert L. Lukaszewski "A Reader's Greek New Testament", ΠΡΟΣ ΚΟΡΙΝΘΙΟΥΖ Α says the word αρσενοκοιτης, ου, ο (arsenokoites) means: male homosexual. Karl Feyerabend "Langenscheidt Pocket Greek Dictionary" translates the word αρσενοκοιτης, ου, ο (arsenokoites) as pederast.

Ruy Barraco Mármol

way: '6:9 Do you know that the unrighteous will not inherit the kingdom of God? Do not be deceived; neither the immoral, nor idolaters, nor adulterers, <u>nor effeminate, nor homosexuals</u>, nor thieves, nor the greedy; nor drunkards, nor revilers, nor robbers will inherit the kingdom of God.'

Independently of the topic of the homosexuals,[91] surely it can be said that being effeminate does not exclude anyone from the kingdom of God.

Neither in the Old Testament, nor in the New Testament, can you find any other condemnations of <u>being effeminate or acting</u> effeminately.

[91] In my opinion, for several natural reasons, voluntary and free homosexual acts (without coertion or an ungovernable inclination to them) are reproachable and not desirable, referring to, with the expression homosexual acts, the sexual relationships between men or between women (which could be called homogender sex), and the unions between men or between women (which could be called homogender unions); and there are explicit condemnations of homosexual acts in the Old Testament and in the New Testament. However, there are not condemnations of effeminate behavior; least of all when it is involuntary. The condemnation in the New Testament of the homosexual acts between men is found in Matthew 15:19, Mark 7:21, and in the book of Acts of the Apostles 15:20. I believe so, because the Greek word (porneia) translated in the K.J.V., in these verses, as 'fornications' refers to the forbidden sexual relationships detailed in the book of Leviticus Chapter 18 of the Bible. In the Catholic Bible, Old Testament, book of Wisdom 14:26, there is a condemnation of unnatural lust of men and women. The Old Testament, book of Leviticus 18, condemns the homosexual acts between men. There are other condemnations. The unions between same sex men or women are illicit according to the Bible, among other reasons, because in the Bible, for instance in the book of Genesis, they go against God's will and plan. It also seems, in my opinion, that the Gospel according to Saint Mark 7:22, condemns all kinds of homosexual acts because I believe the Greek word ασελγεια (aselgeia), translated in the King James Version as lasciviousness, in the Revised Standard Version as licentiousness, in the New American Bible as licentiousness, in the New American Standard Bible as sensuality, in the New International Version as lewdness, in the English Standard Version as sensuality, includes in its concept free homosexual acts between men, and free homosexual acts between women.

Besides, even if effeminacy were condemned in the Bible, or men who committed effeminate acts were condemned, to go from the judgment that says that being effeminate is reproachable, to the judgment that says the effeminate will not enter the kingdom of heaven there is a long distance, way too far to go.

It is not the word of God that effeminates will not inherit the kingdom of God.

Consequences

I believe the consequences of this error are the same indicated for the error about men wearing long hair.

Besides, this error makes people lose respect for the position of the Christian Church in the matter of homosexual acts.

II. 4. About the Sexual Taboo

The Epistle of Paul to Ephesians (R.S.V.), Second Catholic Edition, says: "*5:1 Therefore be imitators of God, as beloved children. 5:2 And walk in love, as Christ loved us and gave himself up for us, a fragrant offering and sacrifice to God. 5:3 But immorality and all impurity or covetousness must not even be named among you, as is fitting among saints. 5:4 Let there be no filthiness, nor silly talk, nor levity, which are not fitting; but instead let there be thanksgiving. 5:5 Be sure of this, that no immoral or impure man, or one who is covetous (that is, an idolater), has any inheritance in the kingdom of Christ and of God. 5:6 Let no one deceive you with empty words, for it is because of these things that the wrath of God comes upon the sons of disobedience. 5:7 Therefore do not associate with them, 5:8 for once you were darkness, but now you are light in the Lord; walk as children of light 5:9 (for the fruit of light is found in all that is good and right and true), 5:10 and try to learn what is pleasing to the Lord. 5:11 Take no part in the unfruitful works of darkness, but instead expose them. 5:12 For it is a shame even to speak of the things that they do in secret; 5:13 but when anything is exposed by the light it becomes visible, for anything that becomes visible is light. 5:14 Therefore it is said, "Awake, O sleeper, and arise from the dead, and Christ shall give you light."*

Error

It is an error to command Christians not even to name immorality and impurity.

Commentary

Paul considered immoral and impure every sexual relationship outside marriage. This is why, for instance, he recommended marriage to those who cannot exercise self-control, saying to those who cannot do it, that it is better for them to marry than to burn (First Epistle of Paul to the Corinthians 7:8-9). When he says 'do not even name immorality and impurity' he is including, the premarital sexual relationships between couples that are in love and have already made the decision of getting married. He includes every sexual relationship outside marriage.

Time has proven that people need to name and need

to talk about sexual relationships, especially about premarital sexual relationships, even about immoral and impure sexual relationships. Talking about them can be very constructive. Of course, there are different ways to talk about them and to name them, and the way I am talking about, is precisely the constructive way of doing so.

Some pretend to excuse these statements of the Epistles of Paul interpreting that Paul only intended to reinforce the idea that those kinds of vices do not have to exist among Christians. But, there would have been no reason to say 'do not name' if what you mean is 'name but do not do'. These statements are not the word of God.

Consequences

These and other statements of Paul have conspired against the understanding of sex in the Christian Church. These and other statements of Paul have conspired against the education about sex, and contributed to turn talking about sex into a taboo, with all the noxious consequences that have resulted with regard to Christians, society and particularly to the image of the Christian Church. Abortion is sometimes in a little part a consequence of lack of education about the matter of sex.

This error to command Christians not even to name immorality and impurity, contributed to a wrong doctrine about sex, and a wrong approach to it by the Christian Church, and consequently by society in general.

II.5. About Who Rules over the Body of the Wife in Marriage

The First Epistle of Paul to the Corinthians (R.S.V.), Second Catholic Edition, says: "*7:1 Now concerning the matters about which you wrote. It is well for a man not to touch a woman. 7:2 But because of the temptation to immorality, each man should have his own wife and each woman her own husband. 7:3 The husband should give to his wife her conjugal rights, and likewise the wife to her husband. 7:4 For the wife does not rule over her own body, but the husband does; likewise the husband does not rule over his own body, but the wife does.*"

Error

It is an error to say that wife does not rule over her body, but her husband, and vice versa.

Commentaries

People do not lose the right to rule over their bodies when they get married. Wives and husbands rule over their own bodies and do not rule over the bodies of their spouses.

The husband that rules over the body of his wife, forcing her to have sex, even in marriage, commits rape. Rape, even in marriage, is seriously immoral.

Certainly husbands and wives are obligated to have sex with their spouses, but not in a different way than they are obligated to love, provide the necessities of life, such as food, clothing, to their spouses; and the fact that spouses are obligated to provide their husbands and wives with those goods, does not mean that husbands and wives can rule over the liberty of their spouses, or their properties, to enjoy them.

It is an error to say that the husband rules over the body of his wife, and the wife over the body of her husband, the same way it would have been a mistake to say that husbands rule over the properties of their spouses. This is not the word of God.

Consequences

This error facilitated the existence in the Christian societies of the idea that says that marital rape is not rape. Thus it has been to some extent the cause of many rapes of wives.

Marital rape is seriously immoral. It often can be more damaging than the other kind of rapes, because the victim might be forced to live with her husband, her offender, because she might not have resources to leave him, and thus might be exposed to the threat of suffering unlimited new offenses.

Moreover, in the presence of a forced marriage, the man forcing a woman to marry him, will acquire throughout the marriage, the title and the right to rape his victim perpetually. Let us not forget there were times, not too far away, in which forced marriages were very frequent, even in Christian societies.

II.6. About Slavery

The First Epistle to the Corinthians (R.S.V.), Second

Catholic Edition, says: "*7:20 Every one should remain in the state in which he was called. 7:21 Were you a slave when called? Never mind. But if you can gain your freedom, avail yourself of the opportunity.*"

The footnote says: "*Or make use of your present condition instead.*"

Error

It is an error to state that everyone should remain in the state in which he was called. It is an error to command or advise a slave that can gain his freedom to make use of his condition of slave instead.

Commentaries

This Verse 7:21 is confusing. The footnote of the Revised Standard Version, Second Catholic Edition, is clarifying. However, the context leads clearly to the correct interpretation.

The King James version translates Verses 7:20-21 in the following way: "*7:20 Let every man abide in the same calling wherein he was called. 7:21 Art thou called being a servant? care not for it: but if thou mayest be made free, use it rather.*" The word servant here is used with the meaning of slave.

The New American Bible translates Verses 7:20-21 in the following way: "*7:20 Everyone should remain in the state in which he was called. 7:21 Were you a slave when you were called? Do not be concerned but, even if you can gain your freedom, make the most of it.*"

The New American Standard Bible translates Verses

7:20-21 in the following way: *"7:20 Let each man remain in that condition in which he was called. 7:21 Were you called while a slave? Do not worry about it; but if you are able also to become free, rather do that."*

The New International Version translates Verses 7:20-21 in the following way: *"7:20 Each one should remain in the situation which he was in when God called him. 7:21 Were you a slave when you were called? Don't let it trouble you-although if you can gain your freedom, do so."*

The English Standard Version translates Verses 7:20-21 in the following way: *"7:20 Each one should remain in the condition in which he was called. 7:21 Were you a slave when called? Do not be concerned about it. But if you can gain your freedom, avail yourself of the opportunity."*

It is clear that these verses command people to remain slaves, because the epistle is commanding everyone to continue in the state in which he was called, and to do that the slave has to continue being a slave, even if he has the chance to gain liberty.

This commandment or advice is an error because certainly, in many cases, I would say in most of the cases, a free person can serve God better than an enslaved one. In most of the cases, at least, a slave who can gain freedom, must do it, not only for himself, but to be able to serve God better. There are people who would rather die before being slaves. To command or advise anyone to choose slavery is wrong. Although in some cases it might be noble and heroic to choose slavery, in general it is an error to do it, to command it and to advise it.

People should not remain in the condition in which they were called. They have to put all their energy in improving their condition to be able to serve God better, of course being prepared to be even in a lowest one if that is what being Christian requires at some point.

This especially applies to those who were in the position of masters. Those who were masters were supposed to change their position, to stop considering themselves masters of other people, including those who were in the position of masters with respect to slaves. Christ taught in the Gospel according to Saint Matthew Verse 23:10 that we should not let anyone call us master. This was a call of Jesus for the end of the institution of slavery, contradicted by Paul.

Consequences

These statements of Paul have contributed to the continuation of slavery, and also have conspired against the diffusion of Christianity.

Deep down they had worse consequences. These statements justified and promoted acceptance of a negative status quo, and discouraged human social improvement in all the areas.

II.7. About the Purpose of Richness

The First Epistle of Paul to Timothy (R.S.V.), Second Catholic Edition, says: "*6:17 As for the rich in this world, charge them not to be haughty, nor to set their hopes on uncertain riches but on God who richly furnishes us with everything to enjoy. 6:18 They are to do good, to be rich in good deeds, liberal and generous, 6:19 thus laying up for themselves a good foundation for the future, so that they may take hold of the life which is life indeed."*

Error

God does not richly furnish people with everything to enjoy. The rich people of this world, including the ones who do good, are rich in good deeds, liberal and generous, will not lay up for themselves a good foundation for the future, to enter the kingdom of God, as long as they believe that they have been richly furnished to enjoy their richness, and they live as if they had been.[92]

---

[92] Indeed, Verse 6:18 of the First Epistle of Paul to Timothy does not seem to say they are to do good, to be rich in good deeds liberal and generous. The verse does not seem to say that they are to do good. The verse just seems to command rich people to do good, to be rich in good deeds, to be ready to distribute, willing to communicate. The Greek text never says they are to do good. The Greek word translated as they are to do good is αγαθοεργειν (agathoergein), which is the active present infinitive tense of the verb αγαθοεργεω (agathoergeo), that means do good. This verb is related with the verb of the Verse 6:17 translated by the R.S.V. as charge them. It should be translated 'charge them ...; to do good...". The King James version translates these verses of the Epistle of Paul to Timothy in the following way: *"6:17 Charge them that are rich in this world, that they be not highminded, nor trust in uncertain riches, but in the living God, who giveth us richly all things to enjoy; 6:18 That they do good, that they be rich in good works, ready to distribute, willing to communicate".* The New American Bible says: *"6:17 Tell the rich in the present age not to be proud and not to rely on so uncertain a thing as wealth but rather on God, who richly provides us with all things for our enjoyment. 6:18 Tell them to do good, to be rich in good works, to be generous, ready to share,"* The New American Standard Bible says: *"6:17 Instruct those who are rich in this present world not to be conceited or to fix their hope on the uncertainty of riches, but on God, who richly supplies us with all things to enjoy. 6:18 Instruct them to do good, to be rich in good works, to be generous and ready to share,"* The New International Version says: *"6:17 Command those who are rich in this present world not to be arrogant nor to put their hope in wealth, which is so uncertain, but to put their hope in God, who richly provides us with everything for our enjoyment. 6:18 Command*

Ruy Barraco Mármol

Commentaries

The ones who have received richness in this life, with which they have received great power to do good, are obligated to God to do as much good as they can with their richness. And even though the rich people can enjoy some of their richness,[93] they have not received the richness to enjoy it, but to serve God with it. It is natural for the rich men, who dedicate themselves to produce with their property the greatest good they are able to, to have and enjoy a higher economic level of life than those who are not rich; but that does not mean that they have received richness to enjoy it. It is a big error to say that God furnishes people with everything to enjoy.

The Gospel according to Saint Luke (R.S.V.), Second Catholic Edition, says: *"19:1 He entered Jericho and was passing through. 19:2 And there was a man named Zacchae'us; he was a chief tax collector, and rich. 19:3 And he sought to see who Jesus was, but could not, on account of the crowd, because he was small of stature. 19:4 So he ran on ahead and climbed up into a sycamore tree to see him,*

---

them to do good, to be rich in good deeds, and to be generous and willing to share. The English Standard Version says: "6:17 As for the rich in this present age, charge them not to be haughty, nor to set their hopes on the uncertainty of riches, but on God, who richly provides us with everything to enjoy. 6:18 They are to do good, to be rich in good works, to be generous and ready to share,"

[93] How much should someone enjoy his wealth? It is my understanding that each individual should judge how much is correct for him or her to enjoy according to their own personal circumstances. The merit of production, the need for his or her work, the necessity of the moment, and many other circumstances may have an influence on the justice or injustice of this enjoyment.

for he was to pass that way. 19:5 And when Jesus came to the place, he looked up and said to him, "Zacchae'us, make haste and come down; for I must stay at your house today." 19:6 So he made haste and came down, and received him joyfully. 19:7 And when they saw it they all murmured, "He has gone in to be the guest of a man who is a sinner. 19:8 And Zachae'us stood and said to the Lord, "Behold, Lord, the half of my goods I give to the poor; and if I have defrauded any one of anything, I restore it fourfold." 19:9 And Jesus said to him, "Today salvation has come to this house, since he also is a son of Abraham. 19:10 For the Son of man came to seek and to save the lost." 19:11 As they heard these things, he proceeded to tell a parable, because he was near to Jerusalem, and because they supposed that the kingdom of God was to appear immediately. 19:12 He said therefore, "A nobleman went into a far country to receive kingly power and then return. 19:13 Calling ten of his servants, he gave them ten pounds, and said to them, 'Trade with these till I come.' 19:14 But his citizens hated him and sent an embassy after him, saying, 'We do not want this man to reign over us.' 19:15 When he returned, having received the kingly power, he commanded these servants, to whom he had given the money, to be called to him, that he might know what they had gained by trading. 19:16 The first came before him, saying, 'Lord, your pound has made ten pounds more.' 19:17 And he said to him, 'Well done, good servant! Because you have been faithful in a very little, you shall have authority over ten cities.' 19:18 And the second came, saying, 'Lord, your pound has made five pounds.' 19:19 And he said to him, 'And you are to be over five cities.' 19:20 Then another came, saying, 'Lord, here is your pound, which I kept laid away in a napkin; 19:21 for I *was afraid of you, because I know you are a severe man; you take up what you did not lay down, and reap what you did not sow.' 19:22 He said to him, 'I will condemn you out of your own mouth, you wicked servant! You knew that I was a severe man, taking up what I did not lay down and reaping what I did not sow? 19:23 Why then did you not put my money into the bank, and at my coming I should have collected it with interest?' 19:24 And he said to those who stood by, 'Take the pound from him, and give it to him who has the ten pounds.' 19:25 (And they said to him, 'Lord, he has ten pounds!') 19:26 'I tell you, that to every one who has will more be given; but from him who has not, even what he has will be taken away. 19:27 But as for these enemies of mine, who did not want me to reign over them, bring them here and slay them before me.'"*

These transcribed verses first narrate the anecdote of the rich Zacchae'us and next they teach the Parable of the Ten Pounds. The fact that Christ exposes the Parable of the Ten Pounds next to the anecdote of the rich Zachae'us, confirms that the parable is a teaching that applies to richness of material goods, even though it is not confined exclusively to that specific matter.

In my opinion, this Parable of the Ten Pounds, very similar to the Parable of the Talents of the Gospel according to Saint Matthew 25:14, teaches that those who have been provided with richness, have been provided with it to produce for God, not to enjoy the richness. It is an error to say that God richly furnishes men to enjoy their richness, and it is contrary to the doctrine taught by Christ to the apostles.

The Gospel according to Saint Matthew (R.S.V.), Second Catholic Edition, says: "*19:16 And behold, one* came up to him, saying, "Teacher, what good deed must I do, to have eternal life?" 19:17 And he said to him, "Why do you ask me about what is good? One there is who is good. If you would enter life, keep the commandments." 19:18 He said to him, "Which?" And Jesus said, "You shall not kill, You shall not commit adultery, You shall not steal, You shall not bear false witness, 19:19 Honor your father and mother, and, You shall love your neighbor as yourself." 19:20 The young man said to him, "All these I have observed; what do I still lack?" 19:21 Jesus said to him, "If you would be perfect, go, sell what you possess and give to the poor, and you will have treasure in heaven; and come, follow me." 19:22 When the young man heard this he went away sorrowful; for he had great possessions. <u>19:23 And Jesus said to his disciples, "Truly, I say to you, it will be hard for a rich man to enter the kingdom of heaven. 19:24 Again I tell you, it is easier for a camel to go through the eye of a needle than for a rich man to enter the kingdom of God." 19:25 When the disciples heard this they were greatly astonished, saying, "Who then can be saved?" 19:26 But Jesus looked at them and said to them, "With men this is impossible, but with God all things are possible."</u> 19:27 Then Peter said in reply, "Behold, we have left everything and followed you. What then shall we have?" 19:28 Jesus said to them, "Truly, I say to you, in the new world, when the Son of man shall sit on his glorious throne, you who have followed me will also sit on twelve thrones, judging the twelve tribes of Israel. 19:29 And every one who has left houses or brothers or sisters or father or mother or children or lands, for my name's sake, will receive a hundredfold, and inherit eternal life. 19:30 But many that are first will be last, and the last first." (Underline emphasis is mine)

These verses of the Gospel according to Saint Matthew make evident another error of Paul. This error is the statement of Paul of this Epistle to Timothy 6:17-20 that tells the rich men that they can lay up for themselves a good foundation for the future, so that they may take hold of the life which is life indeed, doing good, being rich in good deeds, being liberal and generous; saying at the same time that God richly furnishes men with everything to enjoy.

It is an error, because for a rich man to do so it is not as hard as it is for a camel to go through the eye of a needle; and Christ teaches that for a rich man to enter the kingdom of God is harder than for a camel to go through the eye of a needle.

Christ teaches that rich men have to do much more than do good, be rich in good deeds, be generous and liberal, while they enjoy their richness. The Gospel according to Saint Luke (R.S.V.), Second Catholic Edition, says: "6:24 *But woe to you that are rich, for you have received your consolation.*" 6:25 "*Woe to you that are full now, for you shall hunger.* "*Woe to you that laugh now, for you shall mourn and weep.*"

What does Christ teach that rich people have to do? As I said, Christ teaches that they have to live as if they were administrators of the estate they have been provided with. They have to understand that they have received their estate to invest and produce for God, not to enjoy it; although they may enjoy a portion, as I said, and that is natural for them to have, in part because of their commitment, an economic level of life higher than the level of life the unrich people have.

Certainly, for a rich man to live as if he were an

administrator of the estate he has been provided with, to live with a sense of responsibility to God and Society is not as hard as it is for a camel to go through the eye of a needle; but whoever does it, will no longer be a rich man, even though he may have a big estate, because he would be recognizing himself as an administrator of his estate, not considering himself its owner. The one who is rich is the one who is the owner of a big estate, not the administrator of one. The secret is: if a rich man in this life does not consider himself rich before God, but an administrator of God's richness, God will not consider him a rich man at the time of his entering into the kingdom of God. If the rich men do not do that, it will be very hard for them to enter the kingdom of God.

Besides, even though the rich men who do not live as if they were administrators of the estate they have been provided with, will still be rewarded for any good deed they do, for any act of generosity and liberality they do, let us remember that he who gives from poverty gives more than he who gives from abundance. The Gospel according to Saint Luke (R.S.V.), Second Catholic Edition, says about Jesus: "*21:1 He looked up and saw the rich putting their gifts into the treasury; 21:2 and he saw a poor widow put in two copper coins. 21:3 And he said, "Truly I tell you, this poor widow has put in more than all of them; 21:4 for they all contributed out of their abundance, but she out of her poverty put in all the living that she had.*"

What God wants of the rich men is for them to try to invest and produce the most good they are able to, and to be ready to resign all their estate, if it is the only way to follow God in a particular circumstance. To be ready to resign all their estate does not mean necessarily to be ready to donate all of it. Sometimes it involves the courage to oppose an act of corruption that might put in danger the destiny of their business or job, for instance, or their public honor.

Whoever has received money in this life, more often, must produce more money with it, to be able to produce more good with it. Most businessmen might have even a religious duty to invest and seek economic success, or at least commercial success. Economic and commercial success are not bad. The way to get them might be bad sometimes, and what is done with them might be bad sometimes, but they also might be good.

Economic and commercial success give great power to do good. They produce Jobs. Without doubt, Christians should have a lot of desire to do good. And the professions related to the production of tangible goods, in any of its forms, material, temporal (logistics), transportation or commerce, should be also very well esteemed by Christians, without diminution of other professions more or less important.

The servant of The Parable of the Ten Pounds was a good servant because he committed himself to investing, taking risks, and to producing for the noble ten more pounds with the ten pounds he received. And even though, in that parable, the pounds do not only represent tangible goods, it perfectly applies to them.

For many men the result expected by God will be accomplished with economic or commercial success; for many others the result will be accomplished by other ways, working in other professions.

Being a good administrator will not always mean to preserve or increase the material estate received or achieved, but sometimes it will, if in that way the good administrator can produce more good for God.

Consequences

These words of this Epistle of Paul distorted Christian's doctrine about richness. They weakened Christian doctrine. They tempted rich men to believe they have the right to enjoy most of their richness, and that with donations of small percentages of their estate they can buy their way to heaven. They have reduced the number of rich men with a sense of responsibility to God and society, misguiding them away from the kingdom of God, and depriving in that way the world of all the good those rich men could have produced. The lack of commitment of the rich people to society is one of the worst evils a society can have, because rich men are some of the few that have the most power to do good. And because the lack of commitment of the rich to society gives place to a lot of socially vicious, hateful and destructives ideologies and feelings.

II.8. About the Value of Bodily Training

The First Epistle of Paul to Timothy (R.S.V.), Second Catholic Edition, says: 4:8: *"for while bodily training is of some value..."*

Ruy Barraco Mármol

Error

Bodily training is not only of some value, but of great value.

Commentaries

The translation of this verse by the R.S.V. is not the best. The Greek text does not say <u>of some value</u>. It says <u>of limited value.</u> The Greek text says: "η γαρ σωματικη γυμνασια Προς <u>ολιγον</u> εστιν <u>ωφελιμος</u>." The word ολιγον (oligon) means small[94]; and the word ωφελιμοσ (ophelimos) means value[95]. In my opinion the R.S.V. should translate this verse in the following way: "*4:8 for, while physical training is of limited value...*"

This statement of Paul is an error. On the contrary, bodily training is very valuable to develop, especially in young people, spiritual virtues such as faith, hope,

---

[94] Max Zerwick "*Analysis Philologica Novi Testamenti Graeci*" says under Ad Timotheum I, 4:8 that ολιγον (oligon) means in Latin paucus, exiguos, brevis. The Harper Collins Latin Concise Dictionary says that paucus means few, little; and that exiguus means small, short, meagre. Karl Feyerabend in his book "*Langenscheidt Pocket Greek Dictionary*" says that ολιγος (oligos) means few, little; small, short, weak, indifferent.

[95] Max Zerwick "*Analysis Philologica Novi Testamenti Graeci*" says under Ad Timotheum I, 4:8 that the word ωφελιμοσ (ophelimos) means utilis. The Harper Collins Latin Concise Dictionary says under the word *utilis*: adj useful, expedient, profitable; fit (for). The Latin Vulgate version of the Bible says "*4:8 Nam corporalis exercitatio, ad modicum utilis est.* The King James version says: "*4:8 For bodily exercise profiteth little...*" The New American Bible says: "*4:8 for, while physical training is of limited value.* The New American Standard Bible says: "*4:8 for bodily discipline is only of little profit....*" The New International Version says: '*for physical training is of some value.*" The English Standard Version says: "*for while bodily training is of some value.*"

charity, fortitude, justice, prudence, and temperance. It is also of great value for developing perseverance. It is very important for a healthy mind. The old Latin adage teaches "Mens sana in corpore sano." (A sound mind in a healthy body.)

This is especially true when bodily training is carried out in the practice of sports, which is a very important tool for socialization and fraternity. The equality of all men is eloquently verified in sports. I have always seen in the Olympics a very important bastion of international fraternity.

Neither is it the word of God that bodily exercise has limited value, nor only some value.

Consequences

Christianity for a long time did not exploit the full potential of bodily exercise and sport as educational tools, to strengthen the fortitude of Christians, and to bring young people into a Christian life; and still does not.

II.9. About Christian Humility. About the Despisement against the Nonchristians

The First Epistle of Paul to the Corinthians (R.S.V.) Second Catholic Edition, says: "*6:1 When one of you has a grievance against a brother, does he dare go to law before the unrighteous instead of the saints? 6:2 Do you not know that the saints will judge the world? And if the world is to be judged by you, are you incompetent to try trivial cases? 6:3 Do you not know that we are to judge angels? How much* more, matters pertaining to this life! 6:4 If then you have such cases, why do you lay them before those who are least esteemed by the Church? 6:5 I say this to your shame. Can it be that there is no man among you wise enough to decide between members of the brotherhood, 6:6 but brother goes to law against brother, and that before unbelievers?"

The Second Epistle of Paul to the Corinthians (R.S.V.), Second Catholic Edition, says: "6:14 Do not be mismated with unbelievers. For what partnership have righteousness and iniquity? Or what fellowship has light with darkness? 6:15 What accord has Christ with Be'lial? Or what has a believer in common with an unbeliever?"

The First Epistle of Paul to Timothy (R.S.V.), Second Catholic Edition, says: "5:8 If anyone does not provide for his relatives, and especially for his own family, he has disowned the faith and is worse than an unbeliever."

The First Epistle of Paul to the Corinthians (R.S.V.), Second Catholic Edition, says: "7:10 To the married I give charge, not I but the Lord, that the wife should not separate from her husband 7:11 (but if she does, let her remain single or else be reconciled to her husband)-and that the husband should not divorce his wife. 7:12 To the rest I say, not the Lord, that if any brother has a wife who is an unbeliever, and she consents to live with him, he should not divorce her. 7:13 If any woman has a husband who is an unbeliever, and he consents to live with her, she should not divorce him. 7:14 For the unbelieving husband is consecrated through his wife, and the unbelieving wife is consecrated through her husband. Otherwise, your children would be *unclean, but as it is they are holy."*

Error

It is an error to call unrighteous those who are not Christians. It is an error to despise those who are not Christians. It is an error to command Christians to marry only other Christians based on the prejudice that nonchristians are equal to lawlessness, inequity or darkness. It is an error to call demons those who are not Christians. It is an error to say that if someone does not provide for relatives, especially family members, he is worse than an unbeliever. It is an error to say that the sons of the nonchristians are unclean.

Commentaries

It is an error to call unrighteous those who are not Christians, because there certainly were and are righteous men among nonchristians. It is offensive and irritating to despise those who are not Christians, associating them with inequity, lawlessness, darkness, and Be'lial. It is insulting to call the sons of nonchristians unclean, not only to them, but to their relatives.

From the argument of Paul that says that the sons of marriages between believers and unbelievers are clean, because the unbelieving spouse is made holy by the believing spouse, it is inferred that the sons of unbelievers are unclean.

It is one thing to use the word saints to refer to Christians who really live in the way Christ taught that we should, and another very different thing to use the

Ruy Barraco Mármol

word saints to refer to all those who call themselves Christians. Paul is using the word saints to refer to all those who call ourselves Christians.

All these statements of Paul, besides being wrong and unnecessary, are acts of despite. They show lack of love and righteousness. Christians should not be convinced about their own righteousness and despise nonchristians in general, just as nonchristians should not be convinced about their own righteousness and despise Christians; those actions go against Christian values, especially against the obligation to be humble.

In the parable of the Pharisee and the Tax Collector, of the Gospel according to Saint Luke (R.S.V.), Second Catholic Edition, it is said: *"18:9 He also told this parable to some who trusted in themselves that they were righteous and despised others: 18:10 "Two men went up into the temple to pray, one a Pharisee and the other a tax collector. 18:11 The Pharisee stood and prayed thus with himself, 'God, I thank you that I am not like other men, extortioners, unjust, adulterers, or even like this tax collector. 18:12 I fast twice a week, I give tithes of all that I get.' 18:13 But the tax collector, standing far off, would not even lift up his eyes to heaven, but beat his breast, saying, 'God, be merciful to me a sinner!' 18:14 I tell you, this man went down to his house justified rather than the other; for everyone who exalts himself will be humbled, but he who humbles himself will be exalted.""*

Let us Christians never forget that we are not free of sins, that we must not have attitudes like the attitude the Pharisee of the parable had, and that we must not despise nonchristians, unbelievers. Christ taught us to love and treat kindly everybody. He taught us that God loves everybody, Christians, and nonchristians. We must love even our enemies, even those who are or appear to be bad people, Christians and nonchristians. He taught us that we must love our neighbors as ourselves, and that we have neighbors among Christians and nonchristians.

In the parable of the Good Samaritan of the Gospel according to Saint Luke (R.S.V.), Second Catholic Edition, it is said: "*10:29 But he, desiring to justify himself, said to Jesus, "And who is my neighbor?" 10:30 Jesus replied, "A man was going down from Jerusalem to Jericho, and he fell among robbers, who stripped him and beat him, and departed, leaving him half dead. 10:31 Now by chance a priest was going down the road; and when he saw him he passed by on the other side. 10:32 So likewise a Levite, when he came to the place and saw him, passed by on the other side. 10:33 But a Samaritan, as he journeyed, came to where he was; and when he saw him, he had compassion, 10:34 and went to him and bound up his wounds, pouring on oil and wine; then he set him on his own beast and brought him to an inn, and took care of him. 10:35 And the next day he took out two denarii and gave them to the innkeeper, saying, 'Take care of him; and whatever more you spend, I will repay you when I come back.' 10:36 Which of these three, do you think, proved neighbor to the man who fell among the robbers?" 10:37 He said, "The one who showed mercy on him." And Jesus said to him, "Go and do likewise."* The neighbor of the Jew is a Samaritan who practices mercy, and what makes him neighbor, is the way he acts, is his mercy, not the fact that he is Samaritan, his ethno religious condition of Samaritan. That explains the final answer that says: "the one who

Ruy Barraco Mármol

treated him with mercy", without mentioning his condition of Samaritan. His mercy makes him neighbor despite the fact that he was a Samaritan, and the Samaritans and Jews had broken relationship between themselves. There are nonchristians that practice mercy and do good and they are also neighbors of the Christians. It is a serious error to despise nonchristians, especially the nonchristians neighbors of the Christians, and for the only reason of not being Christian.

The error is even worse when the persons despised are children and they are treated as unclean. The book of Acts of the Apostles says that Saint Peter taught, that God showed us that we do not have to call any person unclean or profane. In the book of Acts of the Apostles (R.S.V.), Second Catholic Edition, Saint Peter explicitly says: "*10:28 and said to them, "You yourselves know how unlawful it is for a Jew to associate with or to visit any one of another nation; but God has shown me that I should not call any man common or unclean.*" The Greek word translated as unclean in this verse, which is ακαθαρτον (akatharton) is exactly the same Greek word translated as unclean in Verse 7:14 of the First Epistle of Paul to the Corinthians. Paul says "<u>Otherwise, your children would be unclean.</u>"

The world must not be divided between righteous Christians, and unrighteous nonchristians. The use of terms such as unbelievers, unfaithful, unclean or profane, in the way denounced, is a conduct typical of religious extremists and totalitarians who want to use religion to spread hate instead of love. These are terms very useful for spreading hate not love. These are terms very useful for international hatred, not for international fraternity. These are terms very useful for leading people to war, to conflict, rather than to communion.

All of what has been said regarding this point applies to all religions. For instance, when Muslims despise those who are not Muslims they incur an error. The Muslims who believe that the nonmuslims are the darkness incur an error. The Muslims who believe that the sons of marriages between nonmuslims are unclean, incur a big error.

These statements of the Epistles of Paul were not written under the inspiration of the Holy Spirit, and are not the word of God.

Consequences

A natural effect of mistreatment is to generate more mistreatment, especially among nonchristians. The mistreatment of Christians is less likely to generate mistreatment of others on their part only, because Christ taught us to love even our enemies.

Instructions to despise and mistreat others conspired against the spread of Christianity and facilitated the persecutions against Christians, and also favored religious intolerance and conspired against international fraternity.

Today the Muslim religion is imposed on hundreds of millions of persons by using, among others, expressions like those mentioned above, making many Muslims despise nonmuslims.

Moreover, Muslim terrorists are using similar acts of despisement to promote hatred and wars that are threatening world peace. Christianity must firmly

Ruy Barraco Mármol

condemn these expressions of the Epistles of Paul.

II.10. About the Command to Judge Christians

The First Epistle of Paul to the Corinthians (R.S.V.), Second Catholic Edition, says: *"5:11 But rather I wrote to you not to associate with any one who bears the name of brother if he is guilty of immorality or greed, or is an idolater, reviler, drunkard, or robber — not even to eat with such a one. 5:12 For what have I to do with judging outsiders? Is it not those inside the Church whom you are to judge? 5:13 God judges those outside. "Drive out the wicked person from among you."*

Error

It is an error to say that Christians must judge Christians.

Commentaries

People must try not to judge other people. Especially Christians must try not to do so. This is based on the fact that we all have our sins and vices, and that in most cases, if not all, we do not have the knowledge needed to judge properly other people. A world in which persons try not to judge others is a better world. Our capacity to judge how reprehensible is a sin that another person committed, or the vice that affects another person is always very limited. Our capacity to judge how bad the sins or vices of others are in comparison to our sins and vices is always very limited.

Our knowledge of the personal circumstances, feelings, motives and thoughts of other people is always very limited, as well as our knowledge of whether or not somebody is repented, converted, and has been forgiven by God.

The Gospel according to Saint Matthew (R.S.V.), Second Catholic Edition, says: "7:1 *"Judge not, that you be not judged. 7:2 For with the judgment you pronounce you will be judged, and the measure you give will be the measure you get. 7:3 Why do you see the speck that is in your brother's eye, but you do not notice the log that is in your own eye? 7:4 Or how can you say to your brother, 'Let me take the speck out of your eye,' when there is the log in your own eye? 7:5 You hypocrite, first take the log out of your own eye, and then you will see clearly to take the speck out of your brother's eye."*

The Greek word translated as judge in Verse 7:1 is κρινω (krino) the same Greek word translated as judge in the First Epistle of Paul to the Corinthians Verse 5:13.

The commandment to refrain from judging, that Christ gives us, refers to the kind of judgments the First Epistle of Paul to the Corinthians is promoting. Christ is telling us to refrain from seeing the specks in our brother's eye, and from judging whether other Christians are unclean, greedy, drunkards, revilers or wicked, for instance.[96]

---

[96] Jesus taught that for every word that comes out of our mouth we will be judged (Matt 12:36). The commandment to avoid judging comprises the action of being very careful with any assertion or judgment that we do. The commandment to avoid judging comprises the obligation to be humble, and to remember our own sins, especially when judging. If we need to, we can assert that someone did something wrong. If we need to, we can assert that

Ruy Barraco Mármol

Certainly, there are cases in which a Christian will need to, and even must, judge; but there is a distinct line between authorizing and commanding someone to judge in specific cases, and giving a general commandment for all Christians to judge other Christians.

These statements of the First Epistle of Paul to the Corinthians are mistaken and opposed to the teachings of Christ. They were not written under the inspiration of the Holy Spirit. It is not the word of God that Christians must judge other Christians, in the cases Paul taught that Christians must do it.

Consequences

Besides distorting the virtue of Christianity, the judging attitude promoted by Paul conspired against the growth and progress of Christianity. It is fundamental to the life of the Christian Church to have believers who

---

someone has a vice. If we need to, we can say that someone is reproachable. The commandment to avoid judging comprises to avoid judging if someone will be saved or not; avoid asserting that there is no hope for a person; avoid attributing wrong actions or qualities to anyone. It comprises not being in the look of flaws or sins in other people. And it also comprises not responding evil with evil; it comprises not punishing others, neither for doing 'justice', nor to correct them. It is neither in general our responsibility to judge, nor to correct people by punishment, unless, for instance, in special cases, they are under our authority. On the contrary, in general, we are forbidden to do it. We are forbidden to keep ourselves away from others who are guilty of immorality or greed, or are idolaters, revilers, drunkards or robbers, because of their sins, for the purpose of punishing them, or correcting them. We could keep ourselves away to comply with a most important commandment such as loving God, or our neighbors as ourselves, or ourselves. We are forbidden to drive out the wicked persons from among us, for the purpose of punishing them, or because of their sins. We could do it to comply with a most important commandment. We are forbidden to avoid eating with them.

follow Christ's teaching and commandment not to judge, who judge only when it is absolutely necessary. It is fundamental to the life of any community.

These statements have caused many people to be reluctant to go to churches because of the judging attitude of some Christians, and have made them disbelieve of the truth and goodness of the Christian doctrine.

II.11. About the Obligation of the Christians to Keep Away and Drive Out the Wicked Persons among them

The Second Epistle of Paul to the Thessalonians (R.S.V.), Second Catholic Edition, says: "*3:6 Now we command you, brethren, in the name of our Lord Jesus Christ, that you keep away from any brother who is walking in idleness and not in accord with the tradition that you received from us. 3:7 For you yourselves know how you ought to imitate us; we were not idle when we were with you, 3:8 we did not eat any one's bread without paying, but with toil and labor we worked night and day, that we might not burden any of you. 3:9 It was not because we have not that right, but to give you in our conduct an example to imitate. 3:10 For even when we were with you, we gave you this command: If any one will not work, let him not eat. 3:11 For we hear that some of you are walking in idleness, mere busybodies, not doing any work. 3:12 Now such persons we command and exhort in the Lord Jesus Christ to do their work in quietness and to earn their own living. 3:13 Brethren, do not be weary in well-doing. 3:14 If any one refuses to obey what we say in this letter, note that man, and have nothing to do with him, that he may be ashamed. 3:15 Do not look at him as an enemy, but warn him as a brother."*

The First Epistle of Paul to the Corinthians (R.S.V.), Second Catholic Edition, says: *"5:9 I wrote to you in my letter not to associate with immoral men; 5:10 not at all meaning the immoral of this world, or the greedy and robbers, or idolaters, since then you would need to go out of the world. 5:11 But rather I wrote to you not to associate with any one who bears the name of brother if he is guilty of immorality or greed, or is an idolater, reviler, drunkard, or robber—not even to eat with such a one. 5:12 For what have I to do with judging outsiders? Is it not those inside the Church whom you are to judge? 5:13 God judges those outside. "Drive out the wicked person from among you."*

Error

It is an error to command Christians <u>to keep away</u> from any brother that is walking in idleness. It is an error to command Christians <u>to note</u> the man who refuses to obey what he says in the First Epistle to the Corinthians. It is an error to command <u>not to associate</u> with immoral men. It is an error to command Christians not to associate with brothers guilty of immorality, greed, drunkenness or robbery. It is an error to command us to <u>drive out</u> from among us those brothers, and in general <u>the wicked</u> persons among us.

Commentaries

The Second Epistle of Paul to the Thessalonians

Verse 3:6 is translated by the Revised Standard Version, Second Catholic Edition, in the following way: *"3:6 Now we command you, brethren, in the name of our Lord Jesus Christ, that you keep away from any brother who is walking in idleness and not in accord with the tradition that you received from us."* The Greek word translated as idleness is ατακτως (ataktos), and means inordinate, undisciplined, disorderly.[97]

To command Christians to keep themselves away from any brother that conducts himself in a disorderly way, is walking in idleness, is a drunkard, greedy, a robber, a reviler, or is wicked, is an error, in the first place, because the fulfillment of the commandment requires the conduct of judging and condemning which, I already said, is opposed to the commandment of Christ not to judge, which comprises the commandment not to condemn. The same can be said about the commandment to drive those Christians out from among us.

The Gospel according to Saint Luke (R.S.V.) Second Catholic Edition, says: *"6:37 "Judge not, and you will not be judged; condemn not, and you will not be condemned; forgive, and you will be forgiven."* These commandments of Paul are against the commandment of Jesus Christ not

---

[97] Max Zerwick "Analysis Philologica Novi Testamenti Graeci" says under Ad Thessalonicenses II, 3:6, that the word ατακτως means in Latin in-ordinate, indisciplinate. The Harper Collins Latin Concise dictionary says under the word inordinatus: disordered, irregular. The Latin word used in the Vulgate to translate this word is inordinate. The King James version translates the word as 'disorderly'. The New American Bible translates the word as "disorderly way". The New American Standard Bible translates the word as 'who leads an unruly life'. The New International Version translates that word as 'idle'. The English Standard Version uses the word 'idleness'.

Ruy Barraco Mármol

to judge, not to condemn, and are also against the commandment to love, and to be merciful. Seeking the will of God sometimes we will need to judge others, but that does not mean that we must expel the wicked persons from among us. We are also sinners. We do not know how bad other people's sins in comparison with ours are. On particular occasions it will be necessary or advisable for Christians to keep away from some people who conduct themselves in a disorderly way, or are walking in idleness, or are drunkards, or greedy, or wicked, or even be necessary or advisable to drive some people out from among us; but that does not justify commanding this general instruction, opposed to the commandments not to judge, not to condemn, to love and to be merciful.

Christ taught us that we must love even our enemies. The commandment to love obligates us to do, and to refrain from doing, things for the ones we must love. In principle, to fulfill the commandment of love we should not keep ourselves away from the Christians who conduct themselves in a disorderly way, are walking in idleness, are drunkards, are revilers, greedy or are wicked; and we should also refrain from driving out others, especially Christians, from among us. The Gospel according to Saint Matthew (R.S.V.), Second Catholic Edition, says: "5:43 *"You have heard that it was said, 'You shall love your neighbor and hate your enemy.' 5:44 But I say to you, Love your enemies and pray for those who persecute you, 5:45 so that you may be sons of your Father who is in heaven; for he makes his sun rise on the evil and on the good, and sends rain on the just and on the unjust. 5:46 For if you love those who love you, what reward have you? Do not even the tax collectors do the same? 5:47 And if you salute only your brethren, what more are you doing than others? Do not even the Gentiles do the same? 5:48 You, therefore, must be perfect, as your heavenly Father is perfect."*

This does not mean, as I said, that on particular occasions we are not allowed to keep ourselves away from, or to drive out, somebody. But it does mean that in general we must not. And in those cases in which we may be allowed or need to keep away from somebody because of his conduct, most likely, it will not make any difference whether or not he is a Christian. If it matters, if the reason we have to keep ourselves away from somebody remains in his Christianity, then we will probably be committing an error and a big sin.

The Gospel according to Saint Matthew (R.S.V.), Second Catholic Edition, says: *"9:10 And as he sat at the table in the house, behold, many tax collectors and sinners came and sat down with Jesus and his disciples. 9:11 And when the Pharisees saw this, they said to his disciples, "Why does your teacher eat with tax collectors and sinners?" 9:12 But when he heard it, he said, "Those who are well have no need of a physician, but those who are sick. 9:13 Go and learn what this means, 'I desire mercy, and not sacrifice.' For I came not to call the righteous, but sinners."* Christ taught us in this opportunity that it is not merciful in principle to keep ourselves away from those who seem to be greater sinners than we are, nor to refuse to eat with them. And that teaching, without any doubt, includes the drunkards, the greedy, and the revilers, for instance. Jesus came to call sinners, and he needed to be among sinners to be able to call them. If we are going to try to do the same, we are going to need to eat with sinners,

Ruy Barraco Mármol

such as people who are greedy or drunkards, or revilers, for instance, Christians and nonchristians, always remembering that we are sinners as well. The commandment of Paul to not even eat with drunkards, to keep away from them, and to drive them out from among us, is unmerciful.

The Gospel according to Saint Matthew (R.S.V.), Second Catholic Edition, says: "*13:24 Another parable he put before them, saying, "The kingdom of heaven may be compared to a man who sowed good seed in his field; 13:25 but while men were sleeping, his enemy came and sowed weeds among the wheat, and went away. 13:26 So when the plants came up and bore grain, then the weeds appeared also. 13:27 And the servants of the householder came and said to him, 'Sir, did you not sow good seed in your field? How then has it weeds?' 13:28 He said to them, 'An enemy has done this.' The servants said to him, 'Then do you want us to go and gather them?' 13:29 But he said, 'No; lest in gathering the weeds you root up the wheat along with them. 13:30 Let both grow together until the harvest; and at harvest time I will tell the reapers, Gather the weeds first and bind them in bundles to be burned, but gather the wheat into my barn."'* Explaining this parable the same Gospel according to Saint Matthew (R.S.V.), Second Catholic Edition, says: "*13:36 Then he left the crowds and went into the house. And his disciples came to him, saying, "Explain to us the parable of the weeds of the field." 13:37 He answered, "He who sows the good seed is the Son of man; 13:38 the field is the world, and the good seed means the sons of the kingdom; the weeds are the sons of the evil one; 13:39 and the enemy who sowed them is the devil; the harvest is the close of the age, and the reapers are angels.*

13:40 Just as the weeds are gathered and burned with fire, so will it be at the close of the age. 13:41 The Son of man will send his angels, and they will gather out of his kingdom all causes of sin and all evildoers, 13:42 and throw them into the furnace of fire, where there will be weeping and gnashing of teeth. 13:43 Then the righteous will shine like the sun in the kingdom of their Father. He who has ears, let him hear." In my opinion, Christ tells us in this parable, among other things, that Christians must not drive out of the Christian community, out from among Christians, the wicked persons, who are like weeds growing with the wheat. He teaches us that doing so we might drive out wheat along with weeds. As I said there might be special occasions and reasons that can justify doing so, but these will be exceptions.

In general, whoever worried about keeping himself away from the brother he judged to be living in a disorderly way or being idle, because of the general rule commanded by Paul, might have followed the teachings of Paul, but not the teachings of Christ. The same thing can be said about whoever drove out a drunkard, a greedy person, a reviler, or drove out someone he judged wicked.

Finally, the commandment of Paul that tells us to note whoever refuses to obey the commandments of the First Epistle to the Corinthians, is the worst of all these commandments. Because among the Christians who disobey that commandment of Paul can be some who are doing it to fulfill the commandments of Christ, being a neighbor in the terms of the Parable of the Good Samaritan.

Consequences

These statements contributed to installing among Christians many vices that Christ precisely came to take away. Some of the most important teachings of Christ are contradicted in these statements. Those vices not only affect individuals, but also the community as a whole, because without doubt, among the most important assets the Christian community can have is surely to have humble Christians; Christians who judge only when absolutely necessary; Christians who recognize themselves as sinners; Christians who love the sinners mentioned by Paul and are merciful with them; Christians who eat with them, and who do not try to drive out other Christians they judge wicked; Christians that are tolerant.

II. 12. About the Capacity of Men to Understand the Gospel of Christ. About What Must Be Taught to the New Christians

The First Epistle of Paul to the Corinthians (R.S.V.), Second Catholic Edition, says: "*3:1 But I, brethren, could not address you as spiritual men, but as men of the flesh, as infants in Christ. 3:2 I fed you with milk, not solid food; for you were not ready for it; and even yet you are not ready, 3:3 for you are still of the flesh.*"

Error

It is an error to tell other men that they cannot be addressed as spiritual men, but as men of the flesh, as infants in Christ. It is an error to tell a man that he cannot be fed with solid food.

Commentaries

All men can be addressed as spiritual men, as if they were not men of the flesh, as if they were not infants in Christ. It is up to them to listen or not. All men can be fed with the solid food of Christianity, especially Christians, no matter how new they are as Christians.

Paul in this epistle is telling Christians that he could not address them as spiritual men, but as men of the flesh, as infants in Christ. He is telling Christians, sanctified in Christ Jesus according to his words, that they are still of the flesh, infants in Christ, and are not ready for the solid food he is able to feed them. Paul sent this epistle to the Church of Corinth. In the first paragraph of this epistle (R.S.V.), Second Catholic Edition, he says: "*1:2 To the Church of God which is at Corinth, to those sanctified in Christ Jesus, called to be saints together with all those who in every place call on the name of our Lord Jesus Christ, both their Lord and others.*"

Ministers must not talk down to people putting themselves in a superior position. Ministers must not treat men as if they were incapable of being fed with the solid food of Christianity.

All men can be fed with the solid food of Christianity, even men of the flesh, even sinners as we all are, but especially Christian sinners. Christ came to call all the different kinds of sinners, of men of the flesh, and, "of course", with a message that we can understand.

There is no more solid food in Christianity than the doctrine that Christ taught to the twelve apostles, which was revealed in a way that infants can understand and not just the "wise", in a way even men of the flesh can understand and not just the saints. The twelve apostles taught the doctrine Christ taught them, and they taught it to men of the flesh, to infants in Christ, to infants, like Christ did. Christ talked to people using a language understandable to everyone, and his doctrine was solid food. And Christ thanked his Father for revealing things in that way.

The Gospel according to Saint Matthew (R.S.V.), Second Catholic Edition, says: "*11:25 At the time Jesus declared, "I thank you, Father, Lord of heaven and earth, that you have hidden these things from the wise and understanding and revealed them to infants; 11:26 yes, Father, for such was your gracious will."* The Greek word translated in these verses of the Gospel according to Saint Matthew as infants is νεπιοις (nepiois), exactly the same word translated as infants in Verse 3:1 of the First Epistle of Paul to the Corinthians. This, again, you are most likely noticing by yourselves, is not a coincidence.

If Paul had taught the doctrine of Christ expressed to the twelve apostles the way Christ expressed it, then he would have taught solid food, that even the infants, the ordinary people without special preparation, the ones who were not "wise", the infants of the kingdom, the infants in Christ, would have been able to understand; that even the men of the flesh would have been able to understand. And Paul committed an error by saying the opposite.

If Paul did not teach the doctrine of Christ as Christ

taught it to the apostles, which is the case, when Paul taught that the infants in Christ can only be fed with infant food, he implied that the doctrine that Christ taught was infant food, because Christ also taught and especially taught his doctrine to ordinary people, to infants, to infants in Christ, and to men of the flesh, whom he came to call. Christ also taught his doctrine to new Christians. Infant food is supposed to be given to people for a short period of time to be replaced later by solid food.[98]

Paul was wrong when he wrote these statements and put the doctrine he taught over the doctrine Christ taught to the apostles. The truth is that ordinary people can be fed with the solid food of Christianity, such as the doctrine Christ taught to the apostles. The truth is that the doctrine Christ taught to the apostles can be taught to infants in Christ and to men of the flesh. The truth is that the real solid food, the real bread that gives life, is the word that Jesus taught to the twelve apostles.

Consequences

These statements led some people to think that if Paul's doctrine is solid food, and cannot be taught to infants, the same is true with regard to Christ's doctrine.

For that reason the word of Christ taught to the twelve apostles was not taught to the Christians as it should have been taught. The Catholic Church did not

---

[98] A similar teaching of Paul can be found in the Epistle of Paul to the Hebrews, Verse 5:12.

Ruy Barraco Mármol

undertake the job of making Christians learn and understand the Gospels. For a long time mass itself was celebrated in Latin, a language that the majority of the Christians did not understand, but only the "wise". Even in these days, most of the Christians are not encouraged enough to learn the word of Christ taught to the twelve apostles the way he expressed it, and are not encouraged to be able to understand and interpret the scriptures by themselves. Most Christians do not even know the Gospels.

These wrong statements of Paul also led people to believe that if ordinary people do not have the capacity to understand or judge "the Catholic Doctrine", neither do they have the capacity to rule themselves.

This matter of the capacity of the people that Paul denies put an obstacle in the way of the constitutional democracy that is founded on the premise of the capacity of the people. In constitutional democracy, the freedom of ordinary people is recognized because ordinary people are believed to have the capacity to use that freedom, and to judge how that freedom must be used. Constitutional democracy recognizes that ordinary people have the right to rule through representatives, because people are believed to have the capacity to rule themselves in that way.

The denying of the capacity of the people also promoted the attitude of the Christian ministers to believe themselves over the rest of the men, and to carry out their preaching from that basis. It promoted lack of humility among the Christian ministers. This tempts people to distance themselves from Christianity, especially educated and free-thinking people. It also tempts people not to reflect on, or meditate on the word of Christ. People are not attracted to reading things which they are made to believe incapable of understanding by themselves.

Illustrative Quotes

The epistle "Magno et acerbo" from Pope Pius VII, 1800-1823, to the Archbishop of Mohileff, September 3, 1816 says: "*1604...But, if we grieve that men renowned for piety and wisdom have, by no means rarely, failed in interpreting the Scriptures, what should we not fear if the Scriptures, translated into every vulgar tongue whatsoever, are freely handed on to be read by an inexperienced people who, for the most part, judge not with any skill but with a kind of rashness?...*

1605 Therefore, in that famous letter of his to the faithful of the Church at Meta, our predecessor, Innocent III, quite wisely prescribes as follows: "In truth the secret mysteries of faith are not to be exposed to all everywhere, since they cannot be understood by all everywhere, but only by those who can grasp them with the intellect of faith. Therefore, to the more simple the Apostle says: "I gave you milk to drink as unto little ones in Christ, not meat" (I Cor. 3:2). For solid food is for the elders, as he said: "We speak wisdom...among the perfect (I Cor. 2:6); "for I judged not myself to know anything among you, but Jesus Christ and Him Crucified" (I Cor. 2:2). For so great is the depth of Divine Scripture that not only the simple and the unlettered, but even the learned and prudent are not fully able to explore the understanding of it. Therefore, Scripture says that many "searching have failed in their search" (Ps.

63:7)."[99]

II.13. About Going to Law against Brothers before Nonchristians

The First Epistle of Paul to the Corinthians (R.S.V.) Second Catholic Edition, says: "*6:1 When one of you has a grievance against a brother, does he dare go to law before the unrighteous instead of the saints? 6:2 Do you not know that the saints will judge the world? And if the world is to be judged by you, are you incompetent to try trivial cases? 6:3 Do you not know that we are to judge angels? How much more, matters pertaining to this life! 6:4 If then you have such cases, why do you lay them before those who are least esteemed by the Church? 6:5 I say this to your shame. Can it be that there is no man among you wise enough to decide between members of the brotherhood, 6:6 but brother goes to law against brother, and that before unbelievers?*"

Error

It is an error to present as a fault to go to law against brothers before nonchristians.

Commentaries

To go to law is to go to law courts. To be able to live in society with nonchristians, Christians must have authorities in common with nonchristians. It is not a

---

[99] Denzinger Henry "*The Sources of Catholic Dogma*", (U.S.A.; Loreto Publications, 2002), translated by Roy J. Deferrari, from the thirtieth edition of Enchiridion Symbolorum by Henry Denzinger, revised by Karl Rahner, S.J., published in 1954, by Herder & Co., Freiburg, p. 399.

fault for a Christian, and it has never been a fault, to go to law against a brother before nonchristians. Either all western and Christian societies are wrong today, or Paul was wrong when he made these statements.

The Gospel according to Saint Matthew (R.S.V.), Second Catholic Edition, says: "*18:15 If your brother sins against you, go and tell him his fault, between you and him alone. If he listens to you, you have gained your brother. 18:16 But if he does not listen, take one or two others along with you, that every word may be confirmed by the evidence of two or three witnesses. 18:17 If he refuses to listen to them, tell it to the Church; and if he refuses even to the Church, let him be to you as a Gentile and a tax collector.*" When Jesus says "<u>if he refuses to listen to the Church, let him be to you as a Gentile and a tax collector</u>" he implies that the Church does not have coercive powers. And the word Church here refers to the community of Christians. When Jesus says here "<u>let him be to you as a Gentile and a tax collector</u>", in my opinion, he is saying that after doing what he said, Christians can go in peace against a brother to the courts to settle the dispute, as if he were not a brother.

Christians need to be able to go to court against brothers, on certain occasions, if they do not listen. They need to go to a court with coercive powers that the Church does not have, and should not have.

Christ recognized and encouraged us to recognize civil authorities, "Give to Caesar what is Caesar's, and to God the things that are God's."

Ruy Barraco Mármol

Consequences

The installation of the idea in Christians, that says that Christians must have their own courts, and that the Christians must be judged by Christians, contributed to the intromission of the Christian Church in matters that concern only civil authority. The errors committed by the Christian Church in matters of the civil authority are costly errors, which are still being paid. The Christian Church did not receive, and must not have, any civil power to judge or punish Christians, and much less nonchristians. In order to be able to judge Christians the Christian Church was inevitably going to need coercive powers, and we all know how those powers have been used.

The intromission of the Christian Church in matters that concern only the civil authority was by itself a source of wrongdoings, among which the Inquisition probably comes to mind first, because of the great damage it caused to the Catholic Church, and the Christian community in general.

Whoever asks himself how the Catholic Church went from Christ's commandment not to judge, to the Inquisition, may find the answer in these and other teachings of Paul. Paul commanded Christians to judge Christians, and to believe themselves to be in a better condition to judge than nonchristians.

Also, as we have seen before, Paul was an inquisitor before getting into the Christian Church, and indirectly approved his actions by saying that before being called by God he walked blameless in the justice of the Law, no matter that he was persecuting, torturing, beating to death, men and women of his religion, that believed differently from him.

II. 14. About the Judging Power of the Spiritual Men

The First Epistle of Paul to the Corinthians (R.S.V.), Second Catholic Edition, says: "*2:15 The spiritual man judges all things, but is himself to be judged by no one.*"

Error

The spiritual man does not judge all things and is himself judged in this age the same way the rest of the people are judged.

Commentaries

With the expression "spiritual man", Paul is talking about himself, and seems to refer here to the apostles and ministers of the Christian Church.

This statement is mistaken because Christ did not put the apostles in their earthly life in a position above the rest of the men in the matter of judging. Instead, he told them that they should be the servants of all men, that they are brethren like all the other brethren. The servants of men are judged by men, and of course do not judge all things.

The Gospel according to Saint Matthew (R.S.V.), Second Catholic Edition, says: "*20:25 But Jesus called them to him and said, "You know that the rulers of the Gentiles lord it over them, and their great men exercise their*

Ruy Barraco Mármol

authority over them. 20:26 It shall not be so among you; but whoever would be great among you must be your servant, 20:27 and whoever would be first among you must be your slave; 20:28 even as the Son of man came not to be served but to serve, and to give his life as a ransom for many." Christ teaches the twelve that if they want to be great they have to become servants of each other.

Consequences

This error led ecclesiastic authorities to believe themselves over civil authority, and was also responsible to a great extent for the intromission of the Christian Church in civil matters, and for the inquisition.

Illustrative Quotes

Pope Boniface VIII in his Bull "Unam Sanctam", November 18, 1302 says: "*469 And we are taught by evangelical words that in this power of his are two swords, namely spiritual and temporal. . . . Therefore, each is in the power of the Church, that is, a spiritual and a material sword. But the latter, indeed, must be exercised for the Church, the former by the Church. The former (by the hand) of the priest, the latter by the hand of kings and soldiers, but at the will and sufferance of the priest. For it is necessary that a sword be under a sword and that temporal authority be subject to spiritual power. . . . It is necessary that we confess the more clearly that spiritual power precedes any earthly power both in dignity and nobility, as spiritual matters themselves excel the temporal. . . . For, as truth testifies, spiritual power has to establish earthly power, and* to judge if it was not good. . . . *Therefore, if earthly power deviates, it will be judged by spiritual power; but if a lesser spiritual deviates, by its superior; but if the supreme (spiritual power deviates), it can be judged by God alone, not by man, as the Apostle testifies: "The spiritual man judges all things, but he himself is judged by no one" [1 Cor. 2:15]. But this authority, although it is given to man and is exercised by man, is not human, but rather divine, and has been given by the divine Word to Peter himself and to his successors in him, whom the Lord acknowledged an established rock, when he said to Peter himself: "Whatsoever you shall bind" etc. [Matt. 16:19]. Therefore, "whosoever resists this power so ordained by God, resists the order of God" [cf.Rom. 13:2], unless as a Manichaean he imagines that there are two beginnings, which we judge false and heretical, because, as Moses testifies, not "in the beginnings" but "in the beginning God created the heaven and earth" [cf. Gen. 1:1]. Furthermore, we declare, say, define, and proclaim to every human creature that they by necessity for salvation are entirely subject to the Roman Pontiff."*[100]

II.15. About Submission to Ecclesiastic Authority

The Epistle of Paul to the Hebrews (R.S.V.), Second Catholic Edition, says: *"13:17 Obey your leaders and submit to them; for they are keeping watch over your souls, as men who will have to give account. Let them do this joyfully, and not sadly, for that would be of no advantage to you."*

---

[100] Denzinger Henry *"The Sources of Catholic Dogma"*, (U.S.A.; Loreto Publications, 2002), translated by Roy J. Deferrari, from the thirtieth edition of Enchiridion Symbolorum by Henry Denzinger, revised by Karl Rahner, S.J., published in 1954, by Herder & Co., Freiburg, p. 187.

Error

The statement that commands Christians to obey and submit to our leaders is an error.

Commentaries

The Epistle of Paul to the Hebrews commands us to submit to our leaders. The leaders the Epistle of Paul to the Hebrews is referring to in this Verse 13:17 are the spiritual leaders.[101]

Aside from the fact that the verse we are analyzing says about these leaders that they are keeping watch over our souls, a few verses before, in Verse 13:7, the same Epistle of Paul to the Hebrews (R.S.V.), Second Catholic Edition, says: *"13:7 Remember your leaders, those who spoke to you the word of God; consider the outcome of their life, and imitate their faith. 13:8 Jesus Christ is the same yesterday and today and forever. 13:9 Do not be led away by diverse and strange teachings; for it is well that the heart be strengthened by grace, not by foods, which have not benefited their adherents."* The Greek

---

[101] The Greek word translated as leader here is ηγουμενοις (hegoumenois), which is a tense of the Greek verb ηγεομαι (hegeomai). The Greek verb ηγεομαι (hegeomai) means to lead the way, to go before; to lead the van; to be leader, ruler, or chief; to think, mean, believe. Max Zerwick "Analysis Philologica Novi Testamenti Graeci" under Epistle of Paul to the Hebrews 13:17 and 13:7. Richard J. Goodrich and Lukaszewski Albert. L "A Reader's Greek New Testament" under Epistle of Paul to the Hebrews 13:17, note 61. The English word hegemony shares the same origin. Karl Feyerabend "The Langenscheidt Pocket Greek Dictionary", under the word ηγεομαι (hegeomai) says: to lead the way, to go before; to lead the van; to be leader, ruler, or chief; to think, mean, believe.

word translated in Verse 13:7 as leaders is the same Greek word translated as leaders in Verse 13:17. Verse 13:17 of the Epistle of Paul to the Hebrews says "Obey your leaders and submit to them" meaning with leader the spiritual leaders.

Christ taught us to the contrary. He taught us, that we should not even call anyone but him teacher, or master or leader because we must not have any spiritual teacher, or master or leader other than him. The Gospel according to Saint Matthew (R.S.V.), Second Catholic Edition, says: *"23:1 Then said Jesus to the crowds and to his disciples, 23:2 "The scribes and the Pharisees sit on Moses' seat; 23:3 so practice and observe whatever they tell you, but not what they do; for they preach, but do not practice. 23:4 They bind heavy burdens, hard to bear, and lay them on men's shoulders; but they themselves will not move them with their finger. 23:5 They do all their deeds to be seen by men; for they make their phylacteries broad and their fringes long, 23:6 and they love the place of honor at feasts and the best seats in the synagogues, 23:7 and salutations in the market places, and being called rabbi by men. 23:8 But you are not to be called rabbi, for you have one teacher, and you are all brethren. 23:9 And call no man your father on earth, for you have one Father, who is in heaven. 23:10 Neither be called masters, for you have one master, the Christ. 23:11 He who is greatest among you shall be your servant; 23:12 whoever exalts himself will be humbled, and whoever humbles himself will be exalted".* God does not want us to call our religious authorities rabbi, teacher, master, because he does not want us to have as rabbi, teacher, and master anyone but himself, and he does not want us to submit to any man: he does not want us to submit to any spiritual leader other than him.[102]

---

[102] The Greek words translated in Verse 23:10 of the Gospel according to Saint Matthew (R.S.V.) Second Catholic Edition as 'master' are καθηγηται (kathegetai) and καθηγητης (kathegetes). They both formed by the Greek proposition Καθ (kath) + the Greek verb ηγεομαι (hegeomai), used by Paul when requesting submission to spiritual leaders. Καθ-ηγητης (kathegetes) means chief of the way, magister, praeceptor, who has the power of the moral way, director. Karl Feyerabend in his book "Langenscheidt Pocket Greek Dictionary" says it means: leader, guide, teacher. This Greek word καθ-ηγητης (kath-egetes) is used in the Gospel according to Saint Matthew Verse 23:10 with the meaning of master or leader. Some versions of the Bible translate this word in Verse 23:10 of the Gospel according to Saint Matthew as teacher or instructor. We will see that it is not correct to do it. However, even if it were, if it is not right to call anyone teacher, in a spiritual sense, it is not right to call anyone spiritual leader as well. Jesus gave this teaching talking about the Pharisees and the Scribes who sit in the chair of Moses. The context of Verse 23:10 of the Gospel according to Saint Matthew tells us that it is not right to translate the word καθαγητης (kath-egetes) as teacher or instructor, but as leader or spiritual leader. The English word <u>master</u> admits that meaning. Verse 23:8 of the Gospel according to Saint Matthew says 'one among you is a teacher'. The Greek word translated as teacher in this verse in many of the Bibles is διδασκαλος (didaskalos), which means teacher. The English word didactic shares the same origin of this word. The word διδασκαλος (didaskalos) translated as teacher in Verse 23:8 is different from the word καθηγητησ (kathegetes) used in Verse 23:10. It is not reasonable to interpret that these two verses, Verse 23:8 that says according to the R.S.V. (Second Catholic Edition) "23:8 But you are not to be called rabbi, for you have one teacher, and you are all brethren", and Verse 23:10, that says according to the (R.S.V.), Second Catholic Edition, "Neither be called masters, for you have one master, the Christ", which are not consecutive, repeat the same teaching about being called teacher, using different words. In the middle of these Verses 23:8 and 23:10 there is a verse that refers to the act of calling anyone father. It is not reasonable to interpret that these verses first refer to the act of avoiding being called teacher, then to the act of avoiding being called father, and then to the act of avoiding being called teacher again. What is reasonable is to interpret that Verses 23:8, 23:9 and 23:10 refer to different things. If the word διδασκαλος (didaskalos) of Verse 23:8 means teacher, it is reasonable to translate the word καθηγητησ (kathegetes) of Verse 23:10 as leader, especially because that is its first meaning. The use of the word master in this verse to translate this word is appropriate because it also means leader. Christ taught us in the Gospel according to Saint Matthew 23:10 not to call religious leader or master any person. The Greek word translated as leader in this verse

Commanding submission to our spiritual leaders Paul was contradicting Christ's teachings that tell us not to call teacher or leader anyone but himself. Paul was contradicting the teachings of Jesus that tell us not to have spiritual leaders; and least of all to submit to one. If we submit to a spiritual leader, this spiritual leader becomes our teacher.

If Christ is going to be our teacher, our master, our spiritual leader, we have to follow him, we have to follow his word. And to be able to follow him and his word we must know his word, understand it by ourselves and follow our understanding of the word. If instead of our understanding of the word of God, we are going to follow the interpretation of a spiritual leader that contradicts our understanding, then our leader will no longer be Christ but that spiritual leader: especially if we submit to a spiritual leader other than Christ.

Christian ministers, among other things, must give

---

is a tense of the Greek verb καθ –**ηγεομαι** *(kath-hegeomai)*, and Paul in the Epistle of Paul to the Hebrews taught us not only to have leaders but to submit to them. The Greek word translated as leader in Verse 13:17 of the Epistle of Paul to the Hebrews, in which Paul gives us that teaching, is **ηγεομαι** *(hegeomai).* Some Greek manuscripts, in which very important manuscripts such as Codex Vaticanus and Codex Alexandrinus are not included, read in Verse 23:8 the Greek word καθηγητησ (kathegetes) instead of the Greek word διδασκαλος (didaskalos), and repeat the use of the word καθηγητησ (kathegetes) in Verse 23:10. And some Bibles have chosen to follow these manuscripts translating Verse 23:8 and 23:10 using the same word teacher in both verses instead of leader. It is not reasonable to follow these manuscripts, among other reasons, because of the same reasons it is not reasonable to translate the word in these non-consecutive verses with the same meaning. In any case the teaching is the same, because by teaching not to call or let anyone call us teacher, Jesus taught us not to call or let anyone call us spiritual leader, and taught us not to submit to any man.

Ruy Barraco Mármol

testimony of the word of God, telling us what Christ said, but must not usurp the title of Christ. They must explain to us the word of God, and we must receive them, pay attention to what they say, show them respect, but we must not let them rule what we think or do. We must not submit to them.

This does not mean that we Christians must not obey our religious authorities. Of course we have to obey our religious authorities, in the same way we have to obey our civil authorities, in everything that they command that is at the same time good and contained within the narrow sphere of their competence.

But one thing is to be obedient to authority and other very different thing is to submit to a leader. One thing is to obey an authority within the limited area of his competence, and other thing is to put somebody in a place that belongs to Christ: the place of leader. Christ taught that we must not let other people call us spiritual leader, and that we have only one spiritual leader, Christ.

The word of God is revealed in a way that everyone can understand it. The Gospel according to Saint Matthew (R.S.V.), Second Catholic Edition, says: "*11:25 At that time Jesus declared, "I thank you, Father, Lord of heaven and earth, that you have hidden these things from the wise and understanding and revealed them to infants; 11:26 yes, Father, for such was your gracious will.*"

Whoever understands does not need to submit to a spiritual leader other than Christ. If somebody understands what he said, it is up to him to do God's will or not.

If anyone knows the word of God, and understands

it, he will be able to explain it in a way that other people are able to understand it too. If he cannot explain it, this is because he does not understand it. Nobody needs submission of the believers to preach the word of God.

To have more opportunities to enter to the Kingdom of God men must understand the word of God. It is an obligation of Christians to try to understand. Those who put in their minds interpretations of spiritual leaders other than Christ without understanding those interpretations, are not doing God's will, and are taking the risk of letting a spiritual leader put ideas in their minds as if they were the word of God, when they are not; they are taking the risk of letting the Evil One take away from their minds and their hearts what Christ sowed. The Gospel according to Saint Matthew (R.S.V.), Second Catholic Edition, says: "*13:19. When any one hears the word of the kingdom and does not understand it, the Evil One comes and snatches away what is sown in his heart; this is what was sown along the path.*"

The man that produces good fruit is the one who understands the word of God. The Gospel according to Saint Matthew (R.S.V.), Second Catholic Edition, says: "*13:23. As for what was sown on good soil, this is he who hears the word and understands it; he indeed bears fruit, and yields, in one case a hundredfold, in another sixty, and in another thirty.*"

The lamp of the body is the eye, the mind, not the ear. The Gospel according to Saint Matthew (R.S.V.), Second Catholic Edition, says: "*6:22 "The eye is the lamp of the body. So, if your eye is sound, your whole body will be*

Ruy Barraco Mármol

full of light; 6:23 but if your eye is not sound, your whole body will be full of darkness. If then the light in you is darkness, how great is the darkness."

The Bible, book of the prophet Jeremiah (R.S.V.), Second Catholic Edition, says: *"31:31 "Behold, the days are coming, says the Lord, when I will make a new covenant with the house of Israel and the house of Judah, 31:32 not like the covenant which I made with their fathers when I took them by the hand to bring them out of the land of Egypt, my covenant which they broke, and I showed myself their Master, says the Lord. 31:33 But this is the covenant which I will make with the house of Israel after those days, says the Lord: I will put my law within them, and I will write it upon their hearts; and I will be their God and they shall be my people. 31:34 And no longer shall each man teach his neighbor and each his brother, saying, 'Know the Lord,' for they shall all know me, from the least of them to the greatest, says the Lord; for I will forgive their iniquity, and I will remember their sin no more.""*

A Christian must not submit to the spiritual leaders, he must be a free thinker instead, as Christ requested us, for instance, by telling us not to call anyone teacher, father or master. Christians must make our own judgments and learn to act according to them. Christianity is meant to be essentially a religion of freedom. Christ came to free us from the world, not to submit us to it. And he wants us to love him with freedom, with our mind and with our heart. Christ neither wants us to act because of submission to spiritual leaders, nor because of imitation, nor tradition, but because of love, freedom and understanding. Our religious authorities or ministers are not our spiritual leaders: They are disciples the same way we are. This is what Christ taught in the Gospel according to Saint Matthew Verse 23:9.

To be free thinkers Christians will need to, and will inevitably, disagree sometimes with each other. If Christ asks us to be free thinkers, he also asks us to disagree with each other sometimes. There is no way to be a freethinker without disagreeing with others, and the possibility to disagree must be especially assured as a very valuable treasure. It is wrong to ask for unanimity as Paul did, in the First Epistle to the Corinthians Verse 1:10.

Consequences

This error facilitated people usurping the position of Christ and with the authority derived from it, to command Christians to accept teachings contrary to the word of Christ, and to do things contrary to the teachings of Christ, such as the things done by the priests of the Catholic Church in times of the inquisition.

The man in submission does not think freely, he does not stick to his reason. He acts the way he is told to. A man in submission can be made to think and do things that a free man cannot, or at least cannot be made to think or to do so easily.

All institutions that structure themselves over submission are easier to corrupt. The corruption of men at the top affects all the organization.

This error tempted people to be submissive, and in that way also led them away from the way to salvation.

To be able to enter the kingdom of God people must think for themselves, and act according to their understanding.

These statements tempt and tempted many people, who indeed do not tolerate the idea of submission, to reject Christianity. Democracies are losing many Christian citizens, citizens who being Christians could, because of their faith, do a lot of good to them. People in democracies are taught to believe in freedom of thought; and people who believe in freedom of thought find themselves tempted to get away from Christianity because their ecclesiastic leaders demand submission of thought. People who love freedom of thought find themselves tempted to choose between being free thinkers or Christians, especially in the Catholic countries.

For this reason, you find constitutional democracies that do not work as they should. Constitutional democracies and Christianity should bring out the best of each other, instead of neutralize each other. Submission is good for totalitarianism; it makes Christianity good for totalitarianism and less good for constitutional democracies.

Also, to be able to enforce submission the Catholic Church kept the scriptures out of the reach of the people, kept the people ignorant, and violated their rights of thought and speech. These are also consequences of these statements of Paul.

Illustrative Quotes

The Encyclical of Pope Leo XIII (1878-1903)

"SAPIENTIAE CHRISTIANAE" on Christians as Citizens, says: "22. _Now, as the Apostle Paul urges, this unanimity ought to be perfect._ Christian faith reposes not on human but on divine authority, for what God has revealed "we believe not on account of the intrinsic evidence of the truth perceived by the natural light of our reason, but on account of the authority of God revealing, who cannot be deceived nor Himself deceive." (Constitutio Dei Filius, cap 3). It follows as a consequence that whatever things are manifestly revealed by God we must receive with a similar and equal assent. _To refuse to believe any one of them is equivalent to rejecting them all, for those at once destroy the very groundwork of faith who deny that God has spoken to men, or who bring into doubt His infinite truth and wisdom. To determine, however, which are the doctrines divinely revealed belongs to the teaching Church, to whom God has entrusted the safekeeping and interpretation of His utterances._ But the supreme teacher in the Church is the Roman Pontiff. Union of minds, therefore, requires, together with a perfect accord in the one faith, _complete submission and obedience of will to the Church and to the Roman Pontiff, as to God Himself._ This obedience should, however, be perfect, because it is enjoined by faith itself, and has this in common with faith, that it cannot be given in shreds; nay, were it nor absolute and perfect in every particular, it might wear the name of obedience, but its essence would disappear...".

24. In defining the limits of the obedience owed to the pastors of souls, but most of all to the authority of the Roman Pontiff, it must not be supposed that it is only to be yielded in relation to dogmas of which the obstinate denial cannot be disjoined from the crime of heresy. Nay, further, it

Ruy Barraco Mármol

is not enough sincerely and firmly to assent to doctrines which, though not defined by any solemn pronouncement of the Church, are by her proposed to belief, as divinely revealed, in their common and universal teaching, and which the Vatican Council declared are to be believed "with Catholic and divine faith."((Vatican Council, Constit. De fide catholica, cap. 3, De fide. Cf. H. Denzinger, Enchiridion Symbolorium 11 ed., Feriburg i. Br., 1911), p. 476.)) But this likewise must be reckoned amongst the duties of Christians, that they allow themselves to be ruled and directed by the authority and leadership of bishops, and, above all, of the apostolic see. And how fitting it is that this should be so any one can easily perceive. For the things contained in the divine oracles have reference to God in part, and in part to man, and to whatever is necessary for the attainment of his eternal salvation. <u>Now, both these, that is to say, what we are bound to believe and what we are obliged to do, are laid down, as we have stated, by the Church using her divine right, and in the Church by the supreme Pontiff.</u> Wherefore it belongs to the Pope to judge authoritatively what things the sacred oracles contain, as well as what doctrines are in harmony, and what in disagreement, with them; and also, for the same reason, to show forth what things are to be accepted as right, and what to be rejected as worthless; that it is necessary to do and what to avoid doing, in order to attain eternal salvation. For, otherwise, there would be no sure interpreter of the commands of God, nor would there be any safe guide showing man the way he should live."[103]
(Underline emphasis mine)

---

[103] Pope Leo XIII (1878-1903), Encyclical "sapientiae Christianae", Vatican official web site.

II.16. About the Power of the Civil Authority, its Origin, and the Reasons to Be Afraid of It

The Epistle of Paul to the Romans (R.S.V.), Second Catholic Edition, says: "*13:1 Let every person be subject to the governing authorities. For there is no authority except from God, and those that exist have been instituted by God. 13:2 Therefore he who resists the authorities resists what God has appointed, and those who resist will incur judgment. 13:3 For rulers are not a terror to good conduct, but to bad. Would you have no fear of him who is in authority? Then do what is good, and you will receive his approval, 13:4 for he is God's servant for your good. But if you do wrong, be afraid, for he does not bear the sword in vain; he is the servant of God to execute his wrath on the wrongdoer. 13:5 Therefore one must be subject, not only to avoid God's wrath but also for the sake of conscience. 13:6 For the same reason you also pay taxes, for the authorities are ministers of God, attending to this very thing. 13:7 Pay all of them their dues, taxes to whom taxes are due, revenue to whom revenue is due, respect to whom respect is due, honor to whom honor is due.*"

Error

It is an error to say that all the authorities have been instituted by God, and that we must be subject to them for that reason. It is an error to say that rulers are not a terror to good conduct but to bad. It is an error to say that rulers are the servants of God to execute the wrath of God on the wrongdoer.

Ruy Barraco Mármol

Commentaries

Among all the serious errors that these verses contain I especially want to discuss three. The first is the one that says that all the authorities that exist have been instituted by God and that we must be subject to the governing authorities because of that. The second is the one that says that rulers are not a terror to good conduct but to bad. The third one is the error that says that rulers are the servants of God to execute the wrath of God on the wrongdoer.

Let us start with the first of these three errors. When the Epistle of Paul to the Romans says that all the authorities that exist have been instituted by God, it refers to the persons that exercise the authority, to the rulers. That is why, for instance, a following verse says that authorities are not a terror to good conduct.

It can be admitted that authority in abstract has been created by God, since God is the creator of man and his social nature, but it cannot be admitted as true that the rulers who exercise that authority have all been instituted by God.

It is one thing to say that all authorities have come to be authorities, or are authorities, because God has allowed it, or allows it; and an entirely different thing is to say that God instituted them. It is one thing to say that the rulers have the authority because of God; and another that the authorities have been all instituted by God. It is one thing to say that as a favor or as a punishment God gave power to some authorities; but another thing is to say that God gave power to all.

The Gospel according to Saint Matthew (R.S.V.),

Second Catholic Edition, says: "*4:8 Again, the devil took him to a very high mountain, and showed him all the kingdoms of the world and the glory of them; 4:9 and he said to him, "All these I will give you, if you will fall down and worship me.""* The Gospel according to Saint Luke (R.S.V.), Second Catholic Edition, says: "*4:5 And the devil took him up, and showed him all the kingdoms of the world in a moment of time, 4:6 and said to him, "To you I will give all this authority and their glory; for it has been delivered to me, and I give it to whom I will. 4:7 If you, then, will worship me, it shall all be yours. And Jesus answered him, "It is written, 'You shall worship the Lord your God, and him only shall you serve.""* The question and the answer of these verses strongly suggest that not all authorities are instituted by God, but in some cases by the Devil.

In the book of Revelation, Verse 13:4, the First Beast, with its ten horns and seven heads, receives the throne and great authority from the Devil. Clearly the Bible teaches that not all the authorities are instituted by God.

In the Old Testament we can find many examples of authorities instituted by God, such as Moses, who are exceptions that confirm the rule that says that authorities are not instituted by God.

There are authorities that have been instituted through abominable crimes and certainly have not been instituted by God in authority. With these teachings Paul gave them improperly divine foundation and legitimacy.

There are authorities that do not seem to have been instituted by God. God did not institute Hitler in authority. God did not institute Nero as emperor. It is

Ruy Barraco Mármol

taught that this epistle was written and sent to the Romans while Nero was emperor of Rome. If that were the case Paul would have been teaching the Roman Christians with it, that Nero was instituted as emperor by God.

And even if God instituted them as authorities that did not mean that men were obligated to be subject to them because of that institution. God could have allowed the institution of, or even instituted, some bad authorities as a punishment, but expecting that we learn from that ruling the difference between a bad authority and a good authority, and wanting us to rebel against it. If we have to obey authority, it is not because all authorities are instituted by God, but because authority in abstract is good. We have to obey authority as long as it is good to do it.

In regard to the second error, that says that rulers are not a terror to good conduct but to bad, I want to say, that not only it constitutes an error, but also a teaching directly opposed to Christ's teachings to the apostles.

Christ had good conduct and was crucified. Christ taught that the rulers of the Gentiles lord it over them, and that the great ones make their authority over them felt; and advised Christians that, on the contrary to the teachings of Paul, they were going to be hated by the world, and taken to the kings and governors, precisely for being Christians. Their good conduct was going to make them victims of their rulers.

The Gospel according to Saint Matthew (R.S.V.), Second Catholic Edition, says: "*20:25 But Jesus called them to him and said, "You know that the rulers of the*

Jesus without Paul of Tarsus

Gentiles lord it over them, and their great men exercise their authority over them."

The Gospel according to Saint John (R.S.V.), Second Catholic Edition, says: "*15:18 "If the world hates you, know that it has hated me before it hated you. 15:19 If you were of the world, the world would love its own; but because you are not of the world, but I chose you out of the world, therefore the world hates you. 15:20 Remember the word that I said to you, 'A servant is not greater than his master'. If they persecuted me, they will persecute you; if they kept my word, they will keep yours also. 15:21 But all this they will do to you on my account, because they do not know him who sent me. 15:22 If I had not come and spoken to them, they would not have sin; but now they have no excuse for their sin. 15:23 He who hates me hates my Father also. 15:24 If I had not done among them the works which no one else did, they would not have sin; but now they have seen and hated both me and my Father. 15:25 It is to fulfill the word that is written in their law, 'They hated me without a cause.' 15:26 But when the Counselor comes, whom I shall send to you from the Father, even the Spirit of truth, who proceeds from the Father, he will bear witness to me; and you also are witness, because you have been with me from the beginning.*"

The Gospel according to Saint Luke (R.S.V.), Second Catholic Edition, says: "*21:12 But before all this they will lay their hands on you and persecute you, delivering you up to the synagogues and prisons, and you will be brought before kings and governors for my name's sake.*"

The same person that before "converting himself" persecuted, tortured, and killed innocent Christians who were under his authority, for the only reason of being Christians, apparently not learning any lesson from that, or from the crucifixion of Christ, or the beheading of John the Baptist, had the courage to say, contradicting Christ's teachings: that authorities are not a terror to men with good conduct!

This leads us to the third error. The authorities are not servants of God to execute his wrath over the wrongdoer. They have no way to know for certain what the judgment of God would be in specific cases.

No man should consider himself a servant of God to execute the wrath of God on the wrongdoer. "Do not judge", taught Christ. It is not a function of any man nor of the authorities to execute the wrath of God. Render to Caesar the things that are Caesar's and to God the things that are God's. The power to execute the wrath of God on the wrongdoer does not belong to Caesar, but to God alone, and we should never render it to Caesar.

We have no way to judge God, nor a servant of God executing his wrath. We have very limited ways to judge the conduct of somebody who is a servant of God in charge of executing the wrath of God. God can kill us without doing something wrong. If the authorities were servants of God to execute the wrath of God on the wrongdoer, we would have very limited ways to judge whether or not the wrath they inflict over people is good or bad. They could kill us without doing something wrong. We cannot limit God's power. If the authorities were servants of God to execute the wrath of God on the wrongdoer, we could not limit their power.

Consequences

Saying that the authorities are not a terror to good conduct, Paul contradicted the doctrine Christ taught to the twelve apostles, brought confusion among Christians, and discouraged the preparation of Christians for the great sufferings they would have to face from the authorities, for the only reason of being Christians, especially in earliest times. Let us remember that shortly after this letter was supposed to have been written, Nero was going to start a persecution against Christians, and that persecution was going to be followed by a series of bitter persecutions which challenged the recently born Christianity.

Saying that all authorities have been instituted by God, Paul gave divine foundation, divine legitimacy to all authorities, without considering the way they got their power, facilitating in that manner the consolidation of power of all the illegitimate authorities, including the ones who became rulers through abominable crimes.

In addition, saying that all authorities are servants of God to execute the wrath of God on the wrongdoer he facilitated the commission of bitter crimes by the cruel authorities, especially because he says that authorities are not a terror to good conduct, but to bad. These words imply that if you are the object of bitter crimes you are a wrongdoer, you must have done something wrong. He who executes the wrath of God on the wrongdoer can inflict any kind of bad on people, without necessarily being immoral.

He who was instituted in authority by God, to execute the wrath of God on the wrongdoer, does not need to be limited in his power in the way an authority who was not instituted in authority by God needs to be.

With all these sayings, Paul made the Christian religion a very valuable tool for the most evil and cruel authorities. All those who were opposed to tyrannies in Christian nations since the times of Christ had to fight against the words of Paul.

Paul through these words, and others, discouraged the arrival of constitutional democracies. Constitutional democracy is a form of government founded on the principle that the rulers must be instituted among the governed, deriving their just powers from their consent.

Constitutional democracy is a form of government founded on the principle that rulers do not derive their powers from God; that rulers are not servants of God to execute the wrath of God on the wrongdoer. In constitutional democracy, the people institute their rulers with their vote. Constitutional democracy is a form of government founded on the principle that says that not all authorities are legitimate and instituted by God. Constitutional democracy is a form of government founded on the principle that says that people have the right to institute their own authorities, and to rebel against an authority who has taken away the authority instituted by people.

Constitutional democracy is a form of government in which the power of the rulers is limited because of the tendency of the rulers to lord it over people and to make their authority over them felt. The power of the rulers is limited because they are not considered instituted in authorities by God to execute the wrath of God on the wrongdoer. It is part of the ideology of constitutional democracy that it is a form of government necessary to the common good, because of the tendency of the rulers to lord it over the people. The Constitution of the U.S.A. with its declarations, rights and guaranties, and division of powers, is for the purpose of limiting the power of the rulers, the authorities, the governors.

The Declaration of Independence of the United States says: "2.1 *We hold these truths to be self evident, that all men are created equal, that they are endowed by their Creator with certain inalienable rights, that among these are life, liberty and the pursuit of happiness. That to secure this rights, governments are instituted among men, deriving their just powers from the consent of the governed.*"

Constitutional democracy is a form of government in which the authorities shall not have power to establish a religion or to punish private religious wrongdoings. Saying that authorities are the servants of God to execute the wrath of God over the wrongdoer, Paul delayed the advent of constitutional democracy, with separation of Church and State, with freedom of religion, thought and speech.

Illustrative Quotes

On June 29, 1881, The Catholic Pope, Leo XIII, wrote the Encyclical Diuturnum Illud, that says: "*12. Those who believe civil society to have risen from the free consent of men, looking for the origin of its authority from the same source, say that each individual has given up something of his right, (15) and that voluntarily every person has put himself into the power of the one man in whose* person the whole of those rights has been centered. But it is a great error not to see, what is manifest, that men, as they are not a nomad race, have been created, without their own free will, for a natural community of life. It is plain, moreover, that the pact which they allege is openly a falsehood and a fiction, and that it has no authority to confer on political power such great force, dignity, and firmness as the safety of the State and the common good of the citizens require. Then only will the government have all those ornaments and guarantees, when it is understood to emanate from God as its august and most sacred source.

13. And it is impossible that any should be found not only more true but even more advantageous than this opinion. For the authority of the rulers of a State, if it be a certain communication of divine power, will by that very reason immediately acquire a dignity sometimes desired by heathen emperors when affecting divine honors, but a true and solid one received by a certain divine gift and benefaction. Whence it will behoove citizens to submit themselves and to be obedient to rulers, as to God, not so much through fear of punishment as through respect for their majesty; nor for the sake of pleasing, but through conscience, as doing their duty. And by this means authority will remain far more firmly seated in its place. For the citizens, perceiving the force of this duty, would necessarily avoid dishonesty and contumacy, because they must be persuaded that they who resist State authority resist the divine will, that they who refuse honor to rulers refuse it to God Himself.

14. This doctrine the Apostle Paul particularly inculcated on the Romans; to whom he wrote with so great authority and weight on the reverence to be entertained toward the higher powers, that it seems nothing could be prescribed

more weightily: "Let every soul be subject to higher powers, for there is no power but from God, and those that are, are ordained of God. Therefore he that resisteth the power resisteth the ordinance of God, and they that resist purchase to themselves damnation...wherefore be subject of necessity, not only for wrath, but also for conscience' sake." (Rom. 13:1-2,5). And in agreement with this is the celebrated declaration of Peter, the Prince of the Apostles, on the same subject: "Be ye subject, therefore, to every human creature for God's sake; whether it be to the king as excelling, or to governors, as sent by him for the punishment of evildoers, and for the praise of the good, for so is the will of God (1 Peter 2:13, 15)."

15. The one only reason which men have for not obeying is demanded of them which is openly repugnant to the natural or the divine law, for it is equally unlawful to command to do anything in which the law of nature or the will of God is violated. If, therefore, it should happen to any one to be compelled to prefer one or the other, viz., to disregard either the commands of God or those of rulers, he must obey Jesus Christ, who commands us to "give to Caesar the things that are Caesar's, and to God the things that are God's, "(Matt. 22:21) and must reply courageously after the example of the Apostles: "We ought to obey God rather than men." (Acts 5:9).

II.17. About the Law Given by God to Moses and the Old Covenant

The Epistle of Paul to the Romans (R.S.V.), Second Catholic Edition, says: "4:14 if it is the adherents of the law who are to be the heirs, faith is null and the promise is void. *4:15 For the law brings wrath, but where there is no law there is no transgression"*.

The Epistle of Paul to the Romans (R.S.V.), Second Catholic Edition, says: "*5:20 Law came in, to increase the trespass; but where sin increased, grace abounded all the more, 5:21 so that, as sin reigned in death, grace also might reign through righteousness to eternal life through Jesus Christ our Lord"*.

The First Epistle of Paul to the Corinthians (R.S.V.), Second Catholic Edition, says: "*15:56 The sting of the death is sin, and the power of sin is the law"*.

The Second Epistle of Paul to the Corinthians (R.S.V.), Second Catholic Edition, says: "*3:6 who has qualified us to be ministers of a new covenant, not in a written code but in the Spirit; for the written code kills, but the Spirit Gives life. 3:7 Now if the dispensation of the death, carved in letters on stone, came with such a splendor that the Israelites could not look at Moses' face because of its brightness, fading as it was,*"

Error

The law does not bring wrath. The law did not come in to increase the trespass. The power of sin is not the law. The commandments given by God to Moses were not the dispensation of the death, and did not bring death.

Commentaries

When Paul uses the word law in these verses and in most of his epistles at least, if not all, he refers to the Law of Moses, including in its concept the law given by God to Moses. It can be seen that Paul uses the word law with this meaning in these verses of the Epistle of Paul to the Romans by reading the Epistle of course, and by paying attention to its Verses 5:12-14, for instance. Verse 5:20 of the Epistle of Paul to the Romans tells us that this is also the meaning with which Paul uses the word law in Verse 15:56 of the First Epistle of Paul to the Corinthians.

The Greek word translated as law in these verses is νομος (nomos), the same Greek word translated as law, for instance, in Verse 5:17 of the Gospel according to Saint Matthew, in which Christ says that he did not come to abolish the law but to fulfill it, and that until heaven and earth pass away not the smallest part from the law shall pass away.

When Paul uses the word wrath in these verses he refers to the wrath of God. The word is used with that meaning in the Epistle of Paul to the Romans. In Verse 1:18 (R.S.V.), Second Catholic Edition, it is said: "*1:18 For the wrath of God is revealed from heaven against all ungodliness and wickedness of men who by their wickedness suppress the truth.*" In Verse 2:5 (R.S.V.), Second Catholic Edition, it is said: "*2:5 But by your hard and impenitent heart you are storing up wrath for yourself on the day of wrath when God's righteous judgment will be revealed.*" In Verse 2:8 (R.S.V.), Second Catholic Edition, it is said: "*but for those who are*

Ruy Barraco Mármol

factious and do not obey the truth, but obey wickedness, there will be wrath and fury". In Verse 3:5 (R.S.V.), Second Catholic Edition, it is said: *"But if our wickedness serves to show the justice of God, what shall we say? That God is unjust to inflict wrath on us? (I speak in a human way)."* In Verse 5:9 (R.S.V.), Second Catholic Edition, it is said: *"Since, therefore, we are now justified by his blood, much more shall we be saved by him from the wrath of God"*. In Verse 9:22 (R.S.V.), Second Catholic Edition, it is said: *"What if God, desiring to show his wrath and to make known his power, has endured with much patience the vessels of wrath made for destruction,"* In Verse 12:19 (R.S.V.), Second Catholic Edition, it is said: *"Beloved, never avenge yourselves, but leave it to the wrath of God; for it is written, "Vengeance is mine, I will repay, says the Lord."*

The law given by God to Moses does not bring the wrath of God. The transgressions of men bring the wrath of God. The law given by God to Moses commands us to love God with all our heart, all our soul, and all our strength.[104] The Gospel according to Saint Matthew (R.S.V.), Second Catholic Edition, says: *"22:36 Teacher, which is the great commandment in the Law? 22:37 And he said to him, "You shall love the Lord your God with all your heart, and with all your soul, and with all your mind. 22:38 This is the great and first commandment. 22:39 And a second is like it, You shall love your neighbor as yourself. 22:40 On these two commandments depend all the law and the prophets."* Neither the commandment, nor the action of loving

---

[104] The Bible, book Deuteronomy, Verse 6:5.

God with all our heart, with all our soul and with all our mind, brings the wrath of God. The law given by God to Moses commands us to love our neighbor as ourself.[105] Neither the commandment, nor the action of loving our neighbor as ourself brings the wrath of God.

The law given by God to Moses did not come to increase the trespass. The law given by God to Moses was given to the Jewish nation as instruction and as an instrument to reach salvation. The most important commandments given by God to Moses are to love God and our neighbor as ourselves. The law given by God to Moses did not come to increase the trespass, and it is not the power of sin.

Whoever says that the Law of Moses came to increase the trespass, including in the concept of Law of Moses the law given by God to Moses, is making God responsible for the increasing of the trespass. That is a blasphemy against God.

The book of Exodus (R.S.V.), Second Catholic Edition, says: "*24:12 The Lord said to Moses, "Come up to me on the mountain, and wait there; and I will give you the tables of stone, with law and the commandment, which I have written for their instruction.*"

The book of Psalms (R.S.V.), Second Catholic Edition, says: "*19:7 The law of the Lord is perfect, reviving the soul. The testimony of the Lord is sure, making wise the simple;*"

With regard to the Old Covenant, I want to say that it was also meant to be written in the heart of the Jews, and many Jews had that covenant written in their hearts

---

[105] The Bible, book Leviticus, Verse 19:18.

Ruy Barraco Mármol

and found life with it.

The Gospel according to Saint Matthew (R.S.V.), Second Catholic Edition, says: "*22:31 And as for the resurrection of the dead, have you not read what was said to you by God, 22:32 'I am the God of Abraham, and the God of Isaac, and the God of Jacob'? He is not the God of the dead, but of the living.*" Abraham, Isaac and Jacob had the Old Covenant written in their hearts and they found life, as many other Jews because of this. Many Jews, who were not perfect of course, and did not comply with all and every single work prescribed by the law, found life.

The Gospel according to Saint Matthew (R.S.V.), Second Catholic Edition, says talking about the moments after the crucifixion of Christ: "*27:52 the tombs were also opened, and many bodies of the saints who had fallen asleep were raised, 27:53 and coming out of the tombs after his resurrection they went into the holy city and appeared to many.*" All these resurrected were Jews who found life. Neither the Old Covenant, nor the law given by God to Moses was a dispensation of death. The ministry of the Old Covenant, the ministry of the law given by God to Moses was not a ministry of death. The Old Testament and the law given by God to Moses brought death and life.

The book of Deuteronomy (R.S.V.), Second Catholic Edition, says: "*30:6 <u>And the Lord your God will circumcise your heart and the heart of your offspring</u>, so that you will love the Lord your God with all your heart and with all your soul, that you may live. 30:7 And the Lord your God will put all these curses upon your foes and enemies who persecuted you. 30:8 And you shall again obey the voice of the Lord, and keep all his commandments which I command you this* *day. 30:9 The Lord your God will make you abundantly prosperous in all the work of your hand, in the fruit of your body, and in the fruit of your cattle, and in the fruit of your ground; for the Lord will again take delight in prospering you, as he took delight in your fathers, 30:10 if you obey the voice of the Lord your God, to keep his commandments and his statutes which are written in this book of the law, if you turn to the Lord your God with all your heart and with all your soul. 30:11 says "For this commandment which I command you this day is not too hard for you, neither is it far off. 30:12 It is not in heaven, that you should say, 'Who will go up for us to heaven, and bring it to us, that we may hear it and do it?' 30:13 Neither is it beyond the sea, that you should say, 'Who will go over the sea for us, and bring it to us, that we may hear it or do it?' 30:14 But the word is very near you; it is in your mouth and in your heart, so that you can do it. 30:15 See, I have set before you this day life and good, death and evil. 30:16 If you obey the commandments of the Lord your God which I command you this day, by loving the Lord your God, by walking in his ways, and by keeping his commandments and his statutes and his ordinances, then you shall live and multiply, and the Lord your God will bless you in the land which you are entering to take possession of it."* (Underline emphasis mine)

Consequences

These statements of Paul blaspheme against God, are offensive to the Jewish People, and distract from the coherence and rationality of the Christian religion. They also distort the concept of the law given by God to Moses, which is holy for the Jews and should be

Ruy Barraco Mármol

holy for Christians.

II.18. About the Advice to Look Out for the Dogs, the Evil Workers, for Those Who Mutilate the Flesh

The Epistle of Paul to the Philippians (.R.S.V.) Second Catholic Edition, says: "*3:1 Finally, my brethren, rejoice in the Lord. To write the same things to you is not irksome to me, and is safe for you. 3:2 Look out for the dogs, look out for the evil workers, look out for those who mutilate the flesh. 3:3 For we are the true circumcision, who worship God in the Spirit, and glory in Christ Jesus, and put no confidence in the flesh. 3:4 Though I myself have reason for confidence in the flesh. If any other man thinks he has reason for confidence in the flesh, I have more: 3:5 circumcised on the eighth day, of the people of Israel, of the tribe of Benjamin, a Hebrew born of Hebrews; as to the law a Pharisee; 3:6 as to zeal a persecutor of the church, as to righteousness under the law, blameless.*"

Error

The statement that advises to look out for the dogs, the evil workers, and for those who mutilate the flesh is an error.

Commentaries

The Greek word translated as "those who mutilate the flesh" is κατατομην[106] (katatomen) that means

---

[106] Maw Zerwick "*Analysis Philologica Novi Testamenti Graeci*" says under Ad

mutilation. And as it is taught in the books "La Sagrada Escritura[107]" and "Biblia Comentada,[108] its use is part of a game of words that Paul used to scorn the circumcision, which in Greek is termed πεπιτομη[109] (pepitome).

Paul is using the word mutilation to refer to circumcision and is calling the Jewish people dogs, including the converted Jewish Christians who believed that the Jewish Christians were still obligated to fulfill the part of the Law of Moses that was not opposed to Christ's teachings.

The book of Acts of the Apostles and the Epistles of Paul mention disputes between Paul and the Jewish Christians who wanted to force not only the Jewish Christians, but even the Gentile Christians, to fulfill the Jewish Law in which it was not opposed to Christ's teachings. Verse 15:15 of the book of Acts of the

---

Philippenses Verse 3:2, that κατα-τομη (-τεμνω) means in Latin: con-cisio, mutilatio = mutilati (sarcastice de circumcisione a iudaizantibus praedicata). Karl Feyerabend "Langenscheidt Pocket Greek dictionary" says that the Greek word κατα-τομη, η (kata-tome) means: cutting into pieces, mutilation. Richard J. Goodrich and Lukaszewski "A Readers Greek New Testament" also says under Philippians Verse 3:2 that the Greek word κατα-τομη, ης, η means: mutilation, cutting into pieces.

107 Profesores de la Compañía de Jesús, "Sagrada Escritura", Nuevo Testamento, vol. II, p. 774.

108 Profesores de Salamanca, "Biblia Comentada", Hechos y San Pablo, vol. VI, p. 612.

109 The Latin Vulgate version of the Bible says in the Epistle of Paul to the Philippians:, verse 3:2 "videte concisionem". The King James version says: "beware of the concision". The New American Bible says: "Beware of the mutilation". The New American Standard Bible says: "Beware of the false circumcision" The New International Version says: "those mutilators of the flesh". The English Standard Version says "those who mutilate the flesh."

Ruy Barraco Mármol

Apostles presents converted Pharisees making those claims.[110]

Paul is referring also with the word dogs to those Jewish Christians who believed that the Jewish Christians were still obligated to fulfill the part of the Law of Moses that was not opposed to Christ's teachings.

Let us remember that the twelve apostles neither forbade the Jewish Christians to believe that the Jewish Christians were obligated to fulfill the Jewish Law, in which was not opposed to the teachings of Jesus, nor to observe it. This emerges from the Council of Jerusalem, according to the book of Acts of the Apostles, Chapter 15.

It was neither right, nor necessary, to use the words dogs or mutilation with reference to the Jews or to the circumcision, whether the Jews were Christians or not. It was insulting to do so. It was a big error of Paul, which becomes even more serious because Paul constantly asked the Christians to imitate him. These words of Paul are mistaken, were not written under the inspiration of the Holy Spirit, and are not the word of God.

Some people have tried to excuse Paul of these errors, saying that it was a Jewish custom to call the Gentiles dogs. Although, even if it were a Jewish custom to call the Gentiles dogs, which I believe it was not, it does not justify the action. There are good and bad

[110] The book of Acts of the Apostles (N.K.J.V.) says: "15:1 And certain men came down from Judea and taught the brethren, "'Unless you are circumcised according to the custom of Moses, you cannot be saved.'" The same version and book of the Bible, says: "15:5 But some of the sect of the Pharisees who believed rose up, saying, "It is necessary to circumcise them, and to command them to keep the law of Moses."

customs.

Christ used the word little dogs to answer a Canaanite Woman. The Gospel according to Saint Matthew (R.S.V.), Second Catholic Edition, says: "15:21 And Jesus went away from there and withdrew to the district of Tyre and Si'don. 15:22 And behold, a Canaanite woman from that region came out and cried, "Have mercy on me, O Lord, Son of David; my daughter is severely possessed by a demon"' 15:23 But he did not answer her a word. And his disciples came and begged him, saying, "Send her away, for she is crying after us." 15:24 He answered, "I was sent only to the lost sheep of the house of Israel." 15:25 But she came and knelt before him, saying, "Lord, help me." 15:26 And he answered, 'It is not fair to take the children's bread and throw it to the dogs." 15:27 She said, "Yes, Lord, yet even the dogs eat the crumbs that fall from their masters" table." 15:28 Then Jesus answered her, "O woman, great is your faith! Let it be done for you as you desire." And her daughter was healed instantly." However, Christ was referring to a woman possessed by a demon, and the expression is used in the middle of a metaphor. On the contrary, the expression of Paul is merely an insult.

And even when Paul could have been justified in calling the Gentiles dogs, which is not true, that would not mean that he would have been justified in calling the Jews dogs, and much less the Jewish Christians, who still mistakenly believed that the Jewish Christians were obligated to fulfill the part of the Jewish Law that was not opposed to Jesus's teachings.

The fact that some Jewish Christians wanted all the Christians to be circumcised, although it was an error, was understandable. The fact that some Jewish Christians wanted the Jewish Christians to fulfill the part of the Law of Moses that was not opposed to Christ's teachings, although it was an error, was understandable. Paul committed an error by using the words dogs and evil workers to refer to the Jews, especially to all these Jewish Christians. Paul committed an error by using the word mutilation to refer to the circumcision.

Paul should have had a different approach to the matter–a respectful approach, like the approach Saint Peter had, according to the book of Acts of the Apostles Verse 15:8; and James had, according to the same book, Verse 15:13. These statements of Paul were not written under the inspiration of the Holy Spirit, and are not the word of God.

Consequences

These insulting statements against Jews impeded the spread of Christianity among other Jews, promoted bad relationships between Christians and Jews, were a bad example for Christians, and hid the perfection of the Gospel of Christ.

Illustrative Quotes

Saint Justin Martyr, a saint of the Christian Church, who lived in the second century, in his book "*Dialogue with Trypho*", Chapter 47, made the following distinction: "*But,*" "*Trypho again objected, "if someone knows that what you say is true, and, professing Jesus to be the Christ, believes in and obeys him, yet desires also to observe the commandments of the Mosaic Law, shall he be saved?*"

"In my opinion, Trypho," I replied, *"I say such a man will be saved, unless he exerts every effort to influence other men (I have in mind the Gentiles whom Christ circumcised from all error) to practice the same rites as himself, informing them that they cannot be saved unless they do so. You yourself did this at the opening of our discussion, when you said that I would not be saved unless I kept the Mosaic precepts.*

2. *"But why",* urged Trypho, *"did you say, 'In my opinion such a man will be saved?' There must, therefore, be other Christians who hold a different opinion."*

"Yes, Trypho," I conceded, *"there are some Christians who boldly refuse to have conversation or meals with such persons. I don't agree with such Christians. But if some, due to their instability of will, desire to observe as many of the Mosaic precepts as possible - precepts which we think were instituted because of your hardness of. heart - while at the same time they place their hope in Christ, and if they desire to perform the eternal and natural acts of justice and piety, yet wish to live with us Christians and believers, as I already stated, not persuading them to be circumcised like themselves, or to observe the Sabbath, or to perform similar acts, then it is my opinion that we Christians should receive them and associate with them in every way as kinsmen and brethren.*

3. *"But if any of your people, Trypho, profess their belief in Christ, and at the same time force the Gentiles who believe in Christ to observe the Law instituted through Moses, or refuse to share with them this same common life, I certainly will also not approve of them. But I think that those Gentiles who have been induced to follow the practices of the Jewish Law, and at the same time profess their faith*

in the Christ of God, will probably be saved.

4. "Those persons, however, who had once believed and publicly acknowledged Jesus to be the Christ, and then later, for one reason or another, turned to the observance of the Mosaic Law, and denied that Jesus is the Christ, cannot be saved unless they repent before their death. The same can be said to those descendants of Abraham who follow the Law and refuse to believe in Christ to their very last breath. Especially excluded from eternal salvation are they who in their synagogues have cursed and still do curse those who believe in that very Christ in order that they may attain salvation and escape the avenging fire."

5. "God in his goodness, kindness, and infinite richness considers the repentant sinner to be just and innocent, as he declared through the prophet Ezequiel, and the one who turns from the path of piety and justice to follow that of injustice and impiety God judges to be an impious and unjust sinner. Thus has our Lord Jesus Christ warned us, In whatsoever things I shall apprehend you, in them also shall I judge you."[111]

II.19. Forgiveness of Sins. New Repentance of the Christians Who Abandoned Christianity and then Come Back. Hope. Mercy of God.

The Epistle of Paul to Hebrews (R.S.V.), Second Catholic Edition, says: *"6:4 For it is impossible to restore again to repentance those who have once been enlightened, who have tasted the heavenly gift, and have become*

---

[111] Saint Justin Martyr "Dialogue with Trypho", Translated by Thomas B. Falls, The Catholic University of America Press, Washington D.C., 2003, Chapter 47, p. 71.

partakers of the Holy Spirit, 6:5 and have tasted the goodness of the word of God and the powers of the age to come, 6:6 if they then commit apostasy, since they crucify the Son of God on their own account and hold him up to contempt. 6:7 For land which has drunk the rain that often falls upon it, and brings for vegetation useful to those whose sake it is cultivated, receives the blessing from God. 6:8 But if it bears thorns and thistles, it is worthless and near to being cursed; its end is to be burned."

The Epistle of Paul to the Hebrews, (R.S.V.), Second Catholic Edition, says: "*10:26 For if we sin deliberately after receiving the knowledge of the truth, there no longer remains sacrifice for sins, 10:27 but a fearful prospect of judgment, and a fury of fire which will consume the adversaries.*"

Error

It is not impossible for men, who have once been enlightened and have tasted the heavenly gift and become sharers in the Holy Spirit, when they have tasted the good word of God and the powers of the age to come, and then have fallen away, to repent again. It is not impossible to restore them again to repentance. It is an error to say that they crucify the Son of God again.

Commentaries

It is not impossible for any man to repent again, if he has not committed the sin of blasphemy against the Holy Spirit. Christ taught us that every sin, every blasphemy, will be forgiven to men, but the blasphemy against the

Spirit. The Gospel according to Saint Matthew (R.S.V.), Second Catholic Edition, says: *"12:24 But when the Pharisees heard it they said, "It is only by Be-el'zebul, the prince of the demons, that this man casts out demons." 12:25 Knowing their thoughts, he said to them, "Every kingdom divided against itself is laid waste, and no city or house divided against itself will stand; 12:26 and If Satan cast out Satan, he is divided against himself: how then will his kingdom stand? 12:27 And If I cast out demons by Be-el'zebul, by whom do your sons cast them out? Therefore they shall be your judges. 12:28 But if it is by the Spirit of God that I cast out demons, then the kingdom of God has come upon you. 12:29 Or how can one enter a strong man's house and plunder his goods, unless he first binds the strong man? Then indeed he may plunder his house. 12:30 He who is not with me is against me, and he who does not gather with me scatters. 12:31 Therefore I tell you, every sin and blasphemy will be forgiven men, but the blasphemy against the Spirit will not be forgiven. 12:32 And whoever says a word against the Son of Man will be forgiven: but whoever speaks against the Holy Spirit will not be forgiven, either in this age or in the age to come."*

But, what is the blasphemy against the Spirit that Christ says it is the only sin that will not be forgiven?

The verses in which Christ states that the blasphemy against the Spirit will not be forgiven are found in the Gospels according to Saint Matthew and Saint Mark, and they are given after he was accused of expelling demons with the help of Beelzebul.

Many of the Pharisees, because of their instruction, were able to recognize the Messiah, to recognize Christ as the Son of God, that Christ was God. The coming of the Messiah was prophesied in the Old Testament.

However, regardless of that, many Pharisees rejected the Messiah, because they did not want the kind of salvation he was offering, they did not want the doctrine he was teaching, and they accused Christ of acting with the help of Beelzebul.

I would say that the blasphemy refers to that act, basically slander, committed against the Holy Spirit with freedom, intention and the understanding of the immorality of the act. I believe that slander can be committed against the Holy Spirit being a false prophet and defaming the Holy Spirit by attributing him wrong teachings or actions. This sin I believe will not be forgiven.

The Epistle of Paul to the Hebrews teaches otherwise, by saying that it is impossible for men who have once been enlightened and have tasted the heavenly gift and become sharers in the Holy Spirit, when they have tasted the good word of God and the powers of the age to come, and then have fallen away, to repent again. Those men can fall committing many conducts that do not constitute blasphemy against the Holy Spirit, and still Paul says that is impossible for them to repent again, even though Christ said that people will be forgiven for every sin and blasphemy, but blasphemy against the Spirit

The Gospel has a nice teaching about forgiveness which also shows that these statements of the Epistle of Paul to the Hebrews which we are now discussion are wrong. I am talking about the parable of "The Prodigal and His Brother". The Gospel according to Saint Luke (R.S.V.), Second Catholic Edition, says: "*15:11 And he said, "There was a man who had two sons: 15:12 and the*

Ruy Barraco Mármol

younger of them said to his father, 'Father, give me the share of property that falls to me.' And he divided his living between them. 15:13 Not many days later, the younger son gathered all he had and took his journey into a far country, and there he squandered his property in loose living. 15:14 And when he had spent everything, a great famine arose in that country, and he began to be in want. 15:15 So he went and joined himself to one of the citizens of that country, who sent him into his fields to feed swine. 15:16 And he would gladly have fed on the pods that the swine ate; and no one gave him anything. 15:17 But when he came to himself he said, 'How many of my father's hired servants have bread enough and to spare, but I perish here with hunger! 15:18 I will arise and go to my father, and I will say to him, "Father, I have sinned against heaven and before you; 15:19 I am no longer worthy to be called your son; treat me as one of your hired servants."' 15:20 And he arose and came to his father. But while he was yet at a distance, his father saw him and had compassion, and ran and embraced him and kissed him. 15:21 And the son said to him, 'Father, I have sinned against heaven and before you; I am no longer worthy to be called your son.' 15:22 But the father said to his servants, 'Bring quickly the best robe, and put it on him; and put a ring on his hand and shoes on his feet, 15:23 and bring the fatted calf and kill it, and let us eat and make merry; 15:24 for this my son was dead, and is alive again; he was lost, and is found!' And they began to make merry. 15:25 "Now his elder son was in the field; and as he came and drew near to the house, he heard music and dancing. 15:26 And he called one of the servants and asked what this meant. 15:27 And he said to him, 'Your brother has come, and your father has killed the fatted calf, because he has received him safe and sound.' 15:28 But he was angry and refused to go in. His father came out and entreated him. 15:29 but he answered his father, 'Behold, these many years I have served you, and I never disobeyed your command; yet you never gave me a kid, that I might merry with my friends. 15:30 But when this son of yours came, who has devoured your living with harlots, you killed for him the fatted calf!' 15:31 And he said to him, 'Son, you are always with me, and all that is mine is yours. 15:32 It was fitting to make merry and be glad, for this brother of yours was dead, and is alive; he was lost, and is found.'"" Surely, from these words emerges that these statements of the Epistle of Paul to the Hebrews that we are analyzing are mistaken and are not written under the inspiration of the Holy Spirit and are not the word of God.

Consequences

This issue of the renewal, reconversion, the forgiveness of the fallen Christians, is very important. The forgiveness of our sins, which Christ has announced, is an example of God's mercy, a very important encouragement to reconversion and the most important source of hope for people.

These statements of the Epistle of Paul to the Hebrews might have impeded reconversions, and also might have promoted rejection of Christians that had fallen and wanted to go back to Church. In addition, they might have contributed to mistakes such as those sustained by the believers of montanism and donatism, which have been used for the purpose of promoting divisions and very cruel confrontations among

Ruy Barraco Mármol

Christians.

Illustrative Quotes

The Council of Trent says: "*Chap. 14. The Fallen and Their Restoration 807 Those who by sin have fallen away from the received grace of justification, will again be able to be justified [can. 29] when, roused by God through the sacrament of penance, they by the merit of Christ shall have attended to the recovery of the grace lost. For this manner of justification is the reparation of one fallen, which the holy Fathers * have aptly called a second plank after the shipwreck of lost grace. For on behalf of those who after baptism fall into sin, Christ Jesus instituted the sacrament of penance, when He said: "Receive ye the Holy Ghost; whose sins you shall forgive, they are forgiven them, and whose sins you shall retain, they are retained" [John 20:22, 23]. Hence it must be taught that the repentance of a Christian after his fall is very different from that at his baptism, and that it includes not only a cessation from sins, and a detestation of them, or "a contrite and humble heart" [Ps. 50:19], but also the sacramental confession of the same, at least in desire and to be made in its season, and sacerdotal absolution, as well as satisfaction by fasting, almsgiving, prayers, and other devout exercises of the spiritual life, not indeed for the eternal punishment, which is remitted together with the guilt either by the sacrament or the desire of the sacrament, but for the temporal punishment [can. 30], which (as the Sacred Writings teach) is not always wholly remitted, as is done in baptism, to those who ungrateful to the grace of God which they have received, "have grieved the Holy Spirit" [cf. Eph. 4:30], and have not feared to "violate the temple of God"*

[1 Cor. 3:17]. Of this repentance it is written: "Be mindful, whence thou art fallen, do penance, and do the first works" [Rev. 2:5], and again: "The sorrow which is according to God, worketh penance steadfast unto salvation" [2 Cor. 7:10], and again: "Do penance" [Matt. 3:2; 4:17], and, "Bring forth fruits worthy of penance" [Matt. 3:8]."[112] The teaching of this council is contrary to the teachings of Paul that I have denounced in this point; or at least in contrary to the teachings of the epistle known as Epistle of Paul to the Hebrews, which is not errorless. Whoever sustains that the teachings of this council are right and errorless cannot sustain at the same time that this Epistle was written under the inspiration of the Holy Spirit, is errorless, and is the word of God.

II.20. About the Question if Men are Justified by the Faith Apart from Observance of the Law

The Epistle of Paul to the Romans, New American Standard Bible (N.A.S.B.)[113] says: *"3:27 Where then is boasting? It is excluded. By what kind of law? Of works? No, but by a law of faith. 3:28 For we maintain that a man is justified by faith apart from works of the Law. 3:29 Or is God the God of Jews only? Is He not the God of Gentiles also? Yes, of Gentiles also, 3:30 since indeed God who will justify the circumcised by faith and the uncircumcised through faith is one. 3:31 Do we then nullify the Law*

---

112 Henry Denzinger "The Sources of Catholic Dogma" p.255.

113 Scripture quotations marked in this work with (N.A.S.B.) are taken from the New American Standard Bible, Copyright c 1960, 1962, 1963, 1968, 1971, 1972, 1973, 1975, 1977, 1995, by the Lockman Foundation. Used by permission (www.Lockman.org.)

Ruy Barraco Mármol

through faith? May it never be! On the contrary, we establish the Law."

Error

Man is justified by faith but not apart from works of the law.

Commentaries

Man is justified by faith, but not apart from works of the law. The law given by God to Moses commands that we shall love the Lord our God with all our heart, and with all our soul, and with all our mind. The Gospel according to Saint Matthew (N.A.S.B.) says: "22:36 *"Teacher, which is the great commandment in the Law?" 22:37 And he said to him, "'You shall love the Lord your God with all your heart, and with all your soul, and with all your mind."* This commandment can be found in the book Deuteronomy Verse 6:5.

The law given by God to Moses commands that we shall love our neighbor as ourself. The Gospel according to Saint Matthew (N.AS.B.) says: "*19:16 "And behold, one came to Him and said, "Teacher, what good thing shall I do that I may obtain eternal life?" 19:17 And He said to him, "Why are you asking Me about what is good? There is only One who is good; but If you wish to enter into life, keep the commandments." 19:18 He said to Him, "Which ones?" And Jesus said, "You shall not commit murder; You shall not commit adultery; You shall not steal; You shall not bear false witness; 19:19 Honor your father and mother; and you shall love your neighbor as yourself."*"(underline emphasis is mine) This teaching can be found in the book Leviticus Verse 19:18.

It commands that we shall not murder, commit adultery, steal, bear false witness, among other commandments, as we just have seen. This teaching can be found in the book Exodus 20:13.

Nobody will reach salvation without observing, those commandments of the law given by God to Moses (of course having had the chance to do it). Nobody, who had the chance to do it, will reach salvation without putting in practice those commandments of the law, among others.

The Gospel according to Saint Matthew (N.A.S.B..) says: "*5:17 'Do not think that I came to abolish the Law or the Prophets; I did not come to abolish, but to fulfill. 5:18 "For truly I say to you, until heaven and earth pass away, not the smallest letter or stroke shall pass away from the Law, until all is accomplished. 5:19 "Whoever then annuls one of the least of these commandments, and so teaches others, shall be called least in the kingdom of heaven; but whoever keeps and teaches them, he shall be called great in he kingdom of heaven.*"

One thing is to say that the faith in Jesus brings salvation to man, and another very different thing is to say that man is justified by faith, apart from works of the law.

The Gospel according to Saint Matthew (N.A.S.B.) says: "*7:19 Every tree that does not bear good fruit is cut down and thrown into the fire. 7:20 "So then, you will know them by their fruits. 7:21 "Not everyone who says to Me, 'Lord, Lord,' will enter the kingdom of heaven; but he who does the will of my Father who is in heaven.*"

The Gospel according to Saint Luke (N.A.S.B.) says: "*6:43 For there is no good tree which produces bad fruit; nor, on the other hand, a bad tree which produces good fruit. 6:44 "For each tree is known by its own fruit. For men do not gather figs from thorns, nor do they pick grapes from a briar bush. 6:45 "The good man out of the good treasure of his heart brings forth what is good; and the evil man out of the evil treasure brings forth what is evil; for his mouth speaks from that which fills his heart. 6:46 'And why do you call Me, 'Lord, Lord,' and do not do what I say? 6:47 "Everyone who comes to Me, and hears My words, and acts upon them, I will show you whom he is like: 6:48 he is like a man building a house, who dug deep and laid a foundation upon the rock; and when a flood rose, the torrent burst against that house and could not shake it, because it had been well built. 6:49 "But the one who has heard, and has not acted accordingly, is like a man who built a house upon the ground without any foundation; and the torrent burst against it and immediately it collapsed, and the ruin of that house was great.'*"

Indeed, the man who has faith is the man who not only believes and professes God, and Christ, but also puts in practice the teachings of Christ. Whoever has faith, believes, accepts, trusts, professes, but also understands, and puts in practice the word of God. Reaching salvation is not only about believing or professing Jesus, about believing or professing God. That is why, the Gospel according to Saint Matthew (N.A.S.B.) says: "*7:21 "Not everyone who says to me, 'Lord, Lord', will enter the kingdom of heaven; but he who does the will of My Father who is in heaven. 7:22 "Many will say to Me on that day, 'Lord, Lord, did we not prophesy in*

Your name, and in Your name cast out demons, and in Your name perform many miracles?' 7:23 "And then I will declare to them, 'I never knew you; depart from Me, you who practice lawlessness.'"

Consequences

These and other wrong statements of the Epistles of Paul, about the works prescribed by the law given by God to Moses and faith, about the observance of the law and faith, have been useful for wrong interpretations of Christianity that hold that as long as the man believes in Christ, and professes him, it does not matter how he conducts himself in life, it does not matter what other fruits he produces, in order to reach the kingdom of God.

They have also distorted the concept of the law given by God to Moses. Christ came to teach us the truth about the law. These and other statements of Paul brought confusion to the concept of the law.

The fact that Paul had sustained in other epistle something different, does not mean that what he sustained in this epistle is correct, and does not change the effects that the error of this epistle has had.

II.21. More about the Observance of the Law, Predestination, about God Being Just

The Epistle of Paul to the Romans (N.A.S.B.) says: *"9:10 And not only this, but there was Rebekah also, when she had conceived twins by one man, our father Isaac; 9:11 for though the twins were not yet born, and had not done anything good or bad, in order that God's purpose according to His choice might stand, not because of works, but because of Him who calls, 9:12 it was said to her, "The older will serve the younger." 9:13 Just as it is written, "Jacob I loved, but Essau I hated." 9:14 What shall we say then? There is no injustice with God, is there? May it never be! 9:15 For He says to Moses, "I will have mercy on whom I have mercy, and I will have compassion on whom I have compassion" 9:16 So then it does not depend on the man who wills or the man who runs, but on God who has mercy. 9:17 For the Scripture says to Pharaoh, "For this very purpose I raised you up, to demonstrate My power in you, and that My name might be proclaimed throughout the whole earth".*

Error

Among all the important errors that these verses have, I want to discuss the error that says that it does not depend on the man who wills or the man who runs, but on God who shows mercy.

Commentaries

Being elected by God, reaching the kingdom of God is about willing, doing, exerting, running, and is about God showing and having mercy. Let us remember what the Gospel according to Saint Matthew (N.A.S.B.) says: "*7:19 Every tree that does not bear good fruit is cut down and thrown into the fire. 7:20 So then, you will know them by their fruits. 7:21 'Not everyone who says to Me, 'Lord, Lord', will enter the kingdom of heaven, but he who does the will of my Father who is in heaven."*

Paul says, in Verse 9:16 of the Epistle to the Romans, that it is not about willing, doing, it is not about human exertion, it is not about running, and Christ, in the Gospel according to Saint Matthew (N.A.S.B.), says: "*7:21 Not everyone who says to me, 'Lord, Lord', will enter the kingdom of heaven; but he who does the will of my Father who is in heaven*".

And although God has the right to have mercy with whomever he wishes, and he does not have to answer to anybody, God besides being merciful is just, and keeps his word, so reaching the kingdom of God to some extent is about winning his mercy, or to be more precise, is about not rejecting it. Nobody, who does his will, will be left without the mercy of God. If this is true, then reaching salvation is about willing, doing, running and about God having mercy. He who does not will, does not do, does not run, rejects God's mercy. God has given his word to those who do not reject his mercy, to those who will, to those who do, to those who run, that they will be saved. We are not saved because of our works, but because of the mercy of God. However, we have to accept the mercy of God, and we accept it by willing, doing and running. Salvation is also about willing, doing and running, because of God's will, because of God's mercy, so it is wrong to say that it is not about willing, doing and running.

I have already remarked on the necessity of the fruits to salvation <u>in the point II. 24</u>. These statements contradict the promise of salvation that God made to everyone who has faith and does the will of God. The Gospel according to Saint Matthew (N.A.S.B.) says:

"*12:50 "For whoever does the will of my Father who is in heaven, he is My brother and sister and mother.""*

Consequences

These statements contributed to wrong interpretations of Christianity that hold that as long as the people believe in Christ, and profess their faith in him, it does not matter how they conduct themselves in life in order to reach salvation; it does not matter what other fruits they produce. They gave a wrong image of God, and discouraged people from being Christian.

II. 22. About the Mercy of God

The Epistle of Paul to the Romans (N.A.S.B.) says: "*11:32 For God has shut up all in disobedience that He might show mercy to all.*"

Error

God did not imprison all in disobedience so that he may be merciful to all.

Commentaries

The men that are imprisoned in disobedience, have imprisoned themselves in it. God gave us all freedom. Some of us choose the imprisonment of disobedience; and God is merciful even with those who do it because God is good, and loves all men.

Consequences

I believe statements like this serve only to leave in the mind of the readers wrong and bad ideas about God. More than one man could have taken from them arguments against God.

The ones who are in disobedience are tempted by these statements to find God responsible for their own sins. They are tempted to think that it is God who imprisoned them in disobedience, instead of themselves, and to be angry with God because of that reason. People who do that are less likely to change, to repent, to convert.

II.23. About the Reward of the Well Doing

The Epistle of Paul to the Galatians (N.A.S.B.), says: "*6:7 Do not be deceived, God is not mocked; for whatever a man sows, this he will also reap. 6:8 For the one who sows to his own flesh shall from the flesh reap corruption, but the one who sows to the Spirit shall from the Spirit reap eternal life. 6:9 And let us not lose heart in doing good, for in due time we shall reap if we do not grow weary.*"

Error

It is an error to say that doing good we shall reap in due time, if we do not grow weary.

Commentaries

The King James Version instead of translating in due

time says "in due season". The Revised Standard Version Second Catholic Edition, says "at harvest time". The New American Bible says "in due time". The New International Version says "proper time". The English Standard Version says "in due season".

It is wrong to say that in harvest time or in due time we will reap if we do not grow weary. Doing what is right puts us in grace with God and in a better condition to perceive that condition. It immediately puts us in that grace, to a greater or lesser extent, which should be the most valuable good for us.

Let us remember what the Gospel according to Saint Luke says, which I have already quoted and transcribed when I treated the subject of forgiveness, but I quote and transcribe again (N.A.S.B.) to discuss what Christ teaches us about how Christians should feel about doing good, and expecting a reward for it: "*15:11 And He said, "A certain man had two sons; 15:12 and the younger of them said to his father, 'Father, give me the share of the estate that falls to me.' And he divided his wealth between them. 15:13 "And not many days later, the younger son gathered everything together and went on a journey into a distant country, and there he squandered his estate with loose living. 15:14 "Now when he had spent everything, a severe famine occurred in that country, and he began to be in need. 15:15 "And he went and attached himself to one of the citizens of that country, and he sent him into his fields to feed swine. 15:16 "And he was longing to fill his stomach with the pods that the swine were eating, and no one was giving anything to him. 15:17 "But when he came to his senses, he said, 'How many of my father's hired men have more than enough bread, but I am dying here* with hunger! 15:18 'I will get up and go to my father, and will say to him, "Father, I have sinned against heaven, and in your sight; 15:19 "I am no longer worthy to be called your son; make me as one of your hired men."' 15:20 "And he got up and came to his father. But while he was still a long way off, his father saw him, and felt compassion for him, and ran and embraced him, and kissed him. 15:21 "And the son said to him, 'Father, I have sinned against heaven and in your sight; I am no longer worthy to be called your son.' 15:22 "But the father said to his slaves, 'Quickly bring out the best robe and put it on him, and put a ring on his hand and sandals on his feet; 15:23 and bring the fattened calf, kill it, and let us eat and be merry; 15:24 for this son of mine was dead, and has come to life again; he was lost, and has been found.' And they began to be merry. 15:25 "Now his older son was in the field, and when he came and approached the house, he heard music and dancing. 15:26 "And he summoned one of the servants and began inquiring what these things might be. 15:27 "And he said to him, 'Your brother has come, and your father has killed the fattened calf, because he has received him back safe and sound.' 15:28 " But he became angry, and was not willing to go in; and his father came out and began entreating him. 15:29 "But he answered and said to his father, 'Look! For so many years I have been serving you, and I have never neglected a command of yours; and yet you have never given me a kid, that I might be merry with my friends; 15:30 but when this son of yours came, who has devoured your wealth with harlots, you killed the fattened calf for him.' 15:31 "And he said to him, 'My child, you have always been with me, and all that is mine is yours. 15:32 'But we had to be merry and rejoice, for this brother of yours was dead and has

Ruy Barraco Mármol

begun to live, and was lost and has been found."

In my opinion this parable teaches what I am sustaining, that doing good and having the favor of God is by itself a gift that all men should value above everything else. That is why the father in Verse 15:31 replies to his son: " *"...'My child, you have always been with me, and all that is mine is yours ."* I dare to say that to be a real Christian we must feel, understand, want and accept this fact: the favor of God is our best gift.

In addition, Christ said that every one that makes sacrifices in life for the sake of the kingdom of God will receive his reward in this age and in the other. The Gospel according to Saint Luke (N.A.S.B.) says: "*18:28 And Peter said, "Behold, we have left our own homes, and followed You." 18:29 And he said to them, "Truly I say to you, there is no one who has left house or wife or brothers or parents or children, for the sake of the kingdom of God, 18:30 who shall not receive many times as much at this time and in the age to come, eternal life.""*

These rewards that Jesus says we will receive are not conditioned to the circumstance of not growing weary. These verses teach us that if we do good, we will receive a plentiful return not only in the age to come, but in our current age, independently of whether or not we grow weary. And we must be aware that God might have done us good, or might do us good, that we are not able to perceive. How can we know that because of the sacrifices we made, God did not save our son from a deadly accident for instance? If it is possible that God has already given us a plentiful return, it is wrong to believe that only in due time he will give us that return if we do not grow weary, because that would be to assume that we have not yet received any reward, when as I said, we instantly receive the gift of the grace of God, and we cannot know if he has not rewarded us in another form that we are not able to perceive.

The right state of mind is to understand that the favor of God is the best reward we can have, that God is going to give us a reward even if we grow weary, and that it is possible that God already gave us other rewards for our sacrifices.

Indeed, people should do good just because it is good, because of love, and because of gratitude for the good already received from God, not expecting any other reward; but it is a fact that people do more good if they believe that they will have a reward by doing it.

Consequences

These statements tempt people to overlook that simply having the favor of God is their highest reward, lead people to be unaware that if they did good, they will receive for sure a reward, and to overlook that they might have received a reward in the same moment they were doing good, or even before. People are encouraged to do good when they know for sure that they will receive a reward.

II.24. The Commandment of Paul to Imitate Him – Some other Vices of Paul

The First Epistle of Paul to the Corinthians (N.A.S.B.) says: "*4:16 I exhort you therefore, be imitators*

Ruy Barraco Mármol

of me."

The First Epistle of Paul to the Corinthians (N.A.S.B.) says: *"11:1 Be imitators of me, just as I also am of Christ."*

The Epistle of Paul to the Galatians (N.A.S.B.) says: *"4:12 I beg of you, brethren, become as I am, for I also have become as you are. You have done me no wrong;"*

The Epistle of Paul to the Philippians (N.A.S.B.) says: *"3:17 Brethren, join in following my example, and observe those who walk according to the pattern you have in us."*

The Epistle of Paul to the Philippians (N.A.S.B.) says: *"4:9 The things you have learned and received and heard and seen in me, practice these things; and the God of peace shall be with you."*

The First Epistle of Paul to the Thessalonians (N.A.S.B.) says: *"1:6 You also became imitators of us and of the Lord, having received the word in much tribulation with the joy of the Holy Spirit."*

The Second Epistle of Paul to Thessalonians (N.A.S.B.) says: *"3:7 For you yourselves know how you ought to follow our example, because we did not act in an undisciplined manner among you, 3:8 nor did we eat anyone's bread without paying for it, but with labor and hardship we kept working night and day so that we might not be a burden to any of you; 3:9 not because we do not have the right to this, but in order to offer ourselves as a model for you, that you might follow our example."*

The Epistle of Paul to the Hebrews (N.A.S.B.) says: *"6:12 that you may not be sluggish, but imitators of those who through faith and patience inherit the promises."*

Error

Paul committed an error by asking and commanding to be imitated. It is not the word of God that we should imitate Paul.

Commentaries

One of the first obligations of a man who calls himself a Christian is to acknowledge being a sinner, because we are sinners. Whoever acknowledges being a sinner cannot ask or command others to imitate him, at least in general, because he would be asking or commanding others to sin. Paul asking and commanding to be imitated turned his wrong behaviors, his sins, into teachings.

Christ, for being God, could have attitudes that other men cannot. Christ could act as a man that is free of sin, because he was and is free of sin. He could ask others to imitate him because he was and is blameless. The attitudes of the rest of the men, on the contrary, in all areas, must acknowledge the fact that we are not God, and we are not free of sin. This applied to Paul of course because he was not God.

Whoever asks others to imitate him goes against Christian humility. Christians have somebody to imitate:

Ruy Barraco Mármol

Christ. And Christ, in spite of being God, wanted us to understand him, and wanted us to do good, not as a product of imitation, but as a product of understanding, with will and love. We can see that clearly in the verses that I will transcribe next.

The Gospel according to Saint Matthew (N.A.S.B.) says: "12:7 But if you had known what this means, "I desire compassion, and not a sacrifice,' you would not have condemned the innocent." (Underline emphasis mine)

The Gospel according to Saint Matthew (N.A.S.B.) says: "13:14 And in their case the prophecy of Isaiah is being fulfilled, which says: 'You will keep on hearing, but will not understand. 13:15 And you will keep on seeing, but will not perceive; For the heart of this people has become dull, And with their ears they scarcely hear, And they have closed their eyes lest they should see with their eyes, and hear with their ears, and understand with their heart and return, and I should heal them.'"(Underline emphasis mine)

The Gospel according to Saint Matthew (N.A.S.B.) says: "13:18 "Hear then the parable of the sower. 13:19 When anyone hears the word of the kingdom, and does not understand it, the evil one comes and snatches away what has been sown in his heart. This is the one on whom seed was sown beside the road." (Underline emphasis mine)

The Gospel according to Saint Matthew (N.A.S.B.) says: "13:23 "And the one on whom seed was sown on the good soil, this is the man who hears the word and understands it; who indeed bears fruit, and brings forth, some a hundred fold, some sixty, and some thirty."" (Underline emphasis mine)

The Gospel according to Saint Matthew (N.A.S.B.) says: "16:9 Do you not yet understand or remember the five *loaves of the five thousand, and how many baskets you took up? 16:10 "Or the seven loaves of the four thousand, and how many large baskets you took up? 16:11 "How is it that you do not <u>understand</u> that I did not speak to you concerning bread? But beware of the leaven of the Pharisees and Sadducees." 16:12 Then they <u>understood</u> that He did not say to beware of the leaven of bread, but of the teaching of the Pharisees and Sadducees."* (Underline emphasis mine)

The Gospel according to Saint John (N.A.S.B.) says: "*13:12 And so when He had washed their feet, and taken His garments, and reclined at the table again, He said to them, "Do you <u>know</u> what I have done to you? 13:13 "You call me Teacher and Lord; and you are right, for so I am. 13:14 "If I then, the Lord and the Teacher, washed your feet, you also ought to wash one another's feet. 13:15 "For I gave you an example that you also should do as I did to you."* (Underline emphasis is mine)

All of these verses that I have transcribed show how Christ wants us to understand his doctrine, and how important is for us that understanding in order to reach salvation. Christ did not ask for imitation. He asked for understanding that goes far beyond imitation.

Nobody other than Christ should ask and command to be imitated, much less anyone who has committed as many and as important sins such as the ones Paul committed.

All along this book, I have exposed errors of the Epistles of Paul, which are in fact not simple errors but important sins. Without getting into the question that he attributed words to God that were not the word of God, which is a very serious sin, let us remember that

Paul was a genocidal man who after receiving baptism did not value properly the seriousness of his past acts. Let us look over some of his other sins.

Lack of Repentance and Acknowledgement of the Immorality of the Genocide He Carried Out

As I have previously said in this book, Paul, before becoming a member of the Christian Church, carried out a genocide against Christians, and did not show in his writings proper repentance and acknowledgement of the immorality of the sins he committed during that period of his life.

In the Epistle to the Philippians (N.A.S.B.), about the time just before his baptism, Paul wrote: *"3:5 circumcised the eighth day, of the nation of Israel, of the tribe of Benjamin, a Hebrew of Hebrews; as to the Law, a Pharisee; 3:6 as to zeal, a persecutor of the church; as to righteousness which is in the Law, found blameless."*

With these words, Paul implied that the zeal for the law Given by God to Moses leads to persecution; but to the contrary, neither the law given by God to Moses, nor the zeal for that law, leads to persecution, torture or genocide of men; especially of Christian men, of people teaching a religion of peace and love. The persecution and the genocide of Christians that Paul carried on were not acts of justice based on the Jewish Law. Paul in this verse makes the law given by God to Moses appear as if it would justify these kinds of acts; and makes the zeal for Christianity seem as if it should lead to the same kind of acts. The zeal for the law would have led Paul to be Christian, not a persecutor of

Christians.

Paul was not blameless as to righteousness which is in the Law when he tortured and killed men and women of peace and love for the only reason of being Christians. He carried on his persecution, with knowledge of the great immorality of those acts. He knew his victims were men. He knew it is seriously immoral to kill and to torture these human beings. One of the commandments of the law given by God to Moses is you shall not kill. Nobody should say that he is blameless under the Law given by God to Moses, least of all, somebody who tortured, killed and committed genocide.

Paul in these verses does not acknowledge the immorality of his persecution against Christians, showing lack of repentance about the genocide he perpetrated.

He had no excuse for the persecution he committed against the apostles and the newborn Christian Church, which Christ foretold. The Gospel according to Saint John (N.A.S.B.) says: *"15:18 "If the world hates you, you know that it has hated me before it hated you. 15:19 "If you were of the world, the world would love its own; but because you are not of the world, but I chose you out of the world, therefore the world hates you. 15:20 "Remember the word that I said to you, 'A slave is not greater than his master.' If they persecuted Me, they will also persecute you; if they kept My word, they will keep yours also. 15:21 "But all these things they will do to you for My name's sake, because they do not know the One who sent Me. 15:22 "If I had not come and spoken to them, they would not have sin, but now they have no excuse for their sin; 15:23 "He who hates Me*

Ruy Barraco Mármol

hates My Father also. 15:24 "If I had not done among them the works which no one else did, they would not have sin; but now they have both seen and hated Me and My Father as well."

Arrogance and Lack of Humility of Paul

Christ taught us that we must be humble. In the parable of the Pharisee and the Tax Collector, of the Gospel according to Saint Luke Verse 18:10, he teaches us that the mere act of believing ourselves free of sin is a sin itself. Paul shows in different occasions in his epistles arrogance and lack of humility. We have seen some of them before. Next, I will show some others.

a. The Epistle of Paul to the Romans (N.A.S.B.) says: "*5:8 But God demonstrates His own love toward us, in that while we were yet sinners, Christ died for us.*"

Paul shows lack of humility when he says 'while we still were sinners'. Paul and his disciples were sinners, the same way the rest of men were and are.

b. The First Epistle of Paul to the Corinthians (N.A.S.B.) says: "*2:15. But he who is spiritual appraises all things, yet he himself is appraised by no man. 2:16 For who has known the mind of the Lord, that he should instruct him?' But we have the mind of Christ.*"

It is arrogant to think that you can appraise or judge or scrutinize everything. Paul here says that there are two kinds of people: Spiritual men, and the rest. He counts himself among the spiritual men who judge everything, including everyone, and cannot be judged by anyone. Surely that is an arrogant act. Paul was also arrogant when he said that he had the mind of the Lord and the mind of Christ.

c. The First Epistle of Paul to the Corinthians (N.A.S.B.) says: "*4:4. I am conscious of nothing against myself, yet I am not by this acquitted; but the one who examines me is the Lord.*"

No matter how Christian somebody is, he must be aware of things against himself, he must have always things on his conscience to be repented of. How can you repent if you are not conscious of anything against yourself? Christ teaches us that lesson in the parable of the Pharisee and the Tax Collector, which I have mentioned above. Furthermore, the more Christian somebody is, the more things he will have on his conscience, because the more aware he will be about his obligations and his sins.

d. The First Epistle of Paul to the Thessalonians (N.A.S.B.) says: "*2:10 You are witnesses, as so is God, how devoutly and uprightly and blamelessly we behaved toward you believers.*"

All these verses that I have transcribed here are examples of acts of arrogance and lack of humility of Paul, which are very serious, especially because Paul commands Christians to imitate him.

<u>Disobedience of the Commandment to Avoid Being Called Teacher and Father</u>

The Gospel according to Saint Matthew (N.A.S.B.)

says: "*23:8 But do not be called Rabbi; for One is your Teacher, and you are all brothers. 23:9 "And do not call anyone on earth your father, for One is your Father, He who is in heaven. 23:10 "And do not be called leaders; for One is your Leader, that is, Christ."* Christ is not talking about a biological father. Christ is not telling us not to call father our biological father, or the father who is raising us. What Christ commands us here is precisely not to call father any priest, nor any religious teacher, or authority, nor any other man. The purpose, in my opinion, is to assure freedom, including freedom of thought, to forbid submission, including submission of thought, and to teach equality between men. Paul did not obey these commandments and with his attitude had them ignored by many people. He, who is forbidden to let anyone treat him as a father, is also forbidden to treat others as his sons. The same can be said about the titles of teacher and spiritual leader.

a. The First Epistle of Paul to the Corinthians (N.A.S.B.) says : "*4:14 I do not write these things to shame you, but to admonish you as my beloved children. 4:15 For if you were to have countless tutors in Christ, yet you would not have many fathers; for in Christ Jesus I became your father through the gospel. 4:16 I exhort you therefore, be imitators of me.*" It was Christ who begot all Christians in Christianity. It was Christ with his preaching, and his crucifixion, who did it. If somebody became our Father through the Gospel he was Christ, who is God. But even Christ says that we have only one Father who is in heaven. Paul commits a big fault here treating disciples as his sons, and calling himself their father.

b. The Epistle of Paul to Philemon (N.A.S.B.) says: "1:9 yet for love's sake I rather appeal to you-since I am such a person as Paul, the aged, and now also a prisoner of Christ Jesus- 1:10 I appeal to you for my child, whom I have begotten in my imprisonment, Onesimus,"

c. The Epistle of Paul to the Galatians (N.A.S.B.) says: "4:19 My children, with whom I am again in labor until Christ is formed in you-"

d. The Second Epistle of Paul to Timothy (N.A.S.B.) says: "1:11 for which I was appointed a preacher and an apostle and a teacher."

e. The Second Epistle of Paul to the Corinthians (N.A.S.B.) says: "12:14 Here for this third time I am ready to come to you, and I will not be a burden to you; for I do not seek what is yours, but you; for children are not responsible to save up for their parents, but parents for their children."

f. The First Epistle of Paul to the Thessalonians (N.A.S.B.) says: "2:7 But we proved to be gentle among you, as a nursing mother tenderly cares for her own children."

Other Wrong Behaviors

Paul made wrong statements regarding Saint Peter, the rest of the twelve apostles, and showed himself with desire to be among those in the first positions of the Church, if not in the first. To be among those who are in the first positions he boosted his own image and he diminished the image of the rest. In the following pages, I will remark on some of the statements that give testimony of those misconducts.

a. The First Epistle of Paul to the Corinthians (N.A.S.B.) says: "*12:27 Now you are Christ's body, and individually members of it. 12:28 And God has appointed in the church, first apostles, second prophets, third teachers, then miracles, then gifts of healings, helps, administrations, various kinds of tongues. 12:29 All are not apostles, are they? All are not prophets, are they? All are not teachers, are they? All are not workers of miracles, are they? 12:30 All do not have the gifts of healings, do they? All do not speak with tongues, do they? All do not interpret, do they? 12:31 But earnestly desire the greater gifts. And I show you a still more excellent way.*"

Christ chose for the apostolic ministry twelve apostles, who, still being disciples as all the others, were going to have a higher hierarchy in the newborn church than the rest of the members. The book of Acts of the Apostles (N.A.S.B.) in reference to Judas says: "*1:17 For he was counted among us and, received his portion in this ministry.*" The same book narrating the election of Matthias says "*1:24 And they prayed, and said, "Thou, Lord, who knowest the hearts of all men, show which one of these two Thou hast chosen 1:25 to occupy this ministry and apostleship from which Judas turned aside to go to his own place.*"" These verses show that there was an apostolic ministry, with a number of twelve members. Judas was replaced because the apostles understood that the number of apostles was supposed to be twelve, not more, not less. This is why the apostles gave lots between two of the men who accompanied them the whole time Jesus went among them, and did not name both of them apostles. There was only one place left in the apostolic ministry from which Judas turned away and Matthias was chosen to occupy it.

The title of apostle was first used only to name the twelve apostles chosen by Christ. But in the book of Acts of the Apostles Paul and Barnabas are also called apostles.[114] In the Epistle of Paul to the Romans, Verse 16:7, Andronicus and Junias seem to be called apostles. And Paul in the Second Epistle of Paul to the Corinthians, Verse 8:24, even referred to Titus and other brothers who were sent with him to collect money from the church in Corinthians as apostles. That is why, in referring to the apostles in charge of the apostolic ministry instituted by Christ, formed by twelve apostles, the expression "the twelve" is sometimes used to distinguish them from the other disciples called apostles. The twelve were in a higher position than the rest; they occupied a place in the apostolic ministry. Let us remember that in the book of Revelation, Verse 21:14, the wall of the City of Jerusalem had twelve courses of stones (only twelve) as its foundation, on which were written the names of the twelve apostles of the Lamb, Christ.

The higher hierarchy of the twelve apostles, the ministry of the twelve apostles, is not recognized by Paul in these verses in which he puts himself and the others that have been called apostles at the same level

---

[114] The book of Acts of the Apostles, Verse 14:14.

Ruy Barraco Mármol

of the twelve.

b. The First Epistle of Paul to the Corinthians (N.A.S.B.) says: *"7:32 But I want you to be free from concern. One who is unmarried is concerned about the things of the Lord, how he may please the Lord; 7:33 but one who is married is concerned about the things of the world, how he may please his wife, 7:34 and his interests are divided. And the woman who is unmarried, and the virgin, is concerned about the things of the Lord, that she may be holy both in body and spirit; but one who is married is concerned about the things of the world, how she may please her husband. 7:35 And this I say for your own benefit; not to put a restraint upon you, but to promote what is seemly, and to secure undistracted devotion to the Lord."* Saint Peter was married. The Gospel according to Saint Matthew mentions his mother-in-law.[115] Paul, by saying that the married man is busy with the business of the world and divided regarding the things of the Lord, was unfairly diminishing Saint Peter. And saying that the unmarried are busy with the Lord's affairs was improperly exalting himself.

c. The First Epistle of Paul to the Corinthians (N.A.S.B.) says: *"9:4 Do we not have the right to eat and drink? 9:5 Do we not have a right to take along a believing wife, even as the rest of the apostles, and the brothers of the Lord, and Cephas?"* Then it says: *"9:15 But I have used none of these things. And I am not writing these things that it may be done so in my case; for it would be better for me*

---

[115] The Gospel according to Saint Matthew Verse 8:14.

to die than have any man make my boast an empty one."

Cephas is the apostle Peter. The Gospel according to Saint John (N.A.S.B.) says: *"1:42 He brought him to Jesus, Jesus looked at him, and said, "You are Simon the son of John; you shall be called Cephas" (which translated means Peter)".* The name Cephas is Peter in Aramaic; the language spoken by the Jews in the times of Christ in Israel. The Greek words translated as believing wife, are αδελφην γυναικα (adelphen gunaika). Αδελφην (adelphen) means sister.[116] And γυναικα (gunaika) means woman as a first meaning, and also means wife[117]. Most of the English versions of the Bible translate these words in the same way the N.A.S.B. does, but the King James Version translates these words as "a sister, a wife". The Bible of the Vatican web site in English, New American Bible, reads "Christian wife", but the Bible of the Vatican website in Spanish, *"El libro del Pueblo de Dios"*, reads "mujer creyente" which means "believing woman".

But here, in my opinion, clearly the word is not used to mean wife, because Paul did not have a wife. He is

---

116 Max Zerwick *"Analysis Philologica Novi Testamenti Graeci"* under Ad Corinthios I, Verse 9:5 says that αδελφην (adelphen) means in Latin "christiana". Christiana means Christian woman. The Langenscheidt Pocket Greek Dictionary says under the word αδελφη (adelphe): sister. Richard J Goodrich and Lukaszewski Albert "The A Reader's Greek New Testament", says under corinthians Verse 9:5 that the word means sister, fellow-believer.

117 Max Zerwick *"Analysis Philologica Novi Testamenti Graeci"* says under Ad Corinthios I, Verse 9:5, that γυναικα (gunaika) means in Latin mulier, uxor. The Harper Collins Latin Concise Dictionary says under the word mulier: women; wife- and says under the word uxor: wife. Karl Feyerabend *"The Langenscheidt Pocket Greek Dictionary"* says under the word γυνη (gune), γυναικος (gunaikos) η (e): woman, lady; wife; mistress; widow; servant.

Ruy Barraco Mármol

talking clearly about something that he could have done. That is why he says "but I have used none of these things". So he is talking about taking along a believing woman. Besides, the book of Acts of the Apostles tells us that the apostles were usually not only accompanied by their wives, but also by other Christian women. In the book of Acts of the Apostles (N.A.S.B.) talking about the apostles it is said: "*1:14 These all with one mind were continually devoting themselves to prayer, along with the women, and Mary the mother of Jesus, and with His brothers.*"

In addition, in my opinion, if the author of the epistle had intended here to use the Greek word "γυναικα" (gunaika) with the meaning of wife, he would have used a possessive adjective to indicate that he was talking about wives and not women in general. The same thing would happen in English. If you want to use the word woman with the meaning of wife of a specific man, or the word women with the meaning of wives of specific men, to avoid confusion, you would accompany the word woman with a possessive adjective: you would say "his woman or their women".

I think this verse should be translated in the following way: "Do we not have the right to take a long a women sister like the rest of the apostles, and the brothers of the Lord and Cephas?"

Anyway, I think that Paul here is just remarking that Saint Peter and other apostles were accompanied by women, while he was not, presenting this as a virtue, when it was not. The Gospel according to Saint Luke (N.A.S.B.) says: "*8:1 And it came about soon afterwards, that He began going about from one city and village to another, proclaiming and preaching the kingdom of God; and the twelve were with Him, 8:2 and also some women who had been healed of evil spirits and sicknesses: Mary who was called Magdalene, from whom seven demons had gone out, 8:3 and Joanna the wife of Chuza, Herod's steward, and Susanna, and many others who were contributing to their support out of their private means."*

Even if Paul had been referring to the wives of the apostles, which in my opinion he had not, he would have said something certainly inappropriate.

d. The Epistle of Paul to the Philippians (N.A.S.B.) says: "*3:1 Finally, my brethren, rejoice in the Lord. To write the same things again is no trouble to me, and it is a safeguard for you. 3:2 Beware of the dogs, beware of the evil workers, beware of the false circumcision; 3:3 for we are the true circumcision, who worship in the Spirit of God and glory in Christ Jesus, and put no confidence in the flesh.*"

The Greek word translated as "false circumcision", is κατατομην (katatomen), which we have seen before, in the point II.20 of this book and it means cutting into pieces, mutilation. False circumcision is not a literal translation of this Greek word.

As we saw in the same point II.20, Paul is referring with the expressions dogs, workers of evil, to the Jewish Christians who wanted to force Gentile Christians to be circumcised and bound to the Law of Moses, and probably to all the other Jewish traditions, and is referring with the word mutilation to the circumcision.

According to Paul, Saint Peter, who was a Jew, forced Christians to adopt the Jewish ways. The Epistle

Ruy Barraco Mármol

of Paul to the Galatians (N.A.S.B.) says: "*2:14 But when I saw that they were not straightforward about the truth of the gospel, I said to Cephas in the presence of all, 'If you, being a Jew, live like the Gentiles and not like the Jews, how is that you compel the Gentiles to live like Jews.*" Again, Cephas is Peter in Aramaic. The King James Version says Peter here instead of Cephas.

With the disrespectful expressions dogs, evil workers and mutilation, Paul not only treated disrespectfully the circumcision, and the Jewish Christians that wanted the Gentiles to adopt the Jewish ways, but also treated Saint Peter disrespectfully.

e. The Second Epistle of Paul to the Corinthians (N.A.S.B.) says: "*3:1 Are we beginning to commend ourselves again? Or do we need, as some, letters of commendation to you or from you?*"

For the purpose of protecting the newborn Christian community the Christians sent by the twelve apostles used to carry letters of commendation. This was perfectly natural. To receive or carry a letter of commendation did not diminish anyone; on the contrary. They were very useful for protecting the new community. With these statements, Paul diminished the ones sent by the apostles, and again he put himself at least at the same level of the twelve apostles, saying that he did not need a letter of commendation from anyone. It's clear that he did not accept the superior position and ministry of the twelve.

f. The First Epistle of Paul to the Corinthians (N.A.S.B.) says: "*15:9 For I am the least of the apostles, who am not fit to be called an apostle, because I persecuted the church of God. 15:10 But by the grace of God I am what I am, and His grace toward me did not prove vain; but I labored even more than all of them, yet not I, but the grace of God with me."* Paul exalts himself here as the one who worked hardest or toiled hardest. He says that he worked or toiled harder than Peter and all the others. Even if he were the one who worked or toiled hardest, which from what comes forth from this book he was obviously not, he would have not needed to say it, and would have improperly exalted himself by doing so.

g. The Epistle of Paul to the Galatians (N.A.S.B.) says: *"2:6 But from those who were of high reputation (what they were makes no difference to me; God shows no partiality)- well, those who were of reputation contributed nothing to me. 2:7 But on the contrary, seeing that I had been entrusted with the gospel to the uncircumcised, just as Peter had been to the circumcised. 2:8 (for He who effectually worked for Peter in his apostleship to the circumcised effectually worked for me also to the Gentiles), 2:9 and recognizing the grace that had been given to me, James and Cephas and John, who were reputed to be pillars, gave to me and Barnabas the right hand of fellowship, that we might go to the Gentiles, and they to the circumcised. 2.10 They only asked us to remember the poor-the very thing I also was eager to do."*

In regard to what Paul said about Peter, James and John supposedly recognizing that Paul had been entrusted with the gospel to the uncircumcised, just as Peter had been to the circumcised, and supposedly making some kind of division of competence, this is obviously a lie. The twelve were entrusted with ministering the gospel to the circumcised and the uncircumcised, and Peter, James and John could never have entrusted the mission to the uncircumcised to Paul. This would have been like delegating the mission that was entrusted to them by Christ to fulfill personally. The ministry to the uncircumcised was so important, that its delegation would have been equivalent to abandoning it.

In the book of Acts of the Apostles there are testimonies that the division Paul talks about in these verses did not take place in reality. The book of Acts of the Apostles (N.A.S.B.) says: "*17:1 Now when they had traveled through Amphipolis and Apollonia, they came to Thessalonica, where there was a synagogue of the Jews. 17:2 And according to Paul's custom, he went to them, and from three Sabbaths reasoned with them from the Scriptures.*"

Paul by saying that he was sent to the uncircumcised, just as Peter was sent to the circumcised arrogates himself a title that does not correspond to him, and which would put him on an equal level with Saint Peter and the rest of the apostles in the preaching, if not higher, given the significance of the part Paul was getting, because of the bigger number of the uncircumcised.

The Gospel according to Saint Matthew (N.A.S.B.) says: "*16:17 And Jesus answered and said to him, "Blessed are you, Simon Barjona, because flesh and blood did not reveal this to you, but My Father who is in heaven. 16:18 "And I also say to you that you are Peter, and upon this rock*"

I will build My church; and the gates of Hades shall not overpower it. 16:19 "I will give you the keys of the kingdom of heaven; and whatever you shall bind on earth shall be bound in heaven, and whatever you shall loose on earth shall be loosed in heaven."'

His mission was to give testimony of Jesus and of the word of Jesus to all the people, circumcised and uncircumcised. That is what Peter says in the book of Acts of the Apostles (N.A.S.B.): *"15:5 But certain ones of the sect of the Pharisees who had believed, stood up, saying, "It is necessary to circumcise them, and to direct them to observe the Law of Moses." 15:6 And the apostles and the elders came together to look into this matter. 15:7 And after there had been much debate, Peter stood up and said to them, "Brethren, you know that <u>in the early days God made a choice among you</u>, that by my mouth the Gentiles should hear the word of the gospel and believe. 15:8 "And God, who knows the human heart, bore witness to them, giving them the Holy Spirit, just as He also did to us; 15:9 and He made no distinction between us and them, cleansing their hearts by faith. 15:10 "Now therefore why do you put God to test by placing upon the neck of the disciples a yoke which neither our fathers nor we have been able to bear? 15:11 "But we believe that we are saved through the grace of the Lord Jesus, in the same way as they also are."* (Underline emphasis mine) What Saint Peter says here in the book of Acts of the Apostles directly contradicts what Paul wrote in the Epistle to the Galatians regarding himself being entrusted with the gospel for the uncircumcised or Gentiles, just as Peter was the circumcised. Either the Epistle of Paul to the Galatians is wrong or the book of Acts of the Apostles is wrong.

Ruy Barraco Mármol

In addition, it is worth bringing out that, in Verse 2:6 of this same epistle of Paul to the Galatians, Paul makes some statements that seem diminishing of the twelve apostles, and show some sort of feeling of dislike for them. The Revised Standard Version, Second Catholic Edition, translates this verse in the following way: "*2:6 And from those who were reputed to be something (what they were makes no difference to me; God shows no partiality)-those, I say, who were of repute added nothing to me;*" The King James Version says: "*2:6 But of these who seemed to be somewhat, (whatsoever they were, it maketh no matter to me: God accepteth no man's person:) for they who seemed to be somewhat in conference added nothing to me:*" The New American Bible translates this verse in the following way: "*2:6 But from those who were reputed to be important (what they once were makes no difference to me; God shows no partiality)-those of repute made me add nothing.*" The New American Standard Bible translates this verse in the following way: "*2:6 But from those who were of high reputation (what they were makes no difference to me; God shows no partiality)-well, those who were of reputation contributed nothing to me.*" The New International Version translates this verse in the following way: "*2:6 As for those who seemed to be important —whatever they were makes no difference to me; God does not judge by external appearance-those men added nothing to my message.*" The English Standard Version (E.S.V.) of the Epistle of Paul to the Galatians says: "*2:6 And from those who seemed to be influential (what they were makes no difference to me; God shows no partiality)-those, I say, who seemed influential added nothing to me.*" Paul here is referring to the twelve apostles, particularly among them, to James, Cephas and John, who are explicitly mentioned in Verse 2:9; and he is again being disrespectful, making statements that seem diminishing of them, showing some sort of feeling of dislike for them.

h. The Second Epistle of Paul to the Corinthians (N.A.S.B.) says: "*11:1 I wish that you would bear with me in a little foolishness; but indeed you are bearing with me! 11:2 For I am jealous for you with a godly jealousy; for I betrothed you to one husband, that to Christ I might present you as a pure virgin. 11:3 But I am afraid, lest as the serpent deceived Eve by his craftiness, your minds should be led astray from the simplicity and purity of devotion to Christ. 11:4 For if one comes and preaches another Jesus whom we have not preached, or you received a different spirit which you have not received, or a different gospel which you have not accepted, you bear this beautifully. 11:5 For I consider myself not in the least inferior to the most eminent apostles. 11:6 But even if I am unskilled in speech, yet I am not so in knowledge; in fact, in every way we have made this evident to you in all things. 11:7 Or did I commit a sin in humbling myself that you might be exalted, because I preached the gospel of God to you without charge? 11:8 I robbed other churches, taking wages from them to serve you; 11:9 and when I was present with you and was in need, I was not a burden to anyone; for when brethren came from Macedonia, they fully supplied my need, and in everything I kept myself from being a burden to you, and will continue to do so. 11:10 As the truth of Christ is in me, this boasting of mine will not be stopped in the regions of Achaia. 11:11 Why? Because I do not love you? God knows*

Ruy Barraco Mármol

I do! 11:12 But what I am doing, I will continue to do, that I may cut off opportunity from those who desire and opportunity to be recognized just as we are in the matter about which they are boasting. _11:13 For such men are false apostles, deceitful workers, disguising themselves as apostles of Christ. 11:14 And no wonder, for even Satan disguises himself as an angel of light. 11:15 Therefore it is not surprising if his servants also disguise themselves as servants of righteousness; whose end shall be according to their deeds._ 11:16 "Again I say, let no one think me foolish; but if you do, receive me even as foolish, that I also boast a little. 11:17 That which I am speaking, I am not speaking as the Lord would, but as in foolishness, in this confidence of boasting. 11:18 Since many boast according to the flesh, I will boast also. 11:19 For you, being so wise, bear with the foolish gladly. 11:20 For you bear with anyone if he enslaves you, if he devours you, if he takes advantage of you, if he exalts himself, if he hits you in the face. 11:21 To my shame I must say that we have been weak by comparison. But in whatever respect anyone else is bold (I speak in foolishness), I am just as bold myself. 11:22 Are they Hebrews? So am I. Are they Israelites? So am I. Are they descendants of Abraham? So am I. 11:23 Are they servants of Christ? (I speak as if insane) I more so; in far more labors, in far more imprisonments, beaten times without number, often in danger of death. 11:24 Five times I received from the Jews thirty-nine lashes. 11:25 Three times I was beaten with rods, once I was stoned, three times I was shipwrecked, a night and a day I have spent in the deep. 11:26 I have been on frequent journeys, in dangers from rivers, dangers from robbers, dangers from my countrymen, dangers from the Gentiles, dangers in the city, dangers in *the wilderness, danger on the sea, dangers among false brethren; 11:27 I have been in labor and hardship, through many sleepless nights, in hunger and thirst, often without food, in cold and exposure. 11:28 Apart from such external things, there is the daily pressure upon me of concern for all the churches. 11:29 Who is weak without my being weak? Who is led into sin without my intense concern? 11:30 If I have to boast, I will boast of what pertains to my weakness. 11:31 The God and Father of the Lord Jesus, He who is blessed forever, knows that I am not lying. 11:32 In Damascus the ethnarc under Aretas the king was guarding the city of the Damasceans in order to seize me, 11:33 and I was let down in a basket through a window in the wall, and so escaped his hands.* (Underline emphasis mine)

The eminent apostles Paul is talking about are the twelve apostles. What tells us that he is talking about the twelve apostles? The fact that when this letter was sent to Christians only the twelve and a few more where called apostles. In the book of the Acts of the Apostles only Paul and Saint Barnabas are called apostles, besides the twelve.

The words of Paul say that they were apostles. And no other apostles than the twelve could have been of sufficient importance to justify these statements of Paul. The expression eminent-apostles can only refer to the twelve. The twelve were Hebrews, Israelites, ministers of Christ, and were the eminent apostles. To attack or defend himself from Christians that were not the twelve he would not have needed to say what he said. It would have been enough for him to say that he counted on the blessing of the twelve, of course, if he actually counted on it.

Ruy Barraco Mármol

We already saw how Paul said that he had worked more than the other apostles, that he was not accompanied by women believers as the others, that he was not divided like the apostles that were married, how he treated disrespectfully Peter, James and John, how he called dogs the Jewish Christians that wanted the Gentile Christians to live the Jewish way, and said that Peter did so, and how Paul wanted the title of apostle of the Gentiles that belonged to Peter.

i. Paul says in this Second Epistle to Corinthians (N.A.S.B.): "*12:11 I have become foolish; you yourselves compelled me. Actually I should have been commended by you, for in no respect was I inferior to the most eminent apostles, even though I am a nobody. 12:12 The signs of a true apostle were performed among you with all perseverance, by signs and wonders and miracles. 12:13 For in what respect were you treated as inferior to the rest of the churches, except that I myself did not become a burden to you? Forgive me this wrong!*" A few verses later, in the same epistle, Paul refers again to the most eminent apostles, using the same expression of Verse 11:5, in which he calls the most eminent apostles false apostles, and he says that he has in no respect been inferior to them; and he does it without adding anything that indicates that he is referring to anyone different than the twelve apostles, which confirms that in the previous opportunity, when he was talking about the most eminent apostles, calling them false apostles, he was talking about the twelve.

No doubt, this epistle attacks the twelve apostles and the Church. Probably, not counting Saint John, the twelve apostles never took notice of it. And Saint John most likely took notice of it after Paul of Tarsus' death.

Some Significant Facts Regarding the Life of Paul, His Teachings, His Epistles, and the Church

As I have already said, Paul, at the beginning, did not present himself before the apostles as chosen by Jesus to be a new apostle in charge of preaching to the gentiles; and he did not present himself as privately instructed by Jesus to preach new words of God. At least he did not do so, if he ever did, which I believe he never did, until after his last journey to Jerusalem, which took place later than the year 56 A.D., according to the book of Acts of the Apostles. We can see this by paying attention to the visits of Paul to Jerusalem mentioned in this book.

Verse 9:27 of the book of Acts tells us about Paul's first visit to Jerusalem. This verse says that a disciple of the church, named Barnabas, introduced Paul to the apostles and told them how Paul had seen the Lord, that the Lord had spoken to Paul, and that Paul had preached in Damascus; but it does not say anything, naturally, about Barnabas telling the apostles that Paul had been chosen, named and instructed privately by Jesus to be the apostle to the gentiles, and to preach

---

[118] This first visit to Jerusalem would have occurred three years after the supposed calling of Paul, according to the Epistle of Paul to the Galatians, verse 1:19, and Paul would have talked during this visit of 15 days with Peter, and maybe with James the minor, if James the minor was the James who was a relative of Jesus.

Ruy Barraco Mármol

new words of God. Just imagine how surprised the apostles would have been, and their reaction, had he done so.[118]

It can be seen as well that Paul, in the beginning, did not present himself as a new apostle chosen by Jesus to be the apostle of the gentiles and to preach new words of God, from the book of Acts of the Apostles, Chapter 15, which gives testimony of the Council of Jerusalem (48 to 50 A.D.). In this council Peter highlights how he was chosen so that through his mouth the gentiles would hear the word and believe.

The same thing can be deduced from how Paul, after the council, was sent as if his position within the church was less important than the position of Judas and Silas, who would not even have been apostles. This tells us that not even at the time of the Council of Jerusalem was Paul recognized as a man chosen by Jesus to be the apostle of the gentiles and to preach new words of God; nor had he yet presented himself, nor claimed those titles; least of all before the apostles.

In addition the same conclusion can be drawn from Paul's behavior in Jerusalem with James, in which what is called the last journey of Paul to Jerusalem (58 A.D.). The book of Acts of the Apostles, (E.S.V.) says: "*21:20 And when they heard it, they glorified God. And they said to him, "You see, brother, how many thousands there are among the Jews of those who have believed. They are all zealous for the law, 21:21 and they have been told about you that you teach all the Jews who are among the Gentiles in forsake Moses, telling them not to circumcise their children or walk according to our customs. 21:22 What then is to be done? They will certainly hear that you have come.*

21:23 Do therefore what we tell you. We have four men who are under a vow; 21:24 take these men and purify yourself along with them and pay their expenses, so that they may shave their heads. Thus all will know that there is nothing in what they have been told about you, but that you yourself also live in observance of the law." This passage tells us that James did not know about the teachings of Paul about circumcision and the Law of Moses, and that Paul was not yet recognized as a new apostle chosen by Jesus to be the apostle to the gentiles and to preach new words of God.

Let us remember what Paul taught about the circumcision in the Epistle of Paul to the Galatians (E.S.V.) which says: *"5:1 For freedom Christ has set us free; stand firm therefore, and do not submit again to a yoke of slavery. 5:2 Look: I Paul say to you that if you accept circumcision, Christ will be of no advantage to you: 5:3 I testify again to every man who accepts circumcision that he is obligated to keep the whole law. 5:4 You are severed from Christ, you who would be justified? By the law: you have fallen away from grace."* This is one of the passages in which Paul teaches that the Jews are obligated not to accept the circumcision. Had James known about Paul's teachings and/or had Paul of Tarsus been recognized as the apostle of the Gentiles, and been considered as somebody privately chosen and instructed by Jesus to speak new words of God, he would have not needed to be worried about what the Christian Jews of the Christian Church of Jerusalem had to say.

The transcribed passage of the book of Acts of the Apostles not only lets us know that the Church of Jerusalem did not know about the teachings of Paul, and

Ruy Barraco Mármol

did not know about the Epistle of Paul to the Galatians, but also tells us that Paul up to that moment had not presented himself, and least of all was recognized, as the apostle to the Gentiles, privately instructed by Jesus, to speak new words of God. And this event occurs after the year 56 A.D. It is believed that Peter died during the persecutions of Nero that started in the year 64 A.D. and lasted until the year 68 A.D., year in which Nero died. And it is believed that Peter and Paul were in prison at the same time, but it is not known for certain.

Did apostles from the twelve know for certain, at some moment, what Paul said and taught, and the content of his epistles?

I believe that the Apostle Saint John did know it at some point, after the death of Paul, and thus the book of Revelation, as we will see in the second part of this book. However, with regard to the rest of the apostles it is hard to determine. I believe that they never knew.

We have seen that until the year 56 A.D., most likely the year 58 A.D., at the time of the so called last journey of Paul to Jerusalem, Paul was not recognized by James and by the church of Jerusalem, and that it is very likely therefore that the apostles did not know about the supposed new words of God spoken by Paul of Tarsus, and did not know about his epistles, at least, did not know about all of them.

During most of the time, especially after the council of Jerusalem, Paul was on trips, in which he neither coincided with Peter, nor with any of the other apostles, according to the book of Acts of the Apostles. In the meantime, he would have given credit and authority to disciples who responded to him in all of the places where he preached, giving them instruction to do the same, that is to say to appoint elders in every town.[119]

In that way two groups of communities were developed within the church. The ones who were not under the influence of Paul, who taught principally the words that Jesus taught to his twelve apostles, and the groups that were under the influence of Paul, who taught principally the teachings of Paul, mixed with the teachings of Jesus.

There are testimonies of churches that did not recognize Paul. In the church of Corinth, many who recognized Apollos, who counted with the support of the apostles, did not recognize Paul as the apostle to the gentiles privately instructed by Jesus to preach new words of God. They did not even recognize him as an apostle, or as someone who they had to obey.[120]

In Jerusalem Paul was not recognized. And I believe that it is not risky to say that in all the Jewish Christian world, of Jerusalem, Judea, Galilee and surroundings, Paul was not recognized; which, by the way, were the places in which Jesus preached the most, as well as the twelve apostles in the beginning, and where the people better prepared to dispute with Paul lived. They were the people better prepared because Jesus preached among

---

[119] The Epistle of Paul to Titus (E.S.V.) says: "*1:4 To Titus, my true child in common faith: Grace and peace from God the Father and Christ Jesus our Savior. 1:5 This is why I left you in Crete, so that you might put what remained into order, and appoint elders in every town as I directed you.*"

[120] Book of Acts of the Apostles, verse 18:24. First Epistle of Paul to the Corinthians, verses 1:11; 3:22; 9:2. First Epistle of Clement of Rome, Chapter 47.

them, and because they were Jews, and naturally they had more knowledge of the scriptures than the gentiles.

In addition, the Epistles of Paul, because they were writings originally directed to particular communities, were not immediately known by the rest of the church.[121] I would say that they were known by very few. I believe that they were not known by the apostles, especially considering that it is taught that when the epistles started circulating, the surviving apostles of the twelve were scattered taking the word to faraway places, to all the nations, as Jesus had instructed them, and Paul, as I said, did not coincide with any of them in the journeys he carried out, according to the book of Acts of the Apostles. It is very likely that this had much to do with the fact that they did not hear about the teachings of Paul, and about his epistles, or at least, did not learn about all of them.

In addition, confronted by an apostle, or by a Christian with support of the twelve, Paul could have reacted or behaved in the way he did with James according to the book of Acts of the Apostles, denying and hiding his teachings.

And questioned about one of his epistles he could have denied that he wrote it. In the Second Epistle of Paul to the Thessalonians, verse 2:2, Paul talks about epistles attributed to him that did not belong to him. The epistle just mentioned says (E.S.V.): "*2:2 not to be quickly shaken*

---

[121] De Tuya, Manuel and José Salguero, "Introducción a la Biblia", vol I, p. 364, says: [The writings of the New Testament, because they were in their majority writings directed to particular communities, were not known immediately by the entire Christian Church] "*Los escritos del Nuevo Testamento, por haber sido en su mayoría escritos dirigidos a comunidades particulares, no fueron conocidos inmediatamente por toda la Iglesia Cristiana.*"

in mind or alarmed, either by a spirit or a spoken word or a letter seeming to be from us, to the effect that the day of the Lord has come." This epistle says that Paul said that epistles attributed to him that were not of his authorship were circulating in the church.

Actually, in these verses of the Second Epistle of Paul to the Thessalonians, Paul seems to be denying the First Epistle of Paul to the Thessalonians (E.S.V.), that says *"4:15 For this we declare to you by a word from the Lord, that we who are alive, who are left until the coming of the Lord, will not precede those who have fallen asleep. For the Lord himself will descend from heaven with a cry of command, with the voice of an archangel, and with the sound of the trumpet of God. And the dead in Christ will rise first. Then we who are alive, who are left, will be caught up together with them in the clouds to meet the Lord in the air, and so we will always be with the Lord."* In this First Epistle of Paul to the Thessalonians Paul said that the Second Coming of Jesus would come while he was alive. He said that the Day of the Lord was close or near. He said that he was going to be caught up together with those who were alive to meet the Lord in the air in the Day of the Lord. Saying that he was going to be caught up alive, he said that the Day of the Lord was near, within his lifetime. Notwithstanding, in the Second Epistle of Paul to the Thessalonians Paul tells them not to be shaken by epistles attributed to him that say that the Day of the Lord is near. It would not be strange that in this way Paul had responded had he been questioned about the content and authorship of this and other epistles.

It is possible as well that the apostles learned partially about the wrong teachings, or when it was too late; and that they did nothing to confront him, or to expel Paul's disciples from the church, because of the teaching of the Parable of the Weed, from the Gospel according to Saint Matthew verse 13:24. In this parable Jesus teaches that we should not expel the weed growing in the middle of the church.

Moreover, it is possible, that they thought that it was better for the church not to do anything about it, instead of starting an internal confrontation, when the church was developing, that could put its development in jeopardy. And it is possible that they did not anticipate that the church would eventually consider his epistles the Word of God.

It is very hard, maybe impossible, to know what the book of Acts of the Apostles does not tell us, because the rest of the epistles and testimonies are not trustworthy enough; but what is certain is that the Epistles of Paul of Tarsus contain wrong teachings and vices that were responsible for the worst errors and vices of the Christian Church and that the Epistles of Paul are not the word of God.

The Epistles of Paul Were Not Considered the Word of God During the Life of the Apostles, and Until Long Time After Their Death

Another important thing to consider is that the Epistles of the New Testament were not considered the word of God in the beginning. The first authors of the Christian Church quoted the books of the Old Testament as scripture, quoted the words of Jesus as supreme authority, but did not do the same with the Epistles of the New Testament. At least the great majority of them did not do so.[122]

It is important to understand that the fact that the epistles were read, or that an author or that authors used the words contained in an epistle, or that even used an epistle, does not mean that they considered the epistle the word of God.[123]

The fact that the epistles would have been known or explicitly quoted, if they were not quoted as the word of God, as scripture, would not mean that they were considered or treated as scripture, or the word of God.

Not even the fact that someone would have said that the author of an epistle wrote it moved by the Holy Spirit, would have necessarily implied that he considered that epistle scripture or the word of God. The concept of

---

[122] Metzger, Bruce M. in his book "The Canon of the New Testament", (Oxford: Clarendon Press, 1987), p. 73 says: "In short, we find in both the Jewish and the Hellenistic groups a knowledge of the existence of certain books that later will comprise the New Testament, and more than once they express their thoughts through phrases drawn from these writings. These reminiscences tend to show that an implicit authority of such writings was sensed before a theory of their authority had been developed-in fact, before there was even a consciousness of their authority. This authority, moreover, did not have, to any degree, an exclusive character. On the other hand, we see that the words of Jesus are taken as the supreme authority. Sometimes these quotations are similar to what we find in the four Gospels, at the other times they differ."

[123] The First Epistle of Clement, also known as the Epistle of Clement of Rome to the Corinthians and the Epistle of Ignatius to the Philippians were read in other churches as well. De Tuya, Manuel and José Salguero in "Introducción a la Biblia", says: [The simple liturgical reading does not seem enough reason, because we know by the testimony of several ancient Fathers that they also read in the liturgical assemblies other writings that were never part of the canon of the Holy Scripture.] The note says: [By Saint Dionisius of Corintho we know that the Epistle of Clement of Rome to the Corinthians was read in the liturgical assemblies (cf. En Eusebio, Hist. Eccl., 4,23,1:MG 20,338). In the churches of Asia the Epistle of Saint Polycarp was read (cf. Saint Jerome, De viris Illustr. 17:ML 23,636)...]. De Tuya, Manuel and José Salguero "Introducción a la Biblia", vol I, p. 329.

inspiration was for some, in those times, different than the one that it is given to it, in general, today. It is taught that Clement of Alexandria said that Plato wrote inspired.[124] Clement of Rome, who as we have seen is considered by the majority of Catholic scholars as the third Pope of the Catholic Church, and says in the Epistle called First Epistle of Clement to the Corinthians that Paul of Tarsus wrote inspired by the Holy Spirit, also said in that epistle that himself wrote that First Epistle of Clement moved by the Holy Spirit. And his epistle it is not considered written by him moved by the inspiration of the Holy Spirit.[125]

And it is important to keep in mind that the fact that an author would had treated an Epistle of Paul as the word of God, would not authorize the conclusion that the entire church did so as well, especially in the first two centuries of our age, in which the church was at times still persecuted, and communications were so difficult. The church was not as uniform in the first two centuries

---

[124] The book the "*The Canon of the New Testament*" by Bruce M. Metzger says that Clement refers to Orpheus as "the theologian", and speaks of Plato as being 'under the inspiration of God'. Metzger, Bruce M. "*The Canon of the New Testament*", p. 134. - Manuel de Tuya and José Salguero "*Introducción a la Biblia*", says in this regard and about Clement: [We must highlight, notwithstanding, that along with the canonical books, he quotes others that are not, which suggests that he did not distinguish well the canonical books from the apocryphal.] De Tuya, Manuel and José Salguero "*Introducción a la Biblia*", vol I, p. 367.

[125] The book "*Padres Apostólicos*", Introductions, notes and Spanish version by Daniel Ruiz Bueno, (Madrid: La Editorial Católica S.A., MCML), First Epistle of Clement, p. LXIII (63), p. 236, says: [Happiness and Joy you will give us if, obeying what we just said to you, moved by the Holy Spirit, root out the unrighteous anger of your envy according the entreaty that we have made with this letter for peace and concord.] The Greek text says διὰ του αγιου πνευματος. See book of Acts 21:4 and The Epistle of Paul to the Romans verse 5:5 to find similar expressions.

as it started to be later, when the Roman Empire made Christianity the official religion, and the Empire put its power at the service of the Church, and to some extent the authorities of the Church put themselves at the service of the Empire.

Moreover, one cannot even draw that conclusion, if the author or person has shown lack of judgment in distinguishing what is true from what is false. The Epistle of Clement of Rome, considered within the Catholic Church as the third Pope of the Catholic Church, says about the Phoenix Bird: "*25:1 Let us consider the marvelous sign which is seen in the regions of the east, that is, in the parts about Arabia. There is a bird, which is named the phoenix. This, being the only one of its kind, liveth for five hundred years; and when it hath now reached the time of its dissolution that it should die, it maketh for itself a coffin of frankincense and myrrh and the other spices, into the which in the fullness of time it entereth, and so it dieth. 25:3 But, as the flesh rotteth, a certain worm is engendered, which is nurtured from the moisture of the dead creature and putteth forth wings. Then, when it is grown lusty, it taketh up that coffin where are the bones of its parent, and carrying them journeyeth from the country of Arabia even unto Egypt, to the place called the city of the Sun; 25:4 and in the daytime in the sight of all, flying to the altar of the Sun, it layeth them thereupon; and this done, it setteth forth to return. So the priests examine the registers of the times, and they find that it hath come when the five hundredth year is completed. 26:1 Do we then think it to be a great and marvelous thing, if the Creator of the universe shall bring about the resurrection of them that have served Him with holiness in the assurance of a good faith, seeing that He showeth to us even by a bird the*

*magnificence of His promise? For he saith in a certain place
And Thou shalt raise me up, and I will praise Thee; and; I
went to rest and slept, I was awaked, for Thou art with me.
26:3 And again Job saith And Thou shall raise this my flesh
which hath endured all these things."*[126] The Epistle of
Clement of Rome to the Corinthians presents here this
fiction about the Phoenix bird as if it were a real thing,
not a legend. Immediately before the reference to the
Phoenix, the epistle refers to the fact of how the day
follows the night, and immediately after it quotes the Old
Covenant.[127]

The facts that we know of regarding the first authors
of the Christian Church say that the Epistles of Paul were
not recognized as sacred scripture, and at the same time,
the book of Acts of the Apostles and the Epistles of Paul
give testimony of Christians who did not even recognize
Paul of Tarsus as an apostle, as we have already seen.

The first Chapter of the book of Revelation contains
epistles to the seven churches of Asia. The descriptions
of these churches imply that the churches were
developing with particular characteristics and with
different challenges.

Saint Justyn, who writes around the year 155 A.D., did
not consider the Epistles of Paul as the word of God.

---

[126] Early Christian Writings. The First Epistle of Clement to the Corinthians.
Translated by J.B. Lightfoot. The book "Padres Apostólicos", Introductions, Notes
and Spanish Version by Daniel Ruiz Bueno, p. XXV (25), p. 202.

[127] Even if this were presented as a legend, which is not the case, the context in
which it was inserted this reference to the mythological Phoenix bird would
have been inappropriate, and would have shown lack of judgment by Clement of
Rome.

This can be deduced from the arguments that he uses, and does not use, to defend Christianity in the Epistle that he sent to the Emperor Antoninus Pius. It can also be deduced from the positions that he sustains about women and about the Jewish Christians who were arguing that the Christian Jews still had to comply with the rites of the Law of Moses. Saint Justin converted in Ephesus, and it is believed that he ended up living in Rome, where he became a martyr. His testimony gives account of the existence in the year 150 A.D. of a community of Christians who did not recognize Paul of Tarsus, nor consider his epistles the words of God.[128]

---

[128] Saint Justin Martyr, in a letter that he sent to the Emperor Antoninus Pius, titled "First Apology", p.17, says: "And everywhere we try to pay to those appointed by you more readily than all the people, the taxes and assessments, as we have been taught by Him. For at that time some came and asked Him if it were necessary to pay tribute to Caesar, and He answered, "Tell me, whose image does this coin bear? And they said, Caesar's. And again He answered them, "Give Caesar the things that are Caesar's and to God the things that are God's. So we worship God only, but in other things we gladly serve you, acknowledging you as emperors and rulers of men and women, and praying that with your imperial power you may also be found to possess sound judgment." Ancient Christian Writers, The First and Second Apologies, (New York: Paulist Press, 1997), edited by Walter J. Burghardt, John J. Dillon and Dennis D. McManus. Saint Justin says that the Christians acknowledge the emperors as rulers of men, not as servants of God, instituted by God, to execute the wrath of God over the evildoers as the Epistle of Paul to the Romans, Chapter 13 teaches. The fact that Saint Justin did not mention Paul of Tarsus and did not mention his epistles let us know that he neither acknowledged Paul of Tarsus as the apostle to the gentiles, privately chosen and instructed by Jesus to speak new words of God, nor acknowledged his epistles as the word of God. Similar thing can be said from the fact that Justin neither mentioned nor used the Epistles of Paul, for instance, at the time he was discussing subjects such as the status of women, salvation of the Christian Jews and the Law of Moses. And the opinions of Justin Martyr about these subjects, tell us that he did not consider the Epistles of Paul the word of God, and did not consider Paul a new apostle of Jesus who spoke new words of God, or had the mind of Christ. – Another Christian, named Papias, would have said: "If ever anyone came who had been a follower of the presbyters, I inquired into the words of the presbyters, what Andrew or Peter or Philip or Thomas or James or John or Matthew

Ruy Barraco Mármol

Consequences

Joining the Christian Church, giving credit and authority to new disciples who responded to him in all of the places in which he preached, giving them instructions to do the same, leaving his teachings in epistles, saying that they are the word of God, and commanding the imitation of his conducts, he was able to gain great influence inside the Christian Church, and he was responsible for the installation inside the Christian Church of serious vices, and errors, which were and are responsible for the worst errors and vices of the Christian Church.

---

or any other of the Lord's disciples had said, and what Aristion and the presbyter John, the Lord's disciples were saying. For I did not think that information from books would help me so much as the utterance of a living and surviving voice." He shows great appreciation for the oral tradition and he does not mention Paul of Tarsus at all. *"The Canon of the New Testament"* by Bruce M. Metzger, p. 52. - Arístides, in his Apology written in the beginnings of the II century A.D., not later than the year 150 A.D., would have said the following about Jesus: [He had twelve disciples, who, after the ascension to heaven went out to the provinces of the Empire and taught about the greatness of Jesus, and one of these went out our same places preaching the doctrine of the truth. *Thus the ones who still serve the justice of his preaching, are called Christians.*] He talks about the twelve disciples and does not mention Paul of Tarsus. Ruiz Bueno Daniel, *"Padres Apologistas Griegos (s.II)",* p. 130. (According to the Greek manuscripts).

Chapter III.
Revision

The revision of the Christian doctrine does not admit delay. Christian doctrine cannot be built on the basis of errors. Whether or not Paul is the author of the epistles, the Christian doctrine must be revised. Christian doctrine can neither be built on the basis of fake epistles nor on the basis of the doctrine of a false prophet. The consequences and effects of these errors must be stopped.

However, more important than rebuilding the doctrine built on the doctrine of Paul, is to pay due attention to the true word of Christ the way it was expressed, and to deepen the issues on which Christ put emphasis. The Christian Church has not paid due attention to the issues Christ gave the most, because of the Epistles of Paul. The word of Christ must be the main word quoted in every Christian Church. Christians must demand their ministers to quote Christ.

To live in the mind and in the heart of the people and act as it was meant to be, the word of Christ must be completely learned in the way it was expressed. This does not mean that at the same time we cannot study the interpretation of the most authorized students of the word of God, disciples of Christ. On the contrary, those interpretations must be learned, and of course taught. But the interpretations must be taken as they are: human interpretations that can be mistaken.

Next, I will treat some matters in which Christian doctrine must be revised. Paul himself says in the First Epistle to the Thessalonians (N.A.B.): "*5:19 Do not quench the Spirit. 5:20 Do not despise prophetic utterances. 5:21 Test everything; retain what is good. 5:22 Refrain from every kind of evil.*"

III.1. DIVORCE

The Gospels according to Saint Matthew, Saint Mark and Saint Luke, contain teachings of Christ about divorce.

The Gospel according to Saint Matthew (N.A.B.) says: "*19:1 When Jesus finished these words, he left Galilee and went to the district of Judea across the Jordan. 19:2 Great crowds followed him, and he cured them there. 19:3 Some Pharisees approached him, and tested him, saying, "Is it lawful for a man to divorce his wife for any cause whatever?" 19:4 He said in reply, "Have you not read that from the beginning the Creator 'made them male and female' 19:5 and said, 'For this reason a man shall leave his father and mother and be joined to his wife, and the two shall become one flesh'? 19:6 So they are no longer two, but one flesh. Therefore, what God has joined together, no human being must separate." 19:7 They said to him, "Then why did Moses command that the man give the woman a bill of divorce and dismiss (her)?" 19:8 He said to them, "Because of the hardness of your heart Moses allowed you to divorce your wives, but from the beginning it was not so. 19:9 I say to you, whoever divorces his wife (unless the marriage is unlawful) and marries another commits* adultery." 19:10 His disciples said to him, "If that is the case of a man with his wife, it is better not to marry." 19:11 He answered, "Not all can accept (this) word, but only those to whom that is granted. 19:12 Some are incapable of marriage because they were born so; some, because they were made so by others; some because they have renounced marriage for the sake of the kingdom of God. Whoever can accept this ought to accept it.""

The Gospel according to Saint Matthew (N.A.B) says: "5:31 "It was also said, 'Whoever divorces his wife must give her a bill of divorce.' 5:32 But I say to you, whoever divorces his wife (unless the marriage is unlawful) causes her to commit adultery, and whoever marries a divorced woman commits adultery."

The Gospel according to Saint Mark (N.A.B.) says: "10:1 He set out from there and went into the district of Judea (and) across the Jordan. Again crowds gathered around him and, as was his custom, he again taught them. 10:2 The Pharisees approached and asked, "Is it lawful for a husband to divorce his wife?" 10:3 He said to them in reply, "What did Moses command you?" 10:4 They replied, "Moses permitted him to write a bill of divorce and dismiss her." 10:5 But Jesus told them, "Because of the hardness of your hearts he wrote you this commandment. 10:6 But from the beginning of creation, 'God made them male and female. 10:7 For this reason a man shall leave his father and mother (and be joined to his wife), 10:8 and the two shall become one flesh.' So they are no longer two but one flesh. 10:9 Therefore what God has joined together, no human being must separate." 10:10 In the house the disciples again questioned him about this. 10:11 He said to them, "Whoever divorces his wife and marries another

Ruy Barraco Mármol

commits adultery against her; 10:12 and if she divorces her husband and marries another, she commits adultery."

The Gospel according to Saint Luke (N.A.B.) says: "16:18 Everyone who divorces his wife and marries another commits adultery, and the one who marries a woman divorced from her husband commits adultery."

First Jesus teaches about the case of the man who divorces his wife, and then about the case of the woman who divorces her husband. In his teachings Jesus makes a distinction between the husbands or wives who divorce their spouses and the ones who are victims of the divorce. And, as we can see in the Gospel according to Saint Matthew, Jesus acknowledges an exception in which it is licit to divorce for any reason whatever, that we will analyze in this point. But we will start by discussing the case of the man who divorces his wife.

The Man Who Divorces His Wife

The Gospel according to Saint Matthew (N.A.B.) says: "5:32 But I say to you, whoever divorces his wife (unless the marriage is unlawful) causes her to commit adultery, and whoever marries a divorced woman commits adultery." (Underline emphasis mine)

The Gospel according to Saint Matthew (N.A.B.) says: "19:9 I say to you, whoever divorces his wife (unless the marriage is unlawful) and marries another commits adultery." (Underline emphasis mine)

The Gospel according to Saint Mark (N.A.B.) says: "10:11 He said to them, "Whoever divorces his wife and marries another commits adultery against her; 10:12 and if she divorces her husband and marries another, she commits *adultery.*" (Underline emphasis mine)

The Gospel according to Saint Luke (N.A.B.) says: "*16:18 Everyone who divorces his wife and marries another commits adultery, and the one who marries a woman divorced from her husband commits adultery.*" (Underline emphasis mine)

These verses clearly say that the man who divorces his wife and marries another woman commits adultery.

A man can divorce his wife through direct acts, for instance, telling her that he will no longer be her husband, and that she must leave the marital home, and even forcing his wife to go away from it; and a man can divorce his wife through indirect acts, for instance committing an offense or a series of offenses against his wife that because of their seriousness may make impossible the continuation of the marriage, or unreasonable the exigency of its continuation by the other spouse. The indirect acts may consist, for instance, in one or more cases of physical aggression that threaten her life, or one or more acts of adultery with a family member. This could be called indirect or constructive divorce.

It makes no sense that a spouse can get around the rule that forbids a husband to divorce his wife, by intentionally committing acts that because of their seriousness may make impossible the continuation of the marriage, or unreasonable the exigency of its continuation by the other spouse. This is so because it is a fact that these cases exist. And because these cases exist, if a spouse commits these kinds of acts, even if the purpose of their commission was not to cause a divorce, the commission of them allows the victim to

Ruy Barraco Mármol

consider himself or herself divorced.

The husband that divorces his wife through direct or indirect acts is guilty of the divorce, and if he marries another commits adultery. The gospels clearly establish that in general the man who divorces his wife, and gets married again commits adultery, except for the exception that we will discuss soon afterwards.

The Woman Who Divorces her Husband

After treating the case of the man who divorces his wife, the three mentioned Gospels treat the case in which the woman divorces her husband. This conclusion comes forth from the analysis I will expose next.

Let us start with the Gospel according to Saint Matthew. The Gospel according to Saint Matthew (N.A.B.) says: "*5:32 But I say to you, whoever divorces his wife (unless the marriage is unlawful) causes her to commit adultery, and whoever marries a divorced woman commits adultery.*" (Underline emphasis mine) The underlined sentence is the one we are analyzing now.[129]

---

[129] The Greek word translated as "divorced woman" is απολελυμενην (apolelumenen) which can be either a participle perfect middle or a participle perfect passive. In this case it is a participle perfect middle that should be translated as an active participle, 'the woman who divorced' or 'the woman who has divorced.' We know this for sure because the exact same verb is used in the Gospel according to Saint Luke, Verse 16:18, also teaching about divorce, followed by the expression from her husband and it only makes sense if it is translated as a perfect middle. In the translation of the Gospels the translation that makes the Gospels agree should be preferred to the one that makes them disagree. The King James Version translates this word in Mt. 5:32 as 'her that is divorced' and in Lk 16:18 as 'her that is put away'; the R.S.V. (Second Catholic Edition) as 'divorced woman' in Matthew and 'woman divorced' in Luke; the N.A.S.B. as 'divorced woman' in Mt and 'one who is

This sentence of the Gospel according to Saint Matthew can be interpreted in two ways. One way to interpret this verse says that the man who marries a woman who divorced her husband commits adultery. Under this interpretation, the verse would be the reverse of the one we saw before. It would be contemplating the case in which the woman is responsible for the divorce, and it would be saying that if she marries again she commits adultery; and not only she, but also the man who marries her.

The other possible way to interpret this verse is the one that says that the man who marries the woman divorced by her husband commits adultery, in which case the verse would be contemplating the case in which a man marries a woman divorced by her husband, victim of the divorce of her husband. Under this interpretation, the verse would be saying that if she gets married again, she commits adultery, and not only she, but also the man who marries her, no matter that she was a victim of the divorce, not the perpetrator.

The question is: Is this sentence of the Gospel of Saint Matthew that says 'whoever marries a divorced woman commits adultery' talking about the woman responsible for the divorce, or the woman victim of the divorce?

The answer to the question is given in the Gospel according to Saint Luke, who adds to the same sentence of Verse 5:32 of the Gospel according to Saint Matthew, the expression 'from her husband'. In the Gospel

---

divorced' in Lk; the N.I.V. as 'divorced woman' in Mt. and 'divorced woman' in Lk; the E.S.V. as a 'divorced woman' in Mt. and 'woman divorced' in Lk.

according to Saint Luke, Christ says the same expression, only different in the addition of the expression "from her husband': in Greek απο (apo) ανδρος (andros) γαμων (gamon).[130] The Greek word απο (apo) means from.[131]

The Gospel according to Saint Luke (N.A.B.) says: "*16:18 Everyone who divorces his wife and marries another commits adultery, and the one who marries a woman divorced from her husband commits adultery.*" (Underline emphasis mine)

The King James Version, the Revised Standard Version, Second Catholic Edition, the New American Standard Bible and the English Standard Version, include this expression "from her husband". The New International Version does not.

The expression from her husband that this verse includes strongly suggests that Christ after treating the case of the man who divorces his wife, in which the man is responsible for the divorce, treats the case of the woman who divorces her husband, in which the woman is responsible for the divorce. It tells us that it does not refer to the woman divorced by her husband, victim of the divorce, but to the woman responsible for the

---

[130] Merk, Augustinus in the Bible *"Novum Testamentum Graece et Latine"* septiman editionem includes these Greek words, as well as the book of Goodrich Richard J. and Albert L. Lukaszewski "A Reader's Greek New Testament" second edition. The Nestle-Aland "Greek-English New Testament", also includes these words.

[131] Karl Feyerabend "Langenscheidt Pocket Greek Dictionary Greek-English". Goodrich Richard J. and Albert L. Lukaszewski "A Reader's Greek New Testament" second edition. The Nestle-Aland "Greek-English New Testament", also includes these words.

divorce.

In some versions of the Bible the Gospel according to Saint Matthew repeats in Verse 19:9 the same sentence. Everything said is applicable to this verse too.

This solution harmonizes with the Gospel according to Saint Mark, which also teaches that Christ after treating the case of the man who divorced his wife, treats the case of the woman who divorced her husband. The Gospel according to Saint Mark (N.A.B.) says: "*10:11 He said to them, "Whoever divorces his wife and marries another commits adultery against her; 10:12 and if she divorces her husband and marries another, she commits adultery.*" (Underline emphasis mine)

The interpretation that harmonizes the Gospels should be preferred to others that put them in conflict. So even without considering the expression *from her husband*, not included without explanation in the New International Version, the solution should be the same.

The Husband and the Wife Victims of the Divorce

Jesus makes a distinction between the husband who divorces his wife and the husband who is divorced by his wife. The teaching of Jesus implies that the husband who is divorced by his wife, or the wife who is divorced by her husband, who gets married again, does not commit adultery.

The sentence found in the Gospel according to Saint Matthew (N.A.B.), Verse 5:32, that says: "*But I say to you, whoever divorces his wife (unless the marriage is unlawful) causes her to commit adultery,...*"(underline emphasis mine) does not mean that the wife, victim of

Ruy Barraco Mármol

the divorce, is forbidden to get married again.[132]

In my opinion, it cannot be deduced from the above statement that it is illicit for a victim of divorce to get married again. I believe this, because the responsibility of the adultery is being placed on the guilty spouse. If somebody says, that the person that attacks another with a gun, with the intention to kill him, in a case in which the victim can only defend himself killing the offender, forces his victim to kill him, it would not be right to conclude, from the expression <u>forces the victim to kill him</u>, that the act of self-defense must be forbidden, or is illicit; it would not be right to conclude that you are not allowed to kill in that situation.[133]

---

[132] The Latin Vulgate says: 'facit eam moechari'. The King James version says: "causeth her to commit adultery." The Revised Standard Version says: "makes her an adulteress." The New American Bible says: "causes her to commit adultery". The New American Standard Bible says: "makes her commit adultery." The New International version says: "causes her to become an adulteress." The English Standard Version says: "makes her commit adultery".

[133] Besides, the Greek texts of the most important witnesses say: ποιει (poiei) αυτην (auten) μοιχευθηναι[133] (moicheuthenai). Ποιει (poiei) means 'make', αυτην (auten) means 'her', μοιχευθηναι (moicheuthenai), is a tense of the Greek verb μοιχευω (moicheuo), which means 'to commit adultery.' The name of the tense is infinitive aorist passive, and it does not exist in English. William D. Mounce "Basics of Biblical Greek Grammar", Second Edition (Michigan; Zondervan, 2003) p. 302, teaches that the translation of the infinitive aorist passive tense of the verb λυω (luo), to loose, would be to be loosed in English. The word should be textually translated as 'to be committed adultery,' 'make her to be committed adultery', but it does not make sense in English. The meaning is "makes her victim of an act of adultery." In the passive tenses, the person referred to by the verb is the recipient of the action denoted by the verb. If a verb is in a passive voice the subject is receiving the action of the verb. That verb used in the Bible is being translated as if it were an active infinitive of the indicative mode, and it is not. Karl Feyerabend "Langenscheidt Pocket Greek Dictionary" says under the Greek word ποιεω (poieo): to make, do, produce… William Mounce "Basics of Biblical Greek", (p. 417) says under the Greek word αυτος, η, ο: he, she, it, him/her/itself same.

Jesus without Paul of Tarsus

The Exception of the Gospel according to Saint Matthew, Verses 5:32 and 19:9

Verses 5:32 and 19:9 of the Gospel according to Saint Matthew contain an exception to the rule of divorce. They seem to establish that the case of fornication is the only exception to the general rule that says that the man or the wife who divorces his spouse commits adultery.

The Bibles with which I work in this book use different words to translate this exception.[134]

The best word to translate it is "fornication." It refers to the forbidden sexual acts and unions contained in the book Leviticus Chapter 18. We will see this from the following analysis.

The Greek word that should be translated as fornication is Πορνεια (porneia) and it is used in Verses 5:32 and 19:10 of the Gospel according to Saint Matthew mean.

Richard Goodrich and Lukaszewski Albert "A Reader's Greek New Testament" says under Verse 5:32, Greek word μοιχευθηναι (moicheuthenai), note 78, that the Greek word μοιχευω (moicheuo) means: I commit adultery. - Max Zerwick "Analysis Philologica Novi Testamenti Graeci", says under Verse 5:32 μοιχευθηναι (moicheuthenai): inf. aor. pass. μοδηιχευω (moicheuo) τινα (tina), adulterium committo cum, pass. Seducer ad adult. –

[134] The Greek word translated in the N.A.B. as 'unlawful marriage' is πορνεια (porneia). This word has been translated in different ways. The Latin Vulgate uses the Latin word fornicatio to translate this word. The King James Version uses the word fornication. The Revised Standard Version Second Catholic Edition uses the word unchastity. The New American Bible uses the words marriage is unlawful. The New American Standard Bible uses the word unchastity. The New International Version uses the words marital unfaithfulness. The English Standard Version uses the words sexual immorality.

Ruy Barraco Mármol

It cannot be deduced from the Gospel according to Saint Matthew what the Greek word πορνεια (porneia) means. However, it can be deduced from it that it does not mean adultery.[135]

---

[135] In the same verses in which the exception of πορνεια (porneia) is established the Gospel according to Saint Matthew uses different words to refer to adultery. These different Greek words used in the same verses to refer to adultery are μοιχευθηναι (moicheuthenai) and μοιχται (moichatai) in verse 5:32 of the Gospel according to Saint Matthew, and μοιχαται (moichatai) in verse 19:9 of the Gospel according to Saint Matthew. The Greek word πορνεια (porneia) is used in both verses to refer to a different act which is translated as "fornication." That is also the case of Verse 15:19 in which the Gospel according to Saint Matthew uses the word πορνεια (porneia) with a meaning different from adultery. The Gospel according to Saint Matthew (N.A.B.) says: "*15:19 From the heart come evil thoughts, murder, adultery, unchastity, theft, false witness, blasphemy.*"[135] [135] The Greek word μοιχειαι (moicheiai) is used for "adultery" and πορνεια (porneia) to refer to another act, which is improperly translated as "unchastity." The list of forbidden acts is very similar to the list of commandments of Moses as repeated by Jesus as quoted in Mark 10:19, except that after adultery, is added the act πορνεια (porneia) improperly translated in the N.A.B. as fornication in this verse; and after false witness is βλασφημιαι (blasphemiai) translated in the N.A.B. as blasphemy. The fact that adultery and unchastity (translation of the Greek word πορνεια porneia), are listed separately indicates that the two words do not refer to the same act, which means that fornication does not refer to or mean adultery. The word translated as unchastity here by the New American Bible is the same Greek word πορνεια (porneia) translated as unlawful marriage in Verses 5:32 and 19:9. The Greek word translated as adultery is a different word. The fact that adulterous conduct is included in the listing, even though the list also includes the the Greek word πορνεια (porneia), translated as unchastity, implies that fornication or πορνεια (porneia) has a meaning different from adultery. The Gospel according to Saint Mark (N.A.B.) uses the word πορνεια (porneia) in Verse 7:21 saying: "*7:21 From within people, from their hearts, come evil thoughts, unchastity, theft, murder, adultery, greed, malice, deceit, licentiousness, envy, blasphemy, arrogance, folly.*" The word translated as unchastity in this text of the N.A.B., is also the Greek word πορνεια (porneia). In this verse, the act of unchastity is not even consecutive to adulterous conduct, confirming the conclusion that says the concept of unchastity, the word used to translate the Greek word πορνεια (porneia), is different from the concept of adultery.

In addition, not only can we deduce that it does not mean adultery, we can also deduce that the exception stated in the Gospel according to Saint Matthew is related to the question formulated by the Pharisees to Christ in Verse 19:3 of the Gospel according to Saint Matthew (N.A.B.), that says: "..."*Is it lawful for a man to divorce his wife for any cause whatever?*"" The answer given by Christ is formulated considering the question, which is talking about the divorce for any cause whatever. The answer states the exception of πορνεια (porneia), because the question includes that expression 'for any cause whatever'.

The Gospel according to Saint Mark, Verse 10:1, confirms this conclusion, because it narrates the same event, but omits the part of the question of the Pharisees that says 'for any cause whatever', and omits the exception in the answer. That clearly indicates that the exception mentioned by Christ is related to that part of the question, but this still does not tell us what the meaning of the Greek word πορνεια (porneia) is.

The Gospel according to Saint John uses the Greek word πορνεια (porneia) in Verse 8:41. It says (N.A.B.): "*8:41 You are doing the works of your father!*"(So) they said to him, "*We are not illegitimate. We have one father, God.*" *8:42 Jesus said to them, "if God were your Father, you would love me, for I came from God and am here; I did not come on my own, but he sent me.*" The word translated as illegitimate, in the text of the N.A.B., is πορνεια (porneia). I understand that the word is being used symbolically with the meaning of unfaithfulness to God.

The book of Revelation also uses the word πορνεια (porneia) with the symbolical meaning of unfaithfulness

Ruy Barraco Mármol

to God or idolatry, in Verses 2:21, 9:21, 17:2, 17:4, 18:3 and 19:2.

Unfaithfulness to God is a possible meaning of the word. However it does not relate to the part of the question found in Verse 19:3 of the Gospel according to Saint Matthew, that says 'for any cause whatever', which we know is related to the answer, because it was omitted along with the exception in the Gospel according to Saint Mark.

Besides, in the Gospel according to Saint John, Verse 8:41, where this word is used with the symbolical meaning of being unfaithful to God, Jesus is talking to Pharisees, and speaking of the Pharisees who did not believe in him. Jesus was not saying with the teaching about divorce that all their wives can divorce them because they were being unfaithful to God. In the Gospel according to Saint Mark, Verse 6:24, Jesus talks about those who serve money, saying that you cannot serve God and money. Those who serve money are also unfaithful to God, and Jesus was not saying that a wife can divorce her husband in the case he was serving money, which means that unfaithfulness to God is not the meaning with which this word is being used in this exception.

The book of Acts of the Apostles uses the word three times. The first time is in Verse 15:20, the second time is in Verse 15:28 and the third time is in Verse 21:25.

Verse 15:20 of the book of Acts of the Apostles (N.A.B.) says: "15:20 but tell them by letter to avoid pollution from idols, unlawful marriage, the meat of strangled animals, and blood." The Greek word translated by the New American Bible as 'unlawful marriage' in this verse, and in those following, is also Πορνεια (porneia).

Verse 15:28 of the book of Acts of the Apostles (N.A.B.) says: "*15:28 'It is the decision of the holy Spirit and of us not to place on you any burden beyond these necessities, 15:29 namely, to abstain from meat sacrificed to idols, from blood, from the meat of strangled animals, and from unlawful marriage. If you keep free of these, you will be doing what is right. Farewell.'*"

Verse 21:25 of the book of Acts of the Apostles (N.A.B.) says: "*21:25 As for the Gentiles who have come to believe, we sent them our decision that they abstain from meat sacrificed to idols, from blood, from the meat of strangled animals, and from unlawful marriage.*"

Verse 15:20 narrates the opportunity in which the apostles and presbyters decided which burdens should be laid on the Gentile Converts. They decided that the burdens should be very similar to the ones laid on the aliens residing among the Jews. Verse 15:28 is part of the epistle which resulted from that decision, and Verse 21:25 refers to that epistle. This epistle is only found in the book of Acts of the Apostles.

The similarity between the burdens, which indicates that the apostles and presbyters were considering the burdens that laid on the aliens residing among Jews to make their decision, gives us a very strong reason to think that the Greek word Πορνεια (porneia), the name of the last burden laid by the apostles on the Gentile Converts, refers to the illicit sexual unions and illicit marriages of the Bible, book of Leviticus, Chapter 18, that are altogether the last of the four burdens laid on

Ruy Barraco Mármol

the aliens residing among the Jews. It makes also a lot of sense that they had laid very similar burdens on those very similar cases. The old case: The aliens, or Gentiles, residing among Jews. The new case: the Gentile converts. This meaning should prevail over the symbolical meaning of unfaithfulness to God.

The first burden laid in the book of Leviticus (N.A.B.), Verse 17:8, on the Jews and aliens residing among them, is the obligation to bring any holocaust[136] or sacrifice offered, to the entrance of the meeting tent. In the book of Acts of the Apostles (N.A.B.) Verse 15:29 the first burden laid on the Gentile Converts is the obligation to abstain from meat sacrificed to the idols. These are the only burdens that have significant differences between them. However the difference can be explained because Christ said that he wants mercy not sacrifice, because doing sacrifices is not part of the New Covenant.[137] I believe that, for this reason, the apostles left aside the question of the holocaust and focused on prohibiting Christians from eating meat sacrificed to the idols.

The second burden laid in the book of Leviticus (N.A.B.), Verse 17:10, on the Jews and aliens residing among them, is the obligation to abstain from partaking of any blood. In the book of Acts of the Apostles (N.A.B.) Verse 15:29 the second burden laid on the Gentile Converts is the obligation to abstain from blood.

---

[136] The Holocaust was a type of sacrifice, which was a religious rite.

[137] The Gospel according to Saint Matthew Verses 9:13 and 12:7.

The third burden laid in the book of Leviticus (N.A.B.), Verse 17:15, on the Jews and aliens residing among them, is to abstain from animals that died of themselves or were killed by a wild beast.[138] The third burden laid on the Gentile Converts in the book of Acts of the Apostles (N.A.B.) Verse 15:29 is the obligation to abstain from meat of strangled animals.

The fourth burden laid in the book of Leviticus, Chapter 18 (N.A.B.) on the Jews and aliens residing among them is to abstain from certain illicit sexual unions and illicit marriages. The fourth burden laid on the Gentile Converts in the book of Acts of the Apostles (N.A.B.) Verse 15:29 is the obligation to abstain from fornication.

The order in which the burdens are exposed by the apostles in the epistle is not casual. In Verse 15:20 of the book of Acts of the Apostles, before the epistle was written, the apostles present the burdens in a different order. When the apostles wrote the epistle, Verse 15:28, they made the burdens match the order of the burdens imposed in the book of Leviticus. This fact also supports the argument that says that the Greek word Πορνεια (porneia) refers to the illicit sexual unions and marriages of the book of Leviticus 18.[139]

---

[138] The Bible, book of Deuteronomy, (N.K.J.V.) says: "14:21 "You shall not eat anything that dies of itself; you may give it to the alien who is within your gates, that he may eat it, or you may sell it to a foreigner, for you are a holy people to the LORD your GOD. You shall not boil a young goat in its mother's milk."

[139] The Bible (N.A.B.), book of Leviticus, says: "18:1 The LORD said to Moses, 18:2 "Speak to the Israelites and tell them: I, the Lord, am your God. 18:3 You shall not do as they do in the land of Egypt, where you once lived, nor shall you do as they do in the land of Canaan, where I am bringing you; do not conform to their customs. 18:4 My decrees you shall carry out, and my statutes you shall take care to follow. I,

Ruy Barraco Mármol

Translating the word πορνεια (porneia) with the meaning of the illicit sexual unions and marriages listed

---

the Lord, am your God. _18:5 Keep, then, my statutes and decrees, for the man who carries them out will find life through them._ I am the Lord. 18:6 "None of you shall approach a close relative to have sexual intercourse with her. I am the Lord. 18:7 You shall not disgrace your father by having intercourse with your mother. Besides, since she is your own mother, you shall not have intercourse with her. 18:8 You shall not have intercourse with your father's wife, for that would be a disgrace to your father. 18:9 You shall not have intercourse with your sister, your father's daughter or your mother's daughter, whether she was born in your own household or born elsewhere. 18:10 You shall not have intercourse with your son's daughter or with your daughter's daughter, for that would be a disgrace to your own family. 18:11 You shall not have intercourse with the daughter whom your father's wife bore to him, since she, too, is your sister. 18:12 You shall not have intercourse with your father's sister, since she is your fathers relative. 18:13 You shall not have intercourse with your mother's sister, since she is your mother's relative. 18:14 You shall not disgrace your father's brother by being intimate with his wife, since she, too, is your aunt. 18:15 You shall not have intercourse with your daughter-in-law; she is your son's wife, and therefore you shall not disgrace her. 18:16 You shall not have intercourse with your brother's wife, for that would be a disgrace to your brother. 18:17 You shall not have intercourse with a woman and also with her daughter, nor shall you marry and have intercourse with her son's daughter or her daughter's daughter; this would be shameful, because they are related to her. 18:18 While your wife is still living you shall not marry her sister as her rival; for thus you would disgrace your first wife. 18:19 "You shall not approach a woman to have intercourse with her while she is unclean from menstruation. 18:20 You shall not have carnal relations with your neighbor's wife, defiling yourself with her. 18:21 You shall not offer any of your offspring to be immolated to Molech, thus profaning the name of your God. I am the Lord. 18:22 You shall not lie with a male as with a woman; such a thing is an abomination. 18:23 You shall not have carnal relations with an animal, defiling yourself with it; nor shall a woman set herself in front of an animal to mate with it; such things are abhorrent. 18:24 "Do not defile yourselves by any of these things by which the nations whom I am driving out of your way have defiled themselves. 18:25 Because their land has become defiled, I am punishing it for its wickedness, by making it vomit out its inhabitants. 18:26 You, however, whether natives or resident aliens, must keep my statutes and decrees forbidding all such abominations 18:27 by which the previous inhabitants defiled the land; 18:28 otherwise the land will vomit you out also for having defiled it, just as it vomited out the nations before you 18:29 Everyone who does any of these abominations shall be cut off from among his people. 18:30 Heed my charge, then, not to defile yourselves by observing the abominable customs that have been observed before you. I, the Lord, am your God." (Underline emphasis is mine) in the book of Leviticus, Chapter 18, two possible interpretations come forth from the exception mentioned in the Gospel according to Saint Matthew in the matter of divorce.

The first interpretation says that the exception established by the word πορνεια (porneia), would be the one that says it is licit to divorce and marry again, when the other spouse commits a conduct described in Leviticus 18.

From the expression that says that saving the act of fornication, whoever divorces his spouse and gets married again commits adultery, it would be inferred that in the case of divorce because of fornication the spouses may get married again without committing adultery.

However, under this interpretation it makes no sense the distinction made by Christ with regard to the spouse who divorced his or her husband or wife and the spouse divorced by his husband or wife; the exception established has no relation with the part of the question that says for any cause whatever, that I explained seems to be related; and also it would leave out other exceptions that seem more justified than some of the conducts listed in Leviticus 18. It does not make sense for instance that a woman whose husband had sexual relationships with a neighbor's wife, can divorce and marry again and, for instance, a wife who is a victim of violence cannot.

The second interpretation says that it is not licit to divorce from a spouse with no reason whatever unless the marriage has taken place between persons who are forbidden in the Bible, book of Leviticus, Chapter 18, to

Ruy Barraco Mármol

have sexual union or to get married; for instance, a marriage between a father and a daughter. In those cases divorce is authorized. Indeed, it is commanded.

This interpretation explains the exception referred to by Christ while answering the question formulated to him by the Pharisees. Because it makes sense to say that it is not licit to divorce from a spouse for any reason whatever, except when the marriage involves for instance a father and a daughter.

The Exceptions to the General Rule of Marriage Indissolubility

The fact that Jesus established a general rule of marriage indissolubility does not mean not mean that spouses are not allowed to consider themselves divorced in some cases, or that exceptions are not allowed.

In the first place because Jesus made the distinction between the spouse who divorces his wife or husband and the spouse divorced by his husband or wife. This distinction teaches that the spouse divorced by her or his husband or wife that gets married again does not commit adultery. Let us remember that when one spouse commits an offense or a serious of offenses that because of their seriousness may make impossible the continuation of marriage, or unreasonable to keep the victim bound to the obligations of marriage, the victim of this or these acts may consider himself or herself indirectly divorced by his or her spouse.

In the second place because one of the

commandments of God is "you shall not kill"; nevertheless, homicide in self-defense is permitted and licit. The same way that this exception is licit and permitted, there are other general causes of justification that apply to other commandments that forbid acts, and that command acts.

In fact one of the things for which Christ reproached the Pharisees was that they did not understand that the obligation to keep the Sabbath sometimes was overruled by a more important obligation, and that they did not use their judgment to avoid condemning innocent people.

The Gospel according to Saint Matthew (N.A.B.) says: "*12:1 At that time Jesus was going through a field of grain on the sabath. His disciples were hungry and began to pick the heads of grain and eat them. 12:2 When the Pharisees saw this, they said to him, "See, your disciples are doing what is unlawful to do on the sabbath." 12:3 He said to them, "Have you not read what David did when he and his companions were hungry, 12:4 how he went into the house of God and ate the bread of offering, which neither he nor his companions but only the priests could lawfully eat? 12:5 Or have you not read in the law that on the sabbath the priests serving in the temple violate the sabbath and are innocent? 12:6 I say to you, something greater than the temple is here. 12:7 If you knew what this meant, 'I desire mercy, not sacrifice', you would not have condemned these innocent men. 12:8 For the Son of Man is Lord of the sabbath.""* Christ asked for mercy to understand this and not to condemn the innocent.

The Gospel according to Saint Matthew (N.A.B.) says: "*5:21 You have heard that it was said to your ancestors, 'You shall not kill; and whoever kills will be liable to judgment;"* and nobody intends because of this to exclude the exception of homicide in legitimate defense.

Then the statements of the Gospels quoted do not close the doors to the admission of exceptions in Christianity to the general rule of indissolubility in marriage. The question is: Should Christianity accept any? And the answer is yes. Which ones? The exceptions that justice and mercy rule. Personally I have no doubt that there are cases in which it is licit for a spouse to separate, and after a prudent lapse of time, it is licit for him to marry again.

A good example of a case in which it would be licit to separate and marry again would be the case in which one spouse is a threat to the life of the other, or to their children. In either of those cases, I personally do not have any doubt that it is licit for the victim to consider himself divorced in an indirect way or, if somebody prefers, to separate, divorce, and get married again. Another example is the case of adultery. I have no doubt that it is licit for the victim of adultery to consider himself divorced by the guilty spouse, to separate, divorce and remarry. This exception even has, in my opinion, other biblical basis.

The Gospel according to Saint Matthew (N.A.B.) says: "*1:18 Now this is how the birth of Jesus Christ came about. When his mother Mary was betrothed to Joseph, but before they lived together, she was found with child through the Holy Spirit. 1:19 Joseph her husband, since he was a righteous man, yet unwilling to expose her to the shame, decided to divorce her quietly.*" In my opinion, it comes forth from these expressions that an upright man can think of divorce in case of adultery, and even proceed to divorce himself from his spouse, and of course get married again; and that means in my opinion that it is licit to do it.

The Bible (N.A.B.), book of the prophet Jeremiah, says: "*3:1 If a man sends away his wife and, after leaving him, she marries another man, Does the first husband come back to her? Would not the land be wholly defiled? But you have sinned with many lovers, and yet you would return to me! says the Lord.*"

I believe that we must forgive every sin, and that it may be the best thing to do sometimes to continue the marriage despite this serious offense against it, but the continuation of the marriage cannot be imposed in this case; and I also believe that Christ did not forbid the victim of the divorce to get married again.

This interpretation is strongly supported by the fact that Christ says that whoever divorces himself from his wife or husband and gets married again commits adultery, but it does not say anything about the one that is victim of that divorce. If both cases were the same, there would have not been any need to specify. Obviously, in the reverse case the innocent spouse does not commit adultery.

Concubinage

Some interpret that the exception in which divorce is permitted, mentioned in the Gospel according to Saint Matthew, refers not to unlawful marriage, but to concubinage (cohabitation without a general commitment of staying united until death).

However, in addition to the analysis made before, and to the fact that there is no basis to support that interpretation, the exception would not make sense, because a man and a woman living united together without being formally married, on the contrary, have the obligation not to separate. God's will is that the man leaves his father and mother to unite to a woman, and neither the man, nor the woman, separates this union. It is not up to men or women to unite in a different way, with other rules. This does not mean that such a union must be imposed in the name of God, but it does mean that Christ did not say that those who unite with others in violation of God's will are allowed to separate precisely because they acted against God's will.

The Bible (N.A.B.), book of Exodus, says: "*22:15 When a man seduces a virgin who is not betrothed, and lies with her, he shall pay her marriage price and marry her.*"

Let us remember that marriage is a natural institution, which existed since the beginning, that the ceremonies are a later creation, and that the obligations of marriage exist before the creation of the ceremony, and independently of it.

By the way, the position about concubinage and the obligation of the concubines to stay united until death are very important for the marital institution. People avoid the ceremony of marriage to escape marital obligations. The right interpretation of this matter could contribute to the promotion of marriage because by avoiding the rite of marriage, people would not be avoiding the obligations of marriage.

What Led then the Catholic Church and Other Christian Churches to Be So Closed and Unmerciful in the Matter of Divorce?

The Epistles of Paul led to this. Paul with no authority whatsoever to command, (he did not even have the authority of Peter, nor of the council, nor of the assembly of Christians), talking falsely in the name of God, established an exception that is contrary to the doctrine of Christ, that had the effect of installing in Christianity the idea that no other exceptions are allowed other than the one he established.

The First Epistle of Paul to the Corinthians (N.A.B.) says: "*7:10 To the married, however, I give this instruction (not I, but the Lord): A wife should not separate from her husband- 7:11 and If she does separate she must either remain single or become reconciled to her husband- and a husband should not divorce his wife. 7:12 To the rest I say (not the Lord): If any brother has a wife who is an unbeliever, and she is willing to go on living with him, he should not divorce her; 7:13 and if any woman has a husband who is an unbeliever, and he is willing to go on living with her, she should not divorce her husband. 7:14 For the unbelieving husband is made holy through his wife, and the unbelieving wife is made holy through the brother. Otherwise your children would be unclean, whereas in fact they are holy. 7:15 If the unbeliever separates, however, let him separate. The brother or sister is not bound in such cases: God has called you to peace. 7:16 For how do you know, wife, whether you will save your husband; or how do you know, husband, whether you will save your wife?*"

The exception I am talking about is stated in Verse

Ruy Barraco Mármol

7:15. When he says that in the case in which the unbeliever spouse separates the brother or sister is not bound, he is suggesting and implying that the general rule is that the victims of divorce are bound to their spouses; that in all the other cases the innocent spouses who are victims of the divorces remain bound to their spouses.

The influence of the words of Paul in the interpretation of the Gospel of Christ led the Catholic Church and many other Christian Churches to their present position about divorce and new marriage after divorce, which does not admit the exceptions it should, and has hurt so many people, Christianity and society in general.

In addition, the exception of Paul is, in my opinion, opposed to the teachings of Christ. Christ came to strengthen the idea of marriage indissolubility that admits exception, but, in my opinion, not this one.

The mere separation of the nonbeliever spouse does not untie the Christian spouse from his marital obligations. I do not say here, that divorce would not be justified after a prudent lapse of time, or if the unbeliever spouse is having a relationship with another person. I am not talking about those cases. What I am saying is that until the occurrence of a relevant fact, as serious as the ones mentioned, the spouse is obligated in marriage according to the doctrine of Christ.

In any case, whether the exception of Paul is or is not against Christ's doctrine with this regard just discussed, this First Epistle of Paul to the Corinthians, Verse 7:15, closes the doors to other exceptions and gives place to the unmerciful rule that prohibits the spouse who is the victim of divorce from getting married again.

Correctly interpreting the Bible, only the spouse guilty of divorce commits adultery if he gets married again. Then the ministers would only have reasons to abstain from witnessing a marriage of a spouse guilty of his divorce. They would have no reason whatsoever to abstain from witnessing the marriage of a spouse who was a victim of a divorce and is getting married again. Moreover, since the matter of marital relationships is so hard to judge, the judgment of them should be reserved to God. The ministers neither need to, nor must, nor can, judge in each case which spouse is guilty of the divorce or which spouse should be allowed to get married again or make use the sacraments. This is not the mission of the ministers.

Ministers should consent and witness the celebration of the new weddings according to the Christian rite and of course allow the divorced Christians to make use of the sacraments, respecting their right of presumption of innocence. If someone, who should not have, gets married again, or uses the sacraments, God will do justice to him.

This would not adversely affect the Church in any way; to the contrary. The nonjudgmental attitude would be very good for it. What really harms the Church is the general prohibition, that unfairly affects the spouses who are victims of divorce from getting married again, which is, by the way, ignored by almost all Christians. Today almost nobody gets married thinking that in case they become victim of a divorce they would stay alone, and refrain from getting married again.

Ruy Barraco Mármol

In addition, it is my opinion also, that the spouse guilty of divorce does not commit adultery when his ex-spouse has already gotten married again, because people can only commit adultery when they are married. And I believe that when the spouse victim of divorce gets married again, this frees his or her ex-spouse from marital obligations.

Consequences

The wrong position of Christian Churches in the matter of divorce, caused by the errors of the Epistles of Paul, has caused a huge negative effect on people in many ways. How many lives have been damaged! How many lives are still damaged, and what a big damage is still being done to the Christian Church! How many victims of divorce, who married again, are feeling guilty and fallen out of the grace of God, under the deception of Paul! How many victims of divorce refrained from marrying again believing that in this way they were following the word of God! How many people married again disregarding what they believe the word of God is!; disobeying what they believed the word of God is; What a big damage to the obedience of the word of God this wrong teaching has caused!

III.2. Celibacy

Christ chose married men as apostles. Peter, as I remarked, was married. The Apostles chose married men when they chose seven men to assist them. The book of Acts of the Apostles says in Verse 21:8 that

Saint Philip, one of the seven, had four unmarried daughters who prophesied.

It is true that ministers, on certain occasions, long journeys or persecutions for instance, may find themselves with more freedom and less vulnerable if they are single; but it is also true that sometimes, in other circumstances, they may not.

Moreover, in general, ministers are more vulnerable being unmarried than married, because of the necessity of being married that comes from human nature. And I said necessity of being married, and not necessity of having sexual union, because the necessity of being married goes much farther than the mere necessity of having sexual union.

With regard to soldiers, it could also be said that on some occasions they could be more free and less vulnerable if they were single; and nobody would think about imposing celibacy in the army, especially if becoming a soldier is going to be voluntary.

In my opinion, there is nothing wrong with ministers choosing celibacy. On the contrary, I find it admirable. But I think that celibacy should always remain as a choice for ministers. They should always be allowed to get married. I also believe that for those who are not ministers temporary privation of sexual union is a spiritually good practice, as well as other kinds of temporary abstinence.

However, the imposition of unlimited celibacy on ministers is one of the biggest errors of the Catholic Church. It is the principal cause of the insufficient number of ministers. Celibacy causes the loss of many good ministers, who do not decide to become ministers because of this imposition. The number of ministers that the Catholic Church loses gets incremented because the Catholic Church makes many of its potential ministers believe that they are not called to be ministers because they do not have an inclination to celibacy.

Moreover, the imposition of unlimited celibacy is also the cause of the negative profile and the falling of many of the number of the bad ministers.

The Gospel according to Saint Matthew (N.A.B.) says: "*9:37 Then he said to his disciples, "The harvest is abundant but the laborers are few; 9:38 so ask the master of the harvest to send out laborers for his harvest.""* Laborers are not very easy to find. We should not allow ourselves to dispense of the good persons that do not become ministers because of the imposition of celibacy.

In the Bible, book of Genesis 2:18, God says that it is not good for man to be alone. The teachings of Paul, against this revelation, have caused an enormous damage to many people, to society and to Christianity.

As I said, Christ chose married men as apostles and did not impose celibacy. If he had done so, Peter would not have been chosen as an apostle. In the book of Acts of the Apostles (N.A.B.) talking about the apostles it is said: "*1:14 All these devoted themselves with one accord to prayer, together with some women, and Mary the mother of Jesus, and his brothers.*" The Gospel according to Saint Luke (N.A.B.) says: "*8:1 Afterward he journeyed from one town and village to another, preaching and proclaiming the good news of the kingdom of God. Accompanying him were the Twelve and some women who had been cured of evil spirits and infirmities, Mary, called Magdalene, from whom seven demons had gone out, 8:3 Joanna, the wife of Herod's steward Chuza, Susanna, and many others who provided them out of their resources."*

From the words of the Gospel according to Saint Matthew, Verses 19:10-12, it cannot be concluded that Christ was in favor of celibacy. The Gospel according to Saint Matthew (N.A.B.) says: *"19:10 [His] disciples said to him, "If that is the case of a man and his wife, it is better not to marry." 19:11 He answered, "Not all can accept (this) word, but only those to whom it is granted. 19:12 Some are incapable of marriage because they were born so; some, because they were made so by others; some because they have renounced marriage for the sake of the kingdom of heaven. Whoever can accept this ought to accept it."* The note of the N.A.B. recognizes that the literal translation of the word they translate as <u>incapable of marriage</u> would be "eunuchs." The literal translation of the Gospel according to Saint Matthew, according to the N.A.B. would be something like: *"19:10 [His] disciples said to him, "if that is the case of a man and his wife, it is better not to marry." 19:11 he answered, "Not all can accept [this] word, but only those to whom is granted. 19:12 Some are eunuchs because they were born so; some because they were made so by others; some because they have made themselves eunuchs for the sake of the kingdom of heaven. Whoever can accept this ought to accept it."* The eunuchs were men castrated.

The Greek word translated by the New American Bible as incapable of marriage is ευνουχοι (eunouchoi). The King James Version, the Revised Standard Version, Second Catholic Edition, the New American Standard Bible, the New International Version, and the English

Standard Version translate this word as eunuchs.

These words of Christ cannot be construed as supporting celibacy, because precisely they were said in support of men and women who decided to get married in spite of the general rule of indissolubility that governs the institution. In my opinion, what Christ says in these verses is that getting married and recognizing the general rule of indissolubility are worthy for the sake of God's reign.

Catholic celibacy, in the way is established, is a product of some statements of the Epistles of Paul, which have caused a great damage to the Christian Church.

It is true that married people, especially with children, are more exposed to society; but who says that this is bad? Being exposed, it is harder for ministers to present themselves as superior men in the matters of morality and knowledge. Interacting with others, their wrongdoings and intellectual errors are exposed.

I think the admission by all the Christians Churches of the marriage of ministers would give a spectacular impulse to Christianity.

Christian doctrine about celibacy would have been different if it not were for Paul, and his epistles.

III. 3. Women Ministers

Christ did not choose women as apostles. That fact is a good reason to think carefully about doing otherwise. However, Christ never gave a reason for this; as mentioned earlier, he did have women followers and supporters, who accompanied him and his disciples;

and there were cultural reasons at the time that justified his choice, that today do not exist.

Furthermore, the incorporation of the women into the Christian ministry, especially after the end of the negative imposition of celibacy, seems to me very advisable, and could give Christianity and women's rights a very big impulse all over the world. This impulse could even influence the Islamic world, with significant consequences for international peace and fraternity.

There is no doubt that women have no natural, moral or intellectual incapacity that prevents them from being ministers. And as I said in point II.1 of this book there have been women prophets, and there was at least one woman judge in the times of the Israelite judges.

I believe Christian doctrine about this matter would have been different if it had not been for Paul, and his epistles.

Ruy Barraco Mármol

Chapter IV.
Paul False Prophet

There are strong arguments to sustain that Paul wrote the epistles that are attributed to him. The fact that Paul wrote the epistles that we know as Epistles of Paul seems very well proved. Except for the case of the Epistle of Paul to the Hebrews, in my opinion there are no serious doubts about any of the others. There are people who do not recognize some of them, but they do recognize others that allow us to conclude that Paul was a false prophet. And if he was a false prophet, it is most likely that he was the author of all the epistles attributed to him.

A false prophet is one who says he has had divine dreams, or has heard the word of God, when he has not had those dreams, or has not heard the word of God.[140] Paul said his words were the word of God and they were not. We know that because they were full of errors. That makes him a false prophet.

Paul said that he had seen Christ,[141] that Christ had

---

[140] The Bible, book of the prophet Jeremiah, (N.K.J.V.) says: "23:25 I have heard what the prophets have said who prophesy lies in My name, saying, 'I have dreamed, I have dreamed!' 23:26 "How long will this be in the heart of the prophets who prophesy lies? Indeed they are prophets of the deceit of their own heart,"

[141] The First Epistle of Paul to the Corinthians (N.K.J.V.) says: "9:1 Am I not an apostle? Am I not free? Have I not seen Jesus our Lord? Are you not my work in the Lord?"

Ruy Barraco Mármol

appeared to him[142] and that he was instructed by Christ and not by the Apostles.[143] He also said that he was snatched to the third heaven, and that he heard words that cannot be uttered.[144] He said that Christ speaks in him.[145] He said he was preaching the word of God;[146] that he was revealing the mystery of the Gospel;[147] that he gave instructions in the name of Jesus.[148]

---

[142] The First Epistle of Paul to the Corinthians (N.R.S.V.) says: "*15:8 Then last of all He was seen by me also, as by one born out of due time.*" When did Paul see Christ? Before Christ ascended to Heaven? In which case Paul would have persecuted the Christian Church having seen Christ personally. Or After the ascension of Christ to Heaven? Was not Christ only going to be seen again in the end of times?

[143] The Epistle of Paul to the Galatians (N.K.J.V.) says: "*1:11. But I make known to you, brethren, that the gospel which was preached by me is not according to man; 1:12 For I neither received it from man, nor was I taught it, but It came through the revelation of Jesus Christ.*"

[144] The Second Epistle of Paul to the Corinthians (N.K.J.V.) says: "*12:2 I know a man in Christ who fourteen years ago-whether in the body I do not know. or whether out of the body I do not know, God knows-such a one was caught up to the third heaven. 12:3 And I know such a man—whether in the body or out of the body I do not know, God knows- 12:4 how he was caught up into Paradise and heard inexpressible words, which it is not lawful for a man to utter.*"

[145] The Second Epistle of Paul to the Corinthians (N.K.J.V.) says: "*13:3 since you seek a proof of Christ speaking in me, who is not weak toward you, but mighty in you.*"

[146] The First Epistle of Paul to the Thessalonians (N.K.J.V.) says: "*2:13 For this reason we also thank God without ceasing, because when you received the word of God which you heard from us, you welcomed it not as the word of men, but as it is truth, the word of God, which also effectively works in you who believe.*"

[147] The Epistle of Paul to the Ephesians (N.K.J.V.) says: "*6:19: and for me, that utterance may be given to me, that I may open my mouth boldly to make known the mystery of the gospel, 6:20 for which I am an ambassador in chains; as I ought to speak.*"

[148] The First Epistle of Paul to the Thessalonians (N.K.J.V.) says: "*4:1 Finally*

And he had his doctrine taught and transmitted, and his letters read in all the churches,[149] to teach, for refutation, to correct and train, saying that in that way the man of God may be fully competent and equipped for every good work.[150]

Nevertheless his doctrine was full of errors, which means that it was not true that he was a prophet. He did not preach the word of God, and he intentionally led the Christians to consider his preaching as if it were. All these make him a false prophet.

---

then, brethren, we urge and exhort in the Lord Jesus that you should abound more and more, just as you received from us how you ought to walk and to please God; 4:2 for you know what commandments we gave you through the Lord Jesus."

[149] The Epistle of Paul to the Colossians (N.K.J.V.) says: "4:16 Now when this epistle is read among you, see that it is read also in the church of the Laodiceans, and that you likewise read the epistle from Laodicea. 4:17 And say to Archippus, "Take heed of the ministry which you have received in the Lord, that you may fulfill it.""

[150] The Second Epistle of Paul to Timothy (N.K.J.V.) says: "3:16 All Scripture is given by inspiration of God, and is profitable for doctrine, for reproof, for correction, for instruction in righteousness, 3:17 that the man of God may be complete, thoroughly equipped for every good work."

Ruy Barraco Mármol

Chapter V.
Paul Inspired by the Devil

Since my childhood, I have believed in the existence of the Devil without understanding much about him. The Old and the New Testament talk about the Devil. Christ talked about the Devil. However, it was not until I progressed in the writing of this book, that I think I began to understand some things about him.

The Devil is called Satan, Prince of the Devils, Beelzebul in the Gospel, among other names. In the book of Revelation of the New Testament he is called in many ways as we will see below.

From the Bible it is evident that the Devil is not a sort of opposition to God, in the way evil opposes goodness. He is not the personification of evil. The Bible teaches that he is a being created, as everything else, by God. He is a spiritual being created with greater hierarchy and power than the ordinary angels, with great intelligence and beauty, with capacity to be good, but who chose the wrong way, the evil way.

The Bible, in the book of Ezekiel, talks about the Devil, calling him symbolically King of Tyre. The book of Ezequiel, New American Standard Bible (N.A.S.B.), says: "*28:11 Again the word of the Lord came to me saying, 28:12 "Son of man, take up lamentation over the king of Tyre, and say to him, 'Thus says the Lord God, "You had the seal of perfection, Full of wisdom and perfect beauty. 28:13*

Ruy Barraco Mármol

"You were in Eden, the garden of God; Every precious stone was your covering: The ruby, the topaz, and the diamond; The beryl, the onyx, and the jasper; The lapis lazuli, the turquoise, and the emerald; And the gold, the workmanship of your settings and sockets, Was in you. On the day that you were created They were prepared. 28:14 "You were the anointed cherub who covers [protects], And I placed you there. You were on the holy mountain of God; You walked in the midst of the stones of fire. 28:15 "You were blameless in your ways From the day you were created, Until unrighteousness was found in you,"

The Devil seems to have had the occupation of roaming the earth and patrolling it to accuse and punish the men who sinned. That is why the Gospel according to Saint Luke (N.A.S.B.) says: *"22:31 "Simon, Simon, behold Satan has demanded permission to sift you like wheat, 22:32 but I have prayed for you, that your faith may not fail; and you, when once you have turned again, strengthen your brothers."*

The book of Revelation (N.A.S.B.) says: *"12:9 And the great dragon was thrown down, the serpent of old who is called the devil and Satan, who deceives the whole world; he was thrown down to the earth, and his angels were thrown down with him. 12:10 And I heard a loud voice in heaven, saying, "Now the salvation, and the power, and the kingdom of our God and the authority of His Christ have come, for the accuser of our brethren has been thrown down, who accuses them before our God day and night."*

In the book of Job is the place where I believe the occupation of the Devil is best described. The book of Job (N.A.S.B.) says: *"1:1 There was a man in the Land of Uz, whose name was Job, and that man was blameless, upright, fearing God, and turning away from evil. 1:2 And seven sons and three daughters were born to him. 1:3 His possessions also were 7,000 sheep, 3,000 camels, 500 yoke of oxen, 500 female donkeys, and very many servants; and that man was the greatest of all the men of the east. 1:4 And his sons used to go and hold a feast in the house of each one on his day, and they would send and invite their three sisters to eat and drink with them. 1:5 And it came about, when the days of feasting had completed their cycle, that Job would send and consecrate them, rising up early in the morning and offering burnt offerings according to the number of them all; for Job said, "Perhaps my sons have sinned and cursed God in their hearts." Thus Job did continually. 1:6 Now there was a day when the sons of God came to present themselves before the Lord, and Satan also came among them. 1:7 And the Lord said to Satan, "From where do you come?" Then Satan answered the Lord and said, "From roaming about on the earth and walking around it." 1:8 And the Lord said to Satan, "Have you considered My servant Job? For there is no one like him on the earth, a blameless and upright man, fearing God and turning away from evil." 1:9 Then Satan answered the Lord, "Does Job fear God for nothing? 1:10 "Hast Thou not made a hedge about him and his house and all that he has, on every side? Thou hast blessed the work of his hands, and his possessions have increased in the land. 1:11 "But put forth Thy hand now and touch all that he has; he will surely curse Thee to Thy face." 1:12 Then the Lord said to Satan, "Behold, all that he has is in your power, only do not put forth your hand on him." So Satan departed from the presence of the Lord. 1:13 Now it happened on the day when his sons and his daughters were eating and drinking* wine in their oldest brother's house, 1:14 that a messenger came to Job and said, "The oxen were plowing and the donkeys feeding beside them, 1:15 and the Sabeans attacked and took them. They also slew the servants with the edge of the sword, and I alone have escaped to tell you. 1:16 While he was still speaking, another also came and said, "The fire of God fell from heaven and burned up the sheep and the servants and consumed them, and I alone have escaped to tell you. 1:17 While he was still speaking, another also came and said, "The Chaldeans formed three bands and made a raid on the camels and took them and slew the servants with the edge of the sword; and I alone have escaped to tell you." 1:18 While he was still speaking, another also came and said, "Your sons and your daughters were eating and drinking wine in their oldest brother's house, 1:19 and behold, a great wind came from across the wilderness and struck the four corners of the house, and it fell on the young people and they died; and I alone have escaped to tell you." 1:20 The Job arose and tore his robe and shaved his head, and he fell to the ground and worshiped, 1:21 And he said, "Naked I came from my mother's womb, And naked I shall return there. The Lord gave and the Lord has taken away. Blessed be the name of the Lord. 1:22 Through all this Job did not sin nor did he blame God. 2:1 Again there was a day when the sons of God came to present themselves before the Lord, and Satan also came among them to present himself before the Lord. 2:2 And the Lord said to Satan, "Where have you come from?" Then Satan answered the Lord and said, "From roaming about on the earth, and walking around on it." 2:3 And the Lord said to Satan, "Have you considered My servant Job? For there is no one like him on the earth, a *blameless and upright man fearing God and turning away from evil. And he still holds fast his integrity, although you incited Me against him, to ruin him without cause." 2:4 And Satan answered the Lord and said, "Skin for skin! Yes, all that a man has he will give for his life. 2:5 "However, put forth Thy hand, now, and touch his bone and his flesh; he will curse Thee to Thy face." 2:6 So the Lord said to Satan, "Behold, he is in your power, only spare his life." 2:7 Then Satan went out from the presence of the Lord, and smote Job with sore boils from the sole of his foot to the crown of his head. 2:8 And he took a potsherd to scrape himself while he was sitting among the ashes. 2:9 Then his wife said to him, "Do you still hold fast your integrity? Curse God and die!" 2:10 But he said to her, "You speak as one of the foolish women speaks. Shall we indeed accept good from God and not accept adversity?" In all this Job did not sin with his lips."*

I believe for some reason, it could be envy, the Devil did not limit himself to accusing and punishing with the permission of God, but sinning he started to tempt men. To tempt is not to test but to induce to sin. In the New Testament, the Devil appears tempting Christ with a lot of power.

The number and the importance of the errors of the Epistles of Paul; the conduct of Paul and his background, which do not correspond with those of an Apostle, much less one with the characteristics that Paul attributed to himself; the opposition of his teachings in regard to the teachings of Christ; the nature of some of his teachings; the supernatural signs he carried on to deceive the Christians; the consequences of his errors; lead to the conclusion that he was a false prophet, and not a simple one: one who received his power from the Devil; one inspired by the Devil; maybe, in some way, the Devil himself.

The Gospel according to Saint Matthew (N.A.S.B.) says: "*7:15 "Beware of false prophets, who come to you in sheep's clothing, but inwardly are ravenous wolves. 7:16 "You will know them by their fruits. Grapes are not gathered from thorn bushes, nor figs from thistles, are they? 7:17 "Even so, every good tree bears good fruit; but the bad tree bears bad fruit. 7:18 "A good tree cannot produce bad fruit, nor can a bad tree produce good fruit. 7:19 "Every tree that does not bear good fruit is cut down and thrown into the fire. 7:20 "So then, you will know them by their fruits. 7:21 "Not everyone who says to Me, 'Lord, Lord,' will enter the kingdom of heaven; but he who does the will of My Father who is in heaven. 7:22 "Many will say to Me on that day, 'Lord, Lord, did we not prophesy in Your name, and in Your name cast out demons, and in Your name perform many miracles?' 7:23 "And then I will declare to them, 'I never knew you; Depart from Me, you who practice lawlessness.'"*(Underline emphasis is mine)

V.1.Signs and Wonders

Christ foretold us that false prophets were going to come and be able to make signs and wonders to mislead even the chosen. Then, there is no doubt that a false prophet might have already performed signs and wonders. The Gospel according to Saint Mark (N.A.S.B.), says: "*13:22 for false Christs and false prophets will arise, and will show signs and wonders, in order, if possible, to lead the elect astray. 13:23 "But take heed;*

behold, I have told you everything in advance." The book of Revelation says, in Verse 13:13, that the Second Beast, the false prophet, was going to be able to perform great prodigies.

In the book of Acts of the Apostles, many signs and wonders are attributed to Paul. The calling of Paul occurs when suddenly a light from the sky flashed on him. In the book of Acts of the Apostles, it is said, in Verse 13:11, that he made the magician Elymas temporarily blind, unable so much as to see the sun. In Verse 14:3, that he caused signs and wonders in Iconium. In Verse 14:8, that at Lystra he healed a man who used to sit crippled never having walked. In Verse 16:16, that he made a clairvoyant spirit come out of a slave girl. In Verse 19:6, that he laid his hands on twelve people and the Holy Spirit came down on them and they began to speak in tongues and to utter prophecies. In Verse 19:11, that God worked extraordinary miracles at hands of Paul, so that when handkerchiefs or cloths that had touched his skin were applied to the sick, their diseases were cured and evil spirits departed from them.

In Verse 16:25, it is said that an earthquake liberated him, Silas and other prisoners from a prison in the district of Macedonia.

The fact that Paul, being a false prophet, made signs and wonders in principle indicates that he was inspired and empowered by the Devil.

The Second Epistle of Paul to the Corinthians (N.A.S.B.) says: *"11:14 And no wonder, for even Satan disguises himself as an angel of light."*

Ruy Barraco Mármol

V.2. The Deeds, the Fruits, of Paul

Certainly, the influence of the Jewish Christian religion has been supernaturally great in human history. The moral principles that the Old Testament and the New Testament teach, and the number of secular and nonsecular Jews and Christians who have been educated with them are some of the unequivocal proofs of this. And certainly, there have been a lot of secular and nonsecular Jews and Christians of high moral quality in the world.

But it is also true that, to some extent, although small compared with the goodness the Jewish Christian religion brought, secular and nonsecular Jews and Christians have committed serious errors and sins that have caused great damage in the world. This is in part the consequence of the natural imperfection of men, but in the case of the Christian Church it is also caused to a great extent by Paul who facilitated and promoted those bad actions, which are the kind of bad actions you would expect from somebody inspired by the Devil, or the Devil himself.

The fruits of Paul have been extremely mischievous, and most of their effects still last to the present, producing great harm.

The worst errors and vices of the Catholic Church, and of the Christian Church in general, can trace their source to a greater or lesser extent back to the Epistles of Paul. They would not have been present in the Christian Church to the extent they were and are, if it were not for the action of Paul and his epistles. A good number of them are treated in this book after discussing each error of the epistles, under the title "consequences", but certainly not all. Let us remember some of them.

I explained how Paul by insulting the Jews and the law given by God to Moses, impeded and still impedes the spread of Christianity among them (Points II.18-19).

I explained how Paul by bringing irrationality into the Christian Church, among other errors and vices (II.1,2,3,4,14,26), impeded and still impedes the spread of Christianity among many people.

I explained how Paul by tempting the Christian Church into the intromission in matters of concern only to civil authorities, into the Inquisition (Introduction, II.14; II.15; II.16; II.17 among others), into errors in the matters of freedom, submission, freedom of thought, freedom of religion (II.15,16), divine foundation of authorities and limitation of power of civil authorities (II.17), contradiction of other principles of constitutional democracies, like the capacity of people, impeded and still impedes the spread of Christianity among a lot of people, and the advent of constitutional democracy, which still needs to be spread throughout most of the world (II.13,17).

I explained how Paul has responsibility for the errors of the Christian Church in the matters of Discrimination against women, Women ministry (II.1, V.3.), Divorce (V.1), Approach to sex (II.4), Purpose of richness and mission of people (II.7), Celibacy (V.II), and for the vices of Lack of humility (II.10,11,12,26), Judging and Noting attitude (II.11) that have infected and still infect a lot of secular and nonsecular Christians. I explained how Paul is responsible for the

Ruy Barraco Mármol

bad custom of driving apart Christians who think differently (II.12) and for the mistreatment and despisement of nonchristians (II.10), among others. And I explained how these errors impeded and still impede the spread of Christianity all over the world.

Those who understand the threat that the Muslim International Terrorism poses over the world's sake should be aware that the defeat of this great evil depends on the victory of the values and virtues disregarded by the Epistles of Paul.

International Muslim terrorists exist to the extent and degree they do, because of countries in which submission of all men, discrimination against women, disregard and contempt for freedom in general, and disregard and contempt of freedom of thought, speech and religion in particular are allowed to reign; and people are taught to despise, judge, note, drive apart and punish those who think differently, especially those who are or become Christians or recognize the fundamental individual natural human rights. International Muslim terrorists use general despisement of nonmuslims as a basis for recruiting fanatics, and as a cover-up for their real motives and purposes.

International Muslim terrorists exist, to the extent and degree they do, because of societies in which there is no freedom to love. There is no freedom to love in countries and cultures in which men are forbidden to love those who do not share their same religion, and are taught to despise them, to discriminate against them. There is no freedom to love in countries and cultures in which men are forbidden to get married with someone from another religion.

International Muslim terrorists exist, to the extent and importance they do, because of cultures in which Christianity is forbidden and Islam is imposed, using some of the same errors and vices that Paul introduced into the Christian Church, without which it could not be imposed.

If you are a man coming from a Muslim family, you decide to be Christian, and you are going to be under serious threat because of that, then you are not free to be Christian, you do not have freedom of religion. If you are a Muslim coming from a Muslim family and you are not allowed to exercise your Muslim religion according to your own understanding, you do not have freedom of religion. If you are a Muslim and you are not allowed to believe that the Koran has errors, you do not have freedom of religion. If you are married, you are a woman, and decide to be Christian, and you are going to be under serious threat if you do it, then you are not free to be Christian, and you do not have freedom of religion. If you come from a Muslim family and you are not allowed to have any other religion than the Muslim religion, then you are not Muslim by choice. You are Muslim by imposition. Disregard and contempt of freedom of religion is disregard and contempt of freedom of thought and speech.

International Muslim terrorists exist, to the extent and importance they do, because of the action of the local Muslim terrorists who despise, judge and punish, for instance, those Muslims who decide to change religion, those Muslims who exercise their religion according to their own understanding, or those Muslims who marry nonmuslims, with punishments that could be as severe as death. These local Muslim terrorists, have gained control in some countries of the government and the State.

The local terrorism in Muslim societies is a matter of concern for the international community. I believe that the believers in fundamental individual natural human rights and Christianity should have been taking the same care in having, for instance, Iran recognize the rights of people to institute their authorities, separation of Church and state, freedom of religion, freedom of thought and speech, freedom of love, the principles of international fraternity, equality between men and women, due process, than in keeping this Iran from having nuclear weapons. The key to world peace is constitutional democracy with fundamental individual natural human rights, especially with freedom, with freedom of religion, thought and speech, and with love even for the enemies, which only Christianity teaches.

The Gospels teach us that every single life, every single son of God is important to God. Just as South Africa's apartheid called once for international action against discrimination against black people, today, the action of the local Muslim terrorists requires the same. It is not right to abandon hundreds of millions of people to the Islamic local terrorists and discriminators. This does not mean that we have no choice but to go to war to free them. But it does mean that we must raise our voices and take action to help all those people living in Muslim countries who want freedom to have it. It does mean that there must be international pressure to help them. In that way we will be not only helping them but ourselves.

And when I say people wanting freedom I include Muslims, because I assume that there are Muslims who do not want to impose Muslim religion on anyone; who do not want to impose Muslim religion on their sons, on their spouses, on their neighbors. I assume that there are Muslims, who not only would not hurt or punish, but would even continue to be friend and have relationship with sons, spouses or neighbors who decide not to be Muslim anymore, to be instead Christians; who decide to be Muslim but according to their own understanding of it; who decide to believe that the Koran has errors, or decide to marry a nonmuslim, for instance. I assume that there are Muslims who believe that Christians, just as any other religion of peace, should be allowed to freely preach to everybody all over the world. I assume that there are Muslims who do not want to be terrorists, are not terrorists, and condemn Muslim terrorism. I assume that there are Muslims that do not believe that the believers in fundamental individual human rights and Christians are darkness and are their enemies. I assume that there are Muslims who want to be friend of Christians, Jews, and people of western culture. I assume that there are Muslims who do not want to submit nor be obligated to submit to any other Muslim.

To a great degree the good of today's world and the spread of Christianity depend on the recognition and acknowledgment of those rights and values disregarded and violated by international and local Muslim terrorists.

The defeat of the threat that the secular tyrannies pose over the world depends on this as well. And when I say tyrannies I am including the tyrannies of the majorities. To a great extent the good of the world depends on the defeat of the errors and vices from the Epistles of Paul discussed in this book, and on the recognition of Paul as false prophet.

If constitutional democracies are the key to the well-being of the world we must ask: How are the Christians, Christianity, going to work effectively for the goal of world's sake and the possibility of giving testimony of the word of God freely, while it holds that the Epistles of Paul, with all their errors and vices, are the word of God?

If the recognition of people's right to institute their own authorities is so important for world's sake: How is Christianity going to be able to work effectively for that goal while it holds that the Epistles of Paul, which sustain that all authorities have been instituted by God, are the word of God? How is Christianity going to work effectively against the authorities that commit cruelties in those tyrannies, while it holds that the Epistles of Paul, which sustain that all authorities are servants of God to execute the wrath of God over the wrongdoers, are the word of God? How is Christianity going to work for the limitation of power of the governments, because the authorities have a tendency to abuse their power, while it holds that the Epistles of Paul, that state that the authorities are not a terror to good conduct but to bad conduct, are the word of God?

How is Christianity going to work effectively for freedom of religion, telling people that no Church should be over the civil authorities while it still holds that the Epistles of Paul, which teach that Christians must submit to their religious authorities, are the word of God? How is Christianity going to convince Muslims that no Church should be over the civil authorities, while it still holds that the Epistles of Paul, which say that the spiritual man judges everything and is judged by nobody, and that Christians must judge Christians, are the word of God?

How is Christianity going to work effectively for the recognition of the rights of women while it holds that the Epistles of Paul, that sustain that women must be submissive in everything to their husbands, that no woman should teach or have authority over man, that the head of the woman is her husband, that woman must pray and prophesy with her head veiled "because of the angels", are the word of God?

How is Christianity going to make the Muslims who do it, who despise whoever is not Muslim, understand that it is wrong to do this, while it still holds that the Epistles of Paul that say that the sons of unbelievers are unclean, that call unrighteous those who are not Christians, that command Christians to marry only Christians, based on the prejudice that nonchristians are equal to lawlessness, inequity or darkness, are the word of God?

How is Christianity going to work effectively against the judging attitude of the Muslim fundamentalists, while it still holds that the Epistles of Paul, that not only state that nonchristians are equal to darkness, but also state that Christians should judge Christians, and should expel from among them the drunkards and the wicked Christians, are the word of God?

How is Christianity going to work effectively against the Muslim terrorists while it still holds that the Epistles of Paul, in which Paul says that when he was persecuting, torturing and killing Christians, he was walking blamelessly in the justice of the Law given by God to Moses, are the word of God?

Preventing Christianity from working effectively against those errors and vices was another way with which Paul impeded and still impedes the spread of Christianity among many people.

Distorting Christian doctrine he impeded and impedes many people from seeing the light of the Gospel of Christ, not only in those countries, but in Christian countries too. There are a lot of people in the U.S.A. and in other countries with majority of Christians that cannot see the light of the word of Jesus because of the errors introduced by Paul. Even many Christians do not understand Christ's doctrine and the importance of constitutional democracy because of the Epistles of Paul.

All this should give a good idea as to the great damage Paul and his epistles have caused, and still cause. However, if I had to choose the worst fruit of the Epistles of Paul I would say that it is the following: He is responsible for the fact that the word of Christ was not taught to most of the Christians, especially in the way it was expressed by Christ to the apostles according to the Gospels. Christian ministers should always preach starting from the word of Jesus, while preaching about a subject about which Jesus taught.

With that bad fruit, Paul prevented the word of God from living in the hearts of many men. In that way Paul prevented and prevents many men from learning it, understanding it, and putting it into practice, and impeded and impedes the salvation of many people.

Furthermore, Paul diverted the attention of many Christians, who because of his influence did not pay due attention to the matters that Christ taught us to, and instead led by Paul, put emphasis in matters that Christ did not.

I believe Paul can be recognized as a false prophet by his fruits, and not a simple false prophet, but one inspired by the Devil.

The first goal of the Christian Churches should be to get all members to know the four gospels from the beginning to the end, to promote that all Christians pay due attention to the matters that Christ indicated as most important, and to expunge the doctrine of Paul from the Christian doctrine.

The Christian Church in general and the Catholic Church in particular are in a position to give a spectacular impulsion to Christianity if they carry out these changes, and Christ is ready to assist us in that quest. Christianity must recognize Paul as a false prophet and remain faithful to Jesus. The world needs a faithful to Jesus Christianity.

Ruy Barraco Mármol

Chapter VI.
The Book of Acts of the Apostles

Everything that we have seen up to this moment surely raises questions about the book of Acts of the Apostles. Because the book of Acts of the Apostles says that the Jesus appeared to Paul of Tarsus, to make of him an instrument to bring his name to the gentiles, the kings and the sons of Israel. It says that Paul of Tarsus full of the Holy Spirit made a magician be blind, for instance. And for the reasons explained in this book we know that God did not choose Paul, and we know that neither Jesus, nor the Father, nor the Holy Spirit inspired, guided, nor confirmed the words of the False Apostle Paul. All this was part of the deception of Paul of Tarsus that I have already discussed in this book. The question now is what position should we have regarding the book of Acts of the Apostles, and for that purpose it is convenient to review some aspects about it.

The book of Acts of the Apostles, unlike any other book of the New Covenant, have come to us in two versions of significant different length, one of which is longer than the other in a tenth part: the Western type, which is the longest one, and the Alexandrian type which is the shortest one. Both are regarded as authentic, although the Alexandrian type is the one that modern critical editions follow. This tells us that the original, either one or the other, has been edited. Some say that it has been edited by the same author; although many believe that it was not the same author who did it.

There is also a third type, the Byzantine, however almost all of the scholars seem to believe that it is a later development.

The book could be divided in two parts. The first part tells us about the twelve apostles and the Church in the first times after de death and resurrection of Jesus, and the second part, saying nothing, or very little, about what happened to the twelve afterwards, tells us about the False Apostle Paul. The book starts talking about the twelve to then turn the attention of the reader from the twelve apostles to the False Prophet and False Apostle Paul.

I believe that somebody used authentic and inauthentic sources to write this book for the False Apostle Paul. I do not believe that the editor was just a deceived person. But, this is just a personal opinion. The fact is that it seems to have authentic and inauthentic accounts of facts.

The authorship of the book is attributed to Luke. It is believed that the author of the Gospel is the same author of the book of Acts of the Apostles, among other reasons, because of the introduction of both books, both dedicated to Teophilus.

There are some passages written in the first person plural. These are the so called 'we passages'. They are explained saying that the author was accompanying Paul in those passages, although, in my opinion, the author does not give a proper explanation to them. Anyways, they testify that the author of those passages was not a personal witness of all the other events narrated in the book of Acts, and that he used sources to write about them.

Naturally, the Christians carried on the mission of preserving and transmitting the knowledge of the life and teachings of Jesus and of the Twelve Apostles, so we know that it would have been very hard for someone to make something up about Jesus, but: Can we say the same about Paul? - The Apostles gave testimony of the life and teachings of Jesus, because they were instituted witnesses of it by Jesus, but they could not give testimony of Paul, because they were not present to witness Paul's life and teachings and because naturally they were not instituted witnesses of Paul. This is the big difference between the tradition of the Church regarding Jesus and the Twelve Apostles on one hand and Paul on the other.

The first part of the book of Acts of the Apostles could have had apostolic testimony, but the second part could not, for the simple reason that the apostles were not present when these events happened, and they were neither given commission nor authority to testify about them.

a. About the differences among the supposed calling of the False Apostle Paul

There are three accounts of the story of the calling of the False Apostle Paul in the book of Acts of the Apostles, which have significant differences among them. Before commenting on the matter of the supposed appearance of Jesus after his ascension, I want

Ruy Barraco Mármol

to highlight some of the differences among the accounts, which are principally related to the words attributed to Jesus in them.

Indeed only the first account constitutes an account of the facts of the event. The second and the third are actually accounts of what the False Apostle Paul said about this event, in two different instances.

The book of Acts of the Apostles (N.A.S.B.) says: "*9:1 Now Saul, still breathing threats and murder against the disciples of the Lord, went to the high priest, 9:2 and asked for letters from him to the synagogues at Damascus, so that if he found any belonging to the Way, both men and women, he might bring them bound to Jerusalem. 9:3 And it came about that as he journeyed, he was approaching Damascus, and suddenly a light from heaven flashed around him; 9:4 and he fell to the ground, and heard a voice saying to him, <u>"Saul, Saul, why are you persecuting Me? 9:5 and he said, "Who are Thou, Lord?" And He said, "I am Jesus whom you are persecuting, 9:6 but rise, and enter the city, and it shall be told you what you must do.</u>" 9:7 And the men who traveled with him stood speechless, hearing the voice, but seeing no one. 9:8 And Saul got up from the ground, and though his eyes were open, he could see nothing; and leading him by the hand, they brought him into Damascus. 9:9 And he was three days without sight, and neither ate nor drank. 9:10 Now there was a certain disciple at Damascus, named Ananias; and the Lord said to him in a vision, "Ananias." And he said "Behold, here am I, Lord." 9:11 And the Lord said to him, "Arise and go to the street called Straight, and inquire at the house of Judas for a man from Tarsus named Saul, for behold he is praying, 9:12 and he has seen in a vision a man named Ananias come in and lay* his hands on him, so that he might regain his sight. 9:13 But Ananias answered, "Lord, I have heard from many about this man, how much harm he did to Thy saints at Jerusalem; 9:14 and here he has authority from the chief priests to bind all who call upon Thy name." 9:15 But the Lord said to him, "Go, for he is a chosen instrument of Mine, to bear My name before the Gentiles and kings and the sons of Israel; 9:16 for I will show him how much he must suffer for My name's sake." 9:17 And Ananias departed and entered the house, and after laying his hands on him said, "Brother Saul, the Lord Jesus, who <u>appeared </u>to you on the road by which you were coming, has sent me so that you may regain your sight, and be filled with the Holy Spirit." 9:18 And immediately there fell from his eyes something like scales, and he regained his sight, and he arose and was baptized; 9:19 and he took food and was strengthened. Now for several days he was with the disciples who were at Damascus." (underline emphasis is mine)

The book of Acts of the Apostles (N.A.S.B.) says: "22:6 And it came about that as I was on my way, approaching Damascus about noontime, a very bright light suddenly flashed from heaven all around me, 22:7 and I fell to the ground and heard a voice saying to me, '<u>Saul, Saul, why are you persecuting Me?</u>' 22:8 And I answered, 'Who art Thou, Lord?' And he said to me, '<u>I am Jesus the Nazarene, whom you are persecuting</u>.' 22:9 And those who were with me beheld the light, to be sure, but did not understand the voice of the One who was speaking to me. 22:10 And I said, 'What shall I do Lord?' <u>And the Lord said to me, 'Arise and go into Damascus; and there you will be told of all that has been appointed for you to do.</u>'"22:11 But since I could not see because of the brightness of that light, I *was led by the hand by those who were with me, and came into Damascus. 22:12 And a certain Ananias, a man who was devout by the standard of the Law, and well spoken of by all the Jews who lived there, 22:13 came to me, and standing near said to me, 'Brother Saul, receive your sight!' and at that very time I looked up at him. 22:14 "And he said, 'The God of our fathers has appointed you to know His will, and to see the Righteous One, and to hear an utterance from His mouth. 22:15 'For you will be a witness for Him to all men of what you have seen and heard. 22:16 'And now why do you delay? Arise, and be baptized, and wash away your sins, calling on His name.' 22:17 And it came about when I returned to Jerusalem and was praying in the temple that I fell into trance, 22:18 and I saw Him saying to me, 'Make haste, and get out of Jerusalem quickly, because they will not accept your testimony about Me.' 22:19 And I said, 'Lord, they themselves understand that in one synagogue after another I used to imprison and beat those who believe in Thee. 22:20 And when the blood of Thy witness Stephen was being shed, I also was standing by approving, and watching out for the cloaks of those who were slaying him.' 22:21 And He said to me, 'Go! For I will send you far away to the Gentiles.'"*

The book of Acts of the Apostles (N.A.S.B.) says: "26:13 at midday, O King, I saw on the way a light from heaven, brighter than the sun shining all around me and those who were journeying with me. 26:14 And when we had all fallen to the ground, I heard a voice saying to me in the Hebrew dialect, 'Saul, Saul, why are you persecuting Me? It is hard for you to kick against the goads.' 26:15 And I said, 'Who art Thou, Lord?' And the Lord said, 'I am Jesus whom you are persecuting. 26:16 'But arise, and stand on *your feet; for this purpose I have appeared to you, to appoint you a minister and a witness not only to the things which you have seen, but also to the things in which I will appear to you, 26:17 delivering you from the Jewish people and from the Gentiles, to whom I am sending you, 26:18 to open their eyes so that they may turn from darkness to light and from the dominion of Satan to God, in order that they may receive forgiveness of sins and an inheritance among those who have been sanctified by faith in Me."*

In the first account, the author-editor of the book of Acts of the Apostles gives us the account of the facts; and according to the author-editor Jesus only said to the False Apostle Paul *"Saul, Saul, why are you persecuting Me? 9:5 and he said, "Who are Thou, Lord?" And He said, "I am Jesus whom you are persecuting, 9:6 but rise, and enter the city, and it shall be told you what you must do."*

In the second account, the False Apostle Paul says that Jesus supposedly told him: *"22:10 ...'Arise and go into Damascus; and there you will be told of all that has been appointed for you to do'."*

In the third account the False Apostle Paul says that Jesus supposedly told him: *"I am Jesus whom you are persecuting. 26:16 'But arise, and stand on your feet; for this purpose I have appeared to you, to appoint you a minister and a witness not only to the things which you have seen, but also to the things in which I will appear to you, 26:17 delivering you from the Jewish people and from the Gentiles, to whom I am sending you, 26:18 to open their eyes so that they may turn from darkness to light and from the dominion of Satan to God, in order that they may receive forgiveness of sins and an inheritance among those who have been sanctified by faith in Me."*

Ruy Barraco Mármol

Obviously the first and second accounts of the words of Jesus, on one hand, and the third account, on the other, are substantially different.

Some of the words attributed to Jesus in the third account were attributed previously to Ananias, in the other accounts. In the second account of the event, the book says that the Paul said that Ananias told him: "22.14...*The God of our fathers has appointed you to know His will, and to see the Righteous One, and to hear an utterance from His mouth. 22:15 'For you will be a witness for Him to all men of what you have seen and heard. 22:16 'And now why do you delay? Arise, and be baptized, and wash away your sins, calling on His name.*" In the third account of the story, the book says that Paul said that Jesus, not Ananias, said: "26:16...*I have appeared to you, to appoint you a minister and a witness not only to the things which you have seen, but also to the things in which I will appear to you, 26:17 delivering you from the Jewish people and from the Gentiles, to whom I am sending you, 26:18 to open their eyes so that they may turn from darkness to light and from the dominion of Satan to God, in order that they may receive forgiveness of sins and an inheritance among those who have been sanctified by faith in Me.*" These accounts are incompatible.

It is worth to highlight, based on the 'we passages' of the book of Acts, that the author-editor of the book of Acts seems to have been present in Jerusalem at the time the False Apostle Paul supposedly gave the second account; and that the author seems to have had the opportunity to be with the False Apostle Paul either when he gave the third account or little after he gave it. And he was not present when the facts supposedly happened.

This means that, since in the first account the author presents the facts in one way, and then presents the False Apostle Paul giving not another, but two other different accounts of the same event, the author-editor implies that the False Apostle Paul lied in the other instances, and that the False Apostle Paul put in the mouth of Jesus words that Jesus did not speak. Either Paul put in the mouth of Jesus words that Jesus did not speak, or the author-editor of the book of Acts lied when he attributed those words to the False Apostle Paul. The three accounts cannot be true at the same time. The existence of the three accounts are evidence that one of them, at least, is false, and we know that they are all false because Paul was a false prophet.

It is remarkable that the author-editor of the book of Acts of the Apostles presented Paul attributing words to Jesus that Jesus did not speak, giving false testimony in that way, at the time in which, if he were a true witness of Jesus, he should have been receiving assistance of the Holy Spirit, the Spirit of Truth, to testify the truth against his persecutors and imprisoners. Some say: Why was Paul obligated to tell the truth in these occasions? I respond: we are always obligated to tell the truth, especially about Jesus; and the apostles and the first Christians were especially obligated to tell the truth when giving testimony before authorities for Christ's sake. The Gospel according to Saint Matthew (N.A.S.B.) says: "*10:18 And you shall even be brought before governors and kings for My sake, as a testimony to them and to the Gentiles.*"

And more remarkable is that instead of causing the

Ruy Barraco Mármol

effect of discrediting the False Apostle Paul, the lies attributed to him, that put in the mouth of Jesus words that he did not speak, were used to give authority to the False Apostle Paul, and maybe, used to justify the action of lying for the cause of Jesus: at least and hopefully only until now.

b. About the Matter if Jesus Will Appear to Anyone Before His Second Coming

Leaving aside the deeds of the False Apostle, as I explained in the introduction of this book, the Gospels teach that after the Ascension of Jesus, Jesus would not appear to anyone, until the Second Coming of Jesus. Least of all he would appear to someone other than one of his apostles and for the purpose of bringing more public revelation. Therefore, the alleged appearance to the False Apostle Paul is against the teachings of the Gospels and even contradictory to the teachings of the book of Acts of the Apostles.

The Gospel according to Saint Matthew (N.A.S.B.) says: "24:3 *And as He was sitting on the Mount of Olives, the disciples came to Him privately, saying, "Tell us, when will these things be, and what will be the sign of Your coming and of the end of the age?" 24:4 And Jesus Answered and said to them, "See to it that no one misleads you. 24:5 "For many will come in My name, saying, 'I am the Christ,' and will mislead many."*

The Gospel according to Saint Matthew (N.A.S.B.) says: "24:23 *"Then if anyone says to you, 'Behold, here is the Christ; or There He is, do not believe him." 24:24 For false Christs and false prophets will arise and will show great* signs and wonders, so as to mislead, if possible, even the elect, "24:25 Behold, I have told you in advance, 24:26 "If therefore they say to you, 'Behold He is in the wilderness', do not go forth, or, 'Behold, He is in the inner rooms, 'do not believe them. 24:27 For just as the lightning comes from east, and flashes even to the west, so shall the coming of the Son of Man be." (underline emphasis is mine)

Jesus says if anyone tells you 'here is the Christ' do not believe him. This includes those who say that they were with Christ after his ascension, saying 'here he was'. When Jesus was saying 'do not believe in those who say 'here is Jesus', he was including also those who say 'here was Jesus' and 'this is what Jesus told me'. Nobody should have ever believed in Paul, when he was saying 'he was with Jesus'. Paul came and said 'I was with Jesus' in the road to Damascus and he was believed.

The Gospel according to Saint John (N.A.S.B.) says: "14:2 "In my Father's house are many dwelling places; if it were not so, I would have told you; for I go to prepare a place for you. 14:3 "And if I go and prepare a place for you, I will come again, and receive you to Myself; that where I am, there you may be also. 14:4 And you know the way where I am going." 14:5 Thomas said to Him, "Lord, we do not know where You are going, how do we know the way?" Jesus said to him, "I am the way, and the truth, and the life, no one comes to the Father, but through Me."

Jesus after his ascension was going away to be with the Father to come back only at the time of his Second Coming. He was going to be with us, but not appearing to us to teach us, not choosing another apostle to teach us. He was going to be dwelling in us.

The Gospel according to Saint John (N.A.S.B.) says: "16:5 But now I am going to Him who sent Me; and none of you asks Me, 'Where are You going?' 16:6 "But because I have said these things to you, sorrow has filled your heart. 16:7 "But I tell you the truth, it is to your advantage that I go away; for if I do not go away, the Helper shall not come to you; but If I go, I will send Him to you." After the Holy Spirit came Jesus was going to be with the Father, not appearing to the False Apostle Paul and teaching him.

The book of Acts of the Apostles (N.A.S.B.) says: "1:9 And after He had said these things, He was lifted up while they were looking on, and a cloud received Him out of their sight. 1:10 And as they were gazing intently into the sky while He was departing, behold, two men in white clothing stood, beside them: 1:11 and they also said, "Men of Galilee, why do you stand looking into the sky? This Jesus, who has been taken up from you into heaven, will come in just the same way as you have watched Him go into heaven."

In the Bible there are men who were snatched up to heaven. The book 4 Kings, Verse 2:11 (In the Masoretic text, same verse, book 2 Kings), narrates how Elijah was snatched up to heaven, how his disciples wanted to send men to try to find him, and how Elisha was teaching that it was worthless to search for him. This teaching of the book of Acts of the Apostles, Verse 1:11, suggests the same; says that Jesus was not going to come until the Second Coming.

The book of Acts of the Apostles (N.A.S.B.) says: "3:19 Repent therefore and return, that your sins may be wiped away, in order that times of refreshing may come from the presence of the Lord; 3:20 and that He may send

Jesus, the Christ appointed to you, 3:21 <u>*whom heaven must*</u>
<u>*receive until the period of restoration of all things*</u> *about*
which God spoke by the mouth of His holy prophets from
ancient time." (underline emphasis is mine). Peter said
this after the Ascension of Jesus and before the
supposed appearance of Jesus to Paul.

Moreover, the Gospels teach that not only Jesus was
not going to appear to anyone after his Ascension, but
even before his Ascension, once resurrected, he was
only going to appear to his disciples. The Gospel
according to Saint John (N.A.S.B.) says: *"14:19 After a*
little while the world will behold me no more; but you will
behold Me; because I live, you shall live also. 14:20 In that
day you shall know that I am in My Father, and you in Me,
and I in you. 14:21 He who has My commandments and
keep them, he it is who loves Me; and he who loves Me shall
be loved by My Father and I will love him, and will disclose
Myself to him. 14:22 Judas (not Iscariot) said to Him, "Lord,
what then has happened that You are going to disclose
Yourself to us, and not to the world?" The book of Acts of
the Apostles (N.A.S.B.) says: *"10:40 God raised Him up*
on the third day and granted that He should become visible,
10:41 not to all people, but to witnesses who were chosen
beforehand by God, that is, to us, who ate and drank with
Him after He arose from the dead." These teachings say
that Jesus was not going to appear at the time of his
resurrection to anyone other than a witness who ate
and drank with Jesus during his earthly life, and that
Jesus indeed did not appear to anyone other than them,
after his resurrection. These teachings say that Jesus did
not appear to Paul of Tarsus.

Ruy Barraco Mármol

Conclusion

I think that, despite the errors, we must accept the book of Acts of the Apostles as a book that contains Sacred Scripture, believing that everything that the book says with regard to Jesus and the twelve apostles is true, unless something appears to be evidently wrong, such as the matter of the appearance of Jesus to Paul, or the matter of Paul being full of the Holy Spirit, for instance.

The book of Acts of the Apostles contains words of God, testimony of the ministry of Jesus, of the twelve apostles, and of the action of the Holy Spirit: but at the same time it narrates facts that the twelve apostles did not witness; that contradict the teachings of the Gospels and of Jesus; and that involved a person about whom the twelve apostles did not have the mission to be a witness of, who was a false prophet, who said that Jesus appeared to him. Let us remember that Jesus explicitly told us not to believe if anyone tells us that Jesus was here or there before the Second Coming.

We must believe in the other facts, the ones that involve the action of the twelve apostles and the action of Holy Spirit because we have strong reasons to believe that they constitute apostolic testimony, and they do not contradict the teachings of Jesus and of the Gospels. There are strong reasons to believe that apostles chosen, prepared and credited publically and personally by Jesus were witness and gave testimony of them. The twelve apostles were made apostles to be witnesses of them and the testimony of the apostles was preserved in authentic sources that have been in the hands of the church since their composition, being preserved in the book of Acts of the Apostles. Let us remember that the sources used in the composition of the book of Acts of the Apostles precede the book itself.

Ruy Barraco Mármol

Chapter VII.
Inerrancy and Inspiration of the Epistles of Paul - Catholic's Church Infallibility

I have treated a number of mistaken statements contained in the Epistles of Paul. Without doubt, by virtue of being mistaken, those mistaken statements are not the word of God. In addition, because of the nature and the quantity of the mistakes, the epistles that contain them cannot be taken as written under inspiration of the Holy Spirit. All that is mistaken and bad in the Epistles of Paul is not a work of God, either directly or indirectly.

We are not dealing with a case in which documents that contain the word of God, or have been written under the inspiration of the Holy Spirit, have errors. If documents that contain the word of God may have errors that is another matter. If documents written under the inspiration of the Holy Spirit may have errors that is another matter. If the true sacred scripture may have suffered or can suffer additions and modifications it is also another matter. The Epistles of Paul are not even sacred scripture.

Whoever declared that the Epistles of Paul are errorless, the word of God, and sacred scripture, made very serious mistakes. This is the case of the Catholic Church, and all of the other Christian Churches that I know, which like all the other churches of the world are fallible.

The Catholic Church in the Council of Trent declared: *"And so that no doubt may arise in anyone's mind as to which are the books that are accepted by this Synod, it has decreed that a list of the Sacred books be added to this decree. They are written here below: Books of the Old Testament: The five books of Moses, namely, Genesis, Exodus, Leviticus, Numbers, Deuteronomy; Josue, Judges, Ruth, four book of Kings, two of Paralipomenon, the first book of Esdras, and the second which is called Nehemias, Tobias, Judith, Esther, Job, the Psalter of David consisting of 150 psalms, the Proverbs, Ecclesiastes, the Canticle of Canticles, Wisdom, Ecclesiasticus, Isaias, Jeremias with Baruch, Ezechiel, Daniel, the twelve minor Prophets, that is Osee, Josel, Amos, Abdias, Jonas, Micheas, Nahum, Habacuc, Sophonias, Aggaeus, Zacharias, Malachias; two books of the Machabees, the first and the second. Books of the New Testament: the four Gospels, according to Matthew, Mark, Luke, and John; the Acts of the Apostles, written by Luke the Evangelist, fourteen epistles of Paul the Apostle, to the Romans, to the Corinthians two, to the Galatians, to the Ephesians, to the Philippians, to the Colossians two, to the Thessalonians, two, to Timothy, to Titus, to Philemon, to the Hebrews; two of Peter the Apostle, three of John the Apostle, one of the Apostle James, one of the Apostle Jude, and the Apocalypse of John the Apostle. If anyone, however, should not accept the said books as sacred and canonical, entire with all their parts, as they were wont to be read in the Catholic Church, and as they are contained in the old Latin Vulgate edition, and if both knowingly and deliberately he should condemn the aforesaid traditions let him be anathema. Let all, therefore, understand in what order and in what manner the said Synod, after having laid the foundation of the confession of Faith, will proceed, and what testimonies and authorities it will mainly use in confirming dogmas, and in restoring morals in the Church."*[151]

The Catholic Church in the first Vatican Council, (1893 1870) declared: *"Chapter 2,5. Furthermore, this supernatural revelation, according to the faith of the universal Church, as declared by the holy synod of Trent, is contained "in the written books and in the unwritten traditions which have been received by the apostles from the mouth of Christ Himself; or, through the inspiration of the Holy Spirit have been handed down by the apostles themselves, and have thus come to us" [Council of Trent, see n 783]. And, indeed, these books of the Old and New Testament, whole with all their parts, just as they were enumerated in the decree of the same Council, are contained in the older Vulgate Latin edition, and are to be accepted as sacred and canonical, not because, having been put together by human industry alone, they were then approved by its authority; nor because they contain revelation without error; but because, having been written by the inspiration of the Holy Spirit, they have God as their author and, as such, they have been handed down to the*

---

[151] Council of Trent (1545-1563), fourth session, September 8, 1546, decree concerning the canonical scriptures. Denzinger, Henry "The Sources of Catholic Dogma" p. 244. 783. Under "The Sacred Books and the Traditions of the Apostles are Accepted."

Ruy Barraco Mármol

Church itself (can. 4)."[152]

And the Catholic Church in the second Vatican Council declared: "*11. Those divinely revealed realities which are contained and presented in Sacred Scripture have been committed to writing under the inspiration of the Holy Spirit. For holy mother Church, relying on the belief of the Apostles (see John 20:31; 2 Tim. 3:16; 2 Peter 1:19-20, 3:15-16), holds that the books of the Old and New Testaments in their entirety, with all their parts, are sacred and canonical because written under the inspiration of the Holy Spirit, they have God as their author and have been handed on as such to the Church herself. 1 (cf. First Vatican Council, Dogmatic Constitution on the Catholic Faith, Chap.2 "On Revelation:" Denzinger 1787 (3006); Biblical Commission, Decree of June 18,1915: Denzinger 2180 (3629): EB 420; Holy Office, Epistle of Dec. 22, 1923: EB 499) In composing the sacred books, God chose men and while employed by Him (2) (cf. Pius XII, encyclical "Divino Afflante Spiritu," Sept. 30, 1943: A.A.S. 35 (1943) p. 314; Enchiridion Bible. (EB) 556) they made used of their powers and abilities, so that with Him acting in them and through them, (3) ("In" and "for" man: cf. Heb. 1, and 4,7; ("in"): 2 Sm. 23,2; Matt. 1:22 and various places; ("for"): First Vatican Council, Schema on Catholic Doctrine, note 9: Coll. Lac. VII, 522.) they as true authors, consigned to writing everything and only those things which He wanted. (4) (Leo XIII, encyclical "Providentissimus Deus, "Nov.18,1893: Denzinger 1952 (3293); EB 125).*[153]

---

[152] First Vatican Council, Dogmatic constitution on the Catholic faith, Dei Filius, Session 3, April 24, 1870, Chapter 2. Denzinger, Henry "The Sources of Catholic Dogma" p.444. 1787.

The case of the book of Acts of the Apostles is different, because it contains words of God and apostolic testimony of the life of Jesus, the life of the apostles and of the action of the Holy Spirit. The book of Acts of the Apostles is a case in which authentic sources, and true testimony of facts concerning the life of Jesus, the life of the Apostles and of the action of the Holy Spirit, sacred scripture, was used for the edition of a book that contains sacred scripture and at the same time scripture written by a man that contain errors, and even false testimony.

Christianity under the light of a rational and faithful to Jesus study of the content of the book of Acts of the Apostles must admit that it contains errors that cannot be explained without going against reason and the truth of the teachings of the Gospels.

The fact that the Catholic Church has made a mistake does not mean that everything it did or does is mistaken. The fact that certain points of its doctrine and faith are uncertain or doubtful does not mean that all of its doctrine and faith are uncertain or doubtful. It does not deprive of value all its doctrine and faith. The same thing can be said about the other Christian Churches, which, I understand, have never claimed to be infallible. Infallibility has never been their foundation. Besides, if the Epistles of Paul are full of errors the Christian Church has no other choice but to admit it.

Neither can it be concluded from the fallibility of the

---

[153] Second Vatican Council, Dogmatic Constitution on Divine Revelation DEI VERBUM, solemnly promulgated by his holiness Pope Paul VI on November 18, 1965. Chapter III. Sacred Scripture, Its Inspiration and Divine Interpretation. Point 11. Vatican Official Web Site.

Catholic Church in particular, nor from the fallibility of the Christian Church in general, nor from the serious error of holding the Epistles of Paul as sacred scriptures, that God did not assist the Christian Church permanently and especially in particular circumstances, or that the Christian Church will be, or can be defeated. In the Old Testament God promised assistance and victory to the Jewish nation[154]and he fulfilled the promise, without making their civil, ecclesiastic or military authorities, perfect and infallible people, not even in the strict military area. The Jewish nation was assisted and had victory in spite of having infallible and imperfect authorities. The Christian Church can avoid defeat in spite of the fallibility and imperfection of its authorities and members, if it is the will of God. The Christian Church can reach victory making mistakes.

In any case, what is clear, what can be concluded from the exposition of errors that I just made, is that the Christian Church must recognize its mistakes, and revise all the doctrine and institutions built on the basis of the Epistles of Paul. Christianity does not need the Epistles of Paul to build its doctrine. The word of Christ preserved in the Gospels, and the word of God preserved in the rest of the Bible is more than enough. There is no other option.

All this that I have said is true independently of the question of the identity of the author of the epistles. The Old Covenant and the New Covenant existed before Paul, and before his epistles were mistakenly

---

[154] Book of Exodus 23:22.

considered the word of God, and will not be affected by the acknowledgment of the falsehood of the Epistles of Paul, but certainly reaffirmed.[155] The Epistles of Paul were written around two decades after the ascension of Christ. And they become available to all the churches and started being considered the word of God by all the churches long time after the ascension of Christ. Christianity, at the beginning, fed itself with the word of Jesus, whose word was always recognized by Christianity as the word of God.

---

[155] In my opinion it would have been very hard, I would say impossible, for an outsider to introduce in the Christian Church false writings, and to induce her to consider them sacred scripture; and very hard for someone from the Christian Church. However, in my opinion, for somebody with the position of Paul, or for a well-recognized disciple of his, it would have been possible.

Chapter VIII.
How to Live a Faithful to Jesus Christianity

To live a Christianity faithful to Jesus we have to learn and put in practice the word of Jesus Christ, which we find in the gospels, and the other teachings of the Bible, under the light given by Jesus Christ to understand them; this includes the book of Acts of the Apostles, the other Epistles of the New Testament and the Old Testament. In another book I will contribute to their study and to the building of a Christian doctrine based on the words of Jesus.

He who considers the word of God the words of the False Apostle Paul, or the words of any other man that contradicts Jesus, is not being a faithful disciple of Jesus. He who treats the word of Paul as if it were the word of God it is not being faithful to Jesus.

We can live our Christianity without considering the word of God the Epistles of Paul, and without considering the word of God any other teaching found in the other epistles of the New Testament or in the book of Acts of the Apostles[156] that contradicts the word of Jesus.

If for any reason you do not have a Church with

---

[156] The book of Acts of the Apostles seems to me to be a mix of two different writings. It is strange that Chapters 13 to the end of the book of Acts of the Apostles talk almost exclusively about Paul ignoring the twelve apostles.

whom to join on Sundays to remember Jesus celebrating the Eucharist, and to make use of the other sacraments, among other reasons and purposes, without worshiping Paul or his epistles, or if you do not have a Christian minister to administer the sacraments to you that will not demand you to treat the Epistles of Paul as the word of God, do not forget that any Christian can be a Christian minister, and do not forget that any Christian can be an extraordinary minister of the sacraments. We are all called to be ministers of the Christian Church. The administration of the sacraments is very simple; any Christian can learn to administer them. Sermons in the Christian Church should all start from the word of Jesus. Anyone can read the word of Jesus. Anyone can comment on the word of Jesus, or at least read a comment of another person. There are plenty of comments on the word of Jesus available to us to read at Church.

If you do not have a faithful to Jesus Christian with whom to join on Sundays do not despair. Sooner or later you will find another sheep of Jesus with whom to join on Sundays, who recognizes his voice, and who recognizes that the voice of the False Apostle Paul is not the voice of Jesus.

Not having a Church community cannot be an impediment for the Christianity of any person. Rejecting Paul is not a valid excuse for not being a faithful to Jesus Christian; on the contrary. Search for the information you need. In the first times of the Christian Church, and in times of the persecutions, many Christians found themselves in this situation, and they stepped up and they practiced their faith no matter the difficulties, remaining faithful to Jesus. And they did not count on the education, books, libraries, computers, cars, smart phones, and all the technology with which we count on today.

The only thing that we need to change from our Sunday's meetings, because of the recognition of Paul as a false prophet, is Paul and his epistles. Have faith in Jesus and in the truth.

At the end of this book I will make some comments that might help the reader with the challenge of being a Christian, especially a faithful to Jesus Christian. Next, I will analyze what the book of Revelation says about all this.

-Part II-

Ruy Barraco Mármol

Chapter I.
Paul and the Book of Revelation

If you are shocked by the first part of this book, get ready for more. After a short introduction, you will start to understand one of the most amazing books of the Bible.

As I said in the beginning of this book, the Bible is divided into two parts: The Old Testament and the New Testament. Each one of these two parts is composed of several books. The book of Revelation is part of the New Testament, and Saint John is believed to be its author; the same Saint John, who is the author of one of the Gospels. There are strong arguments to sustain this attribution.[157]

---

[157] In the book *"Biblia Comentada"*, Texto de la Nacar – Colunga VII, Epístolas Católicas. Apocalipsis [In the Commentated Bible, Text of Nacar – Colunga VII, Catholic Epistles. Revelation] by Jose Salguero, O.P. Professor of Sacred Scripture of the Pontifical University of Saint Thomas of Rome, Biblioteca de Autores Cristianos [Library of Christian Authors] Madrid. MCMLXV page 301, he states that around fifty years after the death of Saint John in Ephesus, Saint Justin (153 A.D.) wrote in that very place his Dialogue with Triphon, in which he expressly states 'Also, among us was a man named John, one of Christ's apostles, who prophesied the Revelation (Apocalypse) in which it was held that those who had believed in Christ would pass one thousand years in Jerusalem [symbolically, the New Jerusalem, not the city we know]; Saint Policarp (155 A.D.) who was the immediate disciple of the Apostle Saint John, considered Revelation to have been divinely inspired, and uses expressions that are identical to those in Revelation. Regarding Papias (c. 130 A.D.)

Ruy Barraco Mármol

John was one of the first disciples of Christ, along with his brother James. They were two of the twelve apostles, and John, among the apostles, certainly had an important position.[158]

The book of Revelation, according to the book itself, was written by a man called John when he was exiled on the island of Patmos, in Asia Minor, because of the word of God and the testimony of Jesus.[159] The word

---

Andrew of Caesarea tells us that he confirms the authenticity of Revelation. Also Irenaeus (around 190 A.D.), heir to the Ephesian traditions from having lived in Ephesus for some time, identifies the author of Revelation as the Apostle Saint John. Of equal importance is the testimony of the Canon or list of Moratori , the first list of books in the New Testament (around 170A.D.): Apocalypsis etiam Iohannis...recipimus. [We also received... the book of Revelation from John.] During the rest of the Second Century through the first half of the following century there were many ecclesiastical writers who considered the Apocalypse (Revelation) to be the work of the Apostle Saint John. Clemente of Alexandria around 215 A.D.), Origenes (around 233 A.D.) and Tertulian (around 207 A.D.) all believed this. Some other authors of this epoch, or even the previous century, came to write commentaries on Revelation. Among the latter was Saint Meliton, Bishop of Sardis (around 170 A.D.), one of the cities against which the Apocalypse was directed. The weight of tradition which the unanimous opinion of the first two centuries has regarding the authenticity and canonicity of Revelation is evident. In the book "la Sagrada Escritura", Texto y Comentario por profesores de la Compania de Jesus, Nuevo Testamento Tomo III, Biblioteca de Autores Cristianos, Madrid MCMLXII [The Book of Sacred Scripture, Text and Commentary by professors of the Company of Jesus, New Testament, Tome III, Library of Christian Authors,Madrid MCMLXII] page 564, we can read these basic ideas. Among other things he says that it is obvious that during the first two centuries Revelation was received in the Church as a whole as divinely inspired writing, a work of John the Apostle.

[158] The Gospel according to Saint John (N.I.V.) says: "19:25 Near the cross of Jesus stood his mother, his mother's sister, Mary the wife of Clopas, and Mary Magdalene. 19:26 When Jesus saw his mother there, and the disciple whom he loved standing nearby, he said to his mother, "Dear woman, here is your son," 19:27 and to the disciple, "Here is your mother." From that time on, this disciple took her into his home." The disciple whom Christ loved was Saint John.

Revelation is the translation of the Greek word Απο-καλυψις (Apocalypse).[160] This man according to the book itself, Verse 1:2, bore witness to the word of God and to the testimony of Jesus Christ, even to all that he saw.

There should be no need to say that the reasoning and statements that I have previously formulated in this book are not dependent on the interpretation that I will give about the book of Revelation, which astonishingly seems to confirm them completely; but I want to make this clear anyway.

The book of Revelation is a prophetic book, written in the literary genre called apocalyptic, in which symbolism is frequently used. To understand the book of Revelation its symbolism must be deciphered, and the most authorized sources to use in that labor are the book of Revelation itself and the rest of the books of the Bible; the book of Revelation, the Gospel according to Saint John, the other Gospels, and the rest of the Bible, in principle, in that order.

The book of Revelation itself interprets some of the symbolism that it uses, which is useful in deciphering other symbols. Verse 17:12, about the Beast that has ten horns and seven heads, New International Version (N.I.V.)[161], says: "*17:12 The ten horns you saw are ten*

---

[159] The Bible, book of Revelation, Verse 1:9.

[160] Karl Feyerabend "Langenscheidt Pocket Greek Dictionary Greek-English".

[161] Scripture quotations marked with N.I.V. in this work are taken from the Holy Bible, New International Version®, NIV®. Copyright © 1973, 1978, 1984 by Biblica, Inc.™. Used by permission of Zondervan. All rights reserved worldwide. www.zondervan.com

kings who have not yet received a kingdom, but who for one hour will receive authority as kings along with the beast."

The other books of the New Testament and the Old Testament also use symbolism. In the parables and prophecies of both we can find symbolism. Some of those prophecies have already been fulfilled and some have been interpreted. This is also very useful for deciphering the meaning of the symbolism used in the Bible.

As an example of symbolism used in the Old Testament, and with the intention of guiding the reader not very familiar with the Bible,[162] I will transcribe a prophecy that refers to the first coming of Jesus. The Bible, book of the prophet Isaiah (N.I.V.), says: *"11:1 A shoot will come up from the stump of Jesse; from his roots a Branch will bear fruit. 11:2 The Spirit of the Lord will rest on him— the Spirit of wisdom and of understanding, the Spirit of counsel and of power, the Spirit of knowledge and of the fear of the Lord— 11:3 and he will delight in the fear of the Lord. He will not judge by what he sees with his eyes, or decide by what he hears with his ears; 11:4 but with righteousness he will judge the needy, with justice he will give decisions for the poor of the earth. He will strike the earth with the rod of his mouth; with the breath of his lips he will slay the wicked. 11:5 Righteousness will be his belt and faithfulness the sash around his waist."* The prophecy of Verse 11:4 that says, "He will strike the earth with the rod of his mouth, with the

---

[162] I recommend, for people to better understand the Old Testament the reading of the writings of Saint Justin Martyr "*Dialogue with Trypho*", "*First Apology*" and "*Second Apology*". I also recommend the reading of "the Epistle of Bernabe". These writings can easily be found online. By recommending them I am neither saying that I share what they say, nor saying that I do not share it.

breath of his lips he will slay the wicked" is formulated with symbolism, and it has been symbolically fulfilled by Christ. It is nonsense to waste time trying to find the body of a dead man slain by the breath of the lips of Christ, for the purpose of performing an autopsy to prove its fulfillment, because the prophecy was fulfilled symbolically, not literally.

To pay attention to the fact that this prophecy was fulfilled symbolically is very useful in understanding and interpreting the book of Revelation, because just as this prophecy was fulfilled symbolically, many of the prophecies of the book of Revelation were fulfilled and will be fulfilled symbolically, not literally.

The chapters most related to this book are located in what I will call the second part of the book of Revelation, which goes from Chapter 4 to the end of the book; principally in Chapters 12, 13, 19 and 20.

The events that the book of Revelation describe and prophesy are not all presented in chronological order. For this reason, part of the challenge of interpreting and understanding the book of Revelation is to decipher the chronological order of the events described and prophesied in it.

I will not attempt in this part of the book to interpret and decipher all of what these chapters say (I am not sure if it is even possible for a man to do it) and much less to interpret and decipher all of what the entire second part of the book of Revelation says. However, I will try to interpret its general meaning and I will make some commentaries on it.

1.1. Paul and the Second Beast of the Book of Revelation

In regard to Chapters 12, 13, 19 and 20 of the book of Revelation, as an introduction, I want to say that they reveal, among other things, how the Devil reacted when Christ was born; how he tried to kill Christ and to destroy the newborn Christian Church; the persecution of the Jews by the Devil; the persecution of the Christians by the Devil; and how the Devil used the Roman Empire for those purposes.

These chapters foretold that in the future the Devil was going to use other Empires, States and organizations, and revealed the evil action of a man, a false prophet, at the service of the Devil and empowered by him, who using signs, wonders, and preaching, would achieve enormously negative results in the world: the Second Beast of the book of Revelation. The characterizations of this false prophet apply perfectly to, and to nobody else but, Paul.

They narrate an intervention of Jesus before his second coming, and the beautifying of the Christian Church, that represents to me what would be the return of the Christian Church to the true word of God, purified from the doctrine of Paul.

They describe how the Devil is going to be defeated, and imprisoned, to give start to an indeterminate period of time during which the Devil will be imprisoned, in which those who left this world living in Christ, will be able to influence in the world like angels.

And they reveal details about the second coming of Jesus (the Coming of the Son of Man) and the Final Judgment.

The bases for this interpretation will be seen next, when I analyze each chapter, sometimes dividing chapters in sets of verses for a better understanding. Chapters 17 and 18 are analyzed here because they are very useful for understanding the others.

Chapter 12

Chapter 12 of the book of Revelation (N.I.V.) says: "*12:1 A great and wondrous sign appeared in heaven: a woman clothed with the sun, with the moon under her feet and a crown of twelve stars on her head. 12:2 She was pregnant and cried out in pain as she was about to give birth. 12:3 Then another sign appeared in heaven: an enormous red dragon with seven heads and ten horns and seven crowns on his heads. 12:4 His tail swept a third of the stars out of the sky and flung them to the earth. The dragon stood in front of the woman who was about to give birth, so that he might devour her child the moment it was born. 12:5 She gave birth to a son, a male child, who will rule all the nations with an iron scepter. And her child was snatched up to God and to his throne. 12:6 The woman fled into the desert to a place prepared for her by God, where she might be taken care of for 1,260 days. 12:7 And there was war in heaven. Michael and his angels fought against the dragon, and the dragons and his angels fought back. 12:8 But he was not strong enough, and they lost their place in heaven. 12:9 The great dragon was hurled down—that ancient serpent called the devil, or Satan, who leads the whole world astray. He was hurled to the earth, and his angels with him. 12:10 Then I heard a loud voice in heaven say: "Now have come the salvation and the power and the kingdom of our God, and the authority of his Christ. For the accuser of our brothers, who accuses them before our God day and night, has been hurled down. 12:11 They overcame him by the blood of the Lamb and by the word of their testimony; they did not love their lives so much as to shrink from death. 12:12 Therefore rejoice, you heavens and you who dwell in them! But woe to the earth and the sea, because the devil has gone down to you! He is filled with fury, because he knows that his time is short." 12:13 When the dragon saw that he had been hurled to the earth, he pursued the woman who had given birth to the male child. 12:14 The woman was given the two wings of a great eagle, so that she might fly to the place prepared for her in the desert, where she would be taken care of for a time, times and half a time, out of the serpent's reach. 12:15 Then from his mouth the serpent spewed water like a river, to overtake the woman and sweep her away with the torrent. 12:16 But the earth helped the woman by opening its mouth and swallowing the river that the dragon had spewed out of his mouth. 12:17 Then the dragon was enraged at the woman and went off to make war against the rest of her offspring—those who obey God's commandments and hold to the testimony of Jesus."*

Verses 12:1-2: "*12:1 A great and wondrous sign appeared in heaven: <u>a woman</u> clothed with the sun, with the moon under her feet <u>and a crown of twelve stars on her head. 12:2. She was pregnant</u> and cried out in pain as she was about to give birth."*

This woman that John sees in this Verse 12:1 represents the Jewish community. However, in my opinion, not the entire Jewish community, but only those who were part of the people of God, who loved God, and did his will. The symbolism used to identify her tells us that she represents the Jewish Church.

The fact that the woman has a crown of twelve stars on her head indicates that the woman either represents the Jewish Church, or the Christian Church, because either it refers to the twelve tribes of Israel, in which case it would represent the Jewish Church, or it refers to the twelve apostles, in which case it would represent the Christian Church.

However, the fact that the woman in Verse 12:5 of the book of Revelation will give birth to a male child tells us that the woman represents the Jewish Church and not the Christian Church; because in the study of that verse, we will see that the child is Jesus. If the child is Jesus, we know that the woman, the mother, is not the Christian Church, because the Christian Church did not exist before Christ. The Christian Church was created by Christ.

Furthermore, in Verse 12:17 of the book of Revelation, the Dragon, enraged because of his failure to attack the woman, went off to make war against the rest of her offspring – those who obey God's commandments and hold to the testimony of Jesus, who are the newborn Christian Church, or at least are part of it.[163] If the dragon after failing to attack the woman

---

[163] In the book "Biblia Comentada" by the Profesores de Salamanca [Commentated Bible of the Professors of Salmanca] it is said that those who see in this Woman the representation of Israel base this in reasons which, in our point of view, have a lot of weight. There are many places among the prophets of the Old Testament where Israel is represented by the figure of a woman. Setting aside the wife of the Song of Songs, we could describe the personification of Israel in Hosea (2:19-20), in Jeremiah (3:6-10) and in Ezekiel

Ruy Barraco Mármol

went off to attack the Christian Church, then the woman is not the Christian Church, at least in its entirety.

The use of this symbolism of the woman parturient, or woman in labor, to represent the Jewish people has precedents in the Old Testament of the Bible.

The book of the prophet Micah (N.I.V.) says: "*4:10 Writhe in agony, O Daughter of Zion, like a woman in labor, for now you must leave the city to camp in the open field. You will go to Babylon; there you will be rescued. There the Lord will redeem you out of the hand of your enemies.*" Zion is another symbol which the Bible frequently uses to represent the Jewish people. In this Verse 4:10 the

---

(16:22). The latter introduces us to the two sisters, Oola and Ooliba, (Ezekiel 23) who represent the kingdoms of Samaria and Judah. The apocryphal books follow the same pattern, as may be seen in 4 Esdras (9:38-10:59). And in the New Testament we find these same personifications (Galatians 4:26; Hebrews 11:10; 12:22; 13:14; Apostles 19:8; 21:11). On the other hand, the image of Zion in the pains of labor was not unknown in the Old Testament. The prophet Micah exclaims: 'Writhe in agony;, O Daughter of Zion, Like a woman in labor, for now you must leave the city to camp in the open field. You will go to Babylon;' Micah 4:10. [New International Version] Isaiah presents the oppressed Israelites who cried out to Yahweh: " As a woman with child and about to give birth writhes and cries out in her pain, so were we in your presence, O Lord." (Isaiah 26:17.) And elsewhere the same prophet speaks to us of the multiplication of the new Jerusalem in these terms. Before giving birth she has already given birth. Before feeling labor pains she gave birth to a son. Whoever heard of something like this? Whoever saw it happen? Is a town born in a day? A nation born all at once? Zion has given birth to her children before feeling labor pains (Isaiah 66:7-8). Moreover, the author of Revelation tells us expressly in verse 6 that the Woman fled to the desert where she was fed by God until she was free from the danger of her enemies. From the book of Exodus we know that Israel fled from Egypt to the Sinai desert, where she was fed by God with manna which fell from the sky until she became transformed into a city strong enough to confront and resist her enemies. Profesores de la Universidad Pontificia de Salamanca "Biblia Comentada", Collection of the "Biblioteca de Autores Cristianos, vol. VII, under "Apocalipsis" Verses 12:1-6, p. 427.

Jewish people are represented as a woman in labor.

The book of the prophet Isaiah (N.I.V.) says: "26:17 *As a woman with child and about to give birth writhes and cries out in her pain, so were we in your presence, O Lord. 26:18 We were with child, we writhed in pain, but we gave birth to wind. We have not brought salvation to earth; we have not given birth to people of the world.*" In my opinion the last two expressions must be read as questions: "Have we not brought salvation to earth? Have we not given birth to people of the world?"; and this is another opportunity in which the symbolism of the woman parturient is used in the Bible to represent the Jewish people.

In Chapter 17 of the book of Revelation John also sees a woman but her aspect and descriptions do not at all match the ones of the woman of Chapter 12. Later we will see who the other woman is.

In these first verses John sees and describes the Jewish Church in the moments previous to the birth of Christ and the Christian Church.

Verses 12:3-6 "*12:3 Then another sign appeared in heaven: an enormous red dragon with seven heads and ten horns and seven crowns on his heads. 12:4 His tail swept a third of the stars out of the sky and flung them to the earth. The dragon stood in front of the woman who was about to give birth, so that he might devour her child the moment it was born. 12:5 She gave birth to a son, a male child, who will rule all the nations with an iron scepter. And her child was snatched up to God and to his throne. 12:6 The woman fled into the desert to a place prepared for her by God, where she might be taken care of for 1,260 days.*"

The enormous red Dragon of Verse 12:3 is the Devil. Verse 12:9 of the book of Revelation (N.I.V.) says: "*12:9 The great dragon was hurled down—that ancient serpent called the Devil, or Satan, who leads the whole world astray. He was hurled to the earth, and his angels with him.*"

The stars of Verse 12:4, swept by the tail of the dragon, are his angels, which were nothing less than a third part of the angels. In Verse 1:16-20 of the book of Revelation the seven angels of Jesus are called stars, and in the verse quoted in the previous paragraph, the book of Revelation says the Devil was hurled with his angels. In the Old Testament, the book of Daniel, (N.I.V.) it is said: "*8:9 Out of one of them came another horn, which started small but grew in power to the south and to the east and toward the Beautiful Land. 8:10 It grew until it reached the host of the heavens, and it threw some of the starry host down to the earth and trampled on them.*"

The son of the woman, about whom Verse 12:5 of the book of Revelation is talking about, is Christ, because Christ was snatched up to God and to his throne. This refers to the ascension of Christ to heaven. In addition this Verse 12:5 that we are interpreting says "She gave birth to a male child, who will rule all the nations with an iron scepter"; and this expression is taken from the Old Testament book of Psalms (N.I.V.), Verse 2:7, that talks about the Messiah, the Son of God, saying: "*2:7 I will proclaim the decree of the Lord: He said to me, "You are my Son; today I have become your Father. 2:8 Ask of me, and I will make the nations your inheritance, the ends of the earth your possession. 2:9 You will rule them with an iron scepter; you will dash them to pieces like pottery.*"

The woman who fled into the desert is the Jewish people, but it emerges from Verse 12:13 that this escape happened after the Devil was thrown down from Heaven, which happened after the Ascension of Jesus according to Verse 12:6. And the woman, the Jewish people, the true Jewish people, those who were part of the people of God after the Ascension of Jesus, converted to Christianity. Therefore, the woman who fled to the desert here, are the converted Jewish people. Later in the book of Revelation we will see that the expression woman is used to refer to the Christians.

John sees the Devil appear and prepare himself to devour Christ in the moment of his birth. And John sees Christ's birth and resurrection, and the Jewish people fleeing into the desert, for a period of 1,260 days.

The cipher of 1,260 days is equal to the cipher of 3 years and a half (30x12=360 — 360x3+180), and to the cipher of 42 months (42x30), that are used in the Bible, symbolically, to represent the time of the persecutions, or the time in which the Devil is going to be allowed to cause greater evil.[164] This verse indicates that the Devil was allowed to act with more freedom immediately after the resurrection of Christ.

Verses 12:7-12: "*12:7 And there was war in heaven. Michael and his angels fought against the dragon, and the dragon and his angels fought back. 12:8 But he was not strong enough, and they lost their place in heaven. 12:9 The*

---

[164] In the Bible, book of Daniel, Verses 7:25 and 12:7, this cipher is used.

great dragon was hurled down–that ancient serpent called the devil, or Satan, who leads the whole world astray. He was hurled to the earth, and his angels with him. 12:10 Then I heard a loud voice in heaven say: "Now have come the salvation and the power and the kingdom of our God, and the authority of his Christ. For the accuser of our brothers, who accuses them before our God day and night, has been hurled down. 12:11 They overcame him by the blood of the Lamb and by the word of their testimony; they did not love their lives so much as to shrink from death. 12:12 Therefore rejoice, you heavens and you who dwell in them! But woe to the earth and the sea, because the devil has gone down to you! He is filled with fury, because he knows that his time is short."

Michael is an angel of God.[165] John sees a battle between angels of God, in Michael's command, against the Devil and his angels, that finishes with the defeat of the Devil and his angels, who are hurled from heaven to earth.

It emerges from these verses of the book of Revelation, that originally the Devil was allowed to be in heaven. Let us remember what we saw before about the book Job of the Old Testament. According to this book, the Devil's occupation was to accuse sinners before God and to punish them with the permission of God. The Devil talked personally with God. And let us remember what the New Testament teaches about the Devil in the Gospel according to Saint Luke (N.I.V.), in

---

[165] In the Bible, book of Daniel, Verse 10:13, Michael is also presented as a very important angel. He is called one of the first or chief princes.

which Jesus says to Peter: "*22:31 "Simon, Simon, Satan has asked to sift you as wheat."* It presents the Devil asking God's permission to sift Peter, acting as if he had the right to do it, because of some circumstance.

The book of Revelation seems to say here that after the resurrection of Christ the Devil was deprived of that occupation, and that the Devil was hurled down from heaven to earth. Personally, I believe that from that moment the Devil was not going to be allowed to directly punish or attack those persons who belong to the kingdom of heaven, who are not of this world anymore, at least while they are in grace with God, and while they are walking in the kingdom of God, that is to say, doing the will of God, behaving good. This does not stop the Devil from attacking the people of God through other people who are still of this world. And it probably does not stop the Devil from tempting those who are not of this world anymore, when they, despite belonging to the kingdom of God, are not clean, because they have sins that have not been forgiven yet, and they do not have their spirit in the right disposition.

In my opinion, many times, when the book of Revelation says 'earth' or 'inhabitants of the earth', it is to refer to Christians and Jews, excluding those Christians and Jews who are not of this world anymore, who are not of the earth anymore. They are called inhabitants of the world as opposed to those who are called not of this world anymore, the disciples of Jesus. In Verse 17:8 the book of Revelation says that the inhabitants of the earth were astonished, saying that the inhabitants of the earth are those who have not been written in the book of life from the creation of the world. Something likewise says Verse 13:8 of the book of Revelation. The Gospel according to Saint John (N.I.V.) says: "*3:31 The one who comes from above is above all; the one who is from the earth belongs to the earth, and speaks as one from the earth. The one who comes from heaven is above all. 3:32 He testifies to what he has seen and heard, but no one accepts his testimony. 3:33 The man who has accepted it has certified that God is truthful. 3:34 For the one whom God has sent speaks the words of God, for God gives the Spirit without limit. 3:35 The Father loves the Son and has placed everything in his hands.*"

And when it says 'sea', in my opinion, the book of Revelation is meaning peoples, multitudes, nations, tongues: Gentiles in general. In Verse 17:15 the book of Revelation talks about waters saying that they are peoples, multitudes, nations and languages.

In any case, John sees that the Devil was thrown down to earth and that he would try to do evil to the people; that is why it says in Verse 12:12 of the book of Revelation (N.I.V.): "*...But woe to the earth and the sea, because the devil has gone down to you! He is filled with fury, because he knows that his time is short.*"

In the Gospel according to Saint John (N.I.V.) Jesus says: "*12:28 Father, glorify your name!*" Then a voice came from heaven, "*I have glorified it, and will glorify it again.*" *12:29 The crowd that was there and heard it said it had thundered; others said an angel had spoken to him. 12:30 Jesus said, "This voice was for your benefit, not mine. 12:31 Now is the time for judgment on this world; now the prince of this world will be driven out.*"

The Gospel according to Saint Luke (N.I.V.) says:

"10:17 The seventy-two returned with joy and said, "Lord, even the demons submit to us in your name." 10:18 He replied, "I saw Satan fall like lightning from heaven. 10:19 I have given you authority to trample on snakes and scorpions and to overcome all the power of the enemy; nothing will harm you; 10:20 However, do not rejoice that the spirits submit to you, but rejoice that your names are written in heaven."

Verses 12:13-17. *"12:13 When the dragon saw that he had been hurled to the earth, he pursued the woman who had given birth to the male child. 12:14 The woman was given the two wings of a great eagle, so that she might fly to the place prepared for her in the desert, where she would be taken care of for a time, times and half a time, out of the serpent's reach. 12:15 Then from his mouth the serpent spewed water like a river, to overtake the woman and sweep her away with the torrent. 12:16 But the earth helped the woman by opening its mouth and swallowing the river that the dragon had spewed out of his mouth. 12:17 Then the dragon was enraged at the woman and went off to make war against the rest of her offspring—those who obey God's commandments and hold to the testimony of Jesus."*

These verses say that when the Devil was hurled to the earth, he went after the Jewish people, who were helped to escape from him. And they repeat that the Jewish people were going to be in the desert for a period of time, which represents the times of persecutions. This period of a time, times and half a time, is interpreted to be of three years and a half, each time a year, equal to 42 months, and 1,260 days.

Ruy Barraco Mármol

However, the true Jewish people, the true people of God, as I said, at this time, had already accepted Jesus and converted. Therefore, this persecution refers to a persecution of the converted Jews. This is supported by the fact that Verse 12:17 says that after persecuting the woman, the Devil went off to make war against the rest of her offspring. In my opinion, this passage has the purpose of confirming that the woman that this verse is referring to was at the time the converted Jews. In other chapters of the book of Revelation, the expression "woman" is used to refer to the Christian Church in general.

In this way, what the book of Revelation is saying when it says that the Devil, after the Ascension of Jesus, first persecuted the woman, and that the earth helped the woman, is that the Devil first persecuted the Jews who accepted Jesus, but they were protected by the people from the earth, who were the Jews who did not accept Jesus and were still of this world. It is saying that after this persecution, the Devil went to persecute the rest of the offspring, that is to say, the rest of the Christians, the converted gentiles.

This persecution of the woman, of the converted Jews, refers to the persecution carried on by Paul of Tarsus, who let us remember, counted on the authorization of the Roman Empire, that we will see was the First Beast at the time.

The two wings of a great eagle which were given to the Jewish people reminds us what the Bible, book of Exodus, (N.I.V.) says: *"19:3 Then Moses went up to God, and the Lord called to him from the mountain and said, "This is what you are to say to the house of Jacob and what you are to tell the people of Israel: 19:4 'You yourselves have seen what I did to Egypt, and how I carried you on eagles' wings and brought you to myself. 19:5 Now if you obey my covenant, then out of all nations you will be my treasured possession.*

It is very important to notice that the one who attacks the Jews and the Christians is the Devil,[166] despite the fact that the material perpetrator was not the Devil. How did the Devil attack? We will see later: Through two beasts that are dominated by, and at the service of, the Devil. One of those two beasts was Rome, to be more precise one of the heads of one of those beasts was Rome.

Chapter 13

Verses 13:1-10 of the book of Revelation (N.I.V.): "*13:1. And the dragon stood on the shore of the sea. And I saw a beast coming out of the sea. He had ten horns and seven heads, with ten crowns on his horns, and on each head a blasphemous name. 13:2 The beast I saw resembled a leopard, but had feet like those of a bear and a mouth like that of a lion. The dragon gave the beast his power and his throne and great authority. 13:3 One of the heads of the beast seemed to have had a fatal wound, but the fatal wound had been healed. The whole world was astonished and followed the beast. 13:4 Men worshiped the dragon because he had given authority to the beast, and they also worshiped the beast and asked, "Who is like the beast? Who can make war against him?" 13:5 The beast was given a mouth to utter proud words and blasphemies and to*

---

[166] The book of Revelation, Verse 2:10, also confirms this.

exercise his authority for forty-two months. 13:6 He opened his mouth to blaspheme God, and to slander his name and his dwelling place and those who live in heaven. 13:7 He was given power to make war against the saints and to conquer them. And he was given the authority over every tribe, people, language and nation. 13:8 All inhabitants of the earth will worship the beast-all whose names have not been written in the book of life belonging to the Lamb that was slain from the creation of the world. 13:9 He who has an ear, let him hear. 13:10 If anyone is to go into captivity, into captivity he will go. If anyone is to be killed with the sword, with the sword he will be killed. This calls for patient endurance and faithfulness on the part of the saints."

Saint John sees a beast appear in these verses. This beast comes out when the dragon decides to go after the Jews and the Christians. The beast comes out of the sea, and has seven heads and ten horns. In Verse 17:9 of the book of Revelation John reveals the mystery of the Beast, saying that the seven heads are seven hills on which the woman sits, and also seven kings, and the ten horns are ten kings who have not yet received a kingdom, but who for one hour will receive the authority as kings along with the Beast. The Beast that John sees here is one of the horns of the First Beast. That horn is the Roman Empire that turns into a Beast when the Devil takes control of it. In my opinion, it is not Rome itself. The Rome before Christ was not the First Beast. The Beast appears after the birth of Christ. Rome turns into a Beast after the birth of Christ.

I interpret that the First Beast is the Roman Empire under control of the Devil, because the book of

Revelation says that the Beast comes out of the sea, and to John, the author of the book of Revelation, who was in Patmos, an island of the Aegean sea, which is part of the Mediterranean sea, if the Beast came out of the sea, it came out the Roman Empire. The Roman Empire surrounded and ruled all the Mediterranean sea, the sea called by the Romans in Latin language "Mare Nostrum" (our sea). The Mare Nostrum was Rome's sea. If it came from the sea it came from Rome.

In the first times of Christianity the Roman Empire carried on persecutions against the Christians, and many Christians died at the hands of the authorities of the Roman Empire saintly confessing Christ as their savior.

If it is said that to the Beast was given power to make war against the saints and to conquer them; and we know that it is the Roman Empire who in fact made war against those saints, killing many; the conclusion is that the Beast was acting through the Roman Empire.

Furthermore Verse 17:3 of the book of Revelation says that the seven heads of a Beast, which I argue with strong basis is the First Beast, are also seven hills, as the seven historic hills that formed the heart of the city of Rome: The Aventine hill, the Capitoline hill, the Caelian hill, the Esquiline hill, the Palatine hill, the Quirinal hill and the Viminal hill.

In addition I interpret that when Verse 13:1 of the book of Revelation says that the Beast comes out of the sea it means that it comes out of Rome. I believe so because the word waters in my opinion refers to peoples, multitudes, nations and languages, and I believe the Beast coming out of Rome came out of peoples, multitudes, nations and languages.

The fact that the Roman Empire was under control of the Devil is evident from Verse 2:10 in which the Church in Smyrna is warned that the Devil was going to put some in prison and persecute them, when the material perpetrator of those acts was going to be the Roman Empire. It will be seen later that it also is evident from Verse 17:3 in which John sees another woman, who I interpret with strong basis is the Devil, sitting on a scarlet Beast, who I interpret with an equally strong basis is the Roman Empire. In the analysis of Chapter 17, I will expose the arguments that sustain those interpretations.

A powerful State, in the hands of an authority with unlimited power, who claims to have authority given by God, when it is governed by an immoral ruler, is truly a big source, and a strong tool, of evil. This is especially true if the authority is antichristian and is under control of the Devil, or a Spirit of his acting on his behalf. In that case, it is truly a Beast.

These verses narrate how the Devil taking control of the Roman Empire, personally or through another evil spirit or angel, turned it into a Beast, and how that Beast was allowed to make war on the Saints and even kill many, all of which refers to the historic events of the persecutions and killings of the apostles and Christians of the recently born church. They narrate how the Beast, the Roman Empire, received power over every tribe, people, language and nation, which describes the number and great variety of nations that were part of the Empire.

Maybe the Devil took control of the Beast through a

Spirit of his. Verse 16:13 of the book of Revelation (N.I.V.) says: *"Then I saw three evil spirits that looked like frogs; they came out of the mouth of the dragon, out of the mouth of the beast and out of the mouth of the false prophet."* Sometimes it seems to me that the Devil, the First Beast and the Second Beast constitute an evil trinity, or wanted to imitate one.

Inhabitants of the earth, as I said, are those Jews and Christians who still live in this world. Real Jews and real Christians live under other rules and are not of this world anymore. The statement of Verse 13:8 that says that all the inhabitants of the earth will worship the Beast, all whose names have not been written in the book of life, might refer to the inhabitants of the earth of the Roman Empire who were alive in that time. They worshiped the authority of Rome and Rome as Gods. Only real Christians and real Jews did not worship them. Worshiping the God of Rome, they were worshiping the Dragon, because the Dragon was giving at the time the power to Rome, and because Rome was at the service of the Dragon.

The fact that the book of Revelation uses the future tense for this prophecy, saying that men will worship the Beast, I think was meant to transmit a particular message. In my opinion, these verses are also meant to indicate that in the Great Day of the Wrath of God, which comes after the Coming of the Son of Man, all the inhabitants of the earth that face it, will worship the Beast, because all those who do not die as servants of God will be left on the hands of the Beast. This will be explained in the analysis of other Chapters of the book of Revelation.

Ruy Barraco Mármol

Verses 13:11-18 of the book of Revelation (N.I.V.): "*13:11 Then I saw another beast, coming out of the earth. He had two horns like a lamb, but he spoke like a dragon. 13:12 He exercised all the authority of the first beast on his behalf, and made the earth and its inhabitants worship the first beast, whose fatal wound had been healed. 13:13 And he performed great miraculous signs, even causing fire to come down from heaven to earth in full view of men. 13:14 Because of the signs he was given power to do on behalf of the first beast, he deceived the inhabitants of the earth. He ordered them to set up an image in honor of the beast who was wounded by the sword and yet lived. 13:15 He was given power to give breath to the image of the first beast, so that it could speak and cause all who refused to worship the image to be killed. 13:16 He also forced everyone, small and great, rich and poor, free and slave, to receive a mark on his right hand or on his forehead, 13:17 so that no one could buy or sell unless he had the mark, which is the name of the beast or the number of his name. 13:18 This calls for wisdom. If anyone has insight, let him calculate the number of the beast, for it is man's number. His number is 666.*"

Verse 13:11. "*13:11 Then I saw another beast, coming out of the earth. He had two horns like a lamb, but he spoke like a dragon.*"

This verse starts to talk about another Beast. This Beast comes out of the earth. I join those who interpret that the earth in this verse is Asia Minor, because to John, who was in Patmos, an Island of the Aegean Sea, very close to Asia Minor, the earth was Asia Minor. When this verse says that it comes out of the earth it means that the Second Beast was born in Asia Minor.

I also believe that it means that it came from those Jews who were still of this world. Paul was born in Asia Minor and came from the Jews who were still of this world.

In addition, the book of Revelation says in Verse 13:11 that the Second Beast comes from the earth, and Verse 9:8 of the book of Acts narrating the supposed calling of Paul says that Paul after falling to the ground, got up from the ground. The word translated as ground in this translation is the same Greek word used by the book of Revelation when it says that the Second Beast comes from the earth. The King James Version actually says in this Verse 9:8 of the book of Acts that Paul arose from the earth.

Furthermore, the statement that says that the Second Beast comes out of the earth, in my opinion, is also meant to identify Paul with the Second Beast, calling the attention to the words of John the Baptist that refer to the word of God, and that can be read in the Gospel according to Saint John (N.I.V.) that says: "3:31 *The one who comes from above is above all; the one who is from the earth belongs to the earth, and speaks as one from the earth. The one who comes from heaven is above all. 3:32 He testifies to what he has seen and heard, but no one accepts his testimony. 3:33 The man who has accepted it has certified that God is truthful. 3:34 For the one whom God has sent speaks the words of God, for God gives the Spirit without limit.*" These words teach that only the one whom God has sent speaks the words of God without limit.

Paul, as I explained in Chapter IV of this book, in

which I argue that he is a false prophet, said that Christ spoke in him; he said that the words he preached were the word of God; and he preached as if the word of God had been given to him to instruct in any subject, at any time, without limit.

Other men have received the word of God, but in dreams, angels' appearances, in limited ways, not the way Paul supposedly received it.

In my opinion Saint John, by saying that the Second Beast came out of the earth, wanted to call our attention to these words of the Gospel according to Saint John, that teach that only the Son of God receives the word of God in an unlimited way; that teach that whoever not being the Son of God, preaches as if he received the word of God in an unlimited way, is lying and is a false prophet.

Calling our attention to these words of the Gospel according to Saint John, Saint John was indicating us that Paul was a false prophet, who came from the earth.

Many of the verses of the book of Revelation that are related with the Second Beast are meant to call our attention in passages of the Bible, especially from the Gospel according to Saint John, that let us know that Paul was a false prophet.

The two horns of the Beast are probably an indication that the Second Beast was going to act through two persons of similar characteristics. In the book of Revelation, Chapter 17, it is said that the ten horns of the First Beast are ten kings. This suggests that the horns of the Second Beast indicate that the Second Beast was going to act through two persons, or that there will be two different persons that were going to be the Second Beast. In the Old Testament, book of the prophet Daniel, Verses 8:1-27, there is a prophecy of a Ram with two horns, interpreted by Daniel himself, that says that the two horns represent the kings of Media and Persia.

The fact that the Second Beast had two horns like a lamb indicates that it will give the impression of being a Christian. The word Lamb in the book of Revelation is used exclusively to name Jesus (for instance verse 17:14). In the rest of the Bible, it is only used symbolically to refer to Christ and to his apostles and disciples. The Christians in general are called sheep; the lamb is the young sheep, often used for sacrifices. The Gospel according to Saint Luke (N.I.V.) says: "*10:1 After this the Lord appointed seventy-two others and sent them two by two ahead of him to every town and place where he was about to go. 10:2 He told them, "The harvest is plentiful, but the workers are few. Ask the Lord of the harvest, therefore, to send out workers into his harvest field. 10:3 Go! I am sending you out like lambs among wolves."* The First Epistle of Paul to the Corinthians (N.I.V.) says: "*5:7 Get rid of the old yeast that you may be a new batch without yeast-as you really are. For Christ, our Passover lamb, has been sacrificed.*"

The fact that the Second Beast, or at least its first horn, must have seemed like a Christian is also confirmed by the last part of Verse 13:11, that we are analyzing, which says "but he spoke like a dragon", which means that he spoke like a Devil. This expression corroborates what I said before, because it suggests that talking like a dragon, he was doing the opposite of what could be expected of him, because of the two

Ruy Barraco Mármol

horns he had like a lamb.

No Roman Emperor could fit in these descriptions. Paul fits. The book of Acts of the Apostles teaches that Paul was born in Tarsus in Cilicia,[167] in Asia Minor, he was a Jew still of this world, he preached as if he received the word of God in an unlimited way, he gave the impression he was a Christian, a Lamb, but spoke like a dragon, like a Devil, as I said in the first part of this book.

Verse 13:12 of the book of Revelation (N.I.V.) says: *"13:12 He exercised all the authority of the first beast on his behalf, and made the earth and its inhabitants worship the first beast, whose fatal wound had been healed."*

The first part of this verse says that the Second Beast exercised all the authority of the First Beast in his behalf. As I said before, the First Beast, at the time, is the Roman Empire under control of the Devil, or of a demoniac spirit acting on his behalf.

This verse applies to Paul because everything indicates that he must have counted on the authorization of Rome to carry out the persecution of Christians, which seems to have ended by the time of his supposed calling. He probably carried out the first genocide of Christians authorized and empowered by high authorities of Rome, perhaps by the emperor himself. The Gospel according to Saint John says that Jesus was taken before Pilate because the Jews did not

[167] The book of Acts of the Apostles (N.IV) says: "22:3: *"I am a Jew, born at Tarsus of Cilicia, but brought up in this city. Under Gamaliel I was thoroughly trained in the law of our fathers and was just as zealous for God as any of you are today."*

have authorization to execute the death penalty,[168] which was what the authorities of Jerusalem wanted with regard to Jesus. This suggests that, when shortly after the passion of Christ, more or less two years, Paul pursued, imprisoned and condemned to death Christians, he had authorization and power given by Rome and he was exercising that power of Rome. The book of Acts of the Apostles narrating the release of Peter and John from the hands of the Sanhedrin (N.I.V.) says: "*4:27 Indeed Herod and Pontius Pilate met together with the Gentiles and the people of Israel in this city to conspire against your holy servant Jesus, whom you anointed.*"

In addition, it is curious that for some reason, we do not really know why or how, Paul besides being a Jew was also a Roman citizen, and on one occasion in which he was imprisoned, he received a detachment of two hundred soldiers, seventy horsemen and two hundred spearmen from Rome to protect him.[169] Paul said that he was a Roman Citizen by birth, but it is not clear if so, why or how his parents were Roman citizens.

When the book of Revelation says that the First Beast seemed to have had a fatal wound that had been healed, in my opinion, refers to the persecution of Rome commanded by Paul of Tarsus against the Christians. This persecution, let us remember, was carried out with the authorization of Rome, because

---

[168] The Gospel according to Saint John (N.I.V.) says. "*18:31 Pilate said, "Take him yourselves and judge him by your own law." "But we have no right to execute anyone," the Jews objected.*"

[169] The book of Acts of the Apostles, Verse 23:23.

only Rome had the power and the authority to execute the death penalty. And it happened in times in which according to the book of Acts of the Apostles, Rome had made allegiance with the Jews hierarchy against the Christians. The word of Christ, which is called symbolically sword in the book of Revelation and in other books of the Bible, defeated this persecution, and seemed to have wounded the First Beast with a fatal wound, who was the Roman Empire, but later, with the false conversion of Paul of Tarsus and his preaching, the wound is healed, and the doctrine of Paul of Tarsus makes Christianity less mortal for the Empire and the ideology that sustains it: and thus the First Beast survived.

The second part of this Verse 13:12 of the book of Revelation (N.I.V.) says: "*and made the earth and its inhabitants worship the first beast, whose fatal wound had been healed.*"

This verse says then that the Second Beast made the inhabitants of the earth worship the First Beast, who at the time was the Roman Empire under control of the Devil.

The Gospel according to Saint John (N.I.V.) 4:23 says: "*Yet a time is coming and has now come when the true worshipers will worship the Father in spirit and truth, for they are the kind of worshipers the Father seeks. 4:24 God is spirit and his worshipers must worship in spirit and truth.*" He who does the will of God, worships God in spirit.[170]

---

[170] The book of the prophet Isaiah (N.K.J.V) says: "*1:10 Here the word of the*

The Greek word translated as worship in these verses of the Gospel according to Saint John are the same Greek word translated as worship in the book of Revelation that we are analyzing.[171]

The book of Revelation says that the Beast makes the earth and its inhabitants worship in spirit the Beast, act according to the spirit of the Beast, the doctrine of the Beast.

It can be said that Paul made the inhabitants of the earth worship in spirit the Beast, by making the people act according to the spirit of the Beast, the doctrine of the Beast, contained in the epistles attributed to him.

In addition, the word 'worship' not only means to honor or reverence as a divine being or supernatural power: It also means to regard with extravagant

---

Lord. You rulers of Sodom; Give ear to the law of our God, You people of Gomorrah: 1:11 To what purpose is the multitude of your sacrifices to Me? Says the Lord. "I have had enough of burnt offerings of rams and the fat of the cattle. I do not delight in the blood of bulls, or of lambs or goats. 1:12 When you come to appear beforeMe. Who has required this from your hand, to trample My courts? 1:13 Bring no more futile sacrifices: Incense is an abomination to Me. The New Moons, the Sabbaths, and the calling of assemblies- I cannot endure iniquity and the sacred meeting. 1:14 Your New Moons and your appointed feasts My soul hates. They are a trouble to Me. I am weary of bearing them. 1:15 When you spread out your hands, I will hide My eyes from you. Even though you make many prayers, I will not hear. Your hands are full of blood. 1:16 Wash yourselves, make yourselves clean; put away the evil of your doings from before My eyes, cease to do evil. 1:17 Learn to do good; Seek justice, Rebuke the oppressor; Defend the fatherless, Plead for the widow. 1:18 Come now, and let us reason together, says the Lord." The book of the prophet Isaiah (N.K.J.V) says: "58:6 Is this not the fast that I have chosen: To loose the bonds of wickedness, to undo the heavy burdens. To let the oppressed go free. And that you break every yoke? 58:7 Is it not to share your bread with the hungry, and that you bring to your house the poor who are cast out; when you see the naked, that you cover him, and not hide yourself from your own flesh? Then your light shall break forth like the morning."

[171] The Greek words are προσκυνηται (proskunetai) and προσκυνησουσιν (proskunesousin).

respect, honor or devotion[172]. Verses 22:6-9 of the book of Revelation (N.I.V.), narrating a conversation between John and one of the Angels of the seven bowls, says: *"22:6 The angel said to me, "These words are trustworthy and true. The Lord, the God of the spirits of the prophets, sent his angel to show his servants the things that must soon take place." 22:7 "Behold, I am coming soon! Blessed is he who keeps the words of the prophecy in this book." 22:8 I, John, am the one who heard and saw these things. And when I had heard and seen them, I fell down to worship at the feet of the angel who had been showing them to me. 22:9 But he said to me, "Do not do it! I am a fellow servant with you and with your brothers the prophets and of all who keep the words of this book. Worship God!"* The word worship here is being used with the second meaning, with the meaning <u>to regard with extravagant respect, honor or devotion</u>. Saint John did not have the intention of treating the Angel as a divine being here, even though he was regarding him with extravagant respect, honor and devotion.

The act of giving honor and respect to somebody, as if he were an authority instituted by God to execute the wrath of God upon the wrongdoer, in my opinion, is worshiping; that is, regarding with extravagant respect, honor or devotion, especially when that authority makes himself worshiped as if he were God.

It can be said that Paul made the inhabitants of Rome, at least the Jews and Christians inhabitants of Rome who were of this world, worship the First Beast,

---

[172] The Webster's Seventh New Collegiate Dictionary says under the word worship: vb *"...2 to regard with extravagant respect, honor or devotion...".*

or the Roman Empire, which at that time was the First Beast, because he sent an epistle to the Romans teaching that all the authorities have been instituted by God; teaching that whoever rebels against the authority rebels against the divine order, and that those who do so will bring judgment on themselves; teaching that the rulers hold no terror for those who do right, but for those who do wrong; teaching that the rulers are God's servants to execute the wrath of God upon the wrongdoer, and that everyone has to submit to them giving them respect and honor. Let us remember what the Epistle of Paul to the Romans (N.I.V.) says: "*13:1 Everyone must submit himself to the governing authorities, for there is no authority except that which God has established. The authorities that exist have been established by God. 13:2 Consequently, he who rebels against the authority is rebelling against what God has instituted, and those who do so will bring judgment on themselves. 13:3 For rulers hold no terror for those who do right, but for those who do wrong. Do you want to be free from fear of the one in authority? Then do what is right and he will commend you. 13:4 For he is God's servant to do you good. But if you do wrong, be afraid, for he does not bear the sword for nothing. He is God's servant and agent of the wrath to bring punishment on the wrongdoer. 13:5 Therefore, it is necessary to submit to the authorities, not only because of possible punishment but also because of conscience. 13:6 This is also why you pay taxes, for the authorities are God's Servants, who give their full time to governing. Give everyone what you owe him: If you owe taxes, pay taxes; if revenue, then revenue; if respect, then respect; if honor, then honor.*"[173]

This epistle was sent while Nero was the Emperor of Rome, and Nero was asking Roman citizens to worship and consider Rome and himself as gods. Christians surely were neither taught nor commanded by Paul to call Nero god, at least in the Epistle of Paul to the Romans, nor to worship the Roman Empire, but they were taught to give to the emperor honor and respect, as if he were an authority instituted by God, as if he were an agent of the wrath of God to bring punishment on the wrongdoer, and he was not either. That kind of act fits in the concept of regarding with extravagant respect, honor or devotion. Extravagant means according to the Webster's Seventh New Collegiate Dictionary current definition: "*2.a. exceeding the limits of reason or necessity. 2.b. lacking in moderation balance, and restraint.*"

Verse 13:13 of the book of Revelation (N.I.V.) says: "*And he performed great and miraculous signs, even causing fire to come down from heaven to earth in full view of men.*"

The signs are supernatural acts that God uses to prove that prophets are men of God. In the Gospel according to Saint Mark (N.I.V.), Christ says: "*16:17 And these signs will accompany those who believe: In my name they will drive out demons; they will speak in new tongues; 16:18 they will pick up snakes with their hands; and when they drink deadly poison, it will not hurt them at all; they will place their hands on sick people, and they will get well.*" The Greek word translated as signs is this verse is the same Greek word used in the

---

[173] The Epistle of Paul to the Romans, Verses 13:1-7.

verse of the book of Revelation which we are analyzing. The Greek word is σημεια (semeia). When Verse 13:13 of the book of Revelation says that the Second Beast, performed great and miraculous signs it is saying that he performed acts like these.

Causing fire to come down from heaven is a sign. In the Old Testament, second book of Kings, Verse 1:10, the prophet Elijah asks God to make fire come down from heaven to prove that he is a man of God[174]. In the New Testament, the Gospel according to Saint Luke (N.I.V.) says: "*9:51 As the time approached for him to be taken up to heaven, Jesus resolutely set out for Jerusalem. 9:52 And he sent messengers on ahead, who went into a Samaritan village to get things ready for him; 9:53 but the people there did not welcome him, because he was heading for Jerusalem. 9:54 When the disciples James and John saw this, they asked, "Lord, do you want us to call fire down from heaven to destroy them?" 9:55 But Jesus turned and rebuked them, 9:56 and they went to another village.*"[175]

The Second Beast then, according to the book of Revelation, made signs that could lead people to believe that he was a prophet, a man of God. The Second Beast not only seemed like a lamb, like a man of God, like a Christian, but also made signs that made him look like a

---

[174] *The Bible, the second book of Kings, (N.I.V.) says: "1:10 Elijah answered the captain, "If I am a man of God, may fire come down from heaven and consume you and your fifty men!" Then fire fell from heaven and consumed the captain and his men."*

[175] In the Bible, book of Job, Verse 1:16, the Devil is permitted to put forth his hand on Job's possessions, and he does this by making fire fall from the sky to the earth.

prophet, like an apostle. In the book of Job of the Bible, Old Testament, Satan makes fire fall from the sky over Job's sheep and servants.[176]

These expressions apply to Paul because he made a lot of signs - - at least that is what the book of Acts of the Apostles says - - that made him look like a man of God, like a Christian, which favored the First Beast and the Dragon, by convincing a lot of people that his doctrine, full of vices, was the word of God.

Furthermore, the book of Acts of the Apostles says that his supposed calling happened when a light that came from the sky fell down over him and over those who were accompanying him.[177] I cannot help finding a similarity between fire coming down from the sky and light coming down from the sky. The light that came down from the sky that supposedly preceded the calling of Paul, could have been a sign made by him so that he would seem like a man of God. Besides, the Greek word πυρ (poor) translated in this verse of the book of Revelation as fire, also means lightening, bright.[178] Therefore, what this verse can be saying is that the Second Beast even made brightness, a light, come down from the sky.

The fact that the Second Beast must have seemed a

---

[176] The Bible, book of Job, Verse 1:16.

[177] The book of Acts of the Apostles (N.I.V.) says: "9:3 As he neared Damascus on his journey, suddenly a light from heaven flashed around him. 9:4 He fell to the ground and heard a voice say to him, "Saul, Saul, why do you persecute me?""

[178] Karl Feyerabend "Langenscheidt Pocket Greek Dictionary", says under the Greek word πυρ, πυρος,: fire; lightning; fire-sign; fever-heat; blaze.

false prophet is confirmed in other verses of the book of Revelation; for instance in Verse 19:20, in which the Second Beast is even called a false prophet. It could not have been a man who tried to spread the Imperial religion, or a priest of the Imperial religion. Nobody fits in these descriptions except Paul, much less the way he does.

Verse 13:14: *"Because of the signs he was given power to do on behalf of the first beast, he deceived the inhabitants of the earth. He ordered them to set up an image in honor of the beast who was wounded by the sword and yet lived."*

The first part of this Verse 13:14 says: *"Because of the signs he was given power to do on behalf of the first beast, he deceived the inhabitants of the earth."*

In my opinion, its interpretation does not offer any difficulty. It says that the inhabitants of the earth are deceived because the real Christians, the ones that have come out of the world, the ones who are not of this world anymore, do not get deceived by Paul. They can tell the difference between the word of Christ and the word of Paul, and the fruits of one and the other, or at least ignore or do not put in practice the wrong words of Paul.

This part of Verse 13:14 applies to Paul because, as I said, according to the book of Acts of the Apostles, Paul made a lot of signs, that convinced a lot of people that he was a prophet, that they should imitate him, that they should consider his word, the word of his epistles, the word of God; and in that way he deceived them, which served the First Beast and the Dragon very well.

The second part of this Verse 13:14 says: "*He ordered them to set up an image in honor of the beast who was wounded by the sword and yet lived.*"

Before getting into the interpretation of this part of the verse it is worthwhile to remark that the Greek word translated as "ordered" also means "to say" or "to tell". The King James Version translates this word as "saying", as well as the Revised Standard Version, Second Catholic Edition. The New American Standard Bible translates this word as "bidding". The New American Bible translates "telling", as well as the English Standard Version.

It is also worthwhile to remark that the Greek text of the verse does not say "set up an image in honor of the beast". In no place does it say "honor", and in no place does it say "of". It says 'set up an image "for" or "to" the Beast'. At least this is true of the Greek texts that I am using in this work, quoted in the prologue. The King James Version translates "image to the Beast". The Revised Standard Version translates "image for the Beast". The New American Bible translates "image for the Beast". The New American Standard Bible translates "image to the Beast". The English Standard Version translates "image for the Beast".

The Second Beast told the inhabitants of the earth to set up an image for the Beast. Even though the author is the Second Beast, this verse says that the Second Beast told them to set up an image for the First Beast. The verse ends up saying that the image is for the

Beast "who was wounded by the sword and yet lived" and this leads us to believe that it refers to the First Beast, because Verse 13:3 says about the First Beast: "*One of the heads of the beast seemed to have had a fatal wound, but the fatal wound had been healed.*" And Verse 13:12 says: "*...and made the earth and its inhabitants worship the first beast, whose fatal wound had been healed*".

The word image, according to the Webster's dictionary means: "*1.a reproduction or imitation of the form of a person or a thing; esp: an imitation in solid form. 2.a the optical counterpart of an object produced by a lens, mirror, or other optical system. 2.b any likeness of an object produced on a photographic material. 3: exact likeness. 4.a. A tangible of visible representation: Incarnation. b archaic: an illusory form: Apparition. 5 a (1): a mental picture of something not actually present: Impression (2): a mental conception held in common by members of a group and symbolic of a basic attitude and orientation...*[179]*".* (Underline emphasis is mine)

The Greek word translated as image is εικονα (eikona), which means according to the Langenscheidt Pocket Greek[180] dictionary: likeness, image, picture, painting; simile; phantom; notion. It is the origin of the English word "icon".

The same Greek word εικονα (eikona) translated as image, in the verse of the book of Revelation that we

---

[179] The "Webster's Seventh New Collegiate Dictionary".

[180] Karl Feyerabend "Langenscheidt Pocket Greek Dictionary" under the Greek word εικων, ονος, η. (eikon).

are analyzing, was used by Paul to refer to Christ, saying that Christ is the image of God. The Epistle of Paul to the Colossians (N.I.V.) says, referring to the Son of God: "*1:15 He is the image of the invisible God, the firstborn over all creation.*" The Epistle of Paul to the Hebrews says: "*1:3 The Son is the radiance of God's glory and the exact representation of his being, sustaining all things by his powerful word.*" The Second Epistle of Paul to the Corinthians (N.I.V.) says: "*4:4 The god of this age has blinded the minds of unbelievers, so that they cannot see the light of the gospel of the glory of Christ, who is the image of God.*" In these verses that I have just transcribed, the word image is not a thing. Paul says that Christ is the image of God. They tell us that the image does not necessarily need to be a thing. It can be a thing, but it also can be a person. Christ would be an image of God because he would be a representation of his being and because he irradiates God's glory.

The Epistle of Paul to the Romans (N.I.V.) says: "*8:29 For those God foreknew he also predestined to be conformed to the likeness of his Son, that he might be the firstborn among many brothers.*" The Second Epistle of Paul to the Corinthians (N.I.V.) says: "*3:18 And we, who with unveiled faces all reflect the Lord's glory, are being transformed into his likeness with ever-increasing glory, which comes from the Lord, who is the Spirit.*" The Greek word translated as likeness in these verses is also the same word used in the verse of the book of Revelation that we are analyzing, translated in it as "image". The last verse of these two gives the clue to decipher how the Beast told others to make an image, and how the description applies to Paul.

Let us take a close look at that verse of the Second Epistle of Paul to the Corinthians (N.I.V.) which says: "*3:18 And we, who with unveiled faces all reflect the Lord's glory, are being transformed into his likeness with ever-increasing glory, which comes from the Lord, who is the Spirit.*" This verse implies that Christians should reflect the Lord's Glory and become an image of God. With these words Paul is telling Christians to become an image of God. At the same time Paul is saying that he is becoming an image of God. Saying that Christians should become an image of God, saying that he is becoming an image of God, and asking Christians to imitate himself, with which he made them become an image of God different from the real, he deceived the inhabitants of the earth to set up an image for the Beast. Our ministers and the Christians in general, instead of becoming like Jesus, were deceived to become like Paul.

The First Epistle of Paul to the Thessalonians (N.I.V.) says: "*1:6 You became imitators of us and of the Lord; in spite of severe suffering, you welcomed the message with the joy given by the Holy Spirit. 1:7 And so you became a model to all the believers in Macedonia and Achaia. 1:8 The Lord's message rang out from you not only in Macedonia and Achaia—your faith in God has become known everywhere.*"

In point II.26 of the first part of this book I quoted many verses in which Paul told the inhabitants of the earth to imitate him. In point IV of the first part of this book I quoted many verses with which Paul made the inhabitants of the earth consider his epistles the word of God. We have discussed in this book many important wrong behaviors of Paul and the errors of the Epistles of Paul. Telling the inhabitants of the earth to imitate his conduct and telling them to consider his epistles, which were full of errors, the word of God, he was deceiving them into transforming themselves into an image of God very different from the real God, which was going to be useful and serve the First Beast. Paul was neither an image of the real God with his life, nor with his word. Paul distorted the image of God so that the inhabitants of the earth could not see how God is.

The false image of God that Paul told the inhabitants of the earth to make with their lives is an image for the First Beast, and of the First Beast, because the Second Beast was at the service of the First Beast. It was useful and was prepared to help the constitution and functioning of all the other horns and heads of the First Beast. It was prepared to help the establishment and survival of tyrannies and theocracies. This is the reason why the Epistles of Paul still do this. In addition, it is also an image of the First Beast, because it lets us know how the First Beast is and what the First Beast wants.

In my opinion, by using in this verse of the book of Revelation the figure of the image of God, Saint John wanted to call our attention to the statements of Paul in which he says that Christ, the Son of God, is the image of God. These statements are wrong because Christ, the Son of God, is not the image of God: he is God.

In addition Saint John wanted to call our attention to the Second Epistle of Paul to the Corinthians, Verse 4:4, that says: "*4:4 The god of this age has blinded the minds of unbelievers, so that they cannot see the light of the gospel of the glory of Christ, who is the image of God.*" In this Verse, Paul calls the Devil god, when he says "the god of this age". The Devil is referred to in the Gospel as "prince of the world" but not as god. There is only one God in our world, and he is not the Devil. The Devil in no way is god of anything. It is wrong to call the Devil god.

Moreover, there is another meaning with which the word image can be interpreted. The Second Epistle of Paul to the Corinthians (N.I.V.) says: "*4:4 The god of this age has blinded the minds of unbelievers, so that they cannot see the light of the gospel of the glory of Christ, who is the image of God.*" The Greek word translated as who, in this verse, is "ος". All the English versions of the Bible with which I worked in this book translate this Greek word "ος" (os) as who. However many Spanish versions translate this word as "that" instead of "who". The Spanish version of the Bible of the Vatican Web Site, which is called "El libro del Pueblo de Dios", translates this word as "that". The Spanish word "quien" means who. The Spanish word "que" means that. Next I will explain why the word "ος" can be translated as "that" instead of "who".

The Greek word "ος" (os) is a Greek relative pronoun that means 'who' and 'that', among other meanings. The word ος could refer in this verse of the Epistle to the Corinthians either to the word light or to the word Christ. This is so, because the word ος (os) is the masculine form of the word, and in principle this relative pronoun should match in gender and number with the word to which it refers. The two masculine Greek words with which it could match are the ones translated as light and Christ in this verse. The word

Christ is the closest word to the relative pronoun, but the context indicates that the word ος (os) refers to the word light. Paul is talking about the ministry, about the gospel, about the light of Christ. Besides, the gospel of Christ truly is an image of God, which Christ is not. Christ is God, not his image. All this allows the translation of the word with the meaning of "that" instead of "who".

By translating this word ος (os) as if it refers to the word light the verse would be saying that the light of the Gospel is the image of God. Assuming that the word ος (os) refers to the word light, then this verse of the Second Epistle to the Corinthians should be translated in the following way: "*4:4 The god of this age has blinded the minds of unbelievers, so that they cannot see the light of the gospel of the glory of Christ, that is the image of God.*

The light of the gospel is the image of God, because the Gospel lets us know how God is. The book of Acts of the Apostles (N.I.V.) says: "*26:23 that the Christ would suffer and, as the first to rise from the dead, would proclaim light to his own people and to the Gentiles.*" Here the word light is being used symbolically to refer to the word of God, because what Christ proclaimed was the word of God, his Gospel, which is the image of God.

When Verse 13:14 of the book of Revelation says that the Second Beast ordered them to set up an image to the Beast, it can be saying that the Second Beast ordered them to set up for the Beast a word, a doctrine, a gospel.

This Verse 13:14 of the book of Revelation, interpreted in this sense, would apply to Paul, because he ordered the inhabitants of the earth to set up an image for the Beast, the word of the Beast, which is contained in the Epistles of Paul. The image would be the light of the word for the First Beast that is in the epistles.

We already saw how Paul preached a Gospel different from the Gospel that Christ taught. In Chapter IV of the first part of this book we saw how he made the people consider the epistles he wrote the word of God.

The verse could be saying that Paul ordered the inhabitants of the earth to set up an image of the First Beast when he made them consider his epistles the word of God. The action of the people who read the epistles in the churches, reproduced them, and believed in them as if they were the word of God, set up the epistles as an image of God for the inhabitants of the earth. Those people and Paul set up the Gospel of Paul as an image for all Christians by making it considered the word of God. It was not enough for Paul to say it; he needed people to believe, read and worship the epistles, and set them up as an image for all Christians.

Verse 13:15 of the book of Revelation (N.I.V.) says: *"He was given power to give breath to the image of the first beast, so that it could speak and cause all who refused to worship the image to be killed."*

The first part of this verse says: "He was given power to give breath to the image of the first beast, so that it could speak..." The Greek word translated as breath here is πνευματι (pnyoomati) which means wind,

Ruy Barraco Mármol

air, breath, life, spirit, inspiration.[181] Spirit is one of the meanings of this word. The same Greek word was used in the Gospel according to Saint John (N.I.V.) that says: "*4:23 Yet a time is coming and has now come when the true worshipers will worship the Father in spirit and truth, for they are the kind of worshipers the Father seeks. 4:24 God is spirit and his worshipers must worship in spirit and truth.*" He who does the will of God worships God in spirit.

When Paul made the inhabitants of the earth worship in spirit the Beast and his image, do the will of the Beast, he gave spirit to the image. Making inhabitants of the earth be transformed into images of the Beast he made the image speak. Making the wrong teachings of the Epistles of Paul act in those transformed into images of the Beast he made the images speak. Making the word of the Beast contained in the Epistles of Paul be considered the word of God, he gave word to the image, he made the image speak. All those who teach the errors of the Epistles of Paul, create doctrine upon those errors and imitate the wrong behaviors of Paul, worship in spirit the image of the Beast, and give spirit and word to the image of the Beast, so that it can speak.

The First Epistle of Paul to the Thessalonians (N.I.V.) says: "*1:6 You became imitators of us and of the Lord; in spite of severe suffering, you welcomed the message with the joy given by the Holy Spirit. 1:7 And so you became a model to all the believers in Macedonia and Achaia. 1:8 The Lord's message rang out from you not only in Macedonia and Achaia—your faith in God has become known*

---

[181] Feyerabend, Kart, "Langenscheidt Pocket Greek Dictionary", p. 310.

everywhere."

The First Epistle of Paul to the Thessalonians (N.I.V.) says: "*2:13 And we also thank God continually because, when you received the word of God, which you heard from us, you accepted it not as the word of men, but as it actually is, the word of God, which is at work in you who believe.*"

Not all the Christians, who believe that the Epistles of Paul are sacred scripture, give spirit in their own person to the image of Paul, to the image of the Beast. Only those who really obey and believe what the Epistles of Paul say, and try to live according to them, do. Most Christians do not even know what the epistles say.

However, all of those who sustain that the Epistles of Paul are sacred scripture do contribute in a greater or lesser extent to give spirit to the image of the Beast in others.

The second part of Verse 13:15 says: "*..., so that it could speak and cause all who refused to worship the image to be killed.*"

The Greek word translated as killed is αποκτανθωσιν (apoktanthosin), which is a tense of the verb αποκτεινω (apokteino). The Second Epistle of Paul to the Corinthians (N.I.V.) says: "*3:6 He has made us competent as ministers of a new covenant—not of the letter but of the Spirit; for the letter kills, but the Spirit gives life.*" The Greek word translated as <u>killed</u> in this verse is αποκτεννει (apoktenei), which is also a tense of the verb αποκτεινω (apokteino). The word is used with a symbolical meaning. Paul says that the letter symbolically kills because it makes people sin, and therefore, to be excluded from the people of God. This

Greek word is the same word used in Verse 13:15 of the book of Revelation that we are analyzing, translated in it as <u>killed as well</u>, and it also can be interpreted with that symbolical meaning.

This second part of Verse 13:15 of the book of Revelation applies to Paul because he made people sin tempting them to reject Christianity. Those inhabitants of the earth, who reject Christ because of the teachings of Paul, die. They commit a deadly sin. The teachings of Paul are no excuse for rejecting Christ, because everybody should recognize the Epistles of Paul as false, as well as the teachings of Christ as true. Nobody can reject Christ because of what other men did.

I believe that recognizing the Epistles of Paul as false is an essential part of being a true Christian. We have to win against the Devil who tempts us, the Beasts, the image of the Beast and the number of the Beast.

The ones who are not of this world anymore, the ones who are in the kingdom of God, who continue faithful to Jesus and refuse to worship Paul do not die.

Verse 13:16: "*He also forced everyone, small and great, rich and poor, free and slave, to receive a mark on his right hand or on his forehead.*"

In my opinion, the mark referred to in this verse of the book of Revelation is a mark in the mind, in the soul, in the heart, of the ones who received it.

The book of Revelation (N.I.V.) says: "*7:3 "Do not harm the land or the sea or the trees until we put a seal on the foreheads of the servants of our God." 7:4 Then I heard* the number of those who were sealed: 144,000 from all the tribes of Israel."

The book of Revelation (N.I.V.) says: "14:1 Then I looked, and there before me was the Lamb, standing on Mount Zion, and with him 144,000 who had his name and his Father's name written on their foreheads."

The book of Revelation (N.I.V.) says: "22:3 No longer will there be any curse. The throne of God and of the Lamb will be in the city, and his servants will serve him. 22:4 They will see his face, and his name will be on their foreheads."

The Gospel according to Saint John (N.I.V.) says: "6:27 Do not work for food that spoils, but for food that endures to eternal life, which the Son of Man will give you. On him God the Father has placed his seal of approval."

The Epistle of Paul to the Romans (N.I.V.): "4:11 And he received the sign of circumcision, a seal of the righteousness that he had by faith while he was still uncircumcised."

The First Epistle of Paul to the Corinthians (N.I.V.) says: "9:2: Even though I may not be an apostle to others, surely I am to you! For you are the seal of my apostleship in the Lord."

In the Bible, in the book of Deuteronomy (N.I.V.), following the requirements, decrees, laws and commands of Moses, it is said: "11:18 Fix these words of mine in your hearts and minds; tie them as symbols on your hands and bind them on your foreheads. 11:19 Teach them to your children, talking about them when you sit at home and when you walk along the road, when you lie down and when you get up. 11:20 Write them on the doorframes of your houses and on your gates, 11:21 so that your days and the days of your children may be many in the land that the

Lord swore to give your forefathers, as many as the days that the heavens are above the earth."

Interpreting the word mark of Verse 13:16 symbolically it applies to Paul because he made small and great, rich and poor, free and slave, receive his mark in their mind, receive his doctrine in their mind, the doctrine of the First Beast, of the Dragon, of the Devil. And he made them act according to his doctrine.

In regard to the mark on the right hand, I believe that means that he made people act according to that mark. The right hand is the one with which people write, sign, and do some other very important acts of life.

Verse 13:17: *"so that no one could buy or sell unless he had the mark, which is the name of the beast or the number of his name."*

The words buy and sell are used in the Bible literally and also symbolically, but we will see that the word is being used here with a symbolical meaning. The book of Revelation (N.I.V.) says: *"5:9 And they sang a new song: "You are worthy to take the scroll and to open its seals, because you were slain, and with your blood you purchased men for God from every tribe and language and people and nation."* The word purchased in this verse is being used with a symbolical meaning. Christ was slain, and with his blood he purchased men for God. This is the meaning I understand we have to give the word buy in this Verse 13:17 that we are analyzing._

Paul also uses the word buy with this meaning of getting new disciples. The First Epistle of Paul to the

Corinthians (N.I.V.) says: "*6:19 Do you not know that your body is a temple of the Holy Spirit, who is in you, whom you have received from God? You are not your own; 6:20 you were bought at a price. Therefore honor God with your body.*" The First Epistle of Paul to the Corinthians says: "*7:23 You were bought at a price; do not become slaves of men.*"

Even though the verse talks about a mark with the name or the number of the Beast, it refers to the doctrine. Let us remember what the book of Revelation (N.I.V.) says: "*14:1 Then I looked, and there before me was the Lamb, standing on Mount Zion, and with him 144,000 who had his name and his Father's name written on their foreheads.*" The ones who have the Father's name written on their foreheads, are the ones who have God's doctrine in their minds. The ones who have the Beast's number in their forehead are the ones who have the Beast's doctrine in their minds.

This Verse 13:17 of the book of Revelation applies to Paul because he made it so that nobody could buy or sell Christian disciples, or even be a Christian minister, without accepting his mark, without accepting the mark of the Beast, without putting in their minds the doctrine of Paul.

The mark that Paul made to be put on people's forehead is the mark of the Second Beast because he put it; and it is the mark of the First Beast because the Second Beast, or its first horn, Paul, acted on behalf of it.

Verse 13:18: "*This calls for wisdom! If anyone has insight, let him calculate the number of the beast, for it is man's number. His number is 666."*

In regard to the number, I believe it refers to the Second Beast. It seems that systematically, when the book of Revelation refers to the First Beast, it indicates it expressly, as in Verses 13:12, 13:14; and 13:15.

The number does not need to refer to a name, because the verse says that it is a man's number, not the number of the name of a man. The fact that Verse 15:2 of the book of Revelation (N.I.V.) says, *"And I saw what looked like a sea of glass mixed with fire and, standing beside the sea, those who had been victorious over the beast and his image and over the number of his name"*, does not mean that we must calculate the number of the name of the Beast. There is a number of the man, and there is a number of the name of the man. We must calculate the number of the Beast and be victorious over the number of the name of the Beast. The number of the name of the Second Beast is the number of people who have its mark, who believe in his doctrine. Verse 14:1 of the book of Revelation talks about the 144,000 who had the name of the Lamb and of his Father written on their foreheads. The number of 144,000 men is the number of the name of the Lamb and of his Father.

In order to calculate the number of name of the Beast the book of Revelation gives us the number of the man whose doctrine is followed by those who are the number of the name of the Beast. Realizing who that number belongs to, we will be able to calculate or identify who are the men part of the number of the name of the Beast.

The expression that says that the number of the

Beast is a man's number, also indicates that the Second Beast is a man, not an institution. It is a man, not the Roman Empire for instance.

We already know who the first horn of the Second Beast is: the false Apostle Paul. The consequences of the actions of the Second Beast according to the book of Revelation are very important and transcendent. To occupy the place which the Second Beast has in the book of Revelation, in the history, it must have had a seriously evil and lasting action. If somebody is the Second Beast, or at least its first horn, it is clear that this person is Paul. Therefore this riddle is about discovering how it applies to Paul of Tarsus.

The notorious number of the man, which we find in all the Bibles today is **666**, but there are important documents of antiquity that state the number **616** instead of the number **666**. From the ancient fragments of copies of the book of Revelation, and from the ancient copies of the book of Revelation, it is not certain which one is the right number.[182]

Irenaeous, who lived in the second century A.D.,[183] in his book "Adversus haerenses" 5, 30, 1-3, already gives testimony about the existence of the variant

---

[182] The book "Biblia Comentada", by Profesores de Salamanca, vol. VII, under Apocalipsis Verses 13:11-18, p. 451,. says: "El texto original no es seguro, pues algunos codices dan el número 616, y los otros el 666." The English translation of these words would be - the original text is not sure, because some ancient copies of the Bible give the number 616 and others 666.

[183] Johannes Quasten "Patrologia", Collection of "Biblioteca de Autores Cristianos" Spanish Edition prepared by Ignacio Oñatibia, (Madrid; La Editorial Católica S.A., MCMLXI), p. 276, says that the date of birth of Irenaeous is not known but probably was between 140 and 160 A.D..

Ruy Barraco Mármol

number 616, but he had it as an error.[184] He said that those men who saw the Apostle John face to face held that the correct number is 666.[185] His testimony is an argument in favor of the number 666, but certainly not even close to be important enough to settle the dispute. This is why the number has survived in copies of the Bible for a long time after his book was published, in spite of his opinions, and this is why we are still arguing about it.

I say that his testimony is not important enough to settle the dispute, among other reasons, because Irenaeous also stated, for instance, that Christ lived until Christ was an old man, and that he received this information from disciples of John the apostle, who were taught by John that same thing.[186] We have reasons to disbelieve in the testimony and the judgment of Irenaeous.

In favor of the number 616 it is the fact that some words closely related to the prophecy of the Beast add 617 in Greek Gematria, a type of numerology popular in ancient times. The sum of the Greek words το θηριον (to therion) "the Beast" (book of Revelation 13:18) and τη πονηρα (te ponera) "evil" (Matthew. 12:45) add 617. The sum of the Greek words η ταρση (e tarse) 'tarsus', which were used to individualize Saul in the book of Acts of the Apostles Verses 9:30, 11:25,

---

[184] Profesores de Salamanca (Professors of Salamanca) "Biblia Comentada", vol. VII, under Apocalipsis Verses 13:11-18p. 451.

[185] Irenaeus, "Against Heresies", Book V, Chapter 30, paragraph 1.

[186] Irenaeus "Against Heresies" Book II, Chapter 22.

and 22:3, is 617 as well. It is too much for a coincidence, which makes me wonder if the number of the Beast χις (616) ending with the Greek letter digamma, as it shows on Papyrus 115, was not originally χιζ (617) ending with the Greek letter zeta instead, which is very similar to it.[187]

If the number is 616 it could be said that it points to Paul because it could signify that the Second Beast is the one in middle of the twelve. Paul is the man in middle of the twelve apostles.[188] And the addition of the numbers

---

[187] Washburn, Del, in his book "Theomatics II" (Maryland, Scarborough House, 1994), reveals this and other words and expressions with a meaning related to the Beast that add up to 616, 617 or 615 in Greek or in Hebrew geometry. He also reveals many others that are multiples of 616. He reveals that, among others, the Greek words "the Beast" (book of Revelation 13:18) το θηριον (to therion) and "evil" (Matthew. 12:45) τη πονηρα (te ponera) add up to 617. He argues that it is scientifically proved that this is not casual, teaching about clustering, and that this proves that God wrote the Bible. It is a book that deserves attention. In p. 500, the book says: "My overwhelming conclusion after much research on all related passages, is that 616 is the correct number. Right now I am beginning to get a solid handle on understanding the significance of this number. You will be positively astounded at the content of this chapter. The number 616 does relate to the beast in a way that is unmistakable." –
In Verse 14:12 of the book of Acts of the Apostles the people of Lystra call Paul 'Hermes', and as it can be seen in ancient Greek literary works such as the so called 'Homeric Hymn to Hermes' or in the 'Iliad' Hermes was a Greek god depicted as a messenger of the gods, with great eloquence, and also as a deceiver, a liar, a robber, among other evil attributes. The Greek word Hermes in genitive case, that would have been written Ερμου (Hermou), meaning 'of Hermes', adds up to 615 in Greek Gematria. – Another thing that seems interesting to me is that the Saul from the Old Testament is son of Κις (kis), while the number 616 appears in Papyrus 115 in the following way Χις (Ksis).

[188] The Second Epistle of Paul to the Thessalonians (N.I.V.) says: "*For the secret power of lawlessness is already at work; but the one who holds it back will continue to do so till he is taken out of the way.*" The Greek word translated as 'way' is μεσου (mesou). This word is used with the meaning of middle in John Verses

Ruy Barraco Mármol

6 + 1 + 6 results in 13, whereas it can be said that Paul was the 'apostle' 13.[189]

In addition, the mentioned fact that in Greek geometry the value of the words η ταρση (e tarse) 'tarsus', which were used to individualize Saul or Paul in the book of Acts of the Apostles, Verses 9:30, 11:25, and 22:3, is 617, at the same time that the value of the words το θηριον (to therion) "the Beast", used in this verse 13:18 of the book of Revelation that we are analyzing, is 617, not only suggests that the correct number is 616, but also points out Paul of Tarsus as the Second Beast.

It is also interesting that the Greek words τη πορνε[190] (te porne), which mean "to, with or in, the prostitute" add up to 616; and are used in Verse 6:16 of the First Epistle of Paul to the Corinthians. The numbers of the verses were added after the books were written, but

---

1:26, 19:18 and Revelation Verse 1:13 for instance. Except for the N.A.B. that translates this word as 'scene' the rest of the English translations that I worked with in this book translate this word as way. However, indeed the word means 'middle'. The verse says 'till he is taken out of the middle', and I believe that it is talking about the secret power of lawlessness, Paul, who will be hold back until he is taken out of the middle.

[189] The words 'Saul' and 'Sheol' were very similar in Hebrew, and their writing was identical. In Psalm 18 according to the Masoretic text both words are used, and seem to be part of a play on words. An interesting analysis of this issue has been made by Beaufort Clifton Addison III. Copyright © 1998 Beaufort Clifton Addison III, All Rights Reserved. The word Sheol in Greek is Αδης (Hades). In the vocative case the word is Αδη (Hade). This word is used in the First Epistle of Paul to the Corinthians Verse 15:55 in the vocative case. The addition of the Greek letters of the word Αδη (Hade) results in 13.

[190] The Greek words τη πορνε (te porne) are in the Dative Case. The word τη (te) is the Dative Case of the word ος, η, τω (os, e, to).

notwithstanding it is an amazing "coincidence".

The addition of the values of the letter tau (τ) = 300 + eta (η) = 8 + pi (π) = 80 + omicron (o)= 70 + rho (ρ) = 100 + nu (ν) = 50 + eta (η)= 8 results in 616. The addition of the numbers 300+8+80+70+100+50+8=616.

If somebody asks: who does the cipher refer or belong to? You could answer: to the prostitute. In Chapter 17, as we will see later, the Devil is called prostitute. Was the cipher meant to tell us that Paul was inspired by the Devil; a work of the Devil? Was the Second Beast, Paul, somehow, the Devil himself?

On the other hand, if the number is 666 it applies to Paul of Tarsus, because the Greek words η ταρση (Tarsus), that in Greek gematria add up to 617, if written with Hebrew letters add up to 666.

The addition of the letters Taw (400) + Ahleph (1) + Rehsh (200) + Sahmekh (60) and Heh (5), would add up to 666. The Hebrew Alphabet did not have vowels at the beginning, but some consonants from old started being used as vowels. Two of these consonants were the letters 'Ahleph' and 'He'. The letter 'Ahleph' in the middle of the word was equivalent to the vowel 'a'. The letter 'He' was used at the end of the words to represent the vowels a, e and o.[191] And the letter He is the fifth letter of the Hebrew Alphabet, whereas the fifth letter of the Greek Alphabet is the letter Epsilon (e), all of which would have made it among the consonants used as vowels the most natural choice to write the Greek letter η (e) in the Hebrew language.

---

[191] Goñi, Blas and Juan Labayen "Gramática Hebrea Teórico-Práctica", (Pamplona: Editorial Aramburu, 1945), third edition, p. 3.

Tarsus was the Second Beast: Paul of Tarsus.

I. 2. Paul and the Coming of the Word of God

While I was discovering all this, and writing this book, absolutely astonished, some questions started coming to my mind: How would the world be without the Devil and the Beasts? How would the world be with a Christian Church built from the Christian doctrine expressed by Christ to the apostles, and free from the influence of Paul? How would a world be with the faithful and true word of God acting as it should? Would the world see that day someday? The answer to these questions I believe can be found in the Chapters of the book of Revelation, which I am going to analyze next.

I will start with Chapters 17 and 18. Chapter 17 talks about the Devil and the First Beast. Chapter 18 talks about the fall of the Devil. The reading and understanding of these two chapters is very important to the understanding of the book of Revelation and the Old Testament. After a brief analysis of them I will analyze Chapters 19 and 20, which, in my opinion, shed light on some of the questions I mentioned before.

Chapter 17

Chapter 17 of the book of Revelation (N.I.V.) says: "*17:1 One of the seven angels who had the seven bowls came and said to me, "Come, I will show you the punishment of the great prostitute, who sits on many waters. 17:2 With her the kings of the earth committed adultery and the inhabitants of the earth were intoxicated, with the wine of her adulteries." 17:3 Then the angel carried me away in the Spirit into a desert. There I saw a woman sitting on a scarlet beast that was covered with blasphemous names and had seven heads and ten horns. 17:4 The woman was dressed in purple and scarlet, and was glittering with gold, precious stones and pearls. She held a golden cup in her hand, filled with abominable things and the filth of her adulteries. 17:5 This title was written on her forehead: Mystery Babylon the great, the mother of prostitutes and of the abominations on the earth. 17:6 I saw that the woman was drunk with the blood of the saints, the blood of those who bore testimony to Jesus. When I saw her, I was greatly astonished. 17:7 Then the angel said to me: "Why are you astonished? I will explain to you the mystery of the woman and of the beast she rides, which has the seven heads and ten horns. 17:8 The beast, which you saw, once was, now is not, and will come up out of the Abyss and go to his destruction. The inhabitants of the earth whose names have not been written in the book of life from the creation of the world will be astonished when they see the beast, because he once was, now is not, and yet will come. 17:9 "This calls for a mind with wisdom. The seven heads are seven hills on which the woman sits. 17:10 They are also seven kings. Five have fallen, one is, the other has not yet come; but when he does come, he must remain for a little while. 17:11 The beast who once was, and now is not, is an eighth king. He belongs to the seven and is going to his destruction. 17:12 "The ten horns you saw are ten kings who have not yet received a kingdom, but who for one hour will receive authority as kings along with the beast. 17:13 They have one purpose and will give their power and authority to the beast. 17:14 They will make war against the Lamb, but the Lamb will overcome them because he is Lord of lords and King of kings—and with him will be his called, chosen and faithful followers." 17:15 Then the angel said to me, "The waters you saw, where the prostitute sits, are peoples, multitudes, nations and languages. 17:16 The beast and the ten horns you saw will hate the prostitute. They will bring her to ruin and leave her naked; they will eat her flesh and burn her with fire. 17:17 For God has put it into their hearts to accomplish his purpose by agreeing to give the beast their power to rule, until God's words are fulfilled. 17:18 The woman you saw is the great city that rules over the kings of the earth."*

This Chapter talks about the judgment of the Great Prostitute and its identity. An angel shows John a woman sitting on a Beast, which is no other than the First Beast of Chapter 13, and the woman sitting on it is the Devil. Next, I will explain the basis for these conclusions.

The Beast of Chapter 17 according to its Verse 3 has seven heads and ten horns, the same as the First Beast of Chapter 13, according to its Verse 1. The Beast of Chapter 17 according to its Verse 6 was getting drunk with the blood of the saints and of those who bore testimony to Jesus; and the First Beast of Chapter 13, according to its Verse 7, was allowed to make war against the saints and conquer them. The seven heads of the Beast of Chapter 17 are seven hills, like the seven historic hills of the ancient city of Rome: The Aventine hill, the Capitoline hill, The Caelian, the Esquiline Hill, the Palatine hill, the Quirinal Hill, and the Viminal Hill; and the First Beast of Chapter 13, or at least one of its heads, was Rome as I said. The Beast of Chapter 17, according to its Verse 3, was covered with blasphemous names, the same way the First Beast of Chapter 13 was, according to its Verse 1.

The woman sitting on the Beast must be distinguished of course, from the Beast on which she is sitting. The woman is not the First Beast, and is not Rome, which is one of the heads of the First Beast.

The woman is the Dragon, the Devil, that led the First Beast. Let us remember that Chapter 13:4 taught that the Dragon gave the First Beast its power, its throne, along with great authority, and that Chapter 12:17 made him responsible for the persecution of Christ and the Christian Church, when the material author was Rome, one of the heads of the First Beast. And let us remember that in Chapter 2:10 it is said to the Church in Smyrna that the Devil was going to put some of them in prison, when the material author of those acts would end up being Rome. This also tells us that the Devil led the First Beast.

In addition it is important to note that the woman is called in Chapter 17:5 the great Babylon, or Babylon the great, the mother of prostitutes and of the abominations of earth; in Chapter 17:18 the woman is called the Great City; and in Chapter 19:2 is called the Great Prostitute. Paying attention to the different ways in which the woman is called it will be seen clearly she is the Devil.

In Chapter 19:2 it is said, for instance, that the Great Prostitute, who is the woman, corrupted the earth by her adulteries. And Chapters 12:9; 20:3; 20:7; and 20:10 say that the Dragon, the Devil, the ancient Serpent leads the world astray. Whoever leads the world astray is who corrupts the world.

In Chapter 18:24 it is said about the Great Prostitute, who is the woman, that in her was found the blood of prophets and saints and all of who have been killed on the earth; and all these things can only be said about the Devil.

In Chapter 17:18 it is said that the woman is the Great City and rules over the kings of the earth; and in the Gospel it is the Devil who is presented in that position. The Gospel according to Saint Matthew (N.I.V.) says: "*4:8 Again, the devil took him to a very high mountain and showed him all the kingdoms of the world and their splendor, 4:9 "All this I will give you", he said, "if you will bow down and worship me." 4:10 Jesus said to him, "Away from me, Satan! For it is written: 'Worship the Lord your God, and serve him only."* The Gospel according to Saint Luke (N.I.V.) says: "*4:5 The devil led him up to a high place and showed him in an instant all the kingdoms of the world. 4:6 And he said to him, "I will give you all their authority and splendor, for it has been given to me, and I can give it to anyone I want to."*

In Chapter 17:2 it is said about the woman, that with her the kings of the earth committed adultery, and the inhabitants of the earth were intoxicated with the wine of her adulteries; and all this can only be said about the Devil.

Finally, Chapter 20:7 describes the times just before the Final Judgment, narrating the fall of Satan; and the Great City is destroyed in Chapter 16:19, in the seventh bowl of God's wrath, the last one, that should be poured just before the Final Judgment. The

Great City, who is the woman according to Verse 17:18, is destroyed just when the last battle against Satan should be taking place, according to Chapter 20:7.

All this clearly indicates that the woman of Chapter 17 is the Devil, the Big Red Dragon, the Ancient Serpent, the Great Prostitute, Babylon, the Mother of Prostitutes, the Mother of the Abominations of the earth.

Besides, it makes sense that the Devil would be judged just before the Final Judgment, along with the ones who lived in the Devil. The Big Babylon, the Great City, is opposed to the Holy City.

When Verse 17:16 says that the Beast and the ten horns will hate the prostitute I think the book of Revelation is saying that the organizations of men under control of the Devil, will abandon the Devil, along with their leaders.

Chapter 18

Chapter 18 of the book of Revelation (N.I.V.) says: "*18:1 After this I saw another angel coming down from heaven. He had great authority, and the earth was illuminated by his splendor. 18:2 With a mighty voice he shouted: "Fallen! Fallen is Babylon the Great! She has become a home for demons and a haunt for every evil spirit, a haunt for every unclean and detestable bird. 18:3 For all the nations have drunk the maddening wine of her adulteries. The kings of the earth committed adultery with her, and the merchants of the earth grew rich from her excessive luxuries." 18:4 Then I heard a voice from heaven*

Ruy Barraco Mármol

say: "Come out of her, my people, so that you will not share in her sins, so that you will not receive any of her plagues; 18:5 for her sins are piled up to heaven and God has remembered her crimes. 18:6 Give back to her as she has given; pay her back double for what she has done. Mix her a double portion from her own cup. 18:7 Give her as much torture and grief as the glory and luxury she gave herself. In her heart she boasts, 'I sit as queen; I am not a widow, and I will never mourn.' 18:8 Therefore in one day her plagues will overtake her: death, mourning and famine. She will be consumed by fire, for mighty is the Lord God who judges her. 18:9 "When the kings of the earth who committed adultery with her and shared her luxury see the smoke of her burning, they will weep and mourn over her. 18:10 Terrified at her torment, they will stand far off and cry: "'Woe! Woe, O great city, O Babylon, city of power! In one hour your doom has come!" 18:11 "The merchants of the earth will weep and mourn over her because no one buys their cargoes any more—18:12 cargoes of gold, silver, precious stones and pearls; fine linen, purple, silk and scarlet cloth; every sort of citron wood, and articles of every kind made of ivory, costly wood, bronze, iron and marble; 18:13 cargoes of cinnamon and spice, of incense, myrrh and frankincense, of wine and olive oil, of fine flour and wheat; cattle and sheep; horses and carriages; and bodies and souls of men. 18:14 "They will say, 'The fruit you longed for is gone from you. All your riches and splendor have vanished, never to be recovered.' 18:15 The merchants who sold these things and gained their wealth from her will stand far off, terrified at her torment. They will weep and mourn 18:16 and cry out: "'Woe! Woe, O great city, dressed in fine linen, purple and scarlet, and glittering with gold, precious stones and pearls!

18:17 In one hour such great wealth has been brought to ruin!' "Every sea captain, and all who travel by ship, the sailors, and all who earn their living from the sea, will stand far off. 18:18 When they see the smoke of her burning, they will exclaim, 'Was there ever a city like this great city?' 18:19 They will throw dust on their heads, and with weeping and mourning cry out: "' Woe! Woe, O great city, where all who had ships on the sea became rich through her wealth! In one hour she has been brought to ruin! 18:20 Rejoice over her, O heaven! Rejoice, saints and apostles and prophets! God has judged her for the way she treated you.'" 18:21 Then a mighty angel picked up a boulder the size of a large millstone and threw it into the sea, and said: "With such violence the great city of Babylon will be thrown down, never to be found again. 18:22 The music of harpists and musicians, flute players and trumpeters, will never be heard in you again. No workman of any trade will ever be found in you again. The sound of millstone will never be heard in you again. 18:23 The light of a lamp will never shine in you again. The voice of bridegroom and bride will never be heard in you again. Your merchants were the world's great men. By your magic spell all the nations were led astray. 18:24 In her was found the blood of prophets and of the saints, and of all who have been killed on the earth."

This chapter talks about the judgment of the Devil, and explains the reasons that led him to his condemnation.

Chapter 19

Chapter 19 of the book of Revelation (N.I.V.) says:

"19:1 After this I heard what sounded like the roar of a great multitude in heaven shouting: "Hallelujah! Salvation and glory and power belong to our God, 19:2 for true and just are his judgments. He has condemned the great prostitute who corrupted the earth by her adulteries. He has avenged on her the blood of his servants." 19:3 And again they shouted: "Hallelujah! The smoke from her goes up for ever and ever." 19:4 The twenty-four elders and the four living creatures fell down and worshiped God, who was seated on the throne. And they cried. "Amen, Hallelujah!" 19:5 Then a voice came from the throne, saying: "Praise our God, all you his servants, you who fear him, both small and great!" 19:6 Then I heard what sounded like a great multitude, like the roar of rushing waters and like loud peals of thunder, shouting: "Hallelujah! For our Lord God Almighty reigns." 19:7 Let us rejoice and be glad and give him glory! For the wedding of the Lamb has come, and his bride has made herself ready. 19:8 Fine linen, bright and clean, was given her to wear." (Fine linen stands for the righteous acts of the saints.) 19:9 Then the angel said to me, "Write: 'Blessed are those who are invited to the wedding supper of the Lamb!'" And he added, "These are the true words of God." 19:10 At this I fell at his feet to worship him. But he said to me, "Do not do it! I am a fellow servant with you and with your brothers who hold to the testimony of Jesus. Worship God! For the testimony of Jesus is the spirit of prophecy." 19:11 I saw heaven standing open and there before me was a white horse, whose rider is called Faithful and True. With justice he judges and makes war. 19:12 His eyes are like blazing fire, and on his head are many crowns. He has a name written on him that no one knows but he himself. 19:13 He is dressed in a robe dipped in blood, and *his name is the Word of God. 19:14 The armies of heaven were following him, riding on white horses and dressed in fine linen, white and clean. 19:15 Out of his mouth comes a sharp sword with which to strike down the nations. "He will rule them with an iron scepter." He treads the wine press of the fury of the wrath of God Almighty. 19:16 On his robe and on his thigh he has this name written: King of Kings and Lord of Lords. 19:17 And I saw an angel standing in the sun, who cried in a loud voice to all the birds flying in midair, "Come, gather together for the great supper of God, 19:18 so that you may eat the flesh of kings, generals, and mighty men, of horses and their riders, and the flesh of all people, free and slave, small and great." 19:19 Then I saw the beast and the kings of the earth and their armies gathered together to make war against the rider on the horse and his army. 19:20 But the beast was captured, and with him the false prophet who had performed the miraculous signs on his behalf. With these signs he had deluded those who had received the mark of the beast and worshiped his image. The two of them were thrown alive into the fiery lake of burning sulfur. 19:21 The rest of them were killed with the sword that came out of the mouth of the rider on the horse, and all the birds gorged themselves on their flesh."*

Verses 19:1-4 says: "*19:1 After this I heard what sounded like the roar of a great multitude in heaven shouting: "Hallelujah! Salvation and glory and power belong to our God, 19:2 for true and just are his judgments. He has condemned the great prostitute who corrupted the earth by her adulteries. He has avenged on her the blood of his servants." 19:3 And again they shouted: "Hallelujah! The smoke from her goes up for ever and ever." 19:4 The twenty-four elders and the four living creatures fell down and worshiped God, who was seated on the throne. And they cried. "Amen, Hallelujah!""*

These verses narrate a celebration in heaven because the Devil has been condemned or judged. In the analysis of Chapter 20 it will be seen that this judgment brings an imprisonment of the Devil for a symbolic period of 1000 years, that can last more or less than a 1000 years, depending on human behavior. And it will be seen that after this period the Devil is released for a short period of time, and then thrown into hell for ever.

Verses 19:5-10: *19:5 Then a voice came from the throne, saying: "Praise our God, all you his servants, you who fear him, both small and great!" 19:6 Then I heard what sounded like a great multitude, like the roar of rushing waters and like loud peals of thunder, shouting: "Hallelujah! For our Lord God Almighty reigns." 19:7 Let us rejoice and be glad and give him glory! For the wedding of the Lamb has come, and his bride has made herself ready. 19:8 Fine linen, bright and clean, was given her to wear." (Fine linen stands for the righteous acts of the saints.) 19:9 Then the angel said to me, "Write: 'Blessed are those who are invited to the wedding supper of the Lamb!'" And he added, "These are the true words of God." 19:10 At this I fell at his feet to worship him. But he said to me, "Do not do it! I am a fellow servant with you and with your brothers who hold to the testimony of Jesus. Worship God! For the testimony of Jesus is the spirit of prophecy."*

The bride of Verse 19:7 is the Christian Church, not in an institutional meaning, but in the meaning of the whole body of Christians. Chapter 21:9 (N.I.V.) says: *"21:9 One of the seven angels who had the seven bowls full of the seven last plagues came and said to me, "Come, I will show you the bride, the wife of the Lamb." 21:10 And he carried me away in the Spirit to a mountain great and high, and showed me the Holy City, Jerusalem, coming down out of heaven from God."* Without any doubt the bride in these verses, the wife of the lamb, is not the building that is described following them, but the men and women that are inside her, the people of God, the men that are allowed to enter to the City of God, to the new Holy City of Jerusalem. Let us remember those words of the Gospel according to Saint Matthew (N.I.V.), where Christ says: *"7:21 Not everyone who says to me, 'Lord, Lord,' will enter the kingdom of heaven, but only he who does the will of my Father who is in heaven."*

Now, returning to the verses in analysis, it comes forth from them that the bride, the wife of the Lamb or bride of the Lamb, who I said is the people of God, the Christian people, made themselves ready, with the righteous acts of the saints. This means that the bride, the Christian Church, was not ready, was not dressed up with the righteous acts of the saints, until that moment. And that preparation is celebrated in heaven, with the figure of the wedding supper. It is said in Verse 19:9: *"...Blessed are those who are invited to the wedding supper of the Lamb"*, bringing to memory that parable of the Gospel according to Saint Matthew (N.I.V.) that says: *"22:1 Jesus spoke to them again in parables, saying: 22:2 "The kingdom of heaven is like a king*

Ruy Barraco Mármol

who prepared a wedding banquet for his son. 22:3 He sent his servants to those who had been invited to the banquet to tell them to come, but they refused to come. 22:4 "Then he sent some more servants and said, 'Tell those who have been invited that I have prepared my dinner: My oxen and fattened cattle have been butchered, and everything is ready. Come to the wedding banquet.' 22:5 "But they paid no attention and went off-one to this field, another to his business. 22:6 The rest seized his servants, mistreated them and killed them. 22:7 The king was enraged. He sent his army and destroyed those murderers and burned their city. 22:8 "Then he said to his servants, 'The wedding banquet is ready, but those I invited did not deserve to come. 22:9 Go to the street corners and invite to the banquet anyone you find.' 22:10 So the servants went out into the streets and gathered all the people they could find, both good and bad, and the wedding hall was filled with guests. 22:11 "But when the king came in to see the guests, he noticed a man there who was not wearing wedding clothes. 22:12 'Friend,' he asked, 'how did you get in here without wedding clothes?' The man was speechless. 22:13 "Then the king told the attendants, 'Tie him hand and foot, and throw him outside, into the darkness, where there will be weeping and gnashing of teeth.' "For many are invited, but few are chosen."

The wedding, it will be seen later, does not happen at this moment, although in my opinion, the preparation of the bride does. In my opinion, the preparation is no other thing than the holiness that the Christian people reach by recognizing Paul as a false prophet, and following Christ's doctrine without the bad influence of Paul. At the end of this Chapter, I believe it will be easier to understand the basis for this opinion.

Verses 19:11-21 says: "*19:11 I saw heaven standing open and there before me was a white horse, whose rider is called Faithful and True. With justice he judges and makes war. 19:12 His eyes are like blazing fire, and on his head are many crowns. He has a name written on him that no one knows but he himself. 19:13 He is dressed in a robe dipped in blood, and his name is the Word of God. 19:14 The armies of heaven were following him, riding on white horses and dressed in fine linen, white and clean. 19:15 Out of his mouth comes a sharp sword with which to strike down the nations. "He will rule them with an iron scepter." He treads the wine press of the fury of the wrath of God Almighty. 19:16 On his robe and on his thigh he has this name written: King of Kings and Lord of Lords. 19:17 And I saw an angel standing in the sun, who cried in a loud voice to all the birds flying in midair, "Come, gather together for the great supper of God, 19:18 so that you may eat the flesh of kings, generals, and mighty men, of horses and their riders, and the flesh of all people, free and slave, small and great." 19:19 Then I saw the beast and the kings of the earth and their armies gathered together to make war against the rider on the horse and his army. 19:20 But the beast was captured, and with him the false prophet who had performed the miraculous signs on his behalf. With these signs he had deluded those who had received the mark of the beast and worshiped his image. The two of them were thrown alive into the fiery lake of burning sulfur. 19:21 The rest of them were killed with the sword that came out of the mouth of the rider on the horse, and all the birds gorged themselves on their flesh."*

The rider of Verse 19:11 is Jesus. The sharp sword that comes out of his mouth is his word. The expression will rule them with an iron scepter refers in my opinion to the firmness of his word, that will rule the nations.

The great supper mentioned in Verse 19:17 is the same supper mentioned in Verse 19:9, which talks about the unity of the chapter.

The Beast captured is the First Beast from Chapters 13 and 17. The book of Revelation seems to be saying that the First Beast will rule an international organization of States, whether formal or informal; It seems so, because Verse 19:19 says that the Beast and the kings of the earth and their armies are seen gathered together to make war against the rider, Jesus, and his army, which implies that those kings are under control of the Beast.

When the First Beast is captured, the Second Beast is captured too. Paul might be captured symbolically when the Christian institutions recognize his doctrine as a work of a false prophet. And if there is a second horn it will be captured too, probably being recognized as a false prophet along with his doctrine.

In the same chapter, in which the preparation of the Christian Church is narrated, the capture of the Second Beast is also foretold. In Chapter 20, it will be seen that this happens before the Coming of the Son of Man. The Coming of the Son of Man is the coming of Jesus that happens in the beginning of the end of the world. I will call that coming with the name "Coming of the Son of

Man", because that is the way the Gospels called it, and as a way to differentiate it from the first coming, which is the incarnation, and from this Coming of the Word of God, from Chapter 19.

The reason we know that the preparation of the Christian Church and the capture of the Second Beast happen before the Coming of the Son of Man (Jesus), is that after them, the Devil and the Beast are imprisoned for 1000 years; and the book of Revelation Verse 20:5 tells us, that the resurrection of the dead, which we know comes right after the Coming of the Son of Man, happens after the 1000 years have ended.

Moreover, the Gospels and the book of Revelation describe the Coming of the Son of Man, and neither the Gospels nor the book of Revelation leave any space for this period of 1000 years after the Coming of the Son of Man, as we will see in detail at the time of the analysis of the rest of the chapters of the book of Revelation.

What does this Chapter 19 narrate?

In my opinion it starts narrating the celebration in heaven because the Devil was judged, and because it was about to start his punishment, his imprisonment for a 1000 years, to be released only for a short period of time, after which he will be sent to hell forever. This celebration must happen before the imprisonment.

Then the celebration of the imminent beginning of the reign of the Lord and the celebration of the preparation of the Bride of the Lamb comes. The Bride of the Lamb is the Christian Church, the Christian people, and the celebration of the preparation of the

Bride is the celebration of the holiness that reaches the Christian Church, when Paul is recognized as a false prophet.

After that, Chapter 19 narrates a special intervention of Christ. Christ makes this special intervention through his word. That is why Verse 19:15 says, "*Out of his mouth comes a sharp sword with which to strike down the nations.*" That is why it is said that the rider is the word of God.

The fact that Christ is named as the word of God in this verse is very meaningful. In my opinion, it is meant to let us know that Christ will not intervene with a coming but with his word.

Except in this verse of the book of Revelation, Saint John does not call Christ the word of God. He calls Christ the Word, but not the Word of God. As far as I know in the rest of the Bible the Son is not called the Word of God.

Saint John uses in the book of Revelation the expression word of God with the meaning of doctrine, message or teachings of God. Chapter 20:4 (N.I.V.), for instance, says: "*I saw thrones on which were seated those who had been given authority to judge. And I saw the souls of those who had been beheaded because of their testimony for Jesus and because of the word of God ...*" In the rest of the Bible the expression word of God is used many times with this same meaning.

Christ acts to make his word come, the true word of God, and with that act, in my opinion, the Christianity of many will be strengthened and will multiply its fruits; many Gentile people will convert, while others will find spiritual death by rejecting Christ.

In my opinion, this will happen when the Christians commit themselves to learn all the word of Christ the way it was expressed to the twelve, and after the Christian doctrine is freed from the influence of Paul.

This coming of the word of God to many people, because of the action of Christ, can only take place when they learn and understand the word, and allow Christ to make his home in them. The Gospel according to Saint John (N.I.V.) says: *"14:23 Jesus replied, "If anyone loves me, he will obey my teaching. My Father will love him, and we will come to him and make our home with him."*

What follows is a great reaction of the First Beast, that prepares itself for a war against the disciples of Christ who are spreading the word of God. But the war does not happen, because Christ captures the First Beast and the Second Beast, the false prophet.

The capture of the First Beast suggests to me that a great international organization of states is set apart. This could happen for instance as a consequence of internal and peaceful revolutions in certain countries. It could happen also as a consequence of violent revolutions. And it could bring constitutional democracies to those countries.

The capture of the Second Beast suggests the acknowledgment of Paul as a false prophet by the Christian Churches, including the Catholic Church, and maybe the same thing in regard to another false prophet, if the horns of the Second Beast represent two persons. I personally believe that the two horns of the Second Beast represent two persons, one of whom is Paul. I believe that the recognition of Paul as a false prophet is the preparation of the bride and the recognition as a false prophet of a second person is the capture of the Second Beast. And I believe it is clear who the second horn was. However, I also believe that before getting into that issue we must first get the wooden beam out of our own eye.[192]

What exactly is going to happen we will not be able to know in detail, but we know that Paul is the Second Beast, at least his first horn; and we certainly can understand, with Paul being a false prophet, how much Christ would value that the Christian Church recognize Paul as such, and how this could be a reason for celebration in heaven. And it is not hard to accept that men need the action of Christ to be able to carry on the purification and to defeat the Devil.

This intervention of Christ is not the first coming of Christ, which is his incarnation, and it is not the second coming of Jesus announced in the Gospel and in the book of Revelation, that brings the resurrection of the death, known as the Coming of the Son of Man. It is an intervention of Christ with his word that happens between those comings.

In regard to the chronological order, with Chapter 19 continuing Chapter 13, there is no problem, because the chapters of the book of Revelation do not follow a chronological order.

In regard to the unity of Chapter 19, and specifically the unity of Verses 19:1-10 and 19:11-21, I think it is very well established through different reasons. The first reason is a context reason. The celebration for the judgment of the Devil reasonably must happen before

---

[192] The Gospel according to Saint Matthew, Verse 7:4.

his imprisonment for a 1000 years, which happens before the action of Christ, with the coming of his word, as I will explain in the analysis of Chapter 20. The second reason is a textual reason. The banquet referred to in Verse 19:9 is the same banquet referred to in Verse 19:17.

Chapter 20

Chapter 20 of the book of Revelation (N.I.V.) says: "*20:1 And I saw an angel coming down out of heaven, having the key to the Abyss and holding in his hand a great chain. 20:2 He seized the dragon, that ancient serpent, who is the devil, or Satan, and bound him for a thousand years. 20:3 He threw him into the Abyss, and locked and sealed it over him, to keep him from deceiving the nations anymore until the thousand years were ended. After that, he must be set free for a short time. 20:4 I saw thrones on which were seated those who had been given authority to judge. And I saw the souls of those who had been beheaded because of their testimony for Jesus and because of the word of God. They had not worshiped the beast or his image and had not received his mark on their foreheads or their hands. They came to life and reigned with Christ a thousand years. 20:5 (The rest of the dead did not come to life until the thousand years were ended.) This is the first resurrection. 20:6 Blessed and holy are those who have part in the first resurrection. The second death has no power over them, but they will be priests of God and of Christ and will reign with him for a thousand years. 20:7 When the thousand years are over, Satan will be released from his prison 20:8 and will go out to deceive the nations in the four corners of the earth-God and*

Ruy Barraco Mármol

Magog- to gather them for battle. In number they are like the sand on the seashore. 20:9 They marched across the breadth of the earth and surrounded the camp of God's people, the city he loves. But fire came down from heaven and devoured them. 20:10 And the devil, who deceived them, was thrown into the lake of burning sulfur, where the beast and the false prophet had been thrown. They will be tormented day and night for ever and ever. 20:11 Then I saw a great white throne and him who was seated on it. Earth and sky fled from his presence, and there was no place for them. 20:12 And I saw the dead, great and small, standing before the throne, and books were opened. Another book was opened, which is the book of life. The dead were judged according to what they had done as recorded in the books. 20:13 The sea gave up the dead that were in it, and death and Hades gave up the dead that were in them, and each person was judged according to what he had done. 20:14 Then death and Hades were thrown into the lake of fire. The lake of fire is the second death. 20:15 If anyone's name was not found written in the book of life, he was thrown into the lake of fire."

Verses 20:1-3: *"20:1 And I saw an angel coming down out of heaven, having the key to the Abyss and holding in his hand a great chain. 20:2 He seized the dragon, that ancient serpent, who is the devil, or Satan, and bound him for a thousand years. 20:3 He threw him into the Abyss, and locked and sealed it over him, to keep him from deceiving the nations anymore until the thousand years were ended. After that, he must be set free for a short time."*

Here the book of Revelation lets us know that after

the purification of the Christian Church, after the Coming of the Word of God, the Devil is imprisoned and starts a period in which neither the Devil nor the Beasts will be allowed to act. The period of 1000 years is a symbolic period. In contrast with the period of 3 years and a half, which is used to indicate the periods of the persecutions, in which the Devil is allowed to cause greater evil, the period of 1000 years suggests a long period, or at least a potentially long period; maybe a complete period.

In the Bible, the symbolic period of 1000 years is used on other opportunities. The book of Psalms (N.I.V.) says: "**90:4** *For a thousand years in your sight are like a day that has just gone by, or like a watch in the night.*" The book of Ecclesiastes says: "*6:6 even if he lives a thousand years twice over but fails to enjoy his prosperity. Do not all go to the same place?*"[193] In my opinion, these precedents allow us to infer that the symbolic period of 1000 years, may either be a long period or a short period, which means that it is an undetermined period of time.

Notice that the book of Revelation does not say that it will be a period of justice, peace and prosperity. It

---

[193] The period of 1000 years is mentioned in the epistle of the Bible known as Second Epistle of Saint Peter (N.I.V.), which says: "*3:3 First of all, you must understand that in the last days scoffers will come, scoffing and following their own evil desires. 3:4 They will say, "Where is this 'coming' he promised? Ever since our fathers died, everything goes on as it has since the beginning of creation." 3:5 But they deliberately forget that long ago by God's word the heavens existed and the earth was formed out of water and by water. 3:6 By these waters also the world of that time was deluged and destroyed. 3:7 By the same word the present heavens and earth are reserved for fire, being kept for the day of judgment and destruction of ungodly men. 3:8 But do not forget this one thing, dear friends: With the Lord a day is like a thousand years, and a thousand years are like a day.*"

only says that the Devil and the Beasts will be imprisoned, and will not act. The Gospel according to Saint John (N.I.V.) says, quoting Jesus: "*17:11 I will remain in the world no longer, but they are still in the world, and I am coming to you. Holy Father, protect them by the power of your name-the name you gave me-so that they may be one as we are one. 17:12 While I was with them, I protected them and kept them safe by that name you gave me. None has been lost except the one doomed to destruction so that Scripture would be fulfilled. 17:13 "I am coming to you now, but I say these things while I am still in the world, so that they may have the full measure of my joy with them. 17:14 I have given them your word and the world has hated them, for they are not of the world any more than I am of the world. 17:15 My prayer is not that you take them out of the world but that you protect them from the evil one.*" The Gospel according to Saint Matthew (N.I.V.) says: "*18:7 "Woe to the world because of the things that cause people to sin! Such things must come, but woe to the man through whom they come!*"

There will be in the 1000 years injustices, wars, hunger, but they will not be caused by the instigation of the Devil. There will be earthquakes, illness, and other natural disasters, but the Devil will not be trying to get the worst of men through them. I even believe, that there will be minor demons, but the Devil will not be acting.

The Devil will be released for a short time only after the 1000 years are fulfilled. Verse 20:3 says that the angel that will imprison the Dragon, will put the seals over him. This expression is remarkable because the book of Revelation also teaches, as I will explain later, that after the seventh and last seal has been opened, the Coming of the Son of Man will occur, followed by the Great Tribulation that those who are not chosen will have to face. In my opinion, the book of Revelation indicates with this reference to the seals, that the Devil will be released in the period of Great Tribulation, also called the Great Day of the Wrath of God, the Cluster of the Vine, and the Great Day of God Almighty, that we still have to discuss.

Verses 20:4-6 says: "*20:4 I saw thrones on which were seated those who had been given authority to judge. And I saw the souls of those who had been beheaded because of their testimony for Jesus and because of the word of God. They had not worshiped the beast or his image and had not received his mark on their foreheads or their hands. They came to life and reigned with Christ a thousand years. 20:5 (The rest of the dead did not come to life until the thousand years were ended.) This is the first resurrection. 20:6 Blessed and holy are those who have part in the first resurrection. The second death has no power over them, but they will be priests of God and of Christ and will reign with him for a thousand years.*"

These verses let us know that certain people, by reaching enough grace in the eyes of God, are resurrected before the rest of the people. The Gospel gives testimony about Moses and Elijah resurrected talking with Christ before his resurrection.[194]

---

[194] The Gospel according to Saint Mark (N.I.V.) says: "*9:1 And he said to them, "I tell you the truth, some who are standing here will not taste death before they see the kingdom of God come with power." 9:2 After six days Jesus took Peter, James*

Ruy Barraco Mármol

The Gospel according to Saint Matthew (N.I.V.) says:
"*27:50 And when Jesus had cried out again in a loud voice, he gave up his spirit. 27:51 At that moment the curtain of the temple was torn in two from top to bottom. The earth shook and the rocks split. 27:52 The tombs broke open and the bodies of many holy people who had died were raised to life. 27:53 They came out of the tombs, and after Jesus' resurrection they went into the holy city and appeared to many people. 27:54 When the centurion and those with him who were guarding Jesus saw the earthquake and all that had happened, they were terrified, and exclaimed, "Surely he was the Son of God!""*

The first resurrected are allowed to be priests with God and reign with Christ when the thousand years with the Devil and the Beasts imprisoned begins. In my opinion, this mission will allow them to influence the earth in the way the angels do; but there will still be human and natural disasters. The fact that they are going to reign during the 1000 years does not mean that they are not allowed to influence in earth before.

This matter of the reign of the first resurrected, as will be seen later in the analysis of Chapters 4, 5 and 6, contributes to the deduction of the chronology of the

---

and John with him and led them up a high mountain, where they were all alone. There he was transfigured before them. 9:3 His clothes became dazzling white, whiter than anyone in the world could bleach them. 9:4 And there appeared before them Elijah and Moses, who were talking with Jesus. 9:5 Peter said to Jesus, "Rabbi, it is good for us to be here. Let us put up three shelters-one for you, one for Moses and one for Elijah." 9:6 (He did not know what to say, they were so frightened.) 9:7 Then a cloud appeared and enveloped them, and a voice came from the cloud: "This is my Son, whom I love. Listen to him!" 9:8 Suddenly, when they looked around, they no longer saw anyone with them except Jesus. 9:9 As they were coming down the mountain, Jesus gave them orders not to tell anyone what they had seen until the Son of Man had risen from the dead."

facts of the book of Revelation.

Verse 20:5, that says that the rest of the death will not come to life until the 1000 years are over, is fundamental because it lets us know for sure that the intervention of Christ through his word is previous to the Coming of the Son of Man, when the resurrection of the dead will occur. It also tells us that the intervention of Christ does not consist in a coming, because the next coming of Christ is in the end of the world.

Verses 20:7-11 say: "*20:7 When the thousand years are over, Satan will be released from his prison 20:8 and will go out to deceive the nations in the four corners of the earth-God and Magog- to gather them for battle. In number they are like the sand on the seashore. 20:9 They marched across the breadth of the earth and surrounded the camp of God's people, the city he loves. But fire came down from heaven and devoured them. 20:10 And the devil, who deceived them, was thrown into the lake of burning sulfur, where the beast and the false prophet had been thrown. They will be tormented day and night for ever and ever. 20:11 Then I saw a great white throne and him who was seated on it. Earth and sky fled from his presence, and there was no place for them.*"

These verses refer to the final battle between the Devil and his angels, and God and his angels. It is the final fall of the Great Prostitute, the Great Babylon, the Great City, the Devil. In no way can this battle be confused with the battle of Chapter 19 for obvious reasons. This battle of Chapter 20 happens when the

1000 years are over; the battle of Chapter 19 happens before the period of a 1000 years starts. The Devil in Chapter 20 is thrown into hell forever and ever; in Chapter 19 the Devil is imprisoned for 1000 years.

Verses 20:11-15: "20:11 *Then I saw a great white throne and him who was seated on it. Earth and sky fled from his presence, and there was no place for them. 20:12 And I saw the dead, great and small, standing before the throne, and books were opened. Another book was opened, which is the book of life. The dead were judged according to what they had done as recorded in the books. 20:13 The sea gave up the dead that were in it, and death and Hades gave up the dead that were in them, and each person was judged according to what he had done. 20:14 Then death and Hades were thrown into the lake of fire. The lake of fire is the second death. 20:15 If anyone's name was not found written in the book of life, he was thrown into the lake of fire.*"

The Final Judgment is described here. This Final Judgment is referred to in the Gospel according to Saint Matthew (N.I.V.) which says: "25:31 *When the Son of Man comes in his glory, and all the angels with him, he will sit on his throne in heavenly glory. 25:32 All the nations will be gathered before him, and he will separate the people one from another as a shepherd separates the sheep from the goats. 25:33 He will put the sheep on his right and the goats on his left. 25:34 "Then the king will say to those on his right, 'Come, you who are blessed by my Father; take your inheritance, the kingdom prepared for you since the creation of the world. 25:35 For I was hungry and you gave me something to eat, I was thirsty and you gave me*

*something to drink, I was a stranger and you invited me in,
25:36 I needed clothes and you clothed me, I was sick and
you looked after me, I was in prison and you came to visit
me.' 25:37 "Then the righteous will answer him, 'Lord, when
did we see you hungry and feed you, or thirsty and give you
something to drink? 25:38 When did we see you a stranger
and invite you in, or needing clothes and clothe you?' 25:39
When did we see you sick or in prison and go to visit you?'
25:40 "The King will reply, 'I tell you the truth, whatever you
did for one of the least of these brothers of mine, you did for
me.' 25:41 "Then he will say to those on his left, 'Depart
from me, you who are cursed, into the eternal fire prepared
for the devil and his angels. 25:42 For I was hungry and you
gave me nothing to eat, I was thirsty and you gave me
nothing to drink, 25:43 I was a stranger and you did not
invite me in, I needed clothes and you did not clothe me, I
was sick and in prison and you did not look after me.' 25:44
"They also will answer, 'Lord, when did we see you hungry or
thirsty or a stranger or needing clothes or sick or in prison,
and did not help you?' 25:45 "He will reply, 'I tell you the
truth, whatever you did not do for one of the least of these,
you did not do for me.' 25:46 "Then they will go away to
eternal punishment, but the righteous to eternal life.'"*

Ruy Barraco Mármol

Chapter II.
The Book of Revelation, the Signs of the Coming of the Son of Man, the Coming of the Son of Man and the Great Tribulation, the Final Judgment and the New Jerusalem

II.1. Introduction

For the purpose of strengthening the conviction of the reader in regard to the interpretation of the book of Revelation that I just made, I will now discuss and interpret the rest of the chapters of the second part of the book of Revelation. And I will do it using the Gospels.

The book of Revelation, after the Gospels, in my opinion, is the most fascinating book that has been written. The general understanding of the book of Revelation not only will bring more conviction to the reader in regard to the interpretation made in this book

Ruy Barraco Mármol

about Chapters 12, 13, 17, 18 and 19, but also will allow the reader to understand better the rest of the Bible, especially the books of the prophets of the Old Testament.

Except for the three first chapters, which contain letters to the Churches of the new-born Christianity,[195]

---

[195] Personally I believe that the three first chapters of the book of Revelation have messages for everybody, and are a lot more than just letters to the churches of Asia. I believe they have clues to help us understand the message of other chapters. The book of Revelation, Chapter 2, letter to the Church in Ephesus (N.I.V) says: "2:2 I know your deeds, your hard work and your perseverance. I know that you cannot tolerate wicked men, that you have tested those who claim to be apostles but are not, and have them found false.". The First Epistle of Paul to the Corinthians (N.I.V.) says: "15:32 If I fought wild beasts in Ephesus for merely human reasons, what have I gained? If the dead are not raised, "Let us eat and drink for tomorrow we die.'"" Considering Paul fought in Ephesus, is the Book of Revelation telling us that Paul was considered there a false apostle?

Verse 2:6 of the book of Revelation (N.I.V.) says: "But you have this in your favor: You hate the practices of the Nicolaitans, which I also hate." Nobody seems to know who were the Nicolaiteans but some people believe that the word 'Nicolaiteans' refers to those who dominate the people; maybe the people chosen by God. This is so because the word 'Nicolaitans' comes from the words 'nika' and 'laos' which would have those meanings. The word 'laos' is used sometimes in the Bible with that meaning of people Chosen by God. For instance in the book of Revelation Verse 5:9 and in the Gospel according to Saint John 11:50. It is also used by Paul in the Epistle of Paul to the Hebrews 7:5. Paul, and the number of Paul, dominated the Christian Church, and especially the most humble people who were taught to submit to ecclesiastic and civil authorities. Is the book of Revelation in these verses calling Paul and his followers 'Nicolaiteans'?

The book of Revelation (N.I.V.), Chapter 2, letter to the Church in Pergamun, says: "2:13 I know where you live- where Satan has his throne." Pergaminus or parchment, is a material in which books were written. The doctrine of the Devil was living and being reproduced in the Epistles of Paul which were written in pergaminus or parchment. It is interesting to notice that the doctrine of Paul was placed in the Bible, which is a Holy Place. In the Bible it is often called Holy Place the place where God talks. It is accurate to call the Bible a Holy Place, a temple. The Gospel according to Saint Matthew 24:15 talks about the destruction of Jerusalem, about which the prophet Daniel also spoke. The prophet Daniel spoke about the one who makes desolate and about the abomination of desolation set up in the wing of the and Chapters 12, 13, 17, 18, 19 and 20 already discussed, the rest of the chapters of the book of Revelation talk exclusively about the following: 1. The signs prior to the Coming of the Son of Man. 2. The Coming of the Son of Man, and what happens right after it. 3. The Final Judgment. 4. The new world with the new heaven and the new earth.

The signs previous to the Coming of the Son of Man are a series of bad events that are going to precede it. Apparently the book of Revelation foretells that first will come a war, then hunger, and finally war, famine, plagues, and pandemic diseases. These could happen literally, or symbolically, or their announcement could be for the purpose of revealing other signs of the Coming of the Son of Man, or its reasons or causes. Personally, I believe that one of its main purposes is to let us know that the Coming of the Son of Man will be the consequence of the behavior of men. There will be a previous tribulation, but we will not know in detail what is going to happen. The basis for this opinion will be discussed in the next pages.

The first thing that occurs when the Son of Man

---

temple. The Epistles of Paul could be considered set up in the wing of the Bible.

The book of Revelation (N.I.V.), Chapter 2, letter to the Church in Thyatira, says: "2:24 Now I say to the rest of you in Thyatira, to you who do not hold her teaching and have not learned Satan's deep secrets (I will not impose any other burden on you)." The First Epistle of Paul to the Corinthians (N.I.V.) says: "2:10 But God has revealed it to us by his Spirit. The Spirit searches all things even the deep things of God." Paul wrote that he taught deep things, deep secrets, which I explained were not of God. Was the book of Revelation talking about the deep secrets which Paul taught?

Besides, I also believe that the first three chapters of the book of Revelation might have messages to those of us who are going to face the Great Day of the Wrath of God.

comes, when the end of the world starts, is the Harvest or Gathering of the Chosen. This event is also called in the book of Revelation "the Forehead-sealing of the Servants of God". Jesus sends his angels to harvest the chosen, to gather certain persons to take them to be with God, and to rescue them from the Cluster of the Grapes, from the Great Day of the Wrath of the Lamb, from the Great Tribulation, that the rest will have to confront.

The Coming of the Son of Man, followed by the Harvest is the time of the resurrection of the dead. The book of Revelation teaches that certain people, because of the grace they found in the eyes of God, will resurrect before the Coming of the Son of Man: but the rest will resurrect when the 1000 years are over, at the time of his coming.

The Harvest, the Gathering of the Chosen, the Forehead-sealing of the Chosen, is made between dead resurrected and living people.

Then the people not chosen, not gathered for the Harvest, not sealed, are thrown to a place where they will have to face the Cluster of Grapes, also called the Cluster of the Vines, the Great Day of the Wrath of the Lamb, the Great Tribulation, and the Great Day of the Lord Almighty, among other similar names. In this place, many people will be purified, will reach holiness, and grace into the eyes of God, and will be rescued from it. It is hard to say what specifically will happen in it.

When the Cluster of Grapes starts, as I said, also called the Great Day of the Wrath of the Lamb, the Great Day of the Wrath of the Lord, and the Great Tribulation, among other names, the Devil is released, and the two witnesses of God give testimony. These two witnesses are killed by the Devil and resurrected by God. It seems that they are two persons, but they might be symbolically referring to two Churches, with the death and resurrection of the two Churches happening symbolically in some way.

The Cluster of Grapes, also called Great Day of the Wrath of the Lamb, Great Day of the Wrath of the Lord, ends with the defeat and final imprisonment of the Devil in hell. The Great Red Dragon, the woman sitting on a scarlet Beast, the Great Prostitute, the Great Babylon, the Great City, is thrown to hell forever.

The Final Judgment follows next. All men have to appear before Jesus to be judged. Then the book of Revelation describes the new world, the new heaven, and the new earth, which is called the New Jerusalem.

There is no place after the Coming of the Son of Man, for the intervention of Christ with his word, described in Chapter 19, and for the 1000 years of reign of Christ and the first resurrected, with the Devil imprisoned, described in Chapter 20. This confirms that the events described in Chapter 19 and 20 happen before the Coming of the Son of Man. Next, I will explain the Basis of this interpretation that I just made as an Introduction.

II.2. The Signs of the Coming of the Son of Man - Chapters 4, 5 and 6

In Chapters 4, 5 and 6 the book of Revelation refers to the times previous to the Coming of the Son of Man, which is the Second Coming of Jesus, the start of the end of this world. As I said, the book of Revelation apparently says that prior to the Coming of the Son of Man first will come wars, then famine, and finally wars, famine, pandemic diseases and plagues. And this can happen literally, or might be a symbolic representation of other events that are going to precede or cause the Coming of the Son of Man.

Chapter 4

Chapter 4 of the book of Revelation (N.I.V.) says: *"4:1 After this I looked, and there before me was a door standing open in heaven. And the voice I had first heard speaking to me like a trumpet said, "Come up here, and I will show you what must take place after this." 4:2 At once I was in the Spirit, and there before me was a throne in heaven with someone sitting on it. 4:3 And the one who sat there had the appearance of jasper and carnelian. A rainbow, resembling an emerald, encircled the throne. 4:4 Surrounding the throne were twenty-four other thrones, and seated on them were twenty four elders. They were dressed in white and had crowns of gold on their heads. 4:5 From the throne came flashes of lightning, rumblings and peals of thunder. Before the throne, seven lamps were blazing. These are the seven spirits of God. 4:6 Also before the throne there was what looked like a sea of glass, clear as crystal. In the center, around the throne, were four living creatures, and they were covered with eyes, in front and in back. 4:7 The first living creature was like a lion, the second was like an ox, the third had a face like a man, the fourth was like a flying eagle. 4:8 Each of the four living creatures had six wings and was covered with eyes all around, even under his wings. Day and night they never stop saying: "Holy, holy, holy is the Lord God Almighty, who was, and is, and is to come." 4:9 Whenever the living creatures give glory, honor and thanks to him who sits on the throne and who lives for ever and ever, 4:10 the twenty-four elders fall down before him who sits on the throne, and worship him who lives for ever and ever. They lay their crowns before the throne and say: 4:11 "You are worthy, our Lord and God, to receive glory and honor and power, for you created all things, and by your will they were created and have their being."*

Chapter 4 is introductory. It presents us God, the 24 elders (Verse 4:4), the seven spirits of God (Verse 4:5), the four living creatures (Verse 4:7) and also the sea of glass that is before God's throne (Verse 4:6).

There are several theories about the 24 elders. Some think that they symbolize the patriarchs of the Old Testament and the twelve apostles of the New Testament.[196] I believe the 24 elders symbolize the holy men of the Old and New Covenants. In the Old Testament, book of the prophet Zechariah (N.I.V.), God tells Joshua: "*3:7 "This is what the Lord Almighty says: 'If you will walk in my ways and keep my requirements, then you will govern my house and have charge of my courts, and I will give you a place among these standing here."*

The seven spirits are the seven angels of the seven churches. Verse 1:20 of the book of Revelation (N.I.V.) says: "*The mystery of the seven stars that you saw in my*

---

[196] Profesores de Salamanca "Biblia Comentada", vol. VII, under "Apocalipsis", Verses 4:1-11, p. 368.

right hand and of the seven golden lampstands is this: The seven stars are the angels of the seven churches, and the seven lampstands are the seven churches." In my opinion, the number seven is a symbolic number used to represent all the angels of all the churches. In seems to say that every Christian Church has an angel.

The four living creatures are a kind of very powerful living being: Seraphs. In general, they are taken as angels, a very important kind of angel. In the Bible, book of the prophet Isaiah (N.I.V.), it is said: *"6:1 In the year that King Uzziah died, I saw the Lord seated on a throne, high and exalted, and the train of his robe filled the temple. 6:2 Above him were seraphs, each with six wings: With two wings they covered their faces, with two they covered their feet, and with two they were flying. 6:3 And they were calling to one another: "Holy, holy, holy is the Lord Almighty; the whole earth is full of his glory." 6:4 At the sound of their voices the doorposts and thresholds shook and the temple was filled with smoke."* These beings identified as seraphs in the Old Testament, share the same characteristics: they are very close to God, have six wings, and say things very similar to what the four living creatures of the book of Revelation say. Let us remember that in Verse 4:8 of the book of Revelation (N.I.V.) the four living creatures say: *"Holy, holy, holy is the Lord God Almighty, who was, and is, and is to come.",* and Verse 6:3 of the book of the prophet Isaiah says: *"6:3 And they were calling to one another: "Holy, holy, holy is the Lord Almighty; the whole earth is full of his glory."* That is why they are taken as seraphs.

With regard to the chronology of the book of Revelation, it is important to notice that Verse 4:1 says that what is going to be shown and described in Chapter 4 is what is going to happen thereafter. This indicates that Chapter 4 narrates events that happen after the first Coming of Jesus, the incarnation. Let us remember that John had these visions after the death and resurrection of Jesus.

Chapter 5

Chapter 5 of the book of Revelation (N.I.V.) says: "*5:1 Then I saw in the right hand of him who sat on the throne a scroll with writing on both sides and sealed with seven seals. 5:2 And I saw a mighty angel proclaiming in a loud voice, "Who is worthy to break the seals and open the scroll?" 5:3 But no one in heaven or on earth or under the earth could open the scroll or even look inside it. 5:4 I wept and wept because no one was found who was worthy to open the scroll or look inside. 5:5 Then one of the elders said to me, "Do not weep! See, the Lion of the tribe of Judah, the Root of David, has triumphed. He is able to open the scroll and its seven seals." 5:6 Then I saw a Lamb, looking as if it had been slain, standing in the center of the throne, encircled by the four living creatures and the elders. He had seven horns and seven eyes, which are the seven spirits of God sent out into all the earth. 5:7 He came and took the scroll from the right hand of him who sat on the throne. 5:8 And when he had taken it, the four living creatures and the twenty-four elders fell down before the Lamb. Each one had a harp and they were holding golden bowls full of incense, which are the prayers of the saints. 5:9 And they sang a new song: "You are worthy to take the scroll and to open its seals, because you were slain, and with your blood you purchased men for God from every tribe and language and people and nation. 5:10 You have made them to be a kingdom and priests to serve our God, and they will reign on the earth." 5:11 Then I looked and heard the voice of many angels, numbering thousands upon thousands, and ten thousand times ten thousand. They encircled the throne and the living creatures and the elders. 5:12 In a loud voice they sang: "Worthy is the Lamb, who was slain, to receive power and wealth and wisdom and strength and honor and glory and praise!" 5:13 Then I heard every creature in heaven and on earth and under the earth and on the sea, and all that is in them, singing: "To him who sits on the throne and to the Lamb be praise and honor and glory and power for ever and ever!" 5:14 The four living creatures said, "Amen," and the elders fell down and worshiped."*

This Chapter 5 talks about the book and the seals which will be opened in the next chapter: Chapter 6. It presents the Lamb, who is Christ, looking as if it had been slain. It calls Christ the Lion of the tribe of Judah, the Root of David, and reveals to us, that the taking of the book and the opening of the seals, as will be seen later, begins the process of the end of the world and the advent of the new world, which Christ can promote because he gave his life for mankind.

I have already mentioned, at the time I was discussing Chapter 13, that Christ is sometimes called symbolically Lamb in the book of Revelation and that the symbol is related to the meaning of sacrifice which the coming of Christ signifies for the forgiveness of sins.

Besides, it is important to notice two things. First, that this Chapter reveals that the opening of the seals happens after the first coming of Christ, the incarnation, and after he triumphed. Secondly, that the Chapter presents men reigning as priests on the earth before the opening of the sixth seal (Verse 5:10). Let us remember that men were going to be reigning as priests after the beginning of the 1000 years, after the imprisonment of the Devil. That indicates that the opening of the seals starts after the beginning of the 1000 years, after the imprisonment of the Devil, and consequently after the intervention of Jesus with his word narrated in Chapter 19. Verse 20:4 says that after the intervention of Jesus the Devil is going to be imprisoned and a period of 1000 years will start in which Christ and the first resurrected would reign on the earth.

Chapter 6

Chapter 6 of the book of Revelation (N.I.V.) says: "*6:1 I watched as the Lamb opened the first of the seven seals. Then I heard one of the four living creatures say in a voice like thunder, "Come!" 6:2 I looked, and there before me was a white horse! Its rider held a bow, and he was given a crown, and he rode out as a conqueror bent on conquest. 6:3 When the Lamb opened the second seal, I heard the second living creature say, "Come!" 6:4 Then another horse came out, a fiery red one. Its rider was given power to take peace from the earth and to make men slay each other. To him was given a large sword. 6:5 When the Lamb opened the third seal, I heard the third living creature say, "Come!" I looked, and there before me was a black horse! Its rider was holding a pair of scales in his hand. 6:6 Then I heard what sounded like a voice among the four living creatures, saying,*

Ruy Barraco Mármol

"A quart of wheat for a day's wages, and three quarts of barley for a day's wages, and do not damage the oil and the wine!" 6:7 When the Lamb opened the fourth seal, I heard the voice of the fourth living creature say, "Come!" 6:8 I looked, and there before me was a pale horse! Its rider was named Death, and Hades was following close behind him. They were given power over a fourth of the earth to kill by sword, famine and plague, and by the wild beasts of the earth. 6:9 When he opened the fifth seal, I saw under the altar the souls of those who had been slain because of the word of God and the testimony they had maintained. 6:10 They called out in a loud voice, "How long, Sovereign Lord, holy and true, until you judge the inhabitants of the earth and avenge our blood?" 6:11 Then each of them was given a white robe, and they were told to wait a little longer, until the number of their fellow servants and brothers who were to be killed as they had been was completed. 6:12 I watched as he opened the sixth seal. There was a great earthquake. The sun turned black like sackcloth made of goat hair, the whole moon turned blood red, 6:13 and the stars in the sky fell to earth, as late figs drop from a fig tree when shaken by a strong wind. 6:14 The sky receded like a scroll, rolling up, and every mountain and island was removed from its place. 6:15 Then the kings of the earth, the princes, the generals, the rich, the mighty, and every slave and every free man hid in caves and among the rocks of the mountains. 6:16 They called to the mountains and the rocks, "Fall on us and hide us from the face of him who sits on the throne and from the wrath of the Lamb! 6:17 For the great day of their wrath has come, and who can stand?"

Verses 6:1-2 *"6:1 I watched as the Lamb opened the*

first of the seven seals. Then I heard one of the four living creatures say in a voice like thunder, "Come!" 6:2 I looked, and there before me was a white horse! Its rider held a bow, and he was given a crown, and he rode out as a conqueror bent on conquest."

Jesus opens the first of the seven seals. John sees a white horse with a rider, that rode out as a conqueror bent on conquest. This rider on the white horse is Jesus. Chapter 19, as we saw, also presents a white horse and reveals that who comes riding the horse is Jesus, in what I call the intervention of Jesus through his word. In my opinion, the white horse of these verses is the same white horse that represents the intervention of Christ through his word of Chapter 19, which we have already discussed. I do not find any reason to take it as a different one.

This vision of the rider and the white horse, who rode out as a conqueror bent on conquest, is confirming that what is going to happen after the opening of this first seal, is going to happen after the intervention of Christ through his word narrated in Chapter 19, which will be followed by the imprisonment of the Devil and the Beasts.

The events that come after the opening of the seals happen after the intervention of Christ through his word and the imprisonment of the Devil, with the initiation of the 1000 years.

Verses 6:3-4: *"6:3 When the Lamb opened the second seal, I heard the second living creature say, "Come!" 6:4 Then another horse came out, a fiery red one. Its rider was given power to take peace from the earth and to make men slay each other. To him was given a large sword."*

These verses seem to indicate that after the second seal is opened there will be wars, or a big war, like a world war. But the expression <u>take peace from the earth</u> might symbolically refer to another kind of war, or to another kind of peace.

In the Gospel according to Saint Matthew (N.I.V.) Jesus says: "*10:34 Do not suppose that I have come to bring peace to the earth. I did not come to bring peace, but a sword. 10:35 For I have come to turn "'a man against his father, a daughter against her mother, a daughter-in-law against her mother-in-law-10:36 a man's enemies will be the members of his own household.' 10:37 "Anyone who loves his father or mother more than me is not worthy of me; anyone who loves his son or daughter more than me is not worthy of me;"* With the sword that Jesus brings there is no peace. Perhaps this expression "<u>take away the peace"</u> means that the sword will be allowed, and sword in the meaning of ideological confrontations among men, maybe religious confrontations, religious persecutions. It does not have to mean necessarily great armed conflicts among nations. Perhaps it only means that God will allow conflicts between men, who will bring to each other condemnation.[197]

---

[197] The Bible, book of the prophet Zechariah, (N.I.V.) says: "*8:10 Before that time there were no wages for man or beast. No one could go about his business safely because of his enemy, for I had turned every man against his neighbor. 8:11 But now I will not deal with the remnant of this people as I did in the past,"* declares the Lord Almighty."

Jesus without Paul of Tarsus

Verses 6:5-6: "*6:5 When the Lamb opened the third seal, I heard the third living creature say, "Come!" I looked, and there before me was a black horse! Its rider was holding a pair of scales in his hand. 6:6 Then I heard what sounded like a voice among the four living creatures, saying, "A quart of wheat for a day's wages, and three quarts of barley for a day's wages, and do not damage the oil and the wine!"*

These verses then, by saying that with a day's wages it will only be possible to buy a quart of wheat, are suggesting that there will be poverty and hunger after the opening of the third seal.

Some versions of the Bible translate denarius instead of day's wages. In the Gospel according to Saint Matthew Verse 20:2 there is a parable in which a landowner agrees with a worker to pay him a denarius for the day. The value of the denarius is associated with the day's wages.

The oil and the wine are used in the Sacraments. The expression <u>and do not damage the oil and the wine</u> may mean that the practice of Christianity will not be impeded. Perhaps the verse says that in spite of the bad events that the opening of this third seal is going to bring, people who reach God, through Jesus, will be allowed to find him. This would favor the idea that the poverty and hunger will relate to natural goods and foods, not spiritual goods and foods.

When the Bible foretells hunger, it does not necessarily mean hunger for natural foods. The Bible, book of the prophet Amos (N.I.V.), foretells days of spiritual hunger: "*8:11 "The days are coming," declares the Sovereign Lord, "when I will send a famine through the land-*

not a famine of food or a thirst of water, but a famine of hearing the words of the Lord. 8:12 Men will stagger from sea to sea and wander from north to east, searching for the word of the Lord, but they will not find it." These words of the book of Amos, in my opinion, refer to the times after the Coming of the Son of Man, which begin the end of the world. If they truly refer to the times after the Coming of the Son of Man, they would strengthen the interpretation that says that the famine that the third seal seems to announce is a famine of natural food. That is so, because they say, <u>days are coming in which there will be famine of hearing the words of the Lord</u>. If the days that will bring hunger of spiritual foods are going to happen after the Coming of the Son of Man, then the hunger of the third seal, which happens before the Coming of the Son of Man, as we will see, is very likely to be hunger for natural foods. In any case it is important to notice that the announcement of famine in the Bible does not necessarily mean famine of natural foods, and we have to be aware of that, even though in this case Verses 6:5-6 seem to announce a famine of natural foods.

Verses 6:7-8: "*6:7 When the Lamb opened the fourth seal, I heard a voice of the fourth living creature say, "Come!" 6:8 I looked, and there before me was a pale horse! Its rider was named Death, and Hades was following close behind him. They were given power over a fourth of the earth to kill by sword, famine and plague, and by the wild beasts of the earth.*"

These verses seem to indicate that after the opening

of this seal, the fourth, there will be more wars, famine, plagues, and wild beasts. The Greek word translated as plagues is θανατω (thanato) which means death. The Greek words translated as wild beasts, are θηριων (therion) της (tes) γης (ges), which mean beasts of the earth.[198] Sword, famine, death, and beasts of the earth are going to come after the opening of this seal. In my opinion, this verse is talking about religious or ideological confrontations, wars, death, pandemic diseases.

However, the bad events announced in these verses can be interpreted in symbolical ways. Furthermore, each one of the bad events may have more than one sense, and the joint interpretation of all the bad events may have its own interpretation.

The expression beasts of the earth, for instance, may not refer to animals, but to false prophets. In the Bible, Old Testament, book of the prophet Ezekiel (N.I.V.) it is said: "*34:4 You have not strengthened the weak or healed the sick or bound up the injured. You have not brought back the strays or searched for the lost. You have ruled them harshly and brutally. 34:5 So they were scattered because there was no shepherd, and when they were scattered they became food for all the wild animals.*" The wild animals in this verse are, in my opinion, false prophets. The beasts of the earth can be the false prophets that capture the sheep because of the lack of shepherd, because of the

[198] The Latin Vulgate Version of the Bible says bestiis terrae. The King James Version says beasts of the earth. The Revised Standard Version says beasts of the earth. The New American Bible says beasts of the earth. The New American Standard Bible says wild beasts of the earth. The New International Version says wild beasts of the earth. The English Standard Version says wild beasts of the earth.

Ruy Barraco Mármol

lack of workers in the harvest field of the Lord, because of the lack of ministers. The Gospel according to Saint Matthew (N.I.V.) says: *"9:36 When he saw the crowds, he had compassion on them, because they were harassed and helpless, like sheep without a shepherd. 9:37 Then he said to his disciples, "The harvest is plentiful but the workers are few. 9:38 Ask the Lord of the harvest, therefore, to send out workers in his harvest field."* The sheep need the shepherd, need Jesus, and need the ministers who are supposed to tend the sheep. The book of Revelation, saying that there will be beasts, can be saying with symbolic language that there will be a lack of ministers, and that the action of the false prophets will be allowed.[199] But it does not seem to me the case, because the Devil will still be imprisoned at the time.

Another possibility is that the joint enumeration of the bad events can be for the purpose of calling attention to the reason that will bring the bad events announced, through the association with passages of the Old Testament, in which those bad events were brought for the same reason.

In the Bible, Old Testament, book of the prophet Ezekiel (N.I.V.), it is said: *"14:21 For this is what the Sovereign Lord says: How much worse will it be when I send*

---

[199] The Bible, book of Genesis (N.I.V.), says: *"3:1 Now the serpent was more crafty than any of the wild animals the LORD God had made. He said to the woman, "Did God really say, 'You must not eat from any tree in the garden'?"* The Bible, book of Genesis (N.I.V.), says: *"3:14 So the LORD God said to the serpent, "Because you have done this, "Cursed are you above all the livestock and all the wild animals! You will crawl on your belly and you will eat dust all the days of your life."* The King James Version says beasts of the field instead of wild animals in these verses. The Serpent, who is Satan, is called wild animal or beasts of the field. This opens another possible interpretation. When the book of Revelation refers to the beasts of the earth: Is it talking about the Devil and his angels?

against Jerusalem my four dreadful judgments-sword and famine and wild beasts and plague-to kill its men and their animals! 14:22 Yet there will be some survivors-sons and daughters who will be brought out of it. They will come to you, and when you see their conduct and their actions, you will be consoled regarding the disaster I have brought upon Jerusalem-every disaster I have brought upon it. 14:23 You will be consoled when you see their conduct and their actions, for you will know that I have done nothing in it without cause, declares the Sovereign Lord."

Verses 6:9-11: *"6:9 When he opened the fifth seal, I saw under the altar the souls of those who had been slain because of the word of God and the testimony they had maintained. 6:10 They called out in a loud voice, "How long, Sovereign Lord, holy and true, until you judge <u>the inhabitants of the earth</u> and avenge our blood?" 6:11 Then each of them was <u>given a white robe,</u> and they were told to wait a little longer, until the number of their fellow servants and brothers who were to be killed as they had been was completed."*

From these verses I would like to remark that in my opinion the expression <u>inhabitants of the earth</u> is used in opposition to the inhabitants of the kingdom of God. The inhabitants of the earth are the inhabitants of this world, those who live in this world, according to its values. Christ was not of this world, neither were his disciples.[200]

---

[200] The Gospel according to Saint John (N.I.V.) says: *"8:23: But he continued, "You are from below; I am from above. You are of this world; I am not of this world."* Verses 15:18-19 of the same Gospel (N.I.V.) say: *"15:18 If the world hates you, keep in*

Ruy Barraco Mármol

And what those who had been slain because of the word of God request, in my opinion, is the arrival of the final punishment of the Devil and the new world. Verse 19:2 of the book of Revelation says, referring to the judgment of the Great Prostitute, who is the Devil: "... *He has avenged on her the blood of his servants.*"

This, as will be seen later, signifies that the days of the Great Tribulation which are about to come will be cut because the final punishment of the Devil will come afterward, in a form previous to the Final Judgment. The Devil was in prison but he has to be released during the Great Tribulation and did not yet receive his final punishment. So, what those who had been slain are asking for is that the tribulation end sooner to give place to the punishment of the Devil and his sons.

The Gospel according to Saint Matthew (N.I.V.) says: "*24:21 For then there will be great distress, unequaled from the beginning of the world until now-and never to be equaled again. 7:22 If those days had not been cut short, no one would survive, but for the sake of the elect those days will be shortened.*" [201]

All this already indicates that everything will happen when the end of the world starts, as will be seen later. And, in my opinion, it also means that in the end of the world there will be some more martyrdoms, and persecutions of Christians.

---

mind that it hated me first. 15:19 If you belonged to the world, it would love you as its own. As it is, you do not belong to the world, but I have chosen you out of the world. That is why the world hates you."

[201] The great distress, is the cluster of the vine, the great day of the wrath of the Lamb.

Verses 6:12-17: "*6:12 I watched as he opened the sixth seal. There was a great earthquake. The sun turned black like sackcloth made of goat hair, the whole moon turned blood red, 6:13 and the stars in the sky fell to earth, as late figs drop from a fig tree when shaken by a strong wind. 6:14 The sky receded like a scroll, rolling up, and every mountain and island was removed from its place. 6:15 Then the kings of the earth, the princes, the generals, the rich, the mighty, and every slave and every free man hid in caves and among the rocks of the mountains. 6:16 They called to the mountains and the rocks, "Fall on us and hide us from the face of him who sits on the throne and from the wrath of the Lamb! 6:17 For the great day of their wrath has come, and who can stand?"*

John sees a great earthquake happening, and then a series of signals in the sky. These verses confirm that Chapters 4, 5 and 6 are previous to the Coming of the Son of Man. The Coming of the Son of Man is the coming of Jesus announced in the Gospel as the beginning of the end of the world. The signs narrated in these verses, that happen after the opening of the sixth seal, are those that the Gospel according to Saint Matthew Verse 24:29 and the Gospel according to Saint Mark Verse 13:24, narrate will happen previously to the Coming of the Son of Man, which brings the beginning of the end of the world.

The Gospel according to Saint Matthew (N.I.V.) says: "*24:29 Immediately after the distress of those days '"the sun will be darkened, and the moon will not give its light; the stars will fall from the sky, and the heavenly bodies will be shaken.' 24:20 "At that time the sign of the Son of Man will appear in the sky, and all the nations of the earth will mourn. They will see the Son of Man coming on the clouds of the sky, with power and great glory."*

The book of Revelation (Verse 6:12) says "the sun turned black"; and the Gospel according to Saint Matthew (Verse 24:29) says "the sun will be darkened". The book of Revelation (Verse 6:12) says "the moon turns blood red"; and the Gospel according to Saint Matthew (Verse 24:29) says "the moon will not give its light". The book of Revelation (Verse 6:13) says "the stars in the sky fell to earth"; and the Gospel according to Saint Matthew (Verse 24:29) says "the stars will fall from the sky". The book of Revelation (Verse 6:13) says "the stars will fall from the sky, as late figs drop from a fig tree when shaken by a strong wind"; and the Gospel according to Saint Matthew (Verse 24:29) says "and the heavenly bodies will be shaken".

The book of Revelation (Chapter 6) presents these events after a series of happenings that constitute, or form, a tribulation; and the Gospel according to Saint Matthew (Verse 24:29) says that this will happen immediately after the distress of those days.

Without any doubt both sets of verses narrate the signals previous to the Coming of the Son of Man. And the Gospel according to Saint Mark (Verse 13:24) narrates in a very similar way to the Gospel according to Saint Matthew, the same events: the signals previous to the Coming of the Son of Man.

In addition, Verses 6:15-17 of the book of Revelation (N.I.V.) say: " *6:15 Then the kings of the earth, the princes, the generals, the rich, the mighty, and every slave and every free man hid in caves and among the rocks of the*

mountains. 6:16 They called to the mountains and the rocks.
"Fall on us and hide us from the face of him who sits on the
throne and from the wrath of the Lamb! 6:17 For the great
day of their wrath has come, and who can stand?" The men
hid in mountains and rocks because the Lamb was in
their sight; and the Gospel according to Saint Matthew
(N.I.V.) says: *"24:30 At that time the sign of the Son of*
Man will appear in the sky, and all the nations of the earth
will mourn. They will see the Son of Man coming on the
clouds of the sky, with power and great glory."

Further, I will present other reasons that give even
more basis to what I said. For instance, I will remark
that the Devil will be released in the Great Day of the
Wrath of the Lamb that follows the opening of this seal,
which indicates that the 1000 years will be over
(Revelation 20:3), and that the dead men will be
resurrected (Revelation 20:5). If the dead men will be
resurrected, then the Coming of the Son of Man will
already have happened.

After the sixth seal is opened, the signals previous to
the Coming of the Son of Man happen, and the end of
the world begins with the Coming of the Son of Man.

But, returning to the matter of the signals, and the
bad events announced, in conclusion it is known that
there is going to be a tribulation before the Coming of
the Son of Man, but little can be known with certainty
about what will happen in concrete.

Personally, I believe the main objective of the bad
events announced in the seals is to warn Christians
about the fact that it will be the behavior and the works
of men which are going to bring the end of the world.

The end of the world will come, when the world has

Ruy Barraco Mármol

turned away from God, when absence of love and injustice reign; when, even though the Devil is imprisoned, and the first to be resurrected are acting, there are very few Christians left. Perhaps there will even be a persecution against Christianity. Perhaps men by themselves will turn to a new religion. Or maybe in the future the Gospel of Paul will be standing again in the holy place, where only the true word of God should be.

If there is something that the Bible teaches, it is that God does not act without reason. The Bible, book of the prophet Isaiah (N.I.V.) says: "*24:4 The earth dries up and withers, the world languishes and withers, the exalted of the earth languish, 24:5 The earth is defiled by its people; they have disobeyed the laws, violated the statutes and broken the everlasting covenant. 24:6 Therefore a curse consumes the earth; its people must bear their guilt. Therefore earth's inhabitants are burned up, and very few are left. 24:7 The new wine dries up and the vine withers;*" The Bible, book of the prophet Jeremiah (N.I.V.) says: "*44:23 Because you have burned incense and have sinned against the Lord and have not obeyed him or followed his law or his decrees or his stipulations, his disaster has come upon you, as you now see.*" The Bible, book of the prophet Ezekiel (N.I.V.) says: "*39:21 "I will display my glory among the nations, and all the nations will see the punishment I inflict and the hand I lay upon them. 39:22 From that day forward the house of Israel will know that I am the Lord their God. 29:23 And the nations will know that the people of Israel went into exile for their sin, because they were unfaithful to me. So I hid my face from them and handed them over to their enemies, and they all*

Jesus without Paul of Tarsus

fell by the sword."

Men need to be prepared to persist in faith in any circumstance, in any tribulation; from circumstances mentioned above, like famine, war, pandemic diseases, big natural disasters, big injustices, religious or ideological persecutions, to others more unlikely to happen like an invasion of aliens, if there are aliens. And I do not say this because I think that the end of the world will start with an invasion of aliens, if they exist. I just say it to illustrate how far the preparation for persistence in faith has to go.

II.3. The Coming of the Son of Man – the Harvest - the Great Day of the Wrath of the Lamb – Chapters 14:14-16; 7:1-8; 8; 9; 10; 11:14-10; 15; 16; 7:9-17; 11:1-14

Chapter 6 ends just before the Coming of the Son of Man, event that begins the end of the world. The last verse of Chapter 6 of the book of Revelation, English Standard Version (E.S.V.)[202] says: *"6:16..."Fall on us and hide us from the face of him who is seated on the throne, and from the wrath of the Lamb, 6:17 for the great day of their wrath has come, and who can stand?"*

In the chapters that we will analyze next, the book of Revelation describes for us what will happen from the Coming of the Son of Man to the Final Judgment.

[202] Scripture quotations marked with E.S.V. in this work are from the Holy Bible, English Standard Version (ESV), copyright © 2001 by Crossway Bibles, a publishing ministry of Good News Publishers. Used by permission. All rights reserved.

Ruy Barraco Mármol

The first thing that happens, after the Coming of the Son of Man, is the Harvest. The Harvest is the Gathering of the Chosen of the Gospel.[203] It is carried out among all men, even those who are dead. The Coming of the Son of Man is the time of the resurrection of the dead. The Harvest is foretold in Chapters 14:14-16 and 7:1-8 of the book of Revelation.

After the Harvest, is the time of the Cluster of the Grapes of the nations, or Cluster of the Vine, which is the Great Day of the Wrath of the Lamb, that was announced in the end of Chapter 6. It is also the Great Day of God Almighty mentioned in Chapter 16:14 of the book of Revelation, and also the Great Tribulation mentioned in the Gospel.[204]

The Cluster of the Grapes, the Great Tribulation, the Great Day of the Wrath of the Lamb, the Great Day of God Almighty, is described in Chapters 14:17-20, 8, 9, 11:14-19, 15, 16, and starts with the opening of the seventh seal, and the sounding of seven trumpets. Some verses of other chapters make references to this event but those mentioned talk specifically about it.

When the seventh trumpet sounds, the seven bowls of God's wrath, with the seven plagues, start to be poured. Chapters 15 and 16 describe the pouring of the seven bowls with the seven plagues.

All this constitutes the Cluster of the Grapes, the Great Tribulation, the Great Day of the Wrath of the

---

[203] Gospel according to Saint Matthew 24:31, and Gospel according to Saint Mark 13:27.

[204] Gospel according to Saint Matthew 24:15; Gospel according to Saint Mark 13:14; Gospel according to Saint Luke 21:20.

Lamb, the Great Day of God Almighty. The Devil is released to act during it. Two witnesses also act, who give testimony of Jesus and his word.

After the Cluster of Grapes the Final Judgment comes. The book of Revelation talks about the Final Judgment in Verse 20:11; the Gospel according to Saint Matthew in Verse 25:31.

This is a summary of the happenings foretold in the chapters of the book of Revelation in analysis. Next, I will discuss in particular all these events.

II.3.1. The Harvest

I said the first thing that happens according to the book of Revelation after the Coming of the Son of Man is the Harvest. This is described in Chapters 14:14-16 and 7:1-8 of the book of Revelation.

Chapters 14:14-16. The Harvest of the Earth and the Gathering of the Chosen

Verses 14:14-16 of the book of Revelation (E.S.V.) say: "*14:14 Then I looked, and behold, a white cloud, and seated on the cloud one like a son of man, with a golden crown on his head, and a sharp sickle in his hand. 14:15 And another angel came out of the temple, calling with a loud voice to him who sat on the cloud, "Put in your sickle, and reap, for the hour to reap has come, for the harvest of the earth is fully ripe." 14:16 So he who sat on the cloud swung his sickle across the earth, and the earth was reaped.*"

The one who is seated on a cloud is the Son of Man, Jesus, and these happenings are also foretold in the

Gospels according to Saint Matthew Verse 24:30 and Saint Mark Verse 13:17. The Gospel according to Saint Matthew (E.S.V.), after describing the signs of the Coming of the Son of Man says: "*24:30 Then will appear in heaven the sign of the Son of Man, and then all the tribes of the earth will mourn, and they will see the Son of Man coming on the clouds of heaven with power and great glory. 24:31 And he will send out his angels with a loud trumpet call, and they will gather his elect from the four winds, from one end of heaven to the other.*" The Harvest that these verses 14:14-16 of the book of Revelation announce is the gathering of the chosen of the Gospel.

It is also the Harvest of the Gospel according to Saint Matthew Verse 13:24. The Gospel according to Saint Matthew (E.S.V.) says: "*13:24 He put another parable before them, saying, "The kingdom of heaven may be compared to a man who sowed good seed in his field, 13:25 but while his men were sleeping his enemy came and sowed weeds among the wheat and went away. 13:26 So when the plants came up and bore grain, then the weeds appeared also. 13:27 And the servants of the master of the house came and said to him, 'Master, did you not sow good seed in your field? How then does it have weeds? 13:28 He said to them, 'An enemy has done this.' So the servants said to him, 'Then do you want us to go and gather them? 13:29 But he said, 'No, lest in gathering the weeds you root up the wheat along with them. 13:30 Let both grow together until the harvest, and at harvest time I will tell the reapers, Gather the weeds first and bind them in bundles to be burned, but gather the wheat into my barn.'*"

"...*13:36 Then he left the crowds and went into the house. And his disciples came to him, saying, "Explain to us the parable of the weeds of the field." 13:37 He answered, "The one who sows the good seed is the Son of Man. 13:38 The field is the world, and the good seed is the children of the kingdom. The weeds are the sons of the evil one. 13:39 and the enemy who sowed them is the devil. The harvest is the close of the age, and the reapers are angels. 13:40 Just as the weeds are gathered and burned with fire, so will it be at the close of the age. 13:41 The Son of Man will send his angels, and they will gather out of his kingdom all causes of sin and all law-breakers, 13:42 and throw them into the fiery furnace. In that place there will be weeping and gnashing of teeth. 13:43 Then the righteous will shine like the sun in the kingdom of their Father. He who has ears, let him hear."*

In addition, the Harvest mentioned in the book of Revelation Verse 14:14 is also the Sealing of the Servants of God of Chapter 7:1-8 of the book of Revelation. The book of Revelation and the Gospel say that the Harvest follows the Coming of the Son of Man.

Chapter 7:1-8. The Sealing of the Servants of God

Chapter 7:1-8 of the book of Revelation (E.S.V.) says: "*7:1 After this I saw four angels standing at the four corners of the earth, holding back the four winds of the earth, that no wind might blow on earth or sea or against any tree. 7:2 Then I saw another angel ascending from the rising of the sun, with the seal of the living God, and he called with a loud voice to the four angels who had been given power to harm earth and sea, 7:3 saying, "Do not harm the earth or the sea or the trees, until we have sealed the servants of our*

God on their foreheads." 7:4 And I heard the number of the sealed, 144,000, sealed from every tribe of the sons of Israel: *12,000 from the tribe of Judah were sealed, 12,000 from the tribe of Reuben, 12,000 from the tribe of Gad, 12,000 from the tribe of Asher, 12,000 from the tribe of Naphtali, 12,000 from the tribe of Manasseh, 12,000 from the tribe of Simeon, 12,000 from the tribe of Levi, 12,000 from the tribe of Issachar, 12,000 from the tribe of Zebulum, 12,000 from the tribe of Joseph, 12,000 from the tribe of Benjamin were sealed."*

Chapter 6 of the book of Revelation ends foretelling the Coming of the Son of Man, and the Great Day of the Wrath of the Lamb. Chapter 7 talks about the Sealing of the Servants of God.

The location of Chapter 7 seems to indicate that the Sealing of the Servants of God is part of the Harvest of Chapter 14:14-16. The Sealing of the Servants of God is foretold in Chapter 7, after Chapter 6, which, as I said, ends talking about the Coming of the Son of Man and of the Great Day of the Wrath of the Lamb; and before Chapter 8 which starts to describe that great day.

The Sealing of the Servants of God, because of its location, seems to follow the Coming of the Son of Man, and we know that the Harvest is what happens following the coming, which is also called the Gathering of the Chosen. In addition, because of its location it seems to happen before the opening of the seventh seal of Chapter 8. This seems to put the Sealing of the Servants of God in the same moment of the Harvest of the Earth of Chapter 14:14, also called the Gathering of the Chosen.

We know that the sealing happens before the opening of the seventh seal of Chapter 8, independently of its location in the book, because Chapter 7, which describes the sealing, starts describing how John sees 4 angels standing at the four corners of the earth holding back the four winds, to whom it is said in Verse 7:3: *"saying, "Do not harm the earth or the sea or the trees until we have sealed the servants of our God on their foreheads.";* and the earth and trees (Revelation 8:7) and the sea (Revelation Chapter 8:8) are harmed after the two first trumpets of Chapter 8 blow, which begin the Great Day of the Wrath of the Lamb.

Moreover, the fact that the angels, who will hold back the four winds until the sealing is done, will be in the four corners of the earth, the place where the angels of the Gathering of the Chosen of the Gospel according to Saint Matthew 24:30 and Saint Mark 13:27 will be, confirms that the sealing happens before Chapter 8, in which the Great Day of the Wrath of the Lamb is described. Let us remember that this Gathering of the Chosen is the Harvest of the book of Revelation, Chapter 14.

The Gospel according to Saint Matthew (E.S.V.) says: *"24:30 Then will appear in heaven the sign of the Son of Man, and then all the tribes of the earth will mourn, and they will see the Son of Man coming on the clouds of heaven with power and great glory. 24:31 And he will send out his angels with a loud trumpet call, and they will gather his elect from the four winds, from one end of heaven to the other."* Chapter 7 of the book of Revelation (E.S.V.) says "*7: 7:1 After this I saw four angels standing at the four corners of the earth, holding back the four winds of the earth, that no*

wind might blow on earth or sea or against any tree."
Clearly, this happens immediately after the Coming of
the Son of Man.

In addition, the book of Revelation teaches that the
product of the Harvest, who are the chosen of the
Gospel according to Saint Matthew 24:31, the children
of the kingdom of the Gospel according to Saint
Matthew 13:38, are saved from the Cluster of the
Grapes, or Cluster of the Vines, which, we will see
later, is the Great Day of the Wrath of the Lamb, the
Great Tribulation; and these people, who are sealed,
are servants of God, and therefore children of the
kingdom. Everything indicates that they must be part of
the Harvest, the gathering of the chosen.

Before describing the Great Day of the Wrath of the
Lamb, with the opening of the seventh seal, and the
blowing of the seven trumpets, and the seven bowls
with the seven plagues of the seventh trumpet, John
places this Chapter 7 to let us know that the servants of
God will be sealed and saved from this great day.

This Harvest, this Gathering of the Chosen, this
Forehead Sealing of the Servants of God, is carried out
among the dead and the living people. The Gospel
teaches that the Coming of the Son of Man, the second
coming of Jesus, brings the resurrection of the dead
people.

The Parable of the Servant of the Gospel according
to Saint Matthew (24:45), located between the Coming
of the Son of Man (24:30), and the Final Judgment
(25:31), which refers to the Coming of the Son of Man,
applies to the living people as well to the dead people.

The Gospel according to Saint Matthew (E.S.V.) says:

"24:44 Therefore you also must be ready, for the Son of Man is coming at an hour you do not expect. 24:45 "Who then is the faithful and wise servant, whom his master has set over his household, to give them their food at the proper time? 24:46 Blessed is that servant whom his master will find so doing when he comes. 24:47 Truly, I say to you, he will set him over all his possessions. 24:48 But if that wicked servant says to himself, 'My master is delayed,' 24:49 and begins to beat his fellow servants and eats and drinks with drunkards, 24:50 the master of that servant will come on a day when he does not expect him and at an hour he does not know 24:51 and will cut him in pieces and put him with the hypocrites. In that place there will be weeping and gnashing of teeth."

The same thing can be said about the Parable of the Ten Virgins of the Gospel according to Saint Matthew (E.S.V.), located in the same place, which says: *"25:1 Then the kingdom of heaven will be like ten virgins who took their lamps and went to meet the bridegroom. Five of them were foolish, and five were wise. 25:3 For when the foolish took their lamps, they took no oil with them, 25:4 but the wise took flasks of oil with their lamps. 25:5 As the bridegroom was delayed, they all became drowsy and slept. 25:6 But at midnight there was a cry, 'Here is the bridegroom! Come out to meet him. 25:7 Then all those virgins rose and trimmed their lamps. 25:8 And the foolish said to the wise, 'Give us some of your oil, for our lamps are going out.' 25:9 But the wise answered, saying, 'Since there will not be enough for us and for you, go rather to the dealers and buy for yourselves.' 25:10 And while they were going to buy, the bridegroom came, and those who were ready went in with him to the marriage feast, and the door was shut. 25:11 Afterward the other virgins came also, saying, 'Lord, lord, open to us.' 25:12 But he answered, Truly, I say to you, I do not know you. 25:13 Watch therefore, for you know neither the day nor the hour."*

And the same thing can be said about the Parable of the Talents of the Gospel according to Saint Matthew (E.S.V.), which says: "*25:14 For it will be like a man going on a journey, who called his servants and entrusted to them his property. 25:15 To one he gave five talents, to another two, to another one, to each according to his ability. The he went away. 25:16 He who had received the five talents went at once and traded with them, and he made five talents more. 25:17 So also he who had the two talents made two talents more. 25:18 But he who had received the one talent went and dug in the ground and hid his master's money. 25:19 Now after a long time the master of those servants came and settled accounts with them. 25:20 And he who had received the five talents came forward, saying, 'Master, you delivered to me five talents; here I have made five talents more.' 25:21 His master said to him, 'Well done, good and faithful servant. You have been faithful over a little; I will set you over much. Enter into the joy of your master.' 25:22 And he also who had the two talents came forward, saying, 'Master, you delivered to me two talents; here I have made two talents more.' 25:23 His master said to him, 'Well done, good and faithful servant. You have been faithful over a little; I will set you over much. Enter into the joy of your master.' 25:24 He also who had received the one talent came forward, saying, 'Master, I knew you to be a hard man, reaping where you did not sow, and gathering where you scattered no seed, 25:25 so I was afraid, and I went and hid your talent in the ground. Here you have what is yours.' 25:26 But his master answered him, 'You wicked and slothful servant! You knew that I reap where I have not sowed and gather where I scattered no seed? 25:27 Then you ought to have invested my money with the bankers, and at my coming I should have received what was my own with interest. 25:28 So take the talent from him and give it to him who has the ten talents. 25:29 For to everyone who has will more be given, and he will have an abundance. But from the one who has not, even what he has will be taken away. 25:30 And cast the worthless servant into the outer darkness. In that place there will be weeping and gnashing of teeth.'''*

In my opinion, the fact that in the Gathering of the Chosen of the Gospel according to Saint Matthew Verse 24:31, which is the Harvest of Chapter 14 of the book of Revelation, and the Forehead Sealing of the Servants of God of Chapter 7 of the book of Revelation, it is said that the chosen will be gathered from the four winds, from one end of heaven to the other, confirms this statement; confirms that the gathering will be carried among the living and the dead.

And in my opinion, the expression 'from one end of heaven to the other' was placed to confirm that the Harvest involves also the resurrected from death. The gathering is not only carried out from the four winds, but from one end of heaven to the other. The dead people are neither in the earth, nor in heaven, but the Gospel, by saying that the gathering is carried out from one end of heaven to the other, is saying that it covers any place in which the dead could be.

II.3.2. The Cluster From the Vine of the Earth – The Great Day of the Wrath of the Lamb – The Great Tribulation

After the Harvest, the Gathering of the Chosen, the Forehead Sealing of the Servants of God, the book of Revelation teaches that the Cluster of the Grapes or Cluster of the Vine of the Earth comes.

Chapter 14:17-20. The Cluster of the Vine of the Earth

Chapter 14:17-20 of the book of Revelation (E.S.V.) says: "*14:17 Then another angel came out of the temple in heaven, and he too had a sharp sickle. 14:18 And another angel came out from the altar, the angel who has authority over the fire, and he called with a loud voice to the one who had the sharp sickle, "Put in your sickle and gather the clusters from the vine of the earth, for its grapes are ripe." 14:19 So the angel swung his sickle across the earth and gathered the grape harvest of the earth and threw it into the great winepress of the wrath of God. 14:20 And the winepress was trodden outside the city, and blood flowed from the winepress, as high as a horse's bridle, for 1,600 stadia.*"

This is described in Chapter 14 following the description of the Harvest, that follows the Coming of the Son of Man.

The Gospel according to Saint Matthew (E.S.V.) says about the Harvest: "*13:36 Then he left the crowds and went into the house. And his disciples came to him, saying, "Explain to us the parable of the weeds of the field." 13:37*

He answered, "The one who sows the good seed is the Son of Man. 13:38 The field is the world, and the good seed is the children of the kingdom. The weeds are the sons of the evil one, 13:39 and the enemy who sowed them is the devil. The harvest is the close of the age, and the reapers are angels. 13:40 Just as the weeds are gathered and burned with fire, so will it be at the close of the age. 13:41 The Son of Man will send his angels, and they will gather out of his kingdom all causes of sin and all law-breakers, 13:42 and throw them into the fiery furnace. In that place there will be weeping and gnashing of teeth. 13:43 Then the righteous will shine like the sun in the kingdom of their Father. He who has ears, let him hear." The fate of the weed is to be thrown to the fiery furnace, where there will be weeping and gnashing of teeth.

The book of Revelation gives us some more details of the fate of all causes of sin and all law-breakers, the fate of the weed, teaching about the Cluster of the Vine of the Earth. Verse 14:19 of the book of Revelation (E.S.V.) says: *"So the angel swung his sickle across the earth and gathered the grape of the harvest of the earth and threw it into the great winepress of the wrath of God."*

The angel swung his sickle over the earth and gathered the grape of the harvest and threw it into the great winepress of the wrath of God, which is where the Cluster of the Vine will be made. This cluster, that takes place in the winepress of the wrath of God, is no other than the Great Day of the Wrath of the Lamb, described with the opening of the seventh seal and with the pouring of the seven bowls of the wrath of God; and it is at the same time the Great Tribulation.

After the Coming of the Son of Man, the Harvest

comes first, followed by the Cluster of the Vine, which is the Great Day of the Wrath of the Lamb. That is why Chapter 6 of the book of Revelation (E.S.V.) finishes saying: "*6:16 ...hide us from the face of him who is seated on the throne, and from the wrath of the Lamb, 6:17 for the great day of their wrath has come, and who can stand?*""

The Cluster of the Vine is the collecting of the fruits of the vine. The use of this figure of the cluster of the vine, to refer to the great day of the wrath of the Lamb, lets us know, that the great day of the wrath of the Lamb has as purpose to obtain fruit, to give the people, who are facing it, chance to reach salvation. In fact, many people will find salvation in the Great Day of the Wrath of the lamb, the Cluster of the Vine, the Great Tribulation. Chapter 7:14 lets us know this.

In addition, this chapter, by saying that the cluster is going to be trodden in the winepress, is letting us know that those who face the cluster, will face a great tribulation, the wrath of God.

The book of Revelation describes the Cluster of the Vine, not only in Chapter 14 but in Chapters 8, 9, 10, 11:14-18, and Chapters 15 and 16, all of which I will start to discuss next.

Chapters 8, 9, 10 and 11:14-18. The Opening of the Seventh Seal and the Seven Trumpets

The Cluster of the Vine, the Great Day of the Wrath of the Lamb, the Great Tribulation, starts to be described with detail in Chapter 8, with the opening of the seventh seal.

We know that Chapter 8 talks about the cluster of

the vines, about the Great Day of the Wrath of the Lamb, among other reasons, because Chapter 6 finishes announcing the Coming of the Son of Man and the Great Day of the Wrath of the Lamb; and the Cluster of the Vine follows the Harvest and the Coming of the Son of Man.

With the opening of the seventh seal, seven trumpets start to sound, following which some events occur. This is what I will comment on next, transcribing Chapters 8, 9, 11:14-18. Although we cannot know concretely very much about them, we can understand their general meaning.

Chapter 8

Chapter 8 of the book of Revelation (E.S.V.) says: "*8:1 When the Lamb opened the seventh seal, there was silence in heaven for about half an hour. 8:2 Then I saw the seven angels who stand before God, and seven trumpets were given to them. 8:3 And another angel came and stood at the altar with a golden censer, and he was given much incense to offer with the prayers of all the saints on the golden altar before the throne, 8:4 and the smoke of the incense, with the prayers of the saints, rose before God from the hand of the angel. 8:5 Then the angel took the censer and filled it with fire from the altar and threw it on the earth, and there were peals of thunder, rumblings, flashes of lightning, and an earthquake. 8:6 Now the seven angels who had the seven trumpets prepared to blow them. 8:7 The first angel blew his trumpet, and there followed hail and fire, mixed with blood, and these were thrown upon the earth. And a third of the earth was burned up, and a third of the trees were burned up, and all green grass was burned up. 8:8 The second angel blew his trumpet, and something like a great mountain, burning with fire, was thrown into the sea, and a third of the sea became blood. 8:9 A third of the living creatures in the sea died, and a third of the ships were destroyed. 8:10 The third angel blew his trumpet, and a great star fell from heaven, blazing like a torch, and it fell on a third of the rivers and on the springs of water. 8:11 The name of the star is Wormwood. A third of the waters became wormwood, and many people died from the water, because it had been made bitter. 8:12 The fourth angel blew his trumpet, and a third of the sun was struck, and a third of the moon, and a third of the stars, so that a third of their light be darkened, and a third of the day might be kept from shining, and likewise a third of the night. 8:13 Then I looked, and I heard an eagle crying with a loud voice as it flew directly overhead, "Woe, woe, woe to those who dwell on the earth, at the blast of the other trumpets that the three angels are about to blow!""*

This Chapter 8 starts to describe a tribulation, such as has not happened until now, and never will be until it comes. There is no doubt about that. But, I think the description of Chapter 8 cannot be taken literally and the symbols seem impossible to decipher at this time.

However, I want to call your attention once again to Verse 8:13, which says: *"Then I looked, and I heard an eagle crying with a loud voice as it flew directly overhead, "Woe, woe, woe, to those who dwell on the earth, at the blasts of the other trumpets that the three angels are about to blow!""* Four trumpets have already blown and this verse mentions three "woes" that are about to come.

Each one of those woes will correspond to each one of the trumpets that are about to be blown. This question will have importance later to locate chronologically the action of the two witnesses of Chapter 11 of the book of Revelation.

Chapter 9

Chapter 9 of the book of Revelation (E.S.V.) says: *"9:1 And the fifth angel blew his trumpet, and I saw a star fallen from heaven to earth, and he was given the key to the shaft of the bottomless pit. 9:2 He opened the shaft of the bottomless pit, and from the shaft rose smoke like the smoke of a great furnace, and the sun and the air were darkened with the smoke from the shaft. 9:3 Then from the smoke came locusts on the earth, and they were given power like the power of scorpions of the earth. 9:4 They were told not to harm the grass of the earth or any green plant or any tree, but only those people who do not have the seal of God on their foreheads. 9:5 They were allowed to torment them for five months, but not to kill them, and their torment was like the torment of a scorpion when it stings someone. 9:6 And in those days people will seek death and will not find it. They will long to die, but death will flee from them. 9:7 In appearance the locusts were like horses prepared for battle: on their heads were what looked like crowns of gold; their faces were like human faces, 9:8 their hair like women's hair, and their teeth like lions teeth; 9:9 they had breastplates like breastplates of iron, and the noise of their wings was like the noise of many chariots with horses rushing into battle. 9:10 They have tails and stings like scorpions, and their power to hurt people for five months is in their tails. 9:11 They have as a king over them the angel of the bottomless pit. His name in Hebrew is Abaddon, and in Greek he is called Apollyon. 9:12 The first woe has passed; behold, two woes are still to come. 9:13 Then the sixth angel blew his trumpet, and I heard a voice from the four horns of the golden altar before God, 9:14 saying to the sixth angel who had the trumpet, "Release the four angels who are bound at the great river Euphrates." 9:15 So the four angels, who had been prepared for the hour, the day, the month, and the year, were released to kill a third of mankind. 9:16 The number of mounted troops was twice ten thousand times ten thousand; I heard their number. 9:17 And this is how I saw the horses in my vision and those who rode them: they wore breastplates the color of fire and of sapphire and of sulfur, and the heads of the horses were like lion's heads, and fire and smoke and sulfur came out of their mouths. 9:18 By these three plagues a third of mankind was killed, by the fire and smoke and sulfur coming out of their mouths. 9:19 For the power of the horses is in their mouths and in their tails, for their tails are like serpents with heads, and by means of them they wound. 9:20 The rest of mankind, who were not killed by these plagues, did not repent of the works of their hands nor give up worshiping demons and idols of gold and silver and bronze and stone and wood, which cannot see or hear or talk, 9:21 nor did they repent of their murders or their sorceries or their sexual immorality or their thefts."*

Chapter 9 continues the description of the Great Tribulation. The bad events announced are similar to the bad events that Moses sent to Egypt for the purpose of persuading the pharaoh to free and let go the Jewish people living in Egypt.[205] Perhaps the purpose of this similarity is to indicate that the intention of these bad events is to make people accept the will of God, and convert themselves.

Independently, it is remarkable that the book of Revelation Verse 9:12 says that the first woe has passed, referring to the fifth trumpet, and then talks about the blowing of the sixth trumpet, but before the seventh is blown, Chapter 10 is inserted.

Chapter 10

Chapter 10 of the book of Revelation (E.S.V.) says: "*10:1 Then I saw another mighty angel coming down from heaven, wrapped in a cloud, with a rainbow over his head, and his face was like the sun, and his legs like pillars of fire. 10:2 He had a little scroll open in his hand. And he set his right foot on the sea, and his left foot on the land, and called out with a loud voice, like a lion roaring. When he called out, the seven thunders sounded. 10:4 And when the seven thunders had sounded, I was about to write, but I heard a voice from heaven saying, "Seal up what the seven thunders have said, and do not write it down." 10:5 And the angel whom I saw standing on the sea and on the land raised his right hand to heaven 10:6 and swore by him who lives forever and ever, who created heaven and what is in it, the earth and what is in it, and the sea and what is in it, that there would be no more delay, 10:7 but that in the days of the trumpet call to be sounded by the seventh angel, the mystery of God would be fulfilled, just as he announced to his servants the prophets. 10:8 Then the voice that I had*

---

[205] The Bible, Exodus, Verse 7:8.

heard from heaven spoke to me again, saying, "Go, take the scroll that is open in the hand of the angel who is standing on the sea and on the land." 10:9 So I went to the angel and told him to give me the little scroll. And he said to me, "Take and eat it; it will make your stomach bitter, but in your mouth it will be sweet as honey." 10:10 and I took the little scroll from the hand of the angel and ate it. It was sweet as honey in my mouth, but when I had eaten it my stomach was made bitter. 10:11 And I was told, "You must again prophesy about many peoples and nations and languages and kings."

From this Chapter I noted with interest that it says in Verses 10:6-7, that after the blowing of the seventh trumpet there will be no more delay, the mystery of God would be fulfilled. This confirms the unity of the tribulation of the seventh seals with their trumpets, and the tribulation of the seven bowls with their seven plagues, which I believe come after the blowing of the seventh trumpet.

Chapter 11:14-19

Chapter of the book of Revelation (E.S.V.) 11:14-19: "*11:14 The second Woe has passed, behold, the third woe is soon to come. 11:15 Then the seventh angel blew his trumpet, and there were loud voices in heaven, saying, "The kingdom of the world has become the kingdom of our Lord and of his Christ, and he shall reign forever and ever." 11:16 And the twenty-four elders who sit on their thrones before God fell on their faces and worshiped God, 11:17 saying, "We give thanks to you, Lord God Almighty, who is and who was, for you have taken your great power and begun to reign. 11:18 The nations raged, but your wrath came, and the time for the dead to be judged, and for rewarding your servants, the prophets and saints, and those who fear your name, both small and great, and for destroying the destroyers of the earth. "11:19 Then God's temple in heaven was opened, and the ark of his covenant was seen within his temple. There were flashes of lightning, rumblings, peals of thunder, an earthquake, and heavy hail."*

When the seventh trumpet blows the final wrath comes. Verse 11:18 says "The nations raged, but your wrath came, and the time for the dead to be judged...".

In regard to what happens after the blowing of the seventh trumpet, this Chapter does not tell much, but in my opinion Chapters 15 and 16 do, which are the continuation of Chapter 11. Chapters 15 and 16 tell about the bowls of the wrath of God.

Chapters 15 and 16. The Seven Bowls with Their Seven Plagues

Chapter 15

Chapter 15 of the book of Revelation (E.S.V.) says: "*15:1 Then I saw another sign in heaven, great and amazing seven angels, with seven plagues, which are the last, for with them the wrath of God is finished. 15:2 And I saw what appeared to be a sea of glass mingled with fire- and also those who had conquered the beast and its image and the number of its name, standing beside the sea of glass with harps of God in their hands. 15:3 And they sing the song of Moses, the servant of God, and the song of the Lamb, saying, "Great and amazing are your deeds, O Lord God the Almighty! Just and true are your ways, O King of the nations! 15:4 Who will not fear, O Lord, and glorify your name? For you alone are holy. All nations will come and worship you, for your righteous acts have been revealed." 15:5 After this I looked, and the sanctuary of the tent of witness in heaven was opened, 15:6 and out of the sanctuary came the seven angels with the seven plagues, clothed in pure, bright linen, with golden sashes around their chests. 15:7 And one of the four living creatures gave to the seven angels seven golden bowls full of the wrath of God who lives forever and ever, 15:8 and the sanctuary was filled with smoke from the glory of God and from his power, and no one could enter the sanctuary until the seven plagues of the seven angels were finished."*

Verse 15:2 says: *"And I saw what looked like a sea of glass mixed with fire and, standing beside the sea, those who had been victorious over the beast and his image and over the number of his name."* In my opinion, those who had been victorious over the Beast and his image are those who have been true Christians in spite of Paul and his epistles. Those who have been victorious over the number of the name of the Beast are those who have discovered to whom the number belongs, who is the Beast, what is his name, and were able to be Christians, real Christians, despite the action of the people who are the number of the name of the Beast.

Verse 15:5 talks about an opening of the temple of God. The sanctuary of the tent is the sanctuary of God or altar of God. Chapter 11, which talks about the blowing of the seventh trumpet of the seventh seal, finishes with the opening of the temple of God, and in Chapter 15:5 there is an opening of the temple of God. In my opinion, they talk about the same opening. Chapter 15 continues Chapter 11. Let us remember what the book of Revelation, Verse 11:18, says *"The nations raged, but your wrath came, and the time for the dead to be judged..."*, and Chapter 16 describes the pouring of the seven bowls of the wrath of God, and the Final Judgment follows Chapter 16.

Chapter 16

Chapter 16 of the book of Revelation (E.S.V.) says: *"16:1 Then I heard a loud voice from the temple telling the seven angels, "Go and pour out on the earth the seven bowls of the wrath of God." 16:2 So the first angel went and poured out this bowl on the earth, and harmful and painful sores came upon the people who bore the mark of the beast and worshiped its image. 16:3 The second angel poured out his bowl into the sea and it became like the blood of a corpse, and every living thing died that was in the sea. 16:4 The third angel poured out his bowl into the rivers and the springs of water, and they became blood. 16:5 And I heard the angel in charge of the waters say, "Just are you, O Holy One, who is and who was, for you brought these judgments. 16:6 For they have shed the blood of saints and prophets, and you have given them blood to drink. It is what they deserve!" 16:7 And I heard the altar saying "Yes, Lord God the Almighty, true and just are your judgments!" 16:8 The fourth angel poured out his bowl on the sun, and it was allowed to scorch people with fire, 16:9 They were scorched by the fierce heat, and they cursed the name of God who had power over these plagues. They did not repent and give him glory. 16:10 The fifth angel poured out his bowl on the throne of the beast, and its kingdom was plunged into darkness. People gnawed their tongues in anguish 16:11 and cursed the God of heaven for their pain and sores. They did not repent of their deeds. 16:12 The sixth angel poured out his bowl on the great river Euphrates, and its water was dried up, to prepare the way for the kings from the east. 16:13 And I saw, coming out of the mouth of the dragon and out of the mouth of the beast and out of the mouth of the false prophet, three unclean spirits like frogs. 16:14 For they are demonic spirits, perform signs, who go abroad to the kings of the world, to assemble them for battle on the great day of God the Almighty. 16:15 ("Behold, I am coming like a thief! Blessed is the one who stays awake, keeping his garments on, that he may not go about naked and be seen exposed!") 16:16 And they assembled them at the place that in Hebrew is called Armageddon. 16:17 The seventh angel poured out his bowl into the air, and a loud voice came out of the temple, from the throne, saying "It is done!" 16:18 And there were flashes of lightning, rumblings, peals of thunder, and a great earthquake such as there had never been since man was on the earth, so great was the earthquake. 16:19 The great city was split into three parts, and the cities of the nations fell, and God remembered Babylon the great, to make her drain the cup of the wine of the fury of his wrath. 16:20 And every island fled away, and no mountains were to be found. 16:21 And great hailstones, about one hundred pounds each, fell from heaven on people; and they cursed God for the plague of the hail, because the plague was so severe."*

Verse 16:14 refers to the Great Day of the Wrath of the Lamb, as the Great Day of the God Almighty. Verse 16:15 reminds us of those words of the Gospel according to Saint Matthew Verse 24:43, which describe how the Coming of the Son of Man would be, and say that he will come as a thief, in an unexpected way, and confirm, first, that the Great Day of God Almighty is the Great Day of the Wrath of the Lamb, and secondly, that the Great Day of the Wrath of the Lamb comes following the Coming of the Son of Man.

Also, this Chapter 16 confirms to us that the pouring of the seven bowls with the seven plagues go after the trumpets. In the pouring of the seventh bowl the Great City, Babylon, who is the Devil, is destroyed. The last verses of Chapter 16 say: "*16:17 The seventh angel poured out his bowl into the air, and a loud voice came out of the temple, from the throne, saying, "It is done!" 16:18 And there were flashes of lightning, rumblings, peals of thunder, and a great earthquake such as there had never been since man was on the earth, so great was that earthquake. 16:19 The great city was split into three parts, and the cities of the nations fell, and God remembered Babylon the great, to make her drain the cup of the wine of the fury of his wrath.*" The defeat of the Devil is the last thing that happen.

Verse 16:17 says that there will be a great earthquake, such as there had never been since man was on the earth. This great earthquake contrasts to the earthquake mentioned in Chapter 11:18, which occurs when the seventh trumpet sounds. In my opinion, this is also indicative that Chapters 15 and 16 constitute the execution of the seventh trumpet, and are the end of the tribulation.

In addition, it can be said, that even though the bad events that come after the trumpets of Chapters 8 and 11 in comparison with the pouring of the bowls of Chapter 16 are very similar, the bad events of the bowls seem definitely more destructive. The book of Revelation says that the damages that come after most of the trumpets only affect the third part of their objectives. The same thing is not true in regard to the damages that follow the pouring of the bowls that seem to affect the entire part of their objectives.

In any case, the Cluster of the Vine, the Great Day of the Wrath of the Lamb, the Great Tribulation, is only one, so the bowls necessarily need to happen after the trumpets.

What follows Chapter 16 is described in Chapter 20:10, the eternal imprisonment of the Devil in the lake of fire and sulfur, that gives place to the Final Judgment of Chapter 20:11 of the book of Revelation, and of Verse 25:31 of the Gospel according to Saint Matthew.

Before getting into those Chapters we will analyze another, which gives more information on the Cluster of the Vine, the Great Tribulation, the Great Day of the Wrath of the Lamb.

Chapter 7:9-17. Salvation in the Cluster of the Vine

Chapter 7:9-17 of the book of Revelation (E.S.V.)

Jesus without Paul of Tarsus

says: *"7:9 After this I looked, and behold, a great multitude that no one could number, from every nation, from all tribes and peoples and languages, standing before the throne and before the Lamb, clothed in white robes, with palm branches in their hands, 7:10 and crying out with a loud voice, "Salvation belongs to our God who sits on the throne, and to the Lamb!" 7:11 And all the angels were standing around the throne and around the elders and the four living creatures, and they fell on their faces before the throne and worshiped God, 7:12 saying, "Amen! Blessing and glory and wisdom and thanksgiving and honor and power and might be to our God forever and ever! Amen." 7:13 Then one of the elders addressed me, saying, "Who are these, clothed in white robes, and from where have they come?" 7:14 I said to him, "Sir, you know." And he said to me, "These are the ones coming out of the great tribulation. They have washed their robes and made them white in the blood of the Lamb. 7:15 "Therefore they are before the throne of God, and serve him day and night in his temple; and he who sits on the throne will shelter them with his presence. 7:16 They shall hunger no more, neither thirst anymore; the sun shall not strike them, nor any scorching heat, 7:17 For the Lamb in the midst of the throne will be their shepherd, and he will guide them to springs of living water, and God will wipe away every tear from their eyes.""*

Before describing the Cluster of the Vine, also called the Great Tribulation, the Great Day of the Wrath of God, which has among its objectives to produce servants of God, Christians, the book of Revelation tells us that even in this Great Tribulation it will be possible to reach salvation. I would dare to say that one of the main objectives of the book of Revelation is to give us

Ruy Barraco Mármol

this message.

The Action of the Devil in the Cluster of the Vine

Chapter 20:1-3 of the book of Revelation (E.S.V.) says: "*20:1. Then I saw an angel coming down from heaven, holding in his hand the key to the bottomless pit and a great chain. 20:2 And he seized the dragon, that ancient serpent, who is the devil and Satan, and bound him for a thousand years, 20:3 and threw him into the pit, and shut it and sealed it over him, so that he might not deceive the nations any longer, until the thousand years were ended. After that he must be released for a little while.*"

Chapter 20:7-10 says: "*20:7 And when the thousand years are ended, Satan will be released from his prison, 20:8 and will come out to deceive the nations that are at the four corners of the earth, Gog and Magog, to gather them for battle; their number is like the sand of the sea. 20:9 And they marched up over the broad plain of the earth and surrounded the camp of the saints and the beloved city, but fire came down from heaven and consumed them, 20:10 and the devil who had deceived them was thrown into the lake of fire and sulfur where the beast and the false prophet were, and they will be tormented day and night for ever and ever.*"

The book of Revelation, Verse 20:3, says that Satan, the Dragon, was imprisoned for a 1000 years by an angel, who threw him into a pit, and shut it and sealed it over him, so that he might not deceive the nations until the thousand years were ended.

We have already seen that the period of one

thousand years finishes with the Coming of the Son of Man, because the Coming of the Son of Man brings the resurrection of the dead, and the resurrection of the dead happens when the 1000 years end[206].

The Devil then is released for the Great Day of the Wrath of the Lamb, the Cluster of the Vine, the Great Tribulation. When the seventh seal is open; that is when all the seals are opened (Chapter 8:1), and before the seventh trumpet is blown, the Devil who was thrown into the pit, which was shut and sealed, is released.

The Resurrection of the Dead in the Cluster of the Vine

Chapter 20:4 of the book of Revelation (E.S.V.): *"Then I saw thrones, and seated on them were those to whom the authority to judge was committed. Also I saw the souls of those who had been beheaded for the testimony of Jesus and for the word of God, and who had not worshiped the beast or its image and had not received its mark on their foreheads or their hands. They came to life and reigned with Christ for a thousand years."*

The book of Revelation 20:4 teaches that some men resurrect first: *"those who had been beheaded for the testimony of Jesus and for the word of God, and who had not worshiped the beast or its image and had not received its mark on their foreheads or their hands."* Those who resurrect first will be those who had been beheaded for the testimony of Jesus and for the word of God, and who had not worshiped the beast, or his image (the

---

[206] The book of Revelation, Verse 20:5.

image of Paul that comes forth from his epistles or the epistles itself), and had not received the mark on their foreheads or their hands, which means that they had neither put in their minds his doctrine, nor put it into practice. I believe that it is accurate to say that those who do not die doing so, have the chance to be part of the first resurrected.

The Gospel according to Saint Matthew (E.S.V.), talking about the death and resurrection of Christ says: " *27:52 The tombs also were opened. And many bodies of the saints who had fallen asleep were raised, 27:53 and coming out of the tombs after his resurrection they went into the holy city and appeared to many.*" The Gospel according to Saint Luke (E.S.V.) says: *23:39 One of the criminals who were hanged railed at him, saying, "Are you not the Christ? Save yourself and us!" 23:40 But the other rebuked him, saying, "Do you not fear God, since you are under the same sentence of condemnation? 23:41 And we indeed justly, for we are receiving the due reward of our deeds; but this man has done nothing wrong." And he said, "Jesus, remember me when you come into your kingdom: And he said to him, "Truly, I say to you, today you will be with me in Paradise.*" These verses teach that some people have already resurrected, and will resurrect first.

For the rest, the resurrection from death comes when the thousand years end, and the thousand years end with the Coming of the Son of Man, Jesus, because the Harvest, the Gathering of the Chosen, the Sealing of the Servants of God, is carried out among the resurrected. The dead people not chosen, and the living people not chosen, face the Great Day of the Wrath of God, the Cluster of the Vine, the Great Tribulation.

That is why Christ warned the people so strongly to be prepared, and talked about the tribulation as something in regard to which everyone must be forewarned, even the ones who were alive at the time of his preaching.

The book of Revelation teaches that everybody, no matter his death date, who does not die as a faithful and wise servant, will face the Great Tribulation, and will be thrown, before the Final Judgment, to the outer darkness of the Parable of the Talents (25:30), to the winepress of the wrath of God of the book of Revelation 14:20. This is the last chance to reach salvation. If we do not die as faithful and wise servants we will face the Great Day of the Wrath of the Lamb. To the kingdom of Heaven people either enter living according to Christ's doctrine or do not enter.

Some of those who die as faithful and wise servants will be part of the first resurrection, as I said above. The rest will resurrect, and jointly with the faithful and wise servants alive at the time of the Coming of the Son of Man, will be sealed and saved from the Great Tribulation, which the rest, those who were not chosen, will have to face.

The Great Tribulation of the Gospel and the Cluster of the Vine

The Gospel according to Saint Matthew (E.S.V.) says: "*24:15 So when you see the abomination of desolation spoken of by the prophet Daniel, standing in the holy place (let the reader understand), 24:16 then let those who are in Judea flee to the mountains. 24:17 Let the one who is on the* housetop not go down to take what is in his house, 24:18 and let the one who is in the field not turn back to take his cloak. 24:19 And alas for women who are pregnant and for those who are nursing infants in those days! 24:20 Pray that your flight may not be in winter or on a Sabbath. 24:21 For then there will be great tribulation, such as has not been from the beginning of the world until now, no, and never will be. 24:22 And if those days had not been cut short, no human being would be saved. But for the sake of the elect those days will be cut short. 24:23 Then if anyone says to you, 'Look, here is the Christ!' or 'There he is!' do not believe it. 24:24 For false christs and false prophets will arise and perform great signs and wonders, so as to lead astray, if possible, even the elect. 24:25 See, I have told you beforehand. 24:26 So, if they say to you, 'Look, he is in the wilderness,' do not go out. If they say, 'Look, he is in the inner rooms,' do not believe it. 24:27 For as the lightning comes from the east and shines as far as the west, so will be the coming of the Son of Man. 24:28 Wherever the corpse is, there the vultures will gather."

The Gospel according to Saint Mark (E.S.V.) says: "13:14 "But when you see the abomination of desolation standing where it ought not to be (let the reader understand), then let those who are in Judea flee to the mountains. 13:15 Let the one who is on the housetop not go down, nor enter his house, to take anything out, 13:16 and let the one who is in the field not turn back to take his cloak. 13:17 And alas for women who are pregnant and for those who are nursing infants in those days! 13:18 Pray that it may not happen in winter. 13:19 For in those days there will be such tribulation as has not been from the beginning of the creation that God created until now, and never will be,

15:20 And if the Lord had not cut short the days, no human being would be saved. But for the sake of the elect, whom he chose, he shortened the days, 15:21 And then if anyone says to you, 'Look, here is the Christ!' or Look, there he is!' do not believe it. 15:22 False christs and false prophets will arise and perform signs and wonders, to lead astray, if possible, the elect. 15:23 But be on guard; I have told you all things beforehand."

The Gospel according to Saint Luke (E.S.V.) says: *"21:20 "But when you see Jerusalem surrounded by armies, then know that its desolation has come near. 21:21 Then let those who are in Judea flee to the mountains, and let those who are inside the city depart, and let not those who are out in the country enter it, 21:22 for these are days of vengeance, to fulfill all that is written. 21:23 Alas for women who are pregnant and for those who are nursing infants in those days! For there will be great distress upon the earth and wrath against this people. 21:24 They will fall by the edge of the sword and be led captive among all nations, and Jerusalem will be trampled underfoot by the Gentiles, until the times of the Gentiles are fulfilled."*

The three Gospels talk about a Great Tribulation. The Gospel according to Saint Luke calls it great distress, saying that there will be a great distress and wrath. They all foretell a great tribulation as will never be again. Without doubt the Great Tribulation is the Great Day of the Wrath of the Lamb, because there will be no wrath such as the one that will take place that day. No doubt, the Great Tribulation is the Great Day of the Wrath of the Lamb; no doubt it is what comes after the seventh seal is opened, while the seven trumpets are sounded and the seven bowls of the wrath of God are poured.

This is why the Gospel according to Saint Luke Verse 21:22 says, 'for these are days of vengeance, to fulfill all that is written." Because the great tribulation of Saint Luke occurs in the final days, which explains why there are not more prophecies to be fulfilled. The days of vengeance refer to the punishment of the Devil, as I already said.

This is why the Gospel according to Saint Luke Verse 21:23 says that there will be, in the great distress, wrath against the people. Because the great distress or Great Tribulation will occur the Great Day of the Wrath of the Lamb, in the Day of the Wrath of God.

This is also why the Gospel according to Saint Luke Verse 21:24 says: "They will fall by the edge of the sword and be led captive among all nations, and Jerusalem will be trampled underfoot by the Gentiles, until the times of the Gentiles are fulfilled"; because the Great Tribulation of the Gospel will happen when the two witnesses of the book of Revelation Chapter 11 act, during the Great Day of the Wrath of the Lord, as I will discuss in the next point.

The Greek word ουαι (ouai) translated as <u>Alas</u> or <u>Woe</u> in the Bibles, included in the Gospel according to Saint Luke is also not by chance. The Gospel according to Saint Luke (E.S.V.) says: "*21:23 Alas for women who are pregnant and for those who are nursing infants in those days! For there will be great distress upon the earth and wrath against this people*". Let us remember that the book of Revelation uses the same Greek word in Verse 8:13, among others, saying (E.S.V.): "…"Woe, woe, woe to those who dwell on the earth at the blasts of the other trumpets that the three angels are about to blow!"

Chapter 11:1-14. The Two Witnesses

Chapter 11:1-14 of the book of Revelation (E.S.V.) says: "*11:1 Then I was given a measuring rod like a staff, and I was told, "Rise and measure the temple of God and the altar and those who worship there, 11:2 but do not measure the court outside the temple; leave that out, for it is given over to the nations, and they will trample the holy city for forty-two months. 11:3 And I will grant authority to my two witnesses, and they will prophesy for 1,260 days, clothed in sackcloth."* 11:4 These are the two olive trees and the two lampstands that stand before the Lord of the earth. 11:5 And if anyone would harm them, fire pours from their mouth and consumes their foes. If anyone would harm them, this is how he is doomed to be killed. 11:6 They have the power to shut the sky, that no rain may fall during the days of their prophesying, and they have power over the waters to turn them into blood and to strike the earth with every kind of plague, as often as they desire. 11:7 And when they have finished their testimony, the beast that rises from the bottomless pit will make war on them and conquer them and kill them, 11:8 and their dead bodies will lie in the street of the great city that symbolically is called Sodom and Egypt, where their Lord was crucified. 11:9 For three and a half days some from the peoples and tribes and languages and nations will gaze at their dead bodies and refuse to let them be placed in a tomb, 11:10 and those who dwell on the earth will rejoice over them and make merry and exchange presents, because these two prophets had been a torment to those who dwell on the earth. 11:11 But after* *the three and a half days a breath of life from God entered them, and they stood up on their feet, and great fear fell on those who saw them. 11:12 Then they heard a loud voice from heaven saying to them, "Come up here!" And they went up to heaven in a cloud, and their enemies watched them. 11:13 And at that hour there was a great earthquake, and a tenth of the city fell. Seven thousand people were killed in the earthquake, and the rest were terrified and gave glory to the God of heaven. 11:14 The second woe has passed; behold, the third woe is soon to come."*

During the Cluster of the Vine, the Great Day of the Wrath of the Lamb, the Great Tribulation, the two witnesses of God mentioned by Chapter 11 act. They will be killed in the Great City, which is no other than the Great Babylon, the Devil,[207] where all the blood of the prophets, saints, and all the beheaded of the world were found. It is a way to say they are going to be killed by the Devil. Verse 18:24 of the book of Revelation (E.S.V.) says about the Great City and the prophets and saints: *"And in her was found the blood of prophets and of the saints, and of all who have been slain on earth."* The fact that the blood of the prophets and of the saints was found in the Great City, who is the Devil, means that they were killed by the Devil; the same way the fact that the two witnesses were killed in the Great City means that their blood was found in the Devil, that the Devil killed them.

The two witnesses act during the 1,260 days, which is the period of the persecutions, the tribulations. This

---

[207] As I said at the time I was discussing Chapter 17.

indicates that the two witnesses act during the tribulation, which cannot be other than the Great Tribulation, in which the Devil is released, and can kill them. Their powers are similar to the ones of the angels of the trumpets, and the bowls with their plagues.

The expression of the first verses of Chapter 11:2 which say 'do not measure the court outside the temple, for it is given over to the nations, and they will trample the holy city for forty-two months', bring to memory the words of the Gospel according to Saint Luke (E.S.V.), that say: *"21:20 "But when you see Jerusalem surrounded by armies, then know that its desolation has come near. 21:21 Then let those who are in Judea flee to the mountains, and let those who are inside the city depart, and let not those who are out in the country enter it, 21:22 for these days are days of vengeance, to fulfill all that is written. 21:23 Alas for women who are pregnant and for those who are nursing infants in those days! For there will be great distress upon the earth and wrath against this people. 21:24 They will fall by the edge of the sword and be led captive among all nations, and Jerusalem will be trampled underfoot by the Gentiles, until the time of the Gentiles are fulfilled."*

Taking the following verse of Saint Luke, the number 21:25, as a separate verse, which describes the moments prior to the Coming of the Son of Man, the Gospel according to Saint Luke harmonizes perfectly with the Gospel according to Saint Matthew and the book of Revelation.

The location of the two witnesses in the book of Revelation also indicates that they act during the Great

Tribulation.

Besides, the expression of Verse 11:14, which says that the second Alas or Woe has passed, seems to indicate that the action of the two witnesses takes place, in part at least, during the second Alas or Woe, during the sixth trumpet of the Great Day of the Wrath of the Lamb, of the Great Tribulation, of the Cluster of the Vine.

In regard to the identity of the two witnesses, considering that Verse 11:4 calls them lampstands, and Chapter 1:20 of the book of Revelation calls the seven churches lampstands, it seems possible to me that they will not be two men, but two churches, perhaps the Christian and the Jewish Churches, and that they are going to be killed and resurrected in a symbolical way, somehow; but they also could be two persons just as well.

Finally, with regard to Verse 11:13 of the book of Revelation that says that the tenth of the city fell, in my opinion this means that what was left of the city, which is the Great City, the Devil, was destroyed, and the number of 7000 deaths, is a symbolic number that represents totality, and tells us that all the people who were meant to die, died.

In the book of the prophet Isaiah (E.S.V.) it is said: "*6:10 Make the heart of this people dull, and their ears heavy, and blind their eyes; lest they see with their eyes, and hear with their ears, and understand with their hearts, and turn and be healed.*" *6:11 Then I said, "How long, O Lord?" And he said: "Until cities lie waste without inhabitant, and houses without people, and the land is a desolate waste, 6:12 and the Lord removes people far away, and the forsaken places are many in the midst of the land. 6:13 And though a tenth remain in it, it will be burned again, like a terebinth or an oak, whose stump remains when it is felled. The holy seed is its stump."*

In my opinion, the destruction of the tenth of the city narrated in Verse 11:13, will happen after the events narrated by Chapter 16:20, after the pouring of the last bowl.

II.4. The Final Judgment –Chapters 20:11-15 and 11:18

Verses 20:11-15 and Verse 11:18 talk about the Final Judgment. Chapter 20:11-15 of the book of Revelation (E.S.V.) says: "*20:11 Then I saw a great white throne and him who was seated on it. From his presence earth and sky fled away, and no place was found for them. 20:12 And I saw the dead, great and small, standing before the throne, and books were opened. Then another book was opened, which is the book of life. And the dead were judged by what was written in the books, according to what they had done. 20:13 And the sea gave up the dead who were in it. Death and Hades gave up the dead who were in them, and they were judged, each one of them, according to what they had done, 20:14 Then Death and Hades were thrown into the lake of fire. This is the second death, the lake of fire. 20:15 And if anyone's name was not found written in the book of life, he was thrown into the lake of fire."* Chapter 11:18 of the book of Revelation (E.S.V.) says: "*The nations raged, but your wrath came, and the time for the dead to be judged, and for rewarding your servants, the prophets and saints, and those who fear your name, both small and great, and for destroying the destroyers of the earth."*

This is the judgment referred to by the Gospel according to Saint Matthew (E.S.V.), which says: *"25:31 When the Son of Man comes in his glory, and all the angels with him, then he will sit on his glorious throne. 25:32 Before him will be gathered all the nations, and he will separate people one from another as a shepherd separates the sheep from the goats. 25:33 And he will place the sheep on his right, but the goats on the left. 25:34 Then the King will say to those on his right, 'Come, you who are blessed by my Father, inherit the kingdom prepared for you from the foundation of the world. 25:35 For I was hungry and you gave me food, I was thirsty and you gave me drink, I was a stranger and you welcomed me, 25:36 I was naked and you clothed me, I was sick and you visited me, I was in prison and you came to me.' 25:37 Then the righteous will answer him, saying, 'Lord, when did we see you hungry and feed you, or thirsty and give you drink? 25:38 And when did we see you a stranger and welcome you, or naked and clothe you? 25:39 And when did we see you sick or in prison and visit you? 25:40 And the King will answer them, 'Truly, I say to you, as you did it to one of the least of these my brothers, you did it to me.' 25:41 "Then he will say to those on his left, 'Depart from me, you cursed, into the eternal fire prepared for the devil and his angels. 25:42 For I was hungry and you gave me no food, I was thirsty and you gave me no drink, 25:43 I was a stranger and you did not welcome me, naked and you did not clothe me, sick and in prison and you did not visit me.' 25:44 Then they also will answer, saying, 'Lord, when did we see you hungry or thirsty or a stranger or naked or sick or in prison, and did not minister to you?' 25:45 Then he will answer them, saying, 'Truly, I say to you as you did not do it to one of the least of these, you did not do it to me.' 25:46 And these will go away into eternal punishment, but the righteous into eternal life."*

The book of Revelation and the Gospel treat the Coming of the Son of Man as an event different from the Final Judgment. The Final Judgment does not happen in the moment of the Coming of the Son of Man. The Coming of the Son of Man is the initiation of the Day of Judgment, which finishes with the Final Judgment. The Gospel according to Saint Matthew (E.S.V.) uses the expression <u>day of judgment</u>. It says: "*11:22 But I tell you, it will be more bearable on the day of judgment for Tyre and Sidon than for you. 11:23 And you, Capernaum, will you be exalted to heaven? You will be brought down to Hades. For if the mighty works done in you had been done in Sodom, it would have remained until this day. 11:24 But I tell you that it will be more tolerable on the day of judgment for the land of Sodom than for you."*

After the Coming of the Son of Man comes the Harvest, and the Cluster of the Vine, which is also called the Great Day of the Wrath of God or Great Tribulation. This Cluster of the Vine, Great Day of the Wrath of the Lamb, Great Tribulation, Great Day of the Judgment, ends with the Final Judgment.

II.5. The New Jerusalem. Chapters 21 and 22

Chapters 21 and 22 talk about the New Jerusalem. There will be a new heaven and a new earth. After the judgment of the nations, the Final Judgment, there will be a New Jerusalem.

Ruy Barraco Mármol

Chapter 21

Chapter 21 of the book of Revelation (E.S.V.) says: "*21:1 Then I saw a new heaven and a new earth, for the first heaven and the first earth had passed away, and the sea was no more. 21:2 And I saw the holy city, new Jerusalem, coming down out of heaven from God, prepared as a bride adorned for her husband. 21:3 And I heard a loud voice from the throne saying, "Behold, the dwelling place of God is with man. He will dwell with them, and they will be his people, and God himself will be with them as their God. He will wipe away every tear from their eyes, and death shall be no more, neither shall there be mourning nor crying nor pain anymore, for the former things have passed away." 21:5 And he who was seated on the throne said, "Behold, I am making all things new." Also he said, "Write this down, for these words are trustworthy and true." 21:6 And he said to me, "It is done! I am the Alpha and the Omega, the beginning and the end. To the thirsty I will give from the spring of the water of life without payment. 21:7 The one who conquers will have this heritage, and I will be his God and he will be my son. 21:8 But as for the cowardly, the faithless, the detestable, as for murderers, the sexually immoral, sorcerers, idolaters, and all liars, their portion will be in the lake that burns with fire and sulfur, which is the second death." 21:9 Then came one of the seven angels who had the seven bowls full of the seven last plagues and spoke to me, saying, "Come, I will show you the Bride, the wife of the Lamb." 21:10 And he carried me away in the Spirit to a great, high mountain, and showed me the holy city Jerusalem coming down out of heaven from God, 21:11 having the glory of God, its radiance like a most rare jewel, like a jasper, clear as crystal. 21:12 It had a great, high wall, with twelve gates, and at the gates twelve angels, and on the gates the names of the twelve tribes of the sons of Israel were inscribed-21:13 on the east three gates, on the north three gates, on the south three gates, and on the west three gates. 21:14 And the wall of the city had twelve foundations, and on them were the twelve names of the twelve apostles of the Lamb. 21:15 And the one who spoke with me had a measuring rod of gold to measure the city and its gates and walls. 21:16 The city lies foursquare; its length the same as its width. And he measured the city with his rod, 12,000 stadia. 21:17 He also measured its wall, 144 cubits by human measurement, which is also an angel's measurement. 21:18 The wall was built of jasper, while the city was pure gold, clear as glass. 21:19 The foundations of the wall of the city were adorned with every kind of jewel. The first was jasper, the second sapphire, the third agate, the fourth emerald, 21:20 the fifth onyx, the sixth carnelian, the seventh chrysolite, the eighth beryl, the ninth topaz, the tenth chrysoprase, the eleventh jacinth, the twelfth amethyst. 21:21 And the twelve gates were twelve pearls, each of the gates made of a single pearl, and the street of the city was pure gold, transparent as glass. 21:22 And I saw no temple in the city, for its temple is the Lord God the Almighty and the Lamb. 21:23 And the city has no need of sun or moon to shine on it, for the glory of God gives it light, and its lamp is the Lamb. 21:24 By its light will the nations walk, and the kings of the earth will bring their glory into it, 21:25 and its gates will never be shut by day-and there will be no night there. 21:26 They will bring into it the glory and the honor of the nations. 21:27 But nothing unclean will ever enter it, nor anyone who does what is detestable or false, but only those who are written in the Lamb's book of life."*

Ruy Barraco Mármol

In my opinion, the dimensions of the city indicate that only those whose lives were sufficiently adequate to the doctrine expressed by Christ to the twelve apostles will be admitted in the New Jerusalem. Verses 21:8 and 21:27 confirm that only the real servants of God will enter the kingdom of heaven; only the true Christians.

Chapter 22

Chapter 22 of the book of Revelation (E.S.V.) says: "*22:1 Then the angel showed me the river of the water of life, bright as crystal, flowing from the throne of God and of the Lamb 22:2 through the middle of the street of the city; also, on either side of the river, the tree of life with its twelve kinds of fruit, yielding its fruit each month. The leaves of the tree were for the healing of the nations. 22:3 No longer will there be anything accursed, but the throne of God and of the Lamb will be in it, and his servants will worship him. 22:4 They will see his face, and his name will be on their foreheads. 22:5 And night will be no more. They will need no light of lamp or sun, for the Lord God will be their light, and they will reign forever and ever. 22:6 And he said to me, "These words are trustworthy and true. And the Lord, the God of the spirits of the prophets, has sent his angel to show his servants what must soon take place." 22:7 "And behold, I am coming soon. Blessed is the one who keeps the words of the prophecy of this book." 22:8 I, John, am the one who heard and saw these things. And when I heard and saw them, I fell down to worship at the feet of the angel who showed them to me, 22:9 but he said to me, "You must not do that! I am a fellow servant with you and your brothers* the prophets, and with those who keep the words of this book, Worship God." 22:10 And he said to me, "Do not seal up the words of the prophecy of this book, for the time is near. 22:11 Let the evildoer still do evil, and the filthy still be filthy, and the righteous still do right, and the holy still be holy." 22:12 "Behold, I am coming soon, bringing my recompense with me, to repay everyone for what he has done. 22:13 I am the Alpha and the Omega, the first and the last, the beginning and the end." 22:14 Blessed are those who wash their robes, so that they may have the right to the tree of life and that they may enter the city by the gates. 22:15 Outside are the dogs and sorcerers and the sexually immoral and murderers and idolaters and everyone who loves and practices falsehood. 22:16 "I, Jesus, have sent my angel to testify to you about these things for the churches. I am the root and the descendant of David, the bright morning star." 22:17 The Spirit and the Bride say, "Come." And let the one who hears say, "Come". And let the one who is thirsty come; let the one who desires take the water of life without price. 22:18 I warn everyone who hears the words of the prophecy of this book: if anyone adds to them, God will add to him the plagues described in this book, 22:19 and if anyone takes away from the words of the book of this prophecy, God will take away his share in the tree of life and in the holy city, which are described in this book. 22:20. He who testifies to these things says, "Surely I am coming soon." Amen. Come, Lord Jesus! 22:21 The grace of the Lord Jesus be with all. Amen."

The Greek word translated in Verse 22:15 as sexually immoral is Πορνοι (pornoi) which means fornicator.[208] In my opinion, this word can be interpreted symbolically as being unfaithful to God, or literally as being a prostitute, adulterer, or committing an act described in Leviticus 18. There is no basis to translate the word as sexually immoral. There are some sexually immoral conducts that are out of the biblical concept of being fornicator, excluding of course the concept that emerges from the Epistles of Paul. In my opinion, the first meaning of being unfaithful to God is the appropriate one.

Once again, we are reminded of this question of worshiping in Verse 22:9. The angel does not want John to worship him. A man should not worship any other man, not even an angel. God does not want us to worship anyone. The angels do not want to be worshipped. No man should demand to be worshipped. A man should not show submission to another man; yes, he must obey the authority, but as an equal, not showing submission to it.

---

[208] Karl Feyerabend "Langenscheidt Pocket Greek Dictionary Greek-English" says under the Greek word "πορνος ο" fornicator.

Chapter III.
The Old Testament

The events prophesied in the New Testament about the signs previous to the Coming of the Son of Man, the Harvest, and the Cluster of the Vine, or Great Day of the Wrath of the Lamb, or Great Tribulation, and the Final Judgment, are also prophesied in the Old Testament. The book of Revelation helps us to see this clearly.

Once the book of Revelation is understood, the study of the Bible gains another dimension, especially the study of the Old Testament. However, it will not be the subject of this book to get deeper into this. I will only transcribe some passages that contain prophecies about the end of times, and I will make brief commentaries about them, which I think are very illustrative, and will strengthen the certainty of the reader about what is said in this book.

Before getting into this, it is important to remember again that there are differences between authorized translations of the Bible, especially of the Old Testament, so to interpret the Bible, it is always advisable to check more than one translation.

Independently, it is very important to know that the Old Testament also uses a lot of symbolism, and its interpretation might have more than one meaning or message. If a symbol in the book of Revelation can have

Ruy Barraco Mármol

more than one meaning,[209] why not also in the Old Testament? And one symbol might apply at the same time to two different historical moments.

In addition, it is very important to consider that just as the book of Revelation refers to the Devil with different symbolism, for instance, Babylon, Egypt, Sodom[210] the same thing happens in the Old Testament, where the Devil is referred to as Babylon, Sodom, Egypt, King of Tyre, etc.

Therefore, it is easier to appreciate the fact that the Great Day of the Lord, which is prophesied so much in the Old Testament, is unique; it occurs at the end of times, and is no other thing than the Great Day of the Wrath of the Lamb, the Cluster of the Vine, the Great Tribulation.

It is also easier to appreciate that many of the prophecies directed to the inhabitants of the earth of the Jewish nation are also directed to the inhabitants of the earth of the Christian nation. In my opinion, when the Bible talks about Judah, in many occasions, it refers to the Christians inhabitants of the earth, or at least it refers to the Christians too; to those people who are called Christians but are still inhabitants of this world.

---

[209] In Chapter 17:9 of the book of Revelation says that the seven heads are seven hills and also seven kings.

[210] The Devil is called Sodom and Egypt in Chapter 11:9 of the book of Revelation, when it is said that the Great City, which is the Devil, as we have seen, would be called symbolically Sodom or Egypt.

III.1. The Great Day of the Lord and the Prophets

Almost all the prophets of the Old Testament prophesy about the Great Day of the Lord, which I said is nothing else than the great Day of the Wrath of the Lamb, the Cluster of the Vine, the Great Tribulation of the book of Revelation and of the Gospels. In fact, in the book of Revelation Verse 16:14, the great Day of the Wrath of the Lamb is called the Great Day of the Lord Almighty. And the Day of the Wrath of the Lamb of Verse 6:17 of the book of Revelation is also the great day of the one who is seated on the throne, which means it is also the Great Day of the Lord Almighty. Many of the prophecies of the prophets of the Old Testament refer to the Great Day of the Lord.

The fact that the Great Day of the Wrath of the Lamb of the book of Revelation is prophesied in the Old Testament is explicitly stated in the book of Revelation. Verses 10:6 and 10:7 of the book of Revelation (E.S.V.) say, before revealing the events that come after the seventh trumpet, which unleashes the pouring of the seven bowls of the wrath of God, the following: *"...that there would be no more delay, 10:7 but that in the days of the trumpet call to be sounded by the seventh angel, the mystery of God would be fulfilled, just as he announced to his servants the prophets."*

This Day has such importance, and God has cared so much to forewarn men about it, that it is incredible how so many Christians and Jews ignore it.

Next, I will transcribe some verses of the Old Testament that teach about that day. But before doing so, let us remember briefly some things the book of Revelation says about the Great Day of the Wrath of the Lamb and the Lord. The book of Revelation talks about the signs previous to the Coming of the Son of Man; then about the Coming of the Son of Man, which is the time of the resurrection of the dead. It says that the Coming of the Son of Man is followed by the Harvest, the Gathering of the Chosen, the Sealing of the Servants of God. After the Harvest, those who are not chosen have to face the Cluster of the Vine, the Great Day of the Wrath of the Lamb, the Great Tribulation, which is meant to punish, but also to purify. The Devil and the beasts act during that day, that starts with the opening of the seventh seal, and continues with the blowing of the seven trumpets, and the pouring of the seven bowls of the wrath of God. It finishes with the defeat of the Devil, that avenges the blood of the servants of God, and with the Final Judgment.

The Prophet Isaiah

a. The Bible (E.S.V.), book of the Prophet Isaiah, says: "*2:10 Enter into the rock and hide in the dust from before the terror of the Lord, and from the splendor of his majesty. 2:11 The haughty looks of man shall be brought low, and the lofty pride of men shall be humbled, and the Lord alone will be exalted in that day. 2:12 For the Lord of hosts has a day against all that is proud and lofty, against all that is lifted up-and it shall be brought low; 2:13 against all the cedars of Lebanon, lofty and lifted up; and against all the oaks of Bashan; 2:14 against all the lofty mountains, and against all the uplifted hills; 2:15 against every high tower, and against every fortified wall; 2:16 against all the ships of Tarshish, and against all the beautiful craft. 2:17 And the haughtiness of man shall be humbled, and the lofty pride of men shall be brought low, and the Lord alone will be exalted in that day. 2:18 And the idols shall utterly pass away. 2:19 And people shall enter the caves of the rocks and the holes of the ground, from before the terror of the Lord, and from the splendor of his majesty, when he rises to terrify the earth. 2:20 In that day mankind will cast away their idols of silver and their idols of gold, which they made for themselves to worship, to the moles and to the bats, 2:21 to enter the caverns of the rocks and the clefts of the cliffs, from before the terror of the Lord, and from the splendor of his majesty, when he rises to terrify the earth."*

Cedars of Lebanon, tall and lofty, all the oaks of Bashan, towering mountains, and high hills, are symbols with which the Bible refers to the powerful men, the haughty men, arrogant men, who will be humbled, according to the book of the prophet Isaiah. Men in the Great Day of the Lord, says the prophet Isaiah, go into the rocks, hide in the ground from dread of the Lord.

The book of Revelation says that the same thing happens after the opening of the sixth seal. The book of Revelation (E.S.V.) says: *"6:14 The sky vanished like a scroll that is being rolled up, and every mountain and island was removed from its place. 6:15 Then the kings of the earth and the great ones and the generals and the rich and the powerful, and everyone, slave and free, hid themselves in the caves and among the rocks of the mountains, 6:16 calling to the mountains and rocks, "Fall on us and hide us from the face of him who is seated on the throne, and from the wrath of the Lamb, 6:17 for the great day of their wrath has come, and who can stand?"*

b. The Bible (E.S.V.), book of the prophet Isaiah, says: *"10:24 Therefore thus says the Lord God of hosts: "O my people, who dwell in Zion, be not afraid of the Assyrians when they strike with the rod and lift up their staff against you as the Egyptians did. 10:25 For in a very little while my fury will come to an end, and my anger will be directed to their destruction."*

The book of Revelation teaches us that the wrath of God ends when the seventh trumpet is blown. The enemies in the book of Revelation are called in different ways. In the book of the prophet Isaiah those who are beating the people of God who live in Zion, are called Assyrians, because in the times Isaiah gave this prophecy, they were the enemies attacking Zion. But they both talk about the same day.

c. The Bible (E.S.V.), book of the prophet Isaiah, says: *"13:6 Wail, for the day of the Lord is near; as destruction from the Almighty it will come! 13:7 Therefore all hands will be feeble, and every human heart will melt. 13:8 They will be dismayed; pangs and agony will seize them; they will be in anguish like a woman in labor. They will look aghast at one another; their faces will be aflame. 13:9 Behold, the day of the Lord comes, cruel, with wrath and fierce anger, to make the land a desolation and to destroy its sinners from it."*

It is remarkable that these verses say that the Day of the Lord will come like destruction from the Almighty, and it is a cruel day, that will come with wrath and fierce anger.

Also noteworthy is the anguish of the people. This day is also called the day of anguish in other prophecies of the Bible.

The Prophet Jeremiah

a. The Bible (E.S.V.), book of the prophet Jeremiah, says: "*46:10 That day is the day of the Lord God of host, a day of vengeance, to avenge himself on his foes. The sword shall devour and be sated and drink its fill of their blood. For the Lord God of hosts holds a sacrifice in the north country by the river Euphrates. 46:11 Go up to Gilead, and take balm, O virgin daughter of Egypt! In vain you have used many medicines; there is no healing for you. 46:12 The nations have heard of your shame, and the earth is full of your cry; for warrior has stumbled against warrior; they have both fallen together.*"

The book of the prophet Jeremiah, the same way the book of Revelation does, presents this day of the Lord Almighty as a day of vengeance of his foes. These verses indicate Egypt as the foe, or one of his foes. Egypt, is one of the names that the Devil receives in the book of Revelation (11:8), and in the Old Testament.

During the Great Day of the Wrath of the Lamb in the book of Revelation, Babylon is destroyed, and the Devil is sent to hell eternally. The book of Revelation, Verse 19:2, presents this as the vengeance of the blood of his servants.

These passages of the book of Jeremiah are prophesying about the same day, only here the Devil is being called Egypt.

Ruy Barraco Mármol

The Prophet Ezekiel

a. The Bible (E.S.V.), book of the prophet Ezekiel, says: " *30:1 The word of the Lord came to me: 30:2 "Son of man, prophesy, and say, 'Thus says the Lord God: "' Wail, 'Alas for the day!' 30:3 For the day is near, the day of the Lord is near; it will be a day of clouds, a time of doom for the nations. A sword shall come upon Egypt, and anguish shall be in Cush, when the slain fall in Egypt, and her wealth is carried away, and her foundations are torn down."* These verses introduce another characteristic of this Great Day of the Lord. It is the time of doom for the nations.

In the book of Revelation, Verse 20:8, the Devil in the Great Day of the Wrath of the Lamb comes out to deceive the nations, which of course were present that day.

b. The Bible (E.S.V.), book of the prophet Ezekiel, says: "*38:18 But on that day, the day that Gog shall come against the land of Israel, declares the Lord God, my wrath will be roused in my anger. 38:19 For in my jealousy and in my blazing wrath I declare, On that day there shall be a great earthquake in the land of Israel. 38:20 The fish of the sea and the birds of the heavens and the beasts of the field and all creeping things that creep on the ground, and all the people who are on the face of the earth, shall quake at my presence. And the mountains shall be thrown down, and the cliffs shall fall, and every wall shall tumble to the ground.*"

The book of the prophet Ezekiel says, referring to the Great Day of the Lord, that Gog attacks the land of Israel. The book of Revelation says in Verse 20:7 that Satan will be released from his prison, 20:8 and will come out to deceive the nations that are at the four corners of the earth, Gog and Magog, to gather them for battle. They both prophesy about the same day.

c. The Bible (E.S.V.), book of the prophet Ezekiel, says: "*39:8 Behold, it is coming and it will be brought about, declares the Lord God. That is the day of which I have spoken.*"

These words confirm what is uncontestable: there is only one Great Day of the Lord.

The Prophet Daniel

a. The Bible (E.S.V.), book of the prophet Daniel, says: "*12:1 "At that time shall arise Michael, the great prince who has charge of your people. And there shall be a time of trouble, such as never has been since there was a nation till that time. But at that time your people shall be delivered, everyone whose name shall be found written in the book. 12:2 And many of those who sleep in the dust of the earth shall awake, some to everlasting life, and some to shame and everlasting contempt. 12:3 And those who are wise shall shine like the brightness of the sky above; and those who turn many to righteousness, like the stars forever and ever. 12:4 But you, Daniel, shut up the words and seal the book, until the time of the end. Many shall run to and fro, and knowledge shall increase.*"

These verses, by saying at that time your people-everyone whose name is found written in the book will be delivered, is confirming that they refer to the end of times. They also refer to the dead that resurrect: "multitudes who sleep in the dust of the earth will

Ruy Barraco Mármol

awake".

b. The Bible (E.S.V.), book of the prophet Daniel, says: *"12:8 I heard, but I did not understand. Then I said, 'Oh my lord, what shall be the outcome of these things?" 12:9 He said, "Go your way, Daniel, for the words are shut up and sealed until the time of the end. 12:10 Many shall purify themselves and make themselves white and be refined, but the wicked shall act wickedly. And none of the wicked shall understand, but those who are wise shall understand."*

These verses, which follow those that we have just seen and which refer to the final times, talk about purification. Let us remember that in the book of Revelation those who are not chosen have to face the Cluster of the Vine, the Great Day of the Wrath of the Lamb, the Great Tribulation, which is not just for the purpose of punishment, but also for purification, and conversion, to reach the kingdom of God. The book of Revelation (E.S.V.) says: *"7:13 Then one of the elders addressed me, saying, "Who are these, clothed in white robes, and from where have they come? 7:14 I said to him, "Sir, you know." And he said to me, "These are the ones coming out of the great tribulation. They have washed their robes and made them white in the blood of the Lamb."*

The Prophet Joel

a. The Bible (E.S.V.), book of the prophet Joel, says: *"2:30 And I will show wonders in the heavens and on the earth, blood and fire and columns of smoke. 2:31 The sun shall be turned to darkness, and the moon to blood, before the great and awesome day of the Lord comes. 2:32 And it shall come to pass that everyone who calls on the name of the Lord shall be saved. For in Mount Zion and In Jerusalem there shall be those who escape, as the Lord has said, and among the survivors shall be those whom the Lord calls.*[211]"

These verses are very similar to those which we discussed in the analysis of Chapter 6 of the book of Revelation, which refer to the signals prior to the Coming of the Son of Man. And they also talk, about the possibility of reaching salvation during the Great Day of the Lord, which, as I said, is the Great Day of the Wrath of the Lamb and the Lord Almighty, the Cluster of the Vine, the Great Tribulation. These verses of the prophet Joel talk about the coming of Yahweh and the calling of the name of the Lord as a way to reach salvation. Now we know that Jesus is the Lord, and the name to call is the name of Jesus.

b. The Bible (E.S.V.), book of the prophet Joel, says: "*1:11 Be ashamed, O tillers of the soil; wail, O vinedressers, for the wheat and the barley, because the harvest of the field has perished. 1:12 The vine dries up; the fig tree languishes. Pomegranate, palm, and apple, all the trees of the field are dried up, and gladness dries up from the children of man. 1:13 Put on sackcloth and lament, O priests; wail, O ministers of the altar. Go in, pass the night in sackcloth, O ministers of my God!*

---

[211] The numbers of these verses are different in some Bibles. The following are the numbers where they can be found in some Bibles: The Latin Vulgate: Joel 2:31. The King James Version: Joel 2:31. The Revised Standard Version: 2:31. The New American Bible: Joel 3,4. The New American Standard Bible: Joel 2:31. The New International Version 2:31. The English Standard Version: 2:31.

Because grain offering and drink offering are withheld from the house of your God. 1:14 Consecrate a fast; call a solemn assembly. Gather the elders and all the inhabitants of the land to the house of the Lord your God, and cry out to the Lord. 1:15 Alas for the day! For the day of the Lord is near, and as destruction from the Almighty it comes."

These Verses describe the times prior to the Great Day of the Lord. When Verse 1:13 says that the grain offering and the drink offering are withheld from God, it means in my opinion that men are separated from God; in this case, it would harmonize with the position sustained in this book about the reasons that will unleash the beginning of the end of the times, the Coming of the Son of Man, with the Harvest and the Cluster of the Vine. The Cluster of the Vine is the Great Tribulation, the Great Day of the Wrath of the Lamb, the day of the Lord, that will bring the destruction from the Almighty, mentioned in Verse 1:15 of the book of Joel, just quoted.

c. The Bible (E.S.V.), book of the prophet Joel, says: "2:1 *Blow a trumpet in Zion; sound an alarm on my holy mountain! Let all the inhabitants of the land tremble, for the day of the Lord is coming; it is near,*"

The Prophet Amos

The Bible (E.S.V.), book of the prophet Amos, says: "5:19 *as if a man fled from a lion, and a bear met him, or went into the house and leaned his hand against the wall, and a serpent bit him. 5:20 Is not the day of the Lord*

Jesus without Paul of Tarsus

darkness, and not light, and gloom with no brightness in it?"

The Prophet Obadiah

a. The Bible (E.S.V.), book of the prophet Obadiah, says: *"1:2 Behold, I will make you small among the nations; you shall be utterly despised. 1:3 The pride of your heart has deceived you, you who live in the clefts of the rock, in your lofty dwelling, who say in your heart, "Who will bring me down to the ground?" 1:4 Though you soar aloft like the eagle, though your nest is set among the stars, from there I will bring you down, declares the Lord."*

b. The Bible (E.S.V.), book of the prophet Obadiah, says: "*1:15 For the day of the Lord is near upon all the nations. As you have done, it shall be done to you; your deeds shall return on your own head. 1:16 For as you have drunk on my holy mountain, so all the nations shall drink continually; they shall drink and swallow, and shall be as though they had never been.* *1:17 But in Mount Zion there shall be those who escape, and it shall be holy, and the house of Jacob shall possess their own possessions."* (Underline emphasis is mine)

The Prophet Micah

a. The Bible (E.S.V.), book of the Prophet Micah, says: *"5:9 Your hand shall be lifted up over your adversaries, and all your enemies shall be cut off. 5:10 And in that day, declares the Lord, I will cut off your horses from among you and will destroy your chariots; 5:11 and I will cut off the cities of your land and throw down all your strongholds; 5:12 and I will cut off sorceries from your hand, and you shall have no more tellers of fortunes; 5:13 and I will cut off your carved images and your pillars from among you, and you shall bow down no more to the work of your hands. 5:14 and I will root out your Asherah images from among you and destroy your cities. 5:15 And in anger and wrath I will execute vengeance on the nations that did not obey."*

The vengeance, the anger, the wrath will be taken upon the nations that have not obeyed God; this means in my opinion, upon all the men that did not obey, dead and alive.

The prophet Nahum

The Bible (E.S.V.), book of the prophet Nahum, says: *"1:6 Who can stand before his indignation? Who can endure the heat of his anger? His wrath is poured out like fire, and the rocks are broken into pieces by him. 1:7 The Lord is good, a stronghold in the day of trouble; he knows those who take refuge in him. 1:8 But with an overflowing flood he will make a complete end of the adversaries, and will pursue his enemies into darkness."*

The Prophet Habakkuk

The Bible (E.S.V.), book of the prophet Habakkuk, says: *"3:3 God came from Teman, and the Holy One from Mount Paran. His splendor covered the heavens, and the earth was full of his praise. 3:4 His brightness was like the light; rays flashed from his hand; and there he veiled his power. 3:5 Before him went pestilence, and plague followed at his heels. 3:6 He stood and measured the earth; he looked and shook the nations; then the eternal mountains were scattered; the everlasting hills sank low. His were the everlasting ways. 3:7 I saw the tents of Cushan in affliction, the curtains of the land of Midian did tremble. 3:8 Was your wrath against the rivers, O Lord? Was your wrath against the rivers, or your indignation against the sea, when you rode on your horses, on your chariot of salvation? 3:9 You stripped the sheath from your bow, calling for many arrows. You split the earth with rivers. 3:10 The mountains saw you and writhed; the raging waters swept on; the deep gave forth its voice; it lifted its hands on high. 3:11 The sun and moon stood still in their place at the light of your arrows as they sped, at the flash of your glittering spear. 3:12 You marched through the earth in fury; you threshed the nations in anger."*

The Prophet Zephaniah

a. The Bible (E.S.V.), book of the prophet Zephaniah, says: "*1:14 The great day of the Lord is near, near and hastening fast. The sound of the day of the Lord is bitter; the mighty man cries aloud there. 1:15 A day of wrath is that day, a day of distress and anguish, a day of ruin and devastation, a day of darkness and gloom, a day of clouds and thick darkness, 1:16 a day of trumpet blast and battle cry against the fortified cities and against the lofty battlements. 1:17 I will bring distress on mankind, so that they shall walk like the blind, because they have sinned against the Lord; their blood shall be poured out like dust and their flesh like dung.*"

b. The Bible (E.S.V.), book of the prophet Zephaniah, says 2:1-3: "*2:1 Gather together, yes gather, o shameless nation, 2:2 before the decree takes effect-before the day passes away like chaff- before there comes upon you the burning anger of the Lord. 2:3 Seek the Lord, all you humble of the land, who do his just commands; seek righteousness; seek humility; perhaps you may be hidden on the day of the anger of the Lord."*

Those who are chosen, the righteous, those who are humble, will be sheltered the day of the Lord's anger. And those who convert themselves during the day, will reach shelter on the day of the Lord's anger, if they persist enough.

The Prophet Zechariah

a. The Bible (E.S.V.), book of the prophet Zechariah, says: *"14:1 Behold, a day is coming for the Lord, when the spoil taken from you will be divided in your midst. 14:2 For I will gather all the nations against Jerusalem to battle, and the city shall be taken and the houses plundered and the women raped. Half of the city shall go out into exile, but the rest of the people shall not be cut off from the city."*

In my opinion, the bad events announced simbolize very bad things that are going to happen, without our knowing exactly what they are going to be.

b. The Bible (E.S.V.), book of the prophet Zechariah, says 14:6: *"On that day there shall be no light, cold, or frost. 14:7 And there shall be a unique day, which is known to the Lord, neither day nor night, but at evening time there shall be light."*

The prophecy of this book explicitly says 'Unique day' to refer to the day of the Lord. As I said, there are not two days of the Lord. There is not one day of the Lord for the Jews and one day of the Lord for the Christians. The day of the Lord is for all nations.

The Prophet Malachi

a. The Bible (E.S.V.), book of the prophet Malachi, says: "*2:17 You have wearied the Lord with your words. But you say, "How have we wearied him?" By saying, "Everyone who does evil is good in the sight of the Lord, and he delights in them." Or by asking, "Where is the God of justice?" 3:1 "Behold, I send my messenger, and he will prepare the way before me. And the Lord whom you seek will suddenly come to his temple; and the messenger of the covenant in whom you delight, behold, he is coming, says the Lord of hosts. 3:2 But who can endure the day of his coming, and who can stand when he appears? For he is like a refiner's fire and like fullers' soap. 3:3 He will sit as a refiner and purifier of silver, and he will purify the sons of Levi and refine them like gold and silver, and they will bring offerings in righteousness to the Lord. 3:4 Then the offering of Judah and Jerusalem will be pleasing to the Lord as in the days of old and in former years. 3:5 "Then I will draw near to you for judgment. I will be swift witness against the sorcerers, against the adulterers, against those who swear falsely, against those who oppress the hired worker in his wages, the widow and the fatherless, against those who thrust aside the sojourner, and do not fear me, says the Lord of hosts.*"

Note the mention of the coming of the Lord, the judgment, and also the reference in Verse 3:3 to the purification.

b. The Bible (E.S.V.), book of the prophet Malachi, says: "*3:17 "They shall be mine, says the Lord of hosts, in the day when I make up my treasured possession, and I will spare them as a man spares his son who serves him. 3:18 Then once more you shall see the distinction between the righteous and the wicked, between one who serves God and one who does not serve him. 4:1 "For behold, the day is coming, burning like an oven, when all the arrogant and all evildoers will be stubble. The day that is coming shall set them ablaze, says the Lord of hosts, so that it will leave them neither root nor branch."*

These verses refer to the Day of the Lord. The day mentioned in Verse 3:17 is the Day of the Lord. In the day there will be distinction between the righteous and the wicked. Verse 4:1 says that it will burn like a furnace. Let us remember that the Gospel according to Saint Matthew Verse 13:36, talking about the Harvest of the end of the world, says that the Son of Man will send his angels, and they will gather out of his kingdom all causes of sin and all law-breakers and throw them into the fiery furnace. The Parable of the Net of the same Gospel, Verses 13:47-50, also says that in the end of the world, the closing of the age, the angels will come out and separate the evil from the righteous to throw them into the fiery furnace.

III.2. The Great Day of the Lord and Other Books of the Old Testament of the Bible

Not only the books of the prophets talk about the Great Day of the Lord.

Jesus without Paul of Tarsus

The Book of Psalms

The Bible (E.S.V.), book of Psalms, says: "88:1 O Lord, God of my salvation; I cry out day and night before you. 88:2 Let my prayer come before you; incline your ear to my cry. 88:3 For my soul is full of troubles, and my life draws near to Sheol. 88:4 I am counted among those who go down to the pit; I am a man who has no strength, 88:5 like one set loose among the dead, like the slain that lie in the grave, like those whom you remember no more, for they are cut off from your hand. 88:6 You have put me in the depths of the pit, in the regions dark and deep. 88:7 Your wrath lies heavy upon me, and you overwhelm me with all your waves. 88:8 You have caused my companions to shun me; you have made me a horror to them. I am shut in so that I cannot escape; 88:9 my eye grows dim through sorrow. Every day I call upon you, O Lord; I spread out my hands to you. 88:10 Do you work wonders for the dead? Do the departed rise up to praise you? 88:11 Is your steadfast love declared in the grave, or your faithfulness in Abaddon? 88:12 Are your wonders known in the darkness, or your righteousness in the land of forgetfulness? 88:13 But I, O Lord, cry to you; in the morning my prayer comes before you. 88:14 O Lord, why do you cast my soul away? Why do you hide your face from me? 88:15 Afflicted and close to death from my youth up, I suffer your terrors; I am helpless. 88:16 Your wrath has swept over me; your dreadful assaults destroy me. 88:17 They surround me like a flood all day long; they close in on me together. 88:18 You have caused my beloved and my friend to shun me; my companions have become darkness."

In my opinion, this psalm is about a person that is living the Great Day of the Lord.

Ruy Barraco Mármol

b. The Bible (E.S.V.), the book of Psalms, says: "*110:4 The Lord has sworn and will not change his mind, "You are a priest forever after the order of Melchizedek". 110:5 The Lord is at your right hand; he will shatter kings on the day of his wrath. 110:6 He will execute judgment among the nations, filling them with corpses; he will shatter chiefs over the wide earth. 110:7 He will drink from the brook by the way; therefore he will lift up his head."*

The Book Deuteronomy

a. The Bible (E.S.V.), book of Deuteronomy, says: "32:35 Vengeance is mine, and recompense, for the time when their foot shall slip; for the day their calamity is at hand, and their doom comes swiftly. *32:36 For the Lord will vindicate his people and have compassion on his servants, when he sees that their power is gone and there is none remaining, bond or free. 32:37 Then he will say, 'Where are their gods, the rock in which they took refuge, 32:38 who ate the fat of their sacrifices and drank the wine of their drink offering? Let them rise up and help you; let them be your protection! 32:39 "See now that I, even I, am he, and there is no god beside me; I kill and I make alive; I wound and I heal; and there is none that can deliver out of my hand. 32:40 For I lift my hand to heaven and swear, As I live forever, 32:41 If I sharpen my flashing sword and my hand takes hold on judgment, I will take vengeance on my adversaries and will repay those who hate me. 32:42 I will make my arrows drunk with blood, and my sword shall devour flesh-with the blood of the slain and the captives, from the long-haired heads of the enemy.' 32:43 "Rejoice with him, O heavens; bow down to him, all gods, for he avenges the blood of his children and takes vengeance on his adversaries. He repays those who hate him and cleanses his people's land."''*

In my opinion, these verses talk about the day of the Lord, which is the Day of Judgment that ends with the Final Judgment. When Verse 32:42 of the book of Deuteronomy (E.S.V.) says *'I will make my arrows drunk with blood, and my sword shall devour flesh-with the blood of the slain and the captives, from the long-haired heads of the enemy'*, in my opinion it is revealing that in that day his sword will fall on those who were not chosen.

The Book Leviticus

The Bible (E.S.V.), book of Leviticus, says: "*26:14 But if you will not listen to me and will not do all these commandments, 26:15 if you spurn my statutes, and if your soul abhors my rules, so that you will not do all my commandments, but break my covenant, 26:16 then I will do this to you: I will visit you with panic, with wasting disease and fever that consume the eyes and make the heart ache. And you shall sow your seed in vain, for your enemies shall eat it. 26:17 I will set my face against you, and you shall be struck down before your enemies. Those who hate you shall rule over you, and you shall flee when none pursues you. 26:18 And if in spite of this you will not listen to me, then I will discipline you again sevenfold for your sins, 26:19 and I will break the pride of your power, and I will make your heavens like iron and your earth like bronze. 26:20 And your strength shall be spent in vain, for your land shall not yield its increase, and the trees of the land shall not yield their fruit. 26:21 "Then if you walk contrary to me and will not*

Ruy Barraco Mármol

listen to me, I will continue striking you, sevenfold for your sins. 26:22 And I will let loose the wild beasts against you, which shall bereave you of your children and destroy your livestock and make you few in number, so that your roads shall be deserted. 26:23 " And if by this discipline you are not turned to me but walk contrary to me, 26:24 then I also will walk contrary to you, and I myself will strike you sevenfold for your sins. 26:25 And I will bring a sword upon you, that shall execute vengeance for the covenant. And if you gather within your cities, I will send pestilence among you, and you shall be delivered into the hand of the enemy. 26:26 When I break your supply of bread, ten women shall bake your bread in a single oven and shall dole out your bread again by weight, and you shall eat and not be satisfied. 26:27 "But if in spite of this you will not listen to me, but walk contrary to me, 26:28 then I will walk contrary to you in fury, and I myself will discipline you sevenfold for your sins. 26:29 You shall eat the flesh of your sons, and you shall eat the flesh of your daughters. 26:30 And I will destroy your high places and cut down your incense altars and cast your dead bodies of your idols, and my soul will abhor you. 26:31 And I will lay your cities waste and will make your sanctuaries desolate, and I will not smell your pleasing aromas. 26:32 And I myself will devastate the land, so that your enemies who settle in it shall be appalled at it. 26:33 And I will scatter you among the nations, and I will unsheathe the sword after you, and your land shall be a desolation, and your cities shall be a waste."

These verses, which describe the end of times, refer to three series of punishments that remind me of the seven seals, the seven trumpets, and the seven bowls with their plagues of the book of Revelation.

III.3. The Old Testament and Christianity

All of the above quotes from the Old Testament allow us to perceive clearly that the Great Day of the Wrath of the Lord, is unique, and it happens at the end of times. No doubt, much about what is said in the Bible concerning the Jews who reject God applies also to the Christians who reject God. The Christians who reject God, who reject Jesus, will receive the same, or worse fate, than the Jews who do the same.

In fact, as I said, in my opinion, many times, when the Old Testament refers to Judah, it also refers, at least at the same time, to the Christians.

Ruy Barraco Mármol

Conclusion

I hope that the day will soon come in which Christians recognize Paul as a false prophet, bringing the change into Christianity which it needs, letting the word of Christ work in the Christians as it should, empowering the Christianity of many, and spreading the Gospel all over the world cleaned of Paul's influence.

In my opinion, only the converted will enter the kingdom of God. Punishment does not bring conversion. It only offers the opportunity to convert. Entering the kingdom of God is not about facing the punishment. In this life, or in the Great Day of the Lord, the men who wish to enter the kingdom of God will have to convert and enter the kingdom of God converted. God did not warn men in vain. I strongly recommend all people to convert in this life and to die converted.

The Bible (E.S.V.), book of prophet Isaiah, says: *"22:12 In that day the Lord God of hosts called for weeping and mourning, for baldness and wearing sackcloth; 22:13 and behold, joy and gladness, killing oxen and slaughtering sheep, eating flesh and drinking wine, "Let us eat and drink, for tomorrow we die." 22:14 The Lord of hosts has revealed himself in my ears: "Surely this iniquity will not be atoned for you until you die," says the Lord God of hosts."*

The Bible (E.S.V.), book of the prophet Jeremiah, says: *"10:19 Woe is me because of my hurt! My wound is grievous. But I said, "Truly this is an affliction, and I must* bear it." *10:20 My tent is destroyed, and all my cords are broken; my children have gone from me, and they are not; there is no one to spread my tent again and to set up my curtains."*

The Bible (E.S.V.), book of prophet Ezekiel, says: *"6:10 And they shall know that I am the Lord, I have not said in vain that I would do this evil to them."*

How Could All This Have Happened?

I personally believe that God allowed the action of Paul so that we could prove our love to Christ and so that we could overcome the Beasts and their doctrine.

When you stop to think about it, it is not that hard to understand. Discrimination against women lasted throughout most of the world until a short time ago, as well as slavery. Abortion, the homicide of our most innocent children, is still being promoted even by governments. Few countries are really democratic. Errors can be transmitted and can be assured, especially with submission, making men submit to authorities.

In my opinion, the reason why at the beginning this truth surprises us so much is because we underestimate the Devil and we overestimate humankind. If you read the epistles several times, after reading this book, you will see the Devil making fun of us, disrespecting us. The Christian Church in general has spent so much time trying to find subliminal messages from the Devil in rock songs, when we have so many in the Epistles of Paul...

Anyway, what is clear and irrefutable is that what this book says is true. If it is true, the question regarding how could it be possible, how could so many people have been mistaken, or how can I be the one discovering or one of those who are rediscovering this truth is secondary.

In the book of John Stuart Mill "On Liberty" pp. 310, it is said: *"The real advantage which truth has, consists in this, that when an opinion is true, it may be extinguished once, twice, or many times, but in the course of ages there will generally be found persons to rediscover it, until some one of its reappearances falls on a time when from favorable circumstances it escapes persecution until it has made such head as to withstand all subsequent attempts to suppress it."*

I believe I must be rediscovering this truth. The questions are: is this a favorable time for this truth to come out? Are we going to let persecution suppress it again? Is this the time for the intervention of Christ to purify the Christian Church and to imprison the Devil and the Beasts, or is it not? Is humanity going to need a tribulation to recognize it? Is our love strong enough to be victorious over the Beast, his image and over the number of his name?

Ruy Barraco Mármol

Some Advice to Have in Mind in the Challenge of Being a Christian, Especially a Faithful to Jesus Christian

1. The Reading of the Word of God

The reading of the Gospels according to Saint Matthew, Saint Mark, Saint Luke and Saint John brings people toward God, leads people to be in grace with God, and to enter to the kingdom of God. The knowledge of the Gospels allows the word of Christ to act and live in us. It is indispensable for Christians to know the Gospels and to understand them, and it is very important to read them as often as possible.

The Gospel according to Saint John (E.S.V.) says: *"6:63 It is the Spirit who gives life; the flesh is no help at all. The words that I have spoken to you are spirit and are life."*

2. The Fulfillment of the Will of God - Jobs

It is very important for us, that all the days of our life, we try to direct our actions to fulfill the word of God, to fulfill God's will, to do what is good to God, which implies to do at the same time what is good to the rest of the people and to ourselves. The Gospel according to Saint John (E.S.V.) says: "*4:34: Jesus said to them, "My food is to do the will of him who sent me and to accomplish his work."*"

This includes our actions in our jobs, our businesses, which must be sealed by Christianity. We cannot leave our jobs or our businesses outside of our Christianity.

Doing God's will is also like eating heaven's bread. It gives life in the kingdom of God, leads people to be in grace with God. The Bible teaches that human beings in general were punished because of the sin of Adam. I understand that the Bible teaches that human beings may suffer adversities because of the sins of one man or a few, and also may share rewards for the good actions of a few men or just one man. Even if we cannot notice it, every single act of love and virtue is good not only for ourselves but for humanity. That is one of the reasons why the great life of one man, Christ, saved us all. Every single life is transcendental. A poor man responding in a good way to adversity may be doing great things not only for himself but for humanity.

3. The Love for God and for People

To love God implies to will what is good. But willing what is good is not enough. We must have our feelings connected to God's feelings. We must share God's feelings. If somebody wants to know if he is on the right track in his life, he should ask himself if he loves God. Ask yourself if you care about God's will, if God's joy makes you happy, if you are thankful to God, if you recognize his goodness, if you daily think of God, and if you talk to God.

He who does not love God must search for love for God. Love can be attained as a consequence of a series of voluntary acts. We must effort ourselves to will what is good for God. Sooner or later our feelings will accompany our will. If you make an effort to will what is good for God, if you are grateful for everything he gave us, if you recognize his goodness, if you daily think of God, talk to God, if you pray, sooner or later you will find yourself with feelings that will make it much easier to will what is good for God, and do what is good for God.

The love for God must be strong. Let us remember what the Gospel according to Saint Matthew (E.S.V.) says: "*10:37 Whoever loves father or mother more than me is not worthy of me. 10:38 And whoever does not take his cross and follow me is not worthy of me. 10:39 Whoever finds his life will lose it, and whoever loses his life for my sake will find it.*"

To follow Jesus, we must be prepared to be mocked, insulted, treated as heretics, and even driven apart by nonchristians and by other Christians still influenced by the doctrine of Paul. The Gospel according to Saint Matthew (E.S.V.) says: "*5:10 "Blessed are those who are persecuted for righteousness sake, for theirs is the kingdom of heaven." 5:11 "Blessed are you when others revile you and persecute you falsely on my account. 5:12 Rejoice and be glad, for your reward is great in heaven, for so they persecuted the prophets who were before you.*" The Gospel according to Saint Luke (E.S.V.) says: "*6:26 Woe to you, when all people speak well of you, for so their fathers did to the false prophets.*"

We must be ready not only to sacrifice our material

goods, but also our public honor and our power. We must prefer the glory that comes from God more than human praise. Maybe there are a lot of people who would die for Christ, but there are not too many who would live for Christ. We must try to live for Christ and if someday we have to die for Christ, so be it.

We must not remain in the state in which we were called if in another condition we can serve God better. We must always try to attain the highest positions in everything we do, in order to serve God better and to fulfill his word, if in the highest positions we think we will get greater opportunities to do it, but we need to be prepared to be in lower positions among men, if following Christ requires so.

We must even be prepared to confront members of our own family and friends, if that is necessary, to follow Jesus and his word. The Gospel according to Saint Matthew (E.S.V.) says: *"10:34 "Do not think that I have come to bring peace to the earth. I have not come to bring peace, but a sword. 10:35 For I have come to set a man against his father, and a daughter against her mother, and a daughter in-law against her mother in-law. 10:36 And a person's enemies will be those of his own household."*

If we need to work full time for God, and we can, we must do it, even if we are not ministers. We must help the men who we see are really working for God. If they are working for God they deserve the help we give them, and they will be eating their own bread if they eat through the help they receive. If we are going to judge men we should not do it considering how much they earn, but how much good they produce. The Gospel according to Saint Matthew (E.S.V.) says: *"10:9 Acquire no gold nor silver nor copper for your belts, 10:10 no bag for your journey, nor two tunics, nor sandals, nor a staff, for the laborer deserves his food."*

In addition, because God loves men, if we love God, we will try to do what is good for all men and we will try to love all men, especially the merciful men. God wants us to love the merciful people as ourselves. I think Christians do not pay enough attention to the commandment to love the merciful people as ourselves. We must love everybody, but we must love our neighbor as ourselves. He who is merciful is our neighbor. This is taught in the Parable of the Good Samaritan.

4. Mercy

We must be merciful. In my opinion, being merciful is about doing good for those who are in need, because of love. God wants us not only to love and will what is good, but also to be merciful, even to our enemies in need; even to those who do not seem to deserve it; even to those who without doubt do not deserve it. If we are not merciful we are not following Jesus.

In my opinion, God wants us to be merciful with regard to people who do not seem to deserve it because the good of every single human is important and valued by God, and because the virtue of mercy is critical to the good of the world. The most important matters of the law, as Christ taught, are mercy, faithfulness, and righteousness.

However, being merciful does not imply doing things for people who do not deserve them, that are not in their best interest and/or that could bring unfair and unreasonable bad for others, whom we must even love more.

To be merciful we must care for everybody who is in need. Being merciful implies being interested in the lives of our families and friends; in the lives of the people of our neighborhood; and in the problems of our country and our world. We will know who is in need if we first look.

Being merciful implies thinking about what we can do for the good of those who are in need. Being merciful implies doing things for our family, friends and community. It implies giving time to our families and friends. It implies working to have a free country, a Constitutional Democracy, in which the natural rights of men are recognized, including the natural right to freedom of religion. It also implies working for the spreading of the word of God.

To be merciful we must look, see, think and do. We have to open our hearts to the pain of others. Nonetheless, this does not mean becoming a permanently sad person; because we also have to open our hearts to the joy of others, and we always have to keep in mind the great gift that life is, and never forget how important it is to be happy, not only for ourselves but for other people.

5. Good Response in a Good Situation

Very often we respond better when things go badly for us. We become strong in the face of adversity. This could turn adversity into something necessary or good for us in order for us to reach salvation. It is very important for us to give our best without the necessity of suffering any adversity, being aware and accepting that in any case we will face adversities, severe adversities, and that some of them might even be good for us. We must try not to complain about any bad situation we suffer. This is also something that should distinguish Christians from the rest of the people. Christians should complain less.

The recognition of the Epistles of Paul as uninspired writings, and the rebuilding of the Christian doctrine unleashed from the influence of Paul, are going to be promoted by God. We must be aware that God might promote this recognition through a tribulation, a series of earthquakes, twisters, or other catastrophes, for instance. Those events might be produced by God in order to stimulate the sense of religiousness of the people, and to lead people to take more seriously the word of Christ. We must try to free the Christian doctrine from the bad influence of Paul without the necessity of any bad.

6. Good Response before Adversity

The Devil according to the book of Revelation is still acting in the World. His power is stronger over those who are more distant from Christ. His tool is to tempt. And his intention is to lead men away from God.

To be protected from the Devil, of course it is very important to do good, but also to respond in the best way before adversity. The Devil will not want to hurt us if he produces good by attempting to hurt us, instead of evil.

And even though men should be prepared to respond in a good way before any adversity or set of circumstances, it is important for us to keep in mind that one of the things that the Devil does is to show himself with greater power than the power he really has. This is what he did when he tried to tempt Christ, telling him that he will give him all the kingdoms of the world in a moment of time.

We must neither underestimate, nor overestimate the Devil. In my opinion, not to overestimate the Devil is also very important. God repeated in the Old Testament, many times, that he is the Lord of the world, that nothing happens if he does not allow it, to help us avoid being deceived by the Devil, and be saved in the Great Day of the Wrath of the Lamb, if we have to face it.

It is important for us, in the analysis of the current affairs, not to underestimate the Devil, but also not to play in his favor, making the evil ones appear to be more powerful than what they really are. We must have on account that the Devil can do things to make himself seem to be in control of things that he really does not control, and that we can change.

In my opinion, not to underestimate and overestimate the evil-ones are part of responding good before adversity.

7. Humility

It is very important for us to be humble, to accept that we do not know, most of the time, what is actually better for us, so that things that present themselves as being good might be bad, and on the contrary, things that seem very bad, might be good. We also should recognize that we are sinners.

The necessity to be humble applies especially to the preaching of the word of God. As I said, Christ, God, could preach with an attitude of knowing everything, but the rest of the people cannot. He could act like somebody free of sin, because he was; but people cannot act in that way.

We should avoid the excessive praise of men, and make sure that it does not become necessary to us.

8. The Acceptance of God's will

It is very important for us to accept life just as it is, with its good moments and its bad moments, and to know how to be thankful for it. We must understand that adversities are opportunities to show the best in us. As I said, if the good reaction of a few men in the face of adversity can be so meaningful for the sake of humanity, adversities are opportunities to do great things for humanity. And sometimes overcoming adversities is the only way to achieve some good. That is one of the reasons why Christ had to face crucifixion, accepting the Father's will. It is very natural for a good man to have to face adversities. We must accept God's will and take life just as it is.

Although some adversities may come as a consequence of wrongdoings, not all of them do. As I already said, adversities are part of life, and are good and necessary for us. We must never forget that the fact that something bad happens to us does not mean that God does not love us. Let us remember that Christ suffered. John the Baptist was beheaded. Very often adversities and sufferings are opportunities to serve, to show the best in us, to have a great role in human history.

9. Thankfulness - Giving Honor to God

Adversities must not stop us from noticing all the good things we have received, we are receiving, and we will receive from God. The Christian must be recognized for being a thankful man, not only to God. The natural effect of being thankful to God is being happy. Being thankful and happy in normal situations is an obligation of men. Of course, it is natural to be sad sometimes, for a while, but part of being a Christian is to defeat sadness, with the spirit and knowledge that God gave us.

If we love God, we must have the best appreciation of God. We must not think that the world he created is naturally unfair, and we must recognize the good that God did and does for us, even in poverty, even without health, even in the midst of persecution. Even in poverty, even sick, in persecution, we must be thankful to God. That is the way we must value our life in those situations, and the way we must value the life of others facing those situations. A life in poverty, with illness, in persecution, is not a bad life. We must work and fight against poverty, illness and persecutions, but we must not dishonor God while we do it. We must accept the will of God, and we must thank God for our existence, and for the existence of our loved ones even in the bad moments. People facing poverty, illness, persecution, can be grateful and even happy. If we cannot help them, at least, let us not convince them that they cannot be grateful and happy, or even worse, that they do not have reasons to be grateful to God and happy. Many people facing poverty, illness, persecution, are good people. If we cannot help people facing these problems, at least, let us not convince them that they have the right to be bad people because of their situation.

We must recognize everything that God does for us, and how without him, we would be nothing. However, this does not mean that we cannot feel proud for doing some things right, and give due credit to ourselves for them. What we should not do is to believe that we did not need God to accomplish those things.

10. Education – Freedom of Thought - Truth

Nobody is really a Christian if he is not hungry for wisdom, for truth. Christians must permanently listen, read and study, and should never accept a teaching as true that they do not believe is true. We must search for the truth, have faith in our reasoning and defend our freedom, especially our freedom of expression and religion.

The Devil is the father of the lie. We must have faith in truth. If we do not have faith in truth, if we do not honor truth, we do not have faith in God, we do not honor God. We do not need to lie. We must not be afraid of truth. If what this book says is true, there is no justification for denying it. Defend your right to believe and express the truth. Let us not submit to any lie.

I find very sad submission in any form, but one of the most shameful and dangerous form of submission is the submission of our youth to their teachers at school. We must listen and respect our teachers at school, but we must not submit to them. The submission of youth to teachers, at school, college, etc., is a very bad thing. It is very shameful and negative to affirm that something false is true, to sustain something wrong, or unfair, in order to attain a better grade at school, or to avoid problems with a "teacher". That is spiritual prostitution. If we want our children to be able to confront a teacher to defend the truth, we must care more for having a good and free child than for having a child with the best grades at school.

Our education programs must care as much for forming free citizens, as for forming obedient students. Parents should work hard to have schools in which our sons are not given better grades for believing or sustaining what is wrong.

11. Meditation and Prayer

It is very important for us to meditate. It is very important to have time alone to think and to be with God; at least a few hours on the weekends; and a half hour on weekdays.

It is very important for us to pray. I really recommend both morning and night prayers. Christ prayed a lot to carry out his mission. If he prayed, evidently we need to pray! We are not going to get everything that we pray for, in part because most of the times it will not be what is best for us, but without doubt prayer will always bring us good, in perceptible and imperceptible ways.

Christ taught that if we have faith our prayers would be very powerful. In my opinion, he who has faith is he who is repentant, has knowledge of the word of God, and does his will. To have faith while praying makes our prayer stronger.

12. Fortitude, Perseverance and Physical Training

People, in order to be able to do what is good, need to have a strong and persistent spirit. Physical training is very important in developing that strength and persistence, as well as in developing moral virtues. Christians should give a great importance to physical training, especially to the practice of sports. We need to have a healthy mind, and physical training contributes to the health of our mind.

13. Avoiding Judging - Giving Importance to Words and Thoughts

It is very important for us to be very careful with our judgments, and with what we say, especially about God. And when it comes to judging whether or not somebody is going to be saved, we must definitely try not to do so, unless it is necessary for some reason. We must certainly try not to be wrong in anything that we think and we say, and we must give importance to any mistake we make thinking and speaking. The Gospel according to Saint Matthew (E.S.V.) says: "*12:36 I tell you, on the day of judgment people will give account for every careless word they speak, for by your words you will be justified, and by your words you will be condemned."*

However, it is important to keep in mind that this does not mean that we should not think or speak to avoid making a mistake. Let us remember the Parable of the Ten Pounds (first part, point II.7).

This commandment of avoiding judging applies of course to those Christians who do not recognize Paul as a false prophet. We must not be judgmental against them.

14. Renouncing Anger

It is also an essential part of being a Christian to refrain from being angry. The Gospel according to Saint Matthew (E.S.V.) says: *"5:22 But I say to you that everyone who is angry with his brother will be liable of judgement; whoever insults his brother will be liable of council; and whoever says, 'You fool!' will be liable to the hell of fire."*

Of course it is natural to be angry on some exceptional occasions; but in general we should not be angry with anyone, especially with a brother, with a neighbor; not even for a second. It is not enough trying to avoid letting the sun go down on our anger. We should try never to be angry with anyone, especially with someone who seems to be a good man.

15. Making Use of the Sacraments

In order to assist us in our challenge of being Christians Jesus instituted sacraments. Baptism in the name of the Father, the Son and the Holy Spirit (Matthew 28:19), Washing of the Feet (John 13:1: 13:14), Forgiveness of the Sins or New Bath (John 13:10; 20:23), Eucharist (Matthew 26:26; Mark 14:22: Luke 22:17), Confirmation or the Sacrament of the Holy Spirit (Matthew 15:26; Luke 11:13, John 7:38, Acts 2:38), Anointing of the Sick (Mark 6:13), in my opinion, are sacraments that were certainly instituted by Jesus, without prejudice of another or others that could have been instituted by Jesus as well. Make use of the sacraments. Making use of the sacraments is putting in practice the word of Jesus. These sacraments are not exclusive to the Catholic Church. If you are a Christian minister you can administer them. Any Christian can become a Christian minister, and any Christian can be an extraordinary minister of the Christian Church. This means that in case of necessity, when there is no minister available to somebody who needs to receive baptism, any Christian can be a minister of the sacrament in the benefit of the man in need. Even the Catholic Church admits that a noncatholic Christian minister can baptize, and that any Christian can be extraordinary minister of Baptism. Baptism according to the Catholic Church brings forgiveness of all past sins (Acts 2:38). The same way a noncatholic Christian minister can be a minister of this sacrament that brings the forgiveness of the sins, he can also be a minister of the sacrament of the forgiveness of sins in the benefit of a baptized Christian who needs a new bath. And any Christian can be an extraordinary minister of this sacrament as well.

Ruy Barraco Mármol

16. Spreading this Truth and Working for a Faithful to Jesus Christian Church

The recognition of Paul as a false prophet and the faithfulness to Jesus of the Christian Church are very important. The good of the world depends on them. If you love God, if you love Christ, you must do your part to work for the recognition of Paul as a false prophet and for a faithful to Jesus Christian Church, and you will get the chance to be one of the first resurrected, and one of those invited to the wedding supper of the Lamb. Do your part to prepare the bride, the Christian Church, for the wedding of the Lamb. Do your part to prepare yourself and the whole body of Christians for Christ.

You are expected to perform according to your talents, according to your capacity. If you understand what this book says do not wait for special instruction: Find a way to live a Christianity faithful to Jesus and to spread this truth. Reveal the mystery of the "False Apostle Paul", and work for a faithful to Jesus Christian Church. I believe that God will especially bless the first ministers who start preaching this truth, and the true word of Gods, and the first Christians that become and remain faithful to Jesus.

Let us remember what the Gospel according to Saint Matthew (E.S.V.) says: *"13:45 Again, the kingdom of heaven is like a merchant in search of fine pearls, 13:46 who, on finding one pearl of great value, went and sold all that he had and bought it."* If you understand the value of Jesus, if you value Jesus, nothing should stop you from being a faithful to Jesus Christian. There is nothing more valuable.

Ruy Barraco Mármol

Bibliography

1. *"The Holy Bible"*, Revised Standard Version, Second Catholic Edition, printed in China, (San Francisco, U.S.A.; published by Thomas Nelson Publishing for Ignatius Press, 2006).

2. *"Biblia de Jerusalén"*, Nueva Edición Revisada y Aumentada. Edición Española. (Spain; Desclee de Brouwer, 1999).

3. Holzner, Josef *"San Pablo Heraldo de Cristo"*, (Barcelona; Editorial Herder, 1959).

4. Barraco Mármol, Mario Domingo, *"La Fecha de Nacimiento de Cristo"*.

5. Juan Leal, S.J. in *"Sinopsis de los Cuatros Evangelios"* [Synopsis of the Four Evangelists] published by the B.A.C. (Biblioteca de Autores Cristianos) [Library of Christian Authors] Madrid; Editorial la Católica S.A., MCMLIV).

6. De Tuya Manuel and José Salguero *"Introducción a la Biblia"* [Introduction to the Bible], Collection of the (Biblioteca de Autores Cristianos), (Madrid; Editorial La Católica S.A., MCMLXVII).

7. *"Second Ecumenical Council of the Vatican"*, Dogmatic

Constitution of Divine Revelation, Dei Verbum.

8. *"Webster's Seventh New Collegiate Dictionary"*, (Springfield, Massachusetts, U.S.A., G.&.C. Merriam Company Publishers, 1965).

9. *"The Holy Bible"* containing the Old and New Testaments, translated out of the original tongues: and with the former translations diligently compared and revised by his majesty's special command. *Authorized King James Version.* Oxford. Printed at the University Press. London: Humphrey Milford Oxford University Press, Amen House, E.C.4. New York and Toronto. The Oxford Self-pronouncing Bible, S.S. Teacher's Edition.

10. *"Biblia Sacra iuxta Vulgatam Clementinam"* [The Latin Vulgate], Nova Editio, Logicis Partitionibus Aliisque Subsidiis Ornata, A R.P. Alberto Colunga, O.P. et Dr. Laurentio Turrado professoribus sacrae scripturae in P. Universitate Eccl. Salmanticensi, Biblioteca de Autores Cristianos, (Editorial la Católica S.A., Matriti – MCMXLVI).

11. NESTLE – ALAND, *"Greek-English New Testament'*, in the tradition of Eberhard Nestle and Erwin Nestle, edited by Barbara and Kurt Aland, Johannes Karavidopoulos, Carlo M. Martini, Bruce M. Metzger – English Text 2nd Edition of the Revised Standard Version – The critical apparatuses prepared and edited together with the Institute for New Testament Textual Research,

Munter/Westphalia by Barbara and Kurt Aland. (Stuttgart, Deutsche Bibelgesellschaft. 1981).

12. Merk, Augustinus *"Novum Testamentum Graece et Latine"* septiman editionem.

13. Goodrich, Richard J. and Albert L. Lukaszewski *"A Reader's Greek New Testament"*, second edition, (China; Zondervan, 2007).

14. Zerwick, Max *"Analysis Philologica Novi Testamenti Graeci"*, (Romae; Sumptibus Pontificii Instituti Biblici, 1953).

15. *"Harper Collins Latin Concise Dictionary"* (Great Britain; Harper Collins Publishers Limited, 2003).

16. Feyerabend, Karl *"Langenscheidt Pocket Greek Dictionary"* Greek-English (Berlin, Munich, Vienna, Zurich: Langenscheidt.). Distributed by: Optimum Book Marketing, 171 Madison Avenue, N.Y.

17. *"The Catholic Study Bible"* Published by Oxford University Press, Inc. 200 Madison Avenue, New York. 1990. Scripture texts used taken from the New American Bible.

18. *"The Holy Bible"* New International Version, (Colorado Springs, Colorado, U.S.A., International Bible Society, 1984).

19. *"The Holy Bible, New Testament, English Standard*

Version" Crossway Bibles, a publishing ministry of Good News Publishers, Wheaton, Illinois, 2007.

20. Denzinger, Henry *"The Sources of Catholic Dogma"*, (U.S.A.; Loreto Publications, 2002), translated by Roy J. Deferrari, from the thirtieth edition of Enchiridion Symbolorum by Henry Denzinger, revised by Karl Rahner, S.J., published in 1954, by Herder & Co., Freiburg.

21. B Llorca, G. Villoslada and F.J. Montalban, *"Historia de la Iglesia Católica"*, Collection of the "Biblioteca de Autores Cristianos", second edition (Madrid, Editorial La Editorial Católica S.A., MCMLV), vol.I., p. 235.

22. Council of Trent (1546-1563), fourth session, September 8, 1546, decree concerning the canonical scriptures.

23. First Vatican Council, Dogmatic constitution on the Catholic faith, Dei Filius.

24. Second Vatican Council, Dogmatic Constitution on Divine Revelation Dei Verbum.

25. Mounce, William D. "Basics of Biblical Greek Grammar", Second Edition (Michigan; Zondervan, 2003).

26. The American Declaration of the Rights and Duties of Man.

27. *"Biblia Comentada"*, Texto de la Nacar – Colunga VII, Epistolas Catolicas. Apocalipsis [In the Commentated Bible, Text of Nacar – Colunga VII, Catholic Epistles. Revelation] by Jose Salguero, O.P. Professor of Sacred Scripture of the Pontifical University of Saint Thomas of Rome, Biblioteca de Autores Cristianos [Library of Christian Authors] Madrid. MCMLXV.

28. *"Sagrada Escritura"*, Texto y Comentario por profesores de la Compania de Jesus, Nuevo Testamento Tomo III, Biblioteca de Autores Cristianos, Madrid MCMLXII [The Book of Sacred Scripture, Text and Commentary by professors of the Company of Jesus, New Testament, Tome III, Library of Christian Authors, Madrid MCMLXII]

29. Quasten, Johannes "Patrologia", Collection of "Biblioteca de Autores Cristianos" Spain Edition prepared by Ignacio Oñatibia, (Madrid; La Editorial Católica S.A., MCMLXI).

30. *"The New American Bible"*, Saint Joseph Edition, New York, Catholic Book Publishing CO, 1970.

31. *"The New American Bible"*, Compact Edition, New York, Oxford University Press, 2004.

32. "The *Holy Bible containing the Old and New Testaments*" NKJV New King James Version, Tennessee, Thomas Nelson, Inc., 1979.

33. *"The Holy Bible N.R.S.V."* New Revised Standard Version Catholic Gift Edition, New York , Harper Catholic Bibles, 1989.

34. *"The Open Bible"* New American Standard Bible, New York, Thomas Nelson Publishers, 1960.

35. Washburn, Del, in his book *"Theomatics II"*, Maryland, Scarborough House, 1994.

36. Suarez, Francisco *"Misterios de la Vida de Cristo"* (Mysteries of the life of Jesus), translated into Spanish by the fathers of the Society of Jesus, Editorial La Católica, Madrid, MCMXLVIII,

37. *"Padres Apostolicos"* (Apostolic Fathers), Bilingual Complete Edition, La Editorial Católica S.A., Madrid, MCML.

38. Irenaeus, *"Against Heresies"*.

39. Robert Young LL.D, *"Analytical Concordance to the Bible"*, Funk & Wagnalls Company, New York, 1912.

40. Saint Justin Martyr, *"Dialogue with Trypho"*, translated by Thomas B. Falls, Edited by Michael Slusser, The Catholic University of American Press, Washington D.C. 2003.

41. Goñi, Blas and Juan Labayen "Gramática Hebrea

Teórico-Práctica", (Pamplona: Editorial Aramburu, 1945), third edition.